D1369963

Testing Theories of Economic Imperialism

Testing Theories of Economic Imperialism

Edited by

Steven J. Rosen
Brandeis University

James R. Kurth
Swarthmore College

Lexington Books
D.C. Heath and Company
Lexington, Massachusetts
Toronto   London

Library of Congress Cataloging in Publication Data

Main entry under title:

Testing theories of economic imperialism.

"Papers ... given in a 1973 symposium in installments at the International Studies Association Convention in New York, the International Political Science Association Ninth World Congress in Montreal, and the Peace Science Society North American Convention in Boston."
1. International economic relations—Addresses, essays, lectures. 2. Imperialism—Addresses, essays, lectures. 3. United States—Foreign economic relations—Addresses, essays, lectures. 4. Russia—Foreign economic relations—Addresses, essays, lectures.
I. Rosen, Steven J., ed. II. Kurth, James R., ed.
HF1411.T4143   382   74-301
ISBN 0-669-91314-6

Contents

List of Figures   vii

List of Tables   ix

Part I   *The Theory of Economic Imperialism*

Chapter 1   **Testing Theories of Economic Imperialism,** *James R. Kurth*   3

Chapter 2   **Theories of Imperialism and Neocolonialism,** *Karl W. Deutsch*   15

Chapter 3   **Comparing Theories of Economic Imperialism,** *Andrew Mack*   35

Chapter 4   **Capitalism, Socialism, and the Sources of Imperialism,** *Thomas E. Weisskopf,* **with a Commentary by** *Harry Magdoff*   57

Chapter 5   **Methodological Issues in the Measurement of Inequality, Dependence, and Exploitation,** *James Caporaso*   87

Part II   *Capitalist Imperialism: Empirical Theory-Testing*

Chapter 6   **The Open Door Imperative and U.S. Foreign Policy,** *Steven J. Rosen*   117

Chapter 7   **Correlates of U.S. Military Assistance and Military Intervention,** *John S. Odell*   143

Chapter 8   **The Theory of International Exploitation in Large Natural Resource Investments,** *Theodore H. Moran*   163

Chapter 9   Trade in Raw Materials: The Benefits of
                 Capitalist Alliances,
                 Stephen D. Krasner   183

Chapter 10   Exploitation in Ocean Resource
                 Development, *Donald E. Milsten*   199

Chapter 11   U.S. Economic Penetration of Western
                 Europe, *Walter Goldstein*   211

Part III   *Soviet Imperialism: Empirical*
                 Theory-Testing

Chapter 12   The Political Economy of Soviet
                 Relations with Eastern Europe,
                 Paul Marer   231

Chapter 13   Soviet Economic Penetration of China,
                 1945-1960: 'Imperialism' as a Level
                 of Analysis Problem, *Roy F. Grow*   261

                 About the Contributors   283

List of Figures

5-1	The Lorenz Curve	99
6-1	U.S. Investment, Exports, and Aid in Brazil	122
6-2	U.S. Investment, Exports, and Aid in Indonesia	125
6-3	U.S. Investment, Exports, and Aid in Chile	128
6-4	U.S. Investment, Exports, and Aid in Greece	131
6-5	U.S. Investment, Exports, and Aid in Peru	134
6-6	Coverage of Greek Economic Affiars in the Wall Street *Journal*	136
8-1	The Sharing of Benefits of Foreign Investment—The Basic Model	168
8-2	The Sharing of Benefits of Foreign Investment—The Revised Model	170

List of Tables

5-1	Illustration of Independence of VSDs and VADs	112
6-1	Condensation of Findings	135
7-1	Relation Between U.S. Military Assistance Given to and Raw Materials Value of Nations	148
7-2	Relation Between U.S. Military Assistance Given to and U.S. Private Investment in Nations	149
7-3	Relation Between U.S. Military Assistance Given to and Economic Value of Nations, Controlling for Gross National Product	150
7-4	Relation Between Extent of U.S. Military Intervention, 1948-1967, and Proportion of U.S. Trade, 1964-1965, with Nations	152
7-5	Relation Between Extent of U.S. Military Intervention and Political Stability of Nations, 1948-1967	153
9-1	Percentage of Export Earnings from Leading Commodity Export	184
9-2	Market Shares of the Four Largest LDC Producers	185
9-3	Reserve Holdings of Primary Producers	187
11-1	The Top Ten MNCs, 1971	218
11-2	American Investments in Europe, 1970	220
12-1	Subvention Transfers to the USSR from East European Countries, Cumulative 1945-1960	238

12-2	USSR Economic Assistance to East European Countries and Balance of the Grant Equivalent of Aid and Subvention Transfers, Cumulative 1945-1960	241
12-3	USSR Imports from Czechoslovakia and East Germany, 1948-1955	249
13-1	Commodity Composition of Sino-Soviet Trade, 1950-1960	268
13-2	Value of Sino-Soviet Trade, 1949-1960	270
13-3	Foreign Trade and National Income of China, 1953-1957	270
13-4	Soviet Loans and China's Capital Investment, 1953-1957	271
13-5	Soviet Aid and Chinese Industry	276

Part I
The Theory of Economic Imperialism

1 Testing Theories of Economic Imperialism

James R. Kurth
Swarthmore College

The Theory of Strategic Deterrence versus the Theory of Economic Imperialism

"War is the father of all things," said Heraclitus. And, he might have added, of most theories. Out of the Second World War emerged conceptions that dominated the analysis of international relations for more than twenty years. For most scholars, the basic model of international politics was the balance of power system that was centered upon states with developed economies. The "relationship of major tension" was between the two superpowers, the United States and the Soviet Union.[1] The major determinants of U.S. foreign policy, these scholars argued, were strategic and were imposed by the international system. The major goals and consequences of U.S. foreign policy were seen as the containment of communism and the deterrence of another major war. Together, these conceptions formed the theory of strategic deterrence. The origins of these conceptions, and the deep conviction with which they were held, lay in the lessons men drew from the appeasement of the Nazis and from the Second World War. As such, the theory of strategic deterrence might be called the Munich paradigm of international relations.[2]

In the 1960s, however, under the impact of the new and different war in Vietnam, another set of interrelated conceptions emerged and contested the dominant theory. For a new group of scholars, the basic model of international politics was the imperialist system that was centered upon states of unequal economic development. The relationship of major tension was between the developed and underdeveloped economies. The major determinants of U.S. foreign policy, these scholars argued, were economic and were imposed by the capitalist system. The major goals and consequences of U.S. foreign policy were seen as the expansion of American influence and interests throughout the world, the exploitation of underdeveloped countries, and the prevention of revolutionary change. Together, these conceptions formed the theory of economic imperialism. Similar conceptions had long been a minor tradition in the analysis of international relations, but that tradition had been dismissed as both radical and peripheral. The spread of these conceptions, and the deep conviction with which they were held, resulted from the lessons many men drew from the Vietnamese War. As such, the theory of economic imperialism might be called the Vietnam paradigm of international relations.

The events of the mid-1970s may not bring about the creation of a new theory of international relations, but they will doubtless force the reinterpretation of the old ones. The most obvious of these events are the final withdrawal of U.S. military forces from Indochina in 1973 and the dramatic rise in the monies received by governments of underdeveloped, but oil-producing countries, especially after the Yom Kippur War of 1973. The first should encourage more detached analysis of the theory of economic imperialism; the second should encourage more sophisticated versions of it.

It is therefore an appropriate time to examine the theory of economic imperialism, to test if possible its propositions with more rigor and more facts than has been done before, and to determine what parts of the theory can be refuted, what parts can be reinforced, and what parts can be refined.

This book contains thirteen original chapters on pivotal propositions in the theory of economic imperialism that carefully refine broad ideological differences as precise empirical and analytical issues. They were first presented as papers given in a 1973 symposium in installments at the International Studies Association convention in New York, the International Political Science Association Ninth World Congress in Montreal, and the Peace Science Society North American convention in Boston. The authors represent a diversity of predispositions on the imperialism question but share a commitment to rigorous research.

In the first half of this introduction we will present an overall view of the basic propositions of the theory of economic imperialism and of how these propositions are tested by our authors. In the second half, we will turn to an examination of the most important and most dramatic of the outcomes which theorists of economic imperialism claim to explain the foreign interventions undertaken by the United States within underdeveloped countries in the era since the Second World War. In the course of that examination we shall illustrate some of the major problems afflicting the theory of economic imperialism in its present form.

Causes and Consequences of Economic Imperialism

What are the basic propositions of the theory of economic imperialism? Two of the chapters in this volume, those by Karl Deutsch and Andrew Mack, provide us with an overall view of the arguments of the various theorists, including those of Hobson and Lenin in the early twentieth century and those of Harry Magdoff and Johan Galtung in recent years.

As Deutsch and Mack point out, along with James Caporaso and John Odell in their chapters, writers on economic imperialism normally have not specified their propositions with care and precision. Indeed, it may be accurate to speak of several theories rather than one theory. But as Mack argues in his chapter, the basic propositions contained in theories of economic imperialism can be grouped into broad categories: (1) propositions about the *causes* of a great power's foreign policies toward other countries and (2) propositions about the *consequences* of a great power's foreign policies or more broadly foreign presence for these countries.

The Causes of a Great Power's Foreign Policies

Theorists of economic imperialism argue that the foreign policies of a great power are determined primarily by its economic system. Capitalist systems are propelled outward by three basic drives: the need for raw materials, the need for foreign markets to compensate for inadequate demand at home, and the need for foreign investment to absorb surplus capital. These result in capitalist states undertaking expansionist, even imperialist, foreign policies. In particular, it is argued, the foreign interventions and the foreign assistance programs undertaken by the United States are primarily determined by the American capitalist system and by the economic interests within it.

A corollary proposition is that since socialist systems with planned economies substantially lack two of these drives—the need for foreign markets to compensate for underconsumption at home and the need for foreign investments to absorb surplus capital—they are far less likely to engage in expansionist or imperialist foreign policies in order to achieve economic ends. This corollary can take several forms. One variant is to argue that the Soviet Union (or China) is unlikely to engage in economic imperialism, since it is not a capitalist economy. Another variant is to argue that a socialist America would be less imperialist than the present capitalist one.

Several of the chapters in this volume attempt to test the above propositions. Two of them directly test the proposition that U.S. foreign policies are primarily determined by economic interests. John Odell, in a statistical analysis using cross-sectional data, finds that the amount of U.S. military assistance to a country correlates with the amount of U.S. economic interests in the country. Further, this correlation is not a spurious one merely generated by the size of the country; the correlation between U.S. military assistance and U.S. economic interests exists even among countries of the same size. But, in a similar cross-sectional statistical analysis, Odell finds no correlation between U.S. military intervention and U.S. economic interests. This suggests that economic factors determine outcomes in one "issue area" in U.S. foreign policy, the relatively minor one of military assistance, but that economic factors do not determine outcomes in another "issue area," the major one of military intervention.

Steven Rosen uses a different methodology to arrive at a similar conclusion.

In a comparative analysis of five major recipients of U.S. military and economic assistance (Brazil, Peru, Chile, Greece, and Indonesia) and using longitudinal data, he finds *inter alia* that the amount of U.S. foreign assistance (military and economic) to a country correlates with the openness of the country to U.S. economic interests (trade and investment).

Together, the studies by Odell and Rosen give substantial support to the proposition that the amount of U.S. foreign assistance to a country is primarily determined by U.S. economic interests in the country. Is it possible to extend the economic proposition from U.S. foreign assistance to U.S. foreign interventions? The statistical analysis by Odell suggests that it is not. In the second half of this chapter, however, I will undertake a brief comparative analysis of the major cases of U.S. intervention since 1945 and will argue that an economic explanation can be applied to each of these cases. But as we shall see, the economic explanation for U.S. interventions is afflicted with serious flaws. And at best it is only equal to several, alternative non-economic explanations for U.S. interventions; it cannot be demonstrated that it is superior to them.

Two other chapters in this volume directly attempt to test the proposition that a non-capitalist system, specifically the Soviet Union, is unlikely to engage in economic imperialism. Paul Marer analyzes Soviet policies and practices toward Eastern Europe. With the use of economic data, he specifies and demonstrates at which times and in which ways the Soviet Union engaged in economically exploitative behavior. Roy Grow does a companion analysis of Soviet policies and practices toward China. Together, the studies by Marer and Grow show that the Soviet Union has engaged in particular forms of exploitative behavior, at least from the end of the Second World War to the mid-1950s. This suggests that economic exploitation of other countries is at least a potentiality of a socialist state. It follows from this that either economic imperialism is not peculiarly a function of capitalism or there are different, but still strong tendencies, toward economic imperialism in a socialist state as well.

Many radicals argue, however, that the Soviet Union is not a true example of a socialist economic system, and therefore it is not a true test of the proposition that a socialist America would be less likely to be imperialist than capitalist America. This particular proposition, of course, cannot be directly tested in any empirical sense. Thomas Weisskopf in his chapter, however, constructs a hypothetical socialist America and argues that for structural reasons it would be far less likely to be imperialist than any capitalist system in the United States. Some readers will find Weisskopf's construction not only hypothetical but also Utopian. If so, the implicit message of Weisskopf's argument may be that any economic system we are likely to experience in the real world will be roughly as imperialist (or as non-imperialist) as the present one.

Finally, in a commentary on Weisskopf's paper, Harry Magdoff presents his own views on some of the issues raised in recent debates about the relationship between capitalism and imperialism.

The Consequences of a Great Power's
Foreign Policies or Foreign Presence

Theorists of economic imperialism argue that large areas of the world—especially the underdeveloped countries of Latin America, Africa, the Middle East, and Southeast Asia—are exploited economically by their incorporation into the international capitalist system. In its more extreme form, the argument holds that economic underdevelopment itself primarily results from this exploitation. A corollary proposition is that underdeveloped countries with socialist regimes are far more likely to achieve balanced economic growth with equitable distribution than those countries integrated into international capitalism through trade and investments.

Three of the chapters in this volume directly attempt to test the proposition that underdeveloped countries have been exploited through their incorporation into the international capitalist system. Theodore Moran, in an empirical analysis of a highly salient case, examines the terms by which American corporations invested in Chilean copper in the 1950s and finds that there was in fact exploitation, in a precisely definable and quantifiable sense. He also finds that this exploitation of Chile by the American copper corporations was aided and abetted by the Chilean business elite—the "bridge-head" of imperialism, in the vernacular of *dependencia* theory.

Stephen Krasner, in a comparative analysis of several recent international commodity agreements, comes to a contrasting conclusion. He finds that underdeveloped countries have benefited from their incorporation into the international capitalist system, especially compared with any alternative international economic regime that is likely in the real world. Specifically, he finds that governments of underdeveloped, producing countries have benefited from the economic alliances that they have concluded with governments of developed, consuming countries and with multinational corporations. This has become especially obvious since 1970 with the cooperation between the governments of oil-producing countries and the multinational oil corporations. Thus, M.A. Adelman sees these corporations as "OPEC tax collectors."[3] It may be true that at one time the oil-producing countries were exploited by the oil corporations. It is now the case that the oil-consuming countries are exploited by them both.

Donald Milsten, in a comparative analysis of three industries (oil, shipping, and fishing) engaged in the increasingly important realm of ocean resource development, finds that there has been economic exploitation of underdeveloped countries in the recent past, specifically in the shipping industry. But he also finds that conditions have changed, and in regard to the present and the future, he arrives at conclusions similar to Krasner's.

Together, the studies by Krasner and Milsten and the events in the oil industry since 1970 suggest that American economic exploitation of particular countries and in particular industries is now much diminished if not extinguished. The golden age of American exploitation of the oil-producing countries turns out to have lasted only a generation, from the end of the Second World War until the end of the 1960s. It is interesting to note that the studies by Paul Marer and Roy Grow arrive at a similar conclusion about the Soviet Union. Soviet economic exploitation of Eastern Europe and China led a brief, but intense, life that lasted only from the end of the Second World War until the mid-1950s.

Theorists of economic imperialism normally focus on the relations between developed countries and underdeveloped ones. The propositions about the causes of U.S. foreign assistance and foreign interventions and about the patterns of American economic exploitation, which we have discussed above, have little meaning in regard to American relations with other developed countries. On the other hand, a discussion of the economic causes and consequences of American foreign relations must give attention to the area that is the largest recipient of American trade and investments—that is, Western Europe. In the theory of Harry Magdoff, the spread of American imperialism was keyed to the displacement of the older European imperial systems, and indeed even to the penetration and near colonization of the domestic economies of the European powers themselves. Accordingly, the chapter by Walter Goldstein presents an overall view of American multinational corporations in that area and addresses two issues: the causes of American investment in Europe and the distribution of economic benefits from that investment. These questions are comparable in structure, if less intense in form, to our earlier questions concerning underdeveloped countries.

Toward Statistical Testing of the
Theory of Economic Imperialism

What should be the next step in testing theories of economic imperialism? Most of the empirical papers in this volume are case or comparative studies. But the statistical analysis presented by John Odell illustrates the possibility of another approach. There is a need to apply statistical methods to a wide array of cross-sectional and longitudinal quantitative data on international economic relations. But as James Caporaso points out in his chapter, certain concepts—inequality, dependence, and exploitation—should be the basis of a theory of economic imperialism but have never been defined in a way that permits their measurement or, therefore, their systematic and statistical comparison across countries and over time. Caporaso's chapter is an effort to define these three concepts in a measurable way. While not in itself a test of the theory of economic imperialism, it represents a necessary condition for the next step down a promising path.

The absence of measurable concepts is not the only methodological problem afflicting the theory of economic imperialism, however. There are others that are far more intractable. These problems become especially evident when we turn to an examination of the most important and most dramatic of the outcomes that the theory is supposed to explain—that is, the foreign interventions undertaken by the United States within underdeveloped countries since the Second World War.

Economic Imperialism and U.S. Interventions

Pro-Capitalist and Anti-Communist Imperatives

Let us begin our consideration of U.S. interventions since the Second World War by presenting a list of the major cases that have to be explained. These are:

1. Military interventions or limited wars: Korea 1950-1953, Lebanon 1958, Dominican Republic 1965-1966, Vietnam 1965-1973 and the associated interventions in Laos 1965-1973 and in Cambodia 1970-1973.
2. Interventions with military advisors: China 1946-1947, Greece 1940s, Vietnam and Laos early 1960s, Bolivia 1967.
3. Interventions with the CIA: Iran 1953, Guatemala 1954, Cuba 1961, British Guiana 1963.

Theorists of economic imperialism explain these U.S. interventions as efforts by American capitalists to protect their investments and markets abroad; U.S. interventions are seen as resulting from what might be called a pro-capitalist imperative.

At their simplest, theorists of economic imperialism argue that a U.S. intervention in a particular country was undertaken in order to protect *existing* American markets and investments within the country itself; the focus of the pro-capitalist imperative was on economic interests that were both local and actual. In the case of many U.S. interventions, however, there were no such American economic interests. Consequently, the theorists have had to expand their conception of the scope of the pro-capitalist imperative in two dimensions: from local areas to regional ones and from actual interests to potential ones. Four varieties of economic explanation result. Classified according to the focus of the pro-capitalist imperative, they are (1) local areas and actual interests, (2) local areas and potential interests, (3) regional areas and actual interests, and (4) regional areas and potential interests. The form of economic explanation gets progressively less concrete and direct. But, as we shall see, each of the major U.S. interventions can be covered by at least one of these forms of economic explanation.

Local Areas and Actual Interests. This simplest form of the pro-capitalist imperative has been used to explain several U.S. interventions in underdeveloped countries since the Second World War. Thus, the CIA intervention in Guatemala in 1954 has been explained on the basis of the interests of the United Fruit Company and has included the fact that several U.S. policy-makers had close connections with the company. John Foster Dulles, who was then Secretary of State, had been for many years a legal counsel for United Fruit; Henry Cabot Lodge, the U.S. Ambassador to the U.N., was on the company's board of directors; and John Moors Cabot, the Assistant Secretary of State for Inter-American Affairs, was a large shareholder in the company. Similarly, the CIA intervention in Cuba in 1961 has been explained by the billion-dollar American investment there. The CIA intervention in British Guiana in 1963 has been explained by American investments in bauxite. The military intervention in the Dominican Republic in 1965 has been explained by American sugar interests and again has included the fact that several U.S. policymakers or advisors had close connections with major sugar corporations: at the time, Ellsworth Bunker was chairman, president, and had been for thirty-eight years a director of National Sugar Refining Corporation; Adolph Berle had been chairman and was still a director of Sucrest Corporation; and Abe Fortas had also been a director of Sucrest.[4]

Local Areas and Potential Interests. If the actual American investments and markets within a country at the time of intervention were small, then the emphasis of the explanation can be on potential ones. China in 1946-1947 held few existing American economic interests. But the intervention with large numbers of military advisors could be explained by dreams of, in the phrases of the time, "oil for the lamps of China" and "four hundred million customers." Similarly, there were few existing American economic interests in Iran in 1953, but the CIA intervention was quickly followed by the entry of American oil corporations. The alleged CIA intervention in Brazil in 1964, far more indirect and less assignable than those in Guatemala and Iran, was quickly followed by a major mining concession to the Hanna Mining Company and by major increases in the already large American investment in Brazilian manufacturing ($700 million in 1964; $1.4 billion in 1971).

This form of explanation is greatly strained, however, when it is stretched to cover such military interventions as Korea in 1950, Lebanon in 1958, or Vietnam in the 1960s, where the investments and markets, actual and potential, were of little significance to any major American corporation.[5] Hence, theorists of economic imperialism have needed to extend the scope of the pro-capitalist imperative from local areas to regional ones.

Regional Areas and Actual Interests. Here, U.S. intervention within a country is explained by existing American investments and markets within a contiguous region. The loss of the country through its take-over by a Communist or revolutionary nationalist regime would lead, by variations on the domino theory, to the loss of the region itself and perhaps of even more. Thus it has been argued, the military intervention in Korea preserved Japan and its markets while intervention in Lebanon preserved the Middle East and its oil. Similar regional explanations have been applied to the interventions with military advisors in Greece in the 1940s and in Bolivia in 1967. And, of course, interventions covered by the local pro-capitalist imperative (i.e., Guatemala, Cuba, Dominican Republic) can be covered by the regional one too.

Regional Areas and Potential Interests. Finally, the most extended form of the pro-capitalist imperative has been applied to the most extensive example of U.S. intervention—that is, the advisory intervention in Vietnam and Laos in the early 1960s and the later military escalation in Vietnam, Laos, and Cambodia. Here, what was presumably preserved was the entire region of Southeast Asia and its vast economic potential.

The above discussion of different forms of the pro-capitalist imperative and different cases of U.S. intervention since the Second World War can be summed up in the following matrix:

The Pro-Capitalist Imperative and United States Interventions

	Area	
Interest	Local	Regional
Actual	Guatemala 1954	Greece 1940s
	Cuba 1961	Korea 1950-1953
	British Guiana 1963	Lebanon 1958
	Dominican Republic 1965-1966	Bolivia 1967
Potential	China 1946-1947	Vietnam, Laos, Cambodia 1961-1973
	Iran 1953	

The regional form of the pro-capitalist imperative has also been used, of course, to explain the American system of military alliances with underdeveloped countries; for example, The Rio Pact, SEATO, the military agreements with CENTO, the bilateral treaties with South Korea, Taiwan, and the Philippines, and the military assistance programs for these allies and for other underdeveloped countries.

As an explanation of U.S. interventions, the pro-capitalist imperative as extended has the important virtue of generality or inclusiveness—that is, it can be applied to each of the major U.S. interventions within underdeveloped countries in the period since the Second World War.

That virtue, however, is not achieved without cost. To most people—be they professional scholars, college students, ordinary citizens, or government officials themselves—the pro-capitalist imperative and other simple economic explanations lack plausibility as decision rules for U.S. policy-makers. That such great events could be explained by such narrow conceptions simply seems incredible. Moreover, there exists virtually no *documentary* evidence to support the proposition that U.S. leaders calculate their policies on intervention in such economic terms. Consequently, the more sophisticated economic theorists, such as William Appleman Williams, Harry Magdoff, and Gabriel Kolko, have cast their economic propositions in a more complex form. They see the capitalist economic system as generating an ideological superstructure that lends political legitimacy and moral energy to the system's foreign policies and the content of the American ideological superstructure as having been anti-Communism. The relationship between economic interests and ideological concerns was stated well long ago by Otto Hintze, the German historian of the European estates, in words that can be applied to American businessmen and American policy-makers:

Everywhere the first impulse to social action is given as a rule by real interests, i.e., by political and economic interests. But ideal interests lend wings to these real interests, given them a spiritual meaning, and serve to justify them. Man does not live by bread alone. He wants to have a good conscience as he pursues his life-interests. And in pursuing them he develops his capacities to the highest extent only if he believes that in so doing he serves a higher rather than a purely egoistic purpose. Interests without such "spiritual wings" are lame; but on the other hand, ideas can win out in history only if and inasfar as they are associated with real interests. . . . Whenever interests are vigorously pursued, an ideology tends to be developed also to give meaning, re-enforcement, and justification to these interests.[6]

When recast into anti-Communist form, the pro-capitalist imperative is slightly narrowed in regard to its targets (no longer including certain nationalist expropriating regimes) but greatly broadened in regard to its support (now including many American classes and groups). And as an explanation of U.S. interventions, it rings much more true.

Overprediction and Overdetermination

Even when recast, however, the pro-capitalist imperative retains at least two important problems. One is what can be called the problem of *overprediction*: the theory would have predicted events that have never occurred. The second is the problem of *overdetermination*: other theories can also explain the events and can do so just as well or better.

Overprediction. We saw that the pro-capitalist and anti-Communist imperatives can explain each of the major U.S. interventions since 1945. A theory that can explain everything, however, may explain too much; it would have predicted events that have never occurred. The pro-capitalist and anti-Communist imperatives surely would have predicted U.S. military intervention against the Chinese Communists sometime in 1948-1949, after the failure of the earlier advisory intervention and for the sake of those "four hundred million customers." The imperatives probably would have predicted five other U.S. military interventions in the period since 1945 that have never been undertaken: (1) against the Communist Viet-Minh in Vietnam (Tonkin) in 1953-1954; (2) against the "Castro-Communist" regime in Cuba in 1960-1961, especially after the failure of the proxy intervention at the Bay of Pigs; (3) against the Communist Pathet-Lao in Laos in 1961-1962; (4) against the Communist supported coup in Iraq in 1958; and (5) perhaps even against the Marxist government in Chile in 1970-1971. Given the perspective of the pro-capitalist and anti-Communist imperatives, the most interesting question about the advisory intervention in China and the proxy intervention at the Bay of Pigs would be not why did they occur but why were they not followed by full military intervention. Indeed, the imperatives would have mispredicted as many or more military interventions that did not occur, as they would have correctly predicted military interventions that did occur (Korea 1950-1953; Lebanon 1958, which they might not have predicted; the Dominican Republic 1965-1966; Vietnam 1965-1973 and the associated interventions in Laos and in Cambodia).

Perhaps efforts could be made to interpret these six non-interventions in strictly economic terms. I believe it likely, however, that such efforts would prove unsuccessful. In order to salvage the theory of economic imperialism from the desert of non-intervention, its advocates will probably have to go beyond economic factors to non-economic ones—and this will be a crucial concession indeed.

Overdetermination. Finally, we turn to what is probably the most intractable problem confronting the theory of economic imperialism. The trouble with questions about the causes of foreign policies is not that there are no answers but that there are too many answers. The various interventions by the United States and more generally the anti-Communist imperative of the United States can be and have been explained not only by the capitalist system and economic interests but also by several alternative factors: (1) the international system and strategic interests, (2) the democratic system and party competition, (3) the interests of particular government bureaucracies, including the military services, and (4) the psychological background of a generation of policy-makers possessed by intense memories of appeasement and the Second World War, which led them to misperceive the nature of Communist threats. Each of these alternative factors can be turned into a *sufficient* explanation for the U.S. interventions since 1945.

Is there any way to establish by an empirical test the superiority of one explanation over another—to prune away at this thicket of theories? In regard to the issue at hand—explaining the U.S. interventions since 1945—I would argue that the answer is no. The number of cases is sufficiently small so that each of the theories can be fitted to each of the cases; none of the cases can serve as a discriminating test—that is, a point that some theories can reach and that others can not. If so, the ultimate grounds for choosing one theory over another will be as much existential as empirical. And the ultimate test of the theory of economic imperialism will be merely its power to command a leap of faith.

Notes

1. The phrase is Arnold Wolfer's. *Discord and Collaboration* (Baltimore: Johns Hopkins University Press, 1962), p. 101.

2. On the role of paradigms in science, see Thomas S. Kuhn, *The Structure of Scientific Revolutions* (Chicago: University of Chicago Press, 1962).

3. M.A. Adelman, "Is the Oil Shortage Real? Oil Companies as OPEC Tax-Collectors," *Foreign Policy*, no. 9, Winter 1972-73, pp. 69-107.

4. See James Petras, *Politics and Social Structure in Latin America* (New York: Monthly Review Press, 1970), pp. 235-236.

5. In regard to Vietnam, of course, offshore oil resources were discovered after the American intervention.

6. Quoted in Reinhard Bendix, *Max Weber: An Intellectual Portrait* (New York: Anchor Books, 1962), p. 47.

2 Theories of Imperialism and Neocolonialism

Karl W. Deutsch
Harvard University

This chapter makes some observations on the problems of imperialism and neocolonialism and their relevance to current peace research. In dealing with this topic, we must first agree on the concepts that will be used. An *empire*, I propose, is a kingdom of kingdoms. It is the largest area and the largest unit under central political control that can be found in history. This central political power is not necessarily equally responsive to all the territories under its jurisdiction. It is, rather, responsive to at least one central need and one central area. The empire is under central political control in regard to social, political, economic, and cultural issues—that is to say, empire implies a substantive domain where power has both a wide scope and a significant weight. Very often it includes areas that do not directly fall within the empire. These used to be called spheres of influence; now-a-days they are referred to as allies.[1]

Imperialism—the striving to expand this domain—is an old practice in history that was vastly intensified and expanded in two waves. The first of these waves occurred in Europe after 1500 with the development of ocean-going shipping. The second wave, occurring after 1875, added a new dimension—*modern imperialism*. *Theories* of modern imperialism, then, have the main task of accounting for the existence, the resurgence, the intensification, and the prospects of imperialism after 1875.

Four "Folk" Theories of Imperialism

I will first briefly refer to four families of theories, which are almost folk theories, that can be found on the editorial pages of many newspapers in various countries and periods. They are less theories that *ex ante* predict what is going to happen; they are rather apologies, *ex post*, for what has happened or what is being done. The folk theories come in four packages.

This chapter is a revised version of the presidential address delivered to the Peace Science Convention at the Sheraton Commander Hotel, Cambridge, Massachusetts, November 6, 1973. Printed with the permission of the Peace Science Society (International). The author gratefully acknowledges the assistance of Horst D. Dornbusch in editing this chapter for publication.

15

The first, which I will call the biological-instinctive package, implies that there are some deep drives in the animal nature of man that make him build empires. This is done either by producing a caricature of the Darwinian model of natural selection or by claiming that the behavior of singing birds, who defend their territories, explains why large empires have to be built by men. The race theories, too, come under this heading. Here, again, usually by flat assertion and loose analogy, it is argued that nature itself intended people of at least some races to have empires. Why nature itself should have suddenly gone into high gear after 1875, the theories, of course, do not explain.

The second family of folk theories can be called demographic-Malthusian. Whereas the biological-instinctive theories suggest that people are driven from deep inside to build empires, the demographic-Malthusian ones say that even if people as individuals do not have the slightest interest in empire-building, the sheer pressure of numbers, the discomfort of crowding, and the threat of starvation forces them eventually to build an empire, lest they be pushed off this crowded earth or be deprived of their basic food supply by the larger numbers of their equally hungry contemporaries in other countries. This theory in vulgarized form is again ubiquitous in both Europe and America and it has been so for a long time. It is probably expressed most eloquently in Hitler's *Mein Kampf*.[2]

The third package of folk theories of imperialism is the geographic-strategic one. In this view, there is something in the inherent logic of spaces that makes it always necessary to get one more piece of space under control. The "heartland" of Europe and Asia together, presumably somewhere around the Urals, would give its rulers control of the "world island"; the world island would give them control of the world. Thus, we get beautiful explanatory sets that are essentially mere chains of assertions garlanded with analogies. But these again are made to serve as the foundation of a theory of imperialism.

Finally, there is a psychological-cultural set of notions arguing that a culture is a pattern, a *Gestalt*, that is highly interdependent. It is maintained and carried by a population. It has a territorial base and is a value in itself. It springs from a kind of mystic desire for self-preservation, and therefore, the history of the world is seen as a struggle among these mega-souls, these personalities writ large. This theory is expressed in the writings of the German historian Karl Lamprecht.[3] It is developed in greater detail by Oswald Spengler.[4] But this notion that empires exist primarily to give expression to a civilization or to a people's spirit is not particular merely to Lamprecht and Spengler. It can be found in such diverse places as Dostoevsky's defense of the Russian empire and his advocacy of pan-Slavistic ideals;[5] in the French notion of the *mission civilisatrice*; and in the pre-World War I notion "*Am deutschen Wesen wird die Welt genesen*," which means that "the German essence will save the world." Each of these concepts assert essentially that a large-scale psychological entity, corresponding to something deep in the individual personalities of its members, requires a territorial domain in order to exist and that it has to demonstrate its vitality by striving to expand its domain.

While these theories I have sketched thus far helped to recruit many supporters of imperialism, they are now intellectually beneath contempt. It is better to look at the serious theories that were developed very late in the nineteenth century and in the twentieth century to see whether there can not be a more step-by-step accounting for the process of imperialism. There are six such theories, which are of interest here and which can be referred to as: (1) the conservative; (2) the liberal; (3) the Marxist; (4) the sociological-psychological, as proposed by J.A. Schumpeter; (5) the *dependencia I*, as stated by Johan Galtung; and (6) the *dependencia II*, as outlined by Samir Amin.

The Conservative Theory of Imperialism

Historically, the first development comes from sociologically conservative statesmen. In this view, the expansion of empires is necessary, as proclaimed by such people as Jules Ferry[6] in France, and Benjamin Disraeli, Cecil Rhodes, Rudyard Kipling, and many others in England. It is this conservative set of theories that says: Imperialism is necessary in order to preserve the existing social order in the highly developed countries; imperialism is indispensable in order to secure trade, to secure markets, to maintain employment and capital exports, and to channel the energies and social conflicts of the metropolitan populations into foreign countries where they can be discharged safely against "lesser breeds without the law," without tearing the homelands to pieces. The alternatives to expansion in Africa, wrote Cecil Rhodes, would be riots of unemployed in Manchester.[7] Jules Ferry and other writers went very much to the same point. It is important to note that this theory—that of capitalism virtually requiring expanding markets and imperial expansion abroad in order not to be destroyed by either economic depressions or social conflicts, or both, at home—is a conservative invention.

The Liberal Theory of Imperialism

As we shall see in the following, the liberal version of the idea of imperialism as developed by John Atkinson Hobson and Sir Norman Angell, among others, represents essentially an intermediate stage, a transition stage, between the conservative notion of imperialism and the Marxist notion.[8]

This theory says that there is indeed an economic process promoting imperialist behavior, but it is an unnecessary one. While the Cecil Rhodes or Jules Ferry theory had asserted the necessity of imperialism, Hobson argued that it was indeed a policy that was convenient to certain interest groups but that it was really unnecessary. Imperialism, according to Hobson, is mainly underconsumption—that is to say, it is caused by large groups of entrepreneurs who tend to combine—to develop monopolies—and to underpay their workers; and this monopolistic aspect of the competitive private enterprise economy produces underconsumption on the part of the population of the metropolitan country. Since the metropolitan population does not consume enough, there remains an unsaleable surplus of goods in the metropolitan industrial economy. This unsaleable surplus must be placed abroad, partly through sales but mainly through capital exports. These capital exports then will have to be secured militarily by the acquisition of direct political and military control of colonies. Since different states will all try to do the same, this will make conflicts inevitable and will therefore lead to wars. These side-effects of imperialism are very unpleasant and they make it, in the long run, unprofitable. The costs of maintaining and defending overseas empires within which one exports capital from one's metropolis are larger than the gains or economic benefits one can extract from them. Moreover, the group that benefits from monopoly, under-consumption, and imperialism is not the whole private enterprise system, as the conservatives had argued. According to the classic liberal argument, these serve mainly *special* interests. It is the task, therefore, of liberal and radical critics to unmask these special interests and to show that they are either illusory, or hostile to the *general* interest of the nation, or both. Hobson, by and large, tended to stress the special interests and the aspect of indignation in this image. Norman Angell rather stressed its illusory aspect. But both agreed that imperial behavior, though probable, was unnecessary and damaging.

The effects of imperialism, according to the conservatives, were likely to invigorate the metropolitan economy and culture and to civilize the colonies. It would, therefore, be really beneficial for both colonies and mother country, and if it led to an endless competition for world conquest, this competition was itself good for it would select the best and strongest nations for survival. That was at least how Ferry or Rhodes in their days saw the world. According to Hobson, however, the imperial behavior would distort the metropolitan economy by promoting monopolies, increasing the power of the great financial houses, and dragging the whole nation into adventures that were by no means in the real interest of the country.

On the other hand, the liberal theorists held that imperialism was probably not bad for the colonies. There was no great accusation from them about imperialism damaging the colonies, and Sir Norman Angell in fact believed that imperialism had a civilizing impact. He suggested that if the Western countries could only give up all this unpleasant competition among each other for empire, an international government could be set up that would then police the colonies jointly. From Norman Angell to Clarence Streit[9] this idea of retaining colonial empires but cartelizing and pooling them came up from time to time and was a minor but identifiable theme in the intellectual arsenal of the classic, upper middle-class liberalism of those days.

The Marxist Theory of Imperialism

The Marxists took off from both the conservatives and Hobson. Since Marxists are fond of expropriating, they expropriated the existing theories of imperialism and eventually converted them into Marxist theory. The conservatives began with the value premise that capitalism was good, and since capitalism needs empire, it follows that imperialist behavior—including the wars that it engenders—must also be good. Later, both liberals and Marxists took the opposite view: War is bad. Imperialism leads to war. Therefore imperialism is bad. Unlike the liberals, the Marxists agreed with conservatives that capitalism requires imperialism. But from this they concluded, unlike the conservatives, that, since war is bad, capitalism is bad too. In Marxist writings we find the same causal chain between capitalism and imperialism as was asserted by the conservatives, with only the value signs reversed. But it is essentially the same theory. In 1917 Lenin wrote his sketch of imperialism, and a brilliant sketch it is with a power of vision in its theorizing. His book is based, in part, on earlier works by Otto Bauer in 1907, Rudolf Hilferding in 1910, and Rosa Luxemburg in 1913.[10]

The Marxists accepted the factual description of Hobson that imperialism was mainly economic—it was based on economics—it was due to underconsumption, and it was due to monopolies. But whereas Hobson had said that imperialist behavior is unnecessary, the Marxists accepted the conservative contention that it is vitally necessary to the survival of the private enterprise system—that is, they took the Hobson diagnosis with a Cecil Rhodes type of causality. Capitalism *could not* exist without the capital glut, without underconsumption at home, without imperial expansion abroad. This meant, therefore, that capitalism would endlessly divide and re-divide the world, and, said Lenin, it would use some of the profits from empire to bribe a small labor aristocracy at home who would get higher wages, and in return accept the ideologies of social patriotism, special privilege for labor groups, dislike for foreigners, and patriotic support of the government in imperial wars against the other rival contenders for world power.

Finally, since it was utterly necessary to invest capital abroad and to compete for empire and since the globe was finite, the moment would come—indeed according to Lenin it had come by 1900—where the world had been divided and every further division of the world could occur only by redivision. This meant that whereas colonial expansion from 1875 to 1900 had involved using machine guns against native tribes armed with muzzle loaders, from 1900 on it meant machine guns, artillery and other modern weapon systems on both sides. It meant a radical change in the nature of imperialist warfare. It would now become more deadly, more devastating, more costly by a whole order of magnitude.

Nevertheless, it was impossible to invest capital abroad without direct political and military control. This in Lenin's view was essential, and therefore the struggle for political and military control was also essential and necessary. Continuing wars among capitalist powers could not possibly be abolished so long as capitalism was not abolished.

The doctrine further went on to say that, as Lenin pointed out, imperialism would bring about the *decay* of the metropolitan power—that is, as imperialism would eventually drive capital from the not very profitable investments in the home country into the more profitable investments in the colonies—since in the home country wages were higher in order to keep the labor aristocracy in a pleasant mood, while native labor out in the colonies was cheap—eventually the heavy industries would all end up in the colonies. Dirty and heavy work would be performed out there. A typical example for Lenin was the shift of the British navy in 1911 from coal firing to oil firing. Coal had still to be dug in dusty and dirty mines by British miners. Oil could be produced by Persian or Mexican natives and the British could then move to more pleasant occupations. Lenin finally envisaged a future for Britain where the British grain fields would be turned into golf courses and shooting preserves while grain would be planted in Argentina. The British would cease to be a nation of farmers, factory workers, mechanics, and coal miners and would become a nation of butlers and game keepers. From P.G. Woodhouse to D.H. Lawrence—we then find that these characters really do make their appearance in British literature!

The metropolis would thus decay. The strength of the colonies, according to Lenin, would be built up, because the colonies would get the new mechanical installations, the new added technology, the oil drilling rigs, the blast furnaces—that is, the colonies would have both a modern infra-structure and a good deal of the progressive productive equipment. And most importantly, *they* would become a people of factory workers and *they* would begin to learn all the skills one acquires while working in a factory. Lenin would have rejoiced if he could have read the new book by Alex Inkeles who has interviewed thousands of peoples in six countries to find out exactly what working in a factory does to them. The factory is a school of modernization.[11]

The Lenin theory implies, therefore, that essentially, and in the long run, imperialism will reverse the balance of power between metropolis and colony. The metropolis will eventually fall behind in installed horsepower, in number of factories, and in sophistication of equipment; the colony will have the really basic industrial strength. To some extent, of course, Lenin was impressed with the ways in which Germany had overtaken England and France and in which possibly Russia might someday overtake Western Europe. For Lenin, of course, all countries in the world could be considered at various stages, either as potential subjects of imperial domination or else as potential competitors in the imperial game. In his view, the two roles of empire and colony could be taken by the same country in succession at different times. It could become an empire, then become a colony, and then become an empire again. But what counted really was that the colonial countries would steadily build up their capabilities and their potential. Since, at the same time, the major burdens of wars—modern wars in particular—would largely fall upon the metropolitan countries, one could derive from Lenin's view a notion of the *self-reversing character of imperialism*. Imperialism might end up, in the Leninist scenario, with the devastation of Berlin, Hamburg, Dresden, or Coventry—that is, military and economic destruction of metropolitan countries—while at the same time the colonies would begin to expand in their economy and would become more powerful. As a result, the old metropolitan countries would end up being not only decayed but inferior in power. One is reminded here, for example, of the development of the two earliest empires of the Western world, Spain and Portugal. They lapsed into imperial decay and some of their colonies, such as the Netherlands and Argentina, eventually outgrew the mother countries.[12] The way in which the United States outgrew Great Britain would be another example of how a colony could overtake a center.

This shift in power to the former colonial dominions, according to Lenin, would have serious repercussions on the imperial country. As the colonies became independent, no longer would they accept on privileged terms the capital from the mother countries or safeguard so securely the investments from the metropolis, which would make it very impractical for the latter to continue the export of capital. The metropolitan countries at the same time would, of course, continue to suffer from underconsumption and the imperative need to export. And the net result, as Lenin expected it, would be recurrent crises and the eventual collapse of capitalism. As colonial power or even as the Western control of quasi-colonies would come to an end, the "chain of world capitalism," which in Lenin's view was girdling the globe, would be broken. It would be broken at its *"weakest links"*—that is, in those countries that are just backward enough to keep their industrial labor and their peasantry thoroughly disgruntled and ready for revolution but that are sufficiently advanced to have enough workers concentrated in enough big factories, close enough to the big intersections of the railroad system, to make such a revolution successful. Lenin named three such weakest-link countries as the best candidates for revolution, to wit, Russia, China, and Spain. And he had hopes for India. If and when revolutions in the colonial or "semicolonial"—i.e., developing—countries should occur in sufficient number, capitalism would become inoperable in Western Europe. Lenin was quoted as having said (although I have found no evidence that he actually said so), that "the way to Paris leads through Peking."

A Sociological and Psychological Theory of Imperialism

Nearly at the same time of Lenin's writings, Joseph Schumpeter, in Austria, in 1918, just before the end of the war, sketched an alternative theory.[13] It argued that imperialism was not—as both the conservatives and the Marxists had asserted—a necessary behavior. In Schumpeter's view imperialism was *learned* behavior, which once learned, was very probable but not inevitable.

Schumpeter's theory was largely sociological and psychological. From this point of view, he argued that imperialism was, in a serious sense, timeless. He deliberately went back to examples of the old Assyrian and Roman empires and argued that one could find—even verbatim at times—very similar arguments or behavior patterns as in modern imperialism. Imperialism, said Schumpeter, is *objectless expansion.* By objectless expansion he meant that a continuing process of military and economic expansion would become more important than any of its changing territorial objects. Military professionals, he suggested, will tell their government that in order to secure their empire's frontier, the district immediately beyond the frontier had to be secured. Once this district has been secured, it then becomes imperative to secure the district immediately adjacent to it. And so one always had to conquer the n + 1st district until one reached the Himalaya Mountains, the edge of the ocean, or a desert, so that it would no longer be practical to expand much further. It turns out, in other words, that the rhetoric of imperialism—now-a-days one would say "national security"—is almost identical, regardless of the geographic labels one might fill in. One could put different places and names into the blanks of the formula for different times and according to different local situations. But the formal line of argument would always be the same.

How does this seemingly irrational behavior come into being? Schumpeter argued that a nation may, in one way or another, acquire a large and highly influential elite that benefits from and lives by warlike behavior. This can happen in one of two forms.

First, the nation may have inherited a warlike aristocracy from the distant past. This aristocracy or warrior class—if it is ruling the society—will again and again lead the society into wars. Having learned the habits of warlike behavior, they will again and again strive to act them out. This tendency is particularly dangerous (there is a parallel here to Lenin's weakest-link theory) only at the upper-class level, if the country is backward enough to be ruled by a warlike aristocracy but advanced enough to have first class military hardware. This would produce an outdated aristocracy using modern weapons in the service of what Schumpeter calls an atavistic, backward policy. Schumpeter, writing in 1918, named in particular two countries as being most dangerous in the world of imperialism, namely, Germany and Japan. It might be interesting to find out whether, by 1918, Schumpeter had read Thorsten Veblen's book on *Imperial Germany and the Industrial Revolution,*[14] which appeared in 1915 and made a comparison of Germany and Japan that followed a roughly similar line of reasoning.

However, there was a second way in which a country could acquire such a warlike elite that would take to the *acting out* of warlike behavior. If a country that, at first, had a very non-militaristic social structure later became the object of a major aggression or otherwise involved in a large conflict, it might develop a major military establishment as part of its effort to survive the conflict. Having survived or even won, it would then be stuck with this large military machine that had now lost its original function. If the establishment were powerful, if its members were now reinforced and rewarded for having behaved in the new warlike way, and if it were running the society, then the military establishment would seek and find new functions for its skills and take the country into a period of imperial warfare.

Schumpeter begins his analysis with the case of Egypt, around 1650 to 1550 B.C., when Nomadic people called the Hyksos had invaded Egypt. The Egyptians, having developed a highly mobile striking force of horse-drawn chariots that had, under King Aahmes I, beaten the Hyksos duly, were left with a very large army and a warrior class that had almost nothing further to do. Egypt then spent the next 100 years in efforts to conquer countries in the fertile crescent since the army wanted to be kept occupied. Schumpeter's suggestion would be to study not only the size of the *military-sociological* complex, if one wants to call it that, that has become established in the country but also its roots, its strength, and its reinforcement mechanisms. Then, one could make an estimate as to how many wars during how long a time this country is likely to be involved.

In other words, in order to gauge the depth and strength of imperialist behavior, one should not look at the size of empire, the number or the extent of possessions on the map, nor even the number of wars in the past. One should look only at the depth of the *war-producing sector* of the social structure.

By the first two tests—that is, the number of wars in the past or numbers of colonies or territories conquered on the map—by 1918 England was the number one imperialist country in the world. It had the biggest empire and it had, as Quincy Wright and recently David Singer have pointed out, waged more wars than any other nation.[15] But in Schumpeter's view, the roots of the war-promoting system in the English body-social were more shallow than in almost any other country. Schumpeter therefore predicted that British imperialism would prove to be skin deep and that Britain would give up her empire with very little trouble.

On the other hand, the giving up of the German empire, which was much smaller and which had engaged in fewer wars, or the giving up of the Japanese empire would require much greater social upheavals within these countries. Schumpeter had similarly pessimistic views about the imperial Russia of his day (this was before 1918) and about Austria-Hungary. He predicted major up-heavals in these countries before imperialism could end.

Later, in 1929, when the German empire had fallen and Germany was a republic, Schumpeter looked at the German statistics of the 1920s and announced that Germany now was going to be stable and peaceful because it, according to the statistics, had a bigger middle-class than most other coun-tries.[16] For the middle-class and capitalism, in Schumpeter's view, were both inherently peaceful. It was only the aristocrats who were warlike. And, therefore, one could be sure, as Schumpeter put it, that no extreme party would come to power in Germany for many many years. This article was published in 1929, four years before Hitler took power. But although Schumpeter had been so badly wrong in 1929, much of the logic of his analysis became applicable again to the German Federal Republic from 1949 onward. After the more thorough and more profound upheaval of World War II, and after the continuing social changes in the quarter-century that followed, many of the social roots of warlike behavior in Germany had been greatly weakened, which might explain why in the end the giving up of German territorial claims in Eastern Europe, recently carried out by Chancellor Willy Brandt, proved so easy and, at least until now, has had so few political repercussions.

The most pessimistic implication of the Schumpeter method occurs when we consider the United States. When Schumpeter wrote his work, the United States had a minimal military establishment. Bruce Russett has since shown that after every war the American military establishment remained permanently bigger than it had been before that war.[17] This process began after the Spanish American war. During World War II, under the colossal psychological impact of Pearl Harbor and the war against the Axis, the American military establishment became huge, has remained large and well connected, and to some extent our Pentagon complex has now become something of a Schumpeterian nightmare. I do not know whether President Eisenhower ever read Schumpeter, or whether anybody gave him a digest of the argument, but there is a very noticeable parallelism between Schumpeter's theory and Eisenhower's phrase of the military-industrial complex in his farewell address.[18]

The Dependencia Theories of
Imperialism—Version I: Johan Galtung

The classic theories have been joined by two more recent ones, published in the late 1960s and early 1970s. They are both variations on what we call the *dependencia* theories, which come out of a complex of writings largely by Latin American, and more recently, Arab economists and which are embellished with additional political comment from various groups on the New Left or neo-Marxist fringe of the intellectual spectrum. The first is the theory of Johan Galtung. Galtung, in an article called "A Structural Theory of Imperialism,"[19] follows the Arab and Latin American writers by dividing the world into *centers* and *peripheries*. The division within a single country had been used originally among Norwegian sociologists in the early 60s for the explanation of Norwegian voting behavior in earlier decades. Stein Rokkan was one of the early researchers to use these phrases.[20] But Galtung divides the *world* into *countries*—those at the center and those at the periphery. *Within* each country, again, there is a center, and therefore in the center countries, there is a *center of the center* and a *periphery of the center*. And in the periphery countries, there is a *center of the periphery* and a *periphery of the periphery*, which is really out in the backwoods. It is a little bit difficult to find out precisely how one knows or determines whether a country is in the center or in the periphery, but Galtung does propose three major tests.

First, there is the test of *partner concentration*. The pattern of international transactions, Galtung says, is "feudal" in nature. By *feudal* he means that there are at least two classes of countries. In one class are privileged or metropolitan countries, which are those with high per capita incomes. These center countries have high levels of transactions, with a wide range of different partners so that no one trade partner has a monopoly, and they trade much with each other. On the other hand countries in the other class—the periphery countries—are victims of monopoly. They concentrate largely on one partner, on whom they are more or less dependent.

By and large, for instance, England trades with France, with Germany, with the United States, and with many other countries. Ireland trades mainly with England. England, therefore, is a center country; Ireland is a periphery country. The same is true of Argentina. Argentina, according to Galtung, mainly trades with few countries whereas a center country like the United States would trade with many. Hence Argentina is a peripheral country in the world at large; only in relation to Paraguay does Argentina play the role of a local center.

All this is not only true of trade. It is similarly true of news services, of movie productions, of television programs, of cultural transactions, of military equipment—where you get the machine guns for your army—and of many other types of exchanges.

Secondly, there is the test of *commodity concentration*. The center countries trade in highly diversified ranges of commodities; the periphery countries are under great pressure to concentrate on a very small range of commodities. They are pushed into *"monoculture"*—that is, the production of particular agricultural goods, such as coffee or bananas, or into concentration on particular minerals, such as nickel or copper. It is argued, for instance, that if a country grows bananas, it is usually encouraged not to grow too much coffee and so on. Galtung sees in all such matters a sign of imperialism.

Finally, there is *vertical trading*. By vertical trading Galtung means those productive activities—agriculture or extractive industries like mining—that are relatively primitive, intensive in labor, low in skill, and relatively low in capital equipment, and are performed by dependent, peripheral countries. On the other hand, activities that are very high in skill and capital equipment take place in the center countries. This is similar to Lenin's argument except that Lenin saw the center countries decay into specialization or service industries and consumer economies, whereas Galtung sees the center countries continue to flourish in the highly worthwhile skilled and capital-intensive industrial occupations. The worthwhile industrial occupations, as Galtung sees them, have high *spin-off effects*. If you work as a designer for IBM or if you work in an aircraft factory, you learn large numbers of skills that are also useful for other industries. Therefore the *external economies* created by the firms in the metropolitan countries are high in amount and highly sophisticated in quality. On the other hand, if you learn how to shovel asphalt in Trinidad, the skills you acquire in this activity are almost useless for anything else. In peripheral countries there are thus, according to Galtung, very low spin-off effects or very simplistic (low) external economies.

Trade between countries of very different levels of economic and technological development is called by Galtung "vertical trading," and he predicts that the inequality between such partners will tend to be self-perpetuating. The trade partner who has the higher end of the bargain will show rapid economic growth and rapid technological innovation. The partner in the inferior part of vertical trading with the low-skilled jobs will show low economic growth and increasing technological backwardness. In this sense, whereas David Ricardo has described the exchange of British textiles for Portuguese wine as an example of the wisdom and excellence of the international division of labor and the greatness of the law of comparative advantage, Galtung would say it just shows that the Portuguese were doing something that had few spin-off effects and was poor in external economies, such as growing wine, while the British were developing the textiles of Manchester with strong spin-off effects that would eventually lead to British railroad, aircraft, and other industries. Therefore both the technological gap and the income gap between Britain and Portugal would perpetually increase. In this sense and on this matter, Galtung, who had the advantage of hindsight, produced the more realistic theory than Ricardo did.

It seems clear that there are fundamental differences between Galtung's and Lenin's theories. Both Galtung and Lenin think imperialism is very bad. Both are against it. But Lenin thinks imperialism is self-liquidating and self-reversing, whereas Galtung thinks imperialism is self-preserving and perpetuates backwardness. And, for Galtung, there is nothing much that anybody in the developing countries or anywhere else can do about it except by a radical act of the will.

The center of the center, of course, gets all the advantages of this international division of labor, this unequal division of labor. The periphery of the center gets less than the center, but somewhat similar to Lenin's argument, it gets a rake-off; its labor can be given a somewhat higher wage. Therefore, on the whole, the periphery of the center will patriotically support the center in its imperial policies.

In the periphery countries, the middle class or the bourgeoisie will become somewhat reactionary. According to the Galtung theory, they are likely to be bought by the imperial system and to make up its bridgehead in the native countries. The middle classes of Buenos Aires, Rio de Janeiro, and Santiago de Chile, who completely accept the West European and North American standards of consumption, complete with bathtubs and television sets, live about as well as, or better than, middle class persons live in the advanced countries. But the poor of Brazil, Argentina, and Chile are poor by the grim standards of the poor in Latin America. The difference between rich and poor is much greater in the developing countries than it is in the metropolitan countries.

Moreover, in the periphery countries the center of the periphery partly dissipates the wealth and the potential capital of the periphery countries in the form of luxury imports; or at best it will sustain industries that mainly work for the luxury consumption habits of the small privileged groups in the centers of the periphery countries. The mass of the population of the periphery countries is the rural mass; they will remain poor and at the periphery of the economy and society, and the difference between the urban sectors, such as Rio de Janeiro, Sao Paulo, and the periphery sector such as North Brazil, will get worse and worse as time goes on. Furthermore, if the peasants should leave their poor, backward countryside and move toward the center, they will there again end up in ghettos and shanty towns of one kind or another. Indeed, even the center countries will import poor devils from the peripheries of the world for the menial jobs, and they will create once again a kind of internal colonialization. This is a point that is implicit in Galtung's theory, but he does not stress it. Arab writers and Latin American writers, however, stress this aspect frequently.

Finally, Galtung points out that imperialism is so splendidly self-supporting that it no longer has any need for direct political control. An empire that controls a colony, says he, is an inefficient empire. There is not the slightest need of controlling a colony by foreign troops if the bridgehead bourgeoisie of the center of the periphery will do the job free of charge. Why send in the marines if you have, say, the Chilean army? This would be essentially a Galtung argument. It is only when an imperial system is in danger of breaking down, says Galtung, that direct intervention is at all necessary. Moreover, it is quite possible, since imperialism is a worldwide system, that several imperialist countries could jointly control one developing country at the periphery. We might get an agreement among imperialist countries, including even the United States and the Soviet Union, in Galtung's view, for the joint exploitation of some helpless coffee or tea growing country on the periphery.

As Galtung sees it, the imperialist system is self-perpetuating. Dependence is permanent. And there is nothing in the Galtung scheme that would objectively show how this should ever end. At this point Galtung, in a manner almost reminiscent of Søren Kierkegaard, makes a leap of faith. He assumes that there will be a *prise de conscience*—a raising of consciousness. Somehow, suddenly the illiterate peasants of the backwoods and the poor devils in the ghettoes and shanty towns will get so indignant about their conditions—and they will presumably be led by indignant and virtuous students and intellectuals—that by a tremendous act of spontaneity they will overthrow the system. There will then be a revolution in the peripheral countries. The bourgeoisie of the center of the periphery will "have to choose" whether they go with their local population or with the imperialist system, and the outcome of these struggles will then determine which way the countries of the periphery will go.

Assuming that the revolution wins, the countries of the periphery should then dissociate themselves from the imperialist system, cut down their contacts with the Western world or with the advanced countries, abandon vertical trading, and replace it with horizontal trading, by which is meant trading among each other at the same level of industrial elaboration and technology. Similarly, they should diversify their commodities and diversify their trade partners. By breaking down the three forms of dependency—vertical trading, partner concentration, and commodity concentration—they can eventually liberate themselves. How they would accumulate the necessary capital is not completely clear, but this is a point both Galtung and other writers on the New Left usually tend to minimize; capital accumulation—capitalist or socialist—is a process they do not like to dwell upon, and it is usually not very much stressed in their writings.

The Dependencia Theory of Imperialism—Version II: Samir Amin

The last writer I would like to mention here is Samir Amin,[21] an Egyptian economist and now the head of a development institute at Dakar in West Africa; one can say that he stands for a large group of theorists including, for instance, Anouar Abdel Malek and others. He derives much of his economics from Raúl Prebisch and other Latin American writers. Samir Amin uses a far more explicitly Marxist language than does Galtung. He accepts the same center vs. periphery pattern as Galtung does. He, too, argues that imperialism distorts the entire colonial socio-economic structure. It drains the wealth out of the colonial country or the peripheral country and he, like Galtung, sees the center of the periphery as an alien beachhead, which is really hostile to the interests of the peripheral country.

Lenin, also, had a theory that the middle class would first collaborate with the imperialist system against the colony, later join in a national independence movement for a time with the masses in the peripheral or colonial country, and then finally become conservative again and resist the further development of the anti-imperialist revolution. Something like this could be seen in the three steps found in the merchants of Shanghai. In the 1890s and 1900s, they were conservative; in the Nationalist, middle class period of the Kuomintang, they formed an alliance with the radical groups, with labor, and with the peasants; and finally they became the new conservatives allied with Chiang Kai-shek. That was more or less the standard script according to Lenin. Whereas Lenin had, therefore, a thorough reversal of fronts in his script, Galtung and Anouar Abdel Malek do not predict any such probable changes of fronts. Galtung at least leaves the middle class a choice; Abdel Malek also thinks there *could* be an alliance with the national bourgeoisie but he is on the whole quite skeptical about it.

The imperialist system, according to Samir Amin, keeps agriculture particularly poor. By denying agriculture capital, it manufactures marginal persons— that is to say, since there is little capital left in the rural areas and since population growth continues, people leave the rural areas and move to the towns. But in the towns there is still not enough capital for them to work with, and they will, therefore, not be employed in any kind of well-equipped industry or enterprise. They instead remain marginals—casual laborers with low skill and little or no technical equipment—and poverty becomes self-perpetuating. However, the peasants of the hinterland and the marginals of the cities are now the vast majorities of the peripheral countries, and they have a common interest. The main enemy, according to Samir Amin's thinking, is the ideology of economic growth and the related ideology among Socialists that he calls "economism." The economist ideologists, Samir Amin says, argue that it is very important to increase the per capita income and the capital equipment of the national economy. This is really quite false, he insists, because it treats labor as a commodity and it alienates the worker. It is perfectly possible to have a peripheral country subject to the imperialist system even if all its industries are owned by the government, says Amin, and even if the official ideology is socialism. These industries could still have alienated labor, and they could still be a subordinate link in the chain of world imperialism. The tip-off will be that they are technologically backward compared to the Western countries. And their peripheral situation will perpetuate their lack of capital and their technological backwardness. This could go on indefinitely for half a century or a century, as Amin sees it, even under a large Red flag. Samir Amin is therefore inclined to think of Communist countries, including the Soviet Union, largely as subjected or subordinated to world capitalism and imperialism, while Galtung thinks of the Soviet Union as a potentially imperialist country, which is a major difference between their two views.

Samir Amin has another difficulty, however. Since he, like Galtung, thinks that imperialism is incurable, self-perpetuating, and could last forever, it is most difficult for him to explain what Galtung simply ignored, namely, the observed fact that many countries that were once non-industrial, like Japan or Russia and many others, have since become highly industrialized. Many countries, once subject to the privileged condition of foreign capital, foreign investments, and all the rest, are no longer so. Samir Amin solves this problem by rechristening the countries in that category. He says simply they never were peripheral countries. They were simply "young capitalist" countries—that is to say, if you are poor and non-industrial and you do not grow, then you are a genuine peripheral country. If you were non-industrial, poor and did grow, that proves you were not a peripheral country at all but rather a young capitalist country. This comes close to making the theory circular and verbal.

There is one bit of evidence that makes this theory somewhat more respectable, namely, that the young capitalist countries are countries that are, as Amin says, "auto-centered"—that is, self-centered; they have, as we should say, their own effective national decision system. They can develop a middle class, they can develop at least small mercantile entrepreneurs, they can make use of the economic opportunities that came from the entry into international trade and the imperial epoch, and they can then therefore emerge on their own power. Nevertheless, the theory is extraordinarily weak because other countries also have small merchants, and many colonial countries have their own national decision centers; indeed, Samir Amin has spent pages and pages explaining how these national decision centers simply are doing the business of imperialism in repressing their own countries. Here I think we see an effort to make economic determinism work overtime and to create a causal and deterministic argument that can only be kept alive by very ingenious use of definitions—by essentially defining the difficult bits out of the argument.

Nevertheless, Amin leaves some room for voluntaristic decision. In certain countries, there has been a borderline situation where the country could have gone one way or the other. Such a country, in Amin's view, is Argentina. Argentina around 1900 had one of the highest living standards in the world and was then considered a highly advanced country. However, the import merchants, import interests, and the landlords of Argentina, in making an alliance with the international imperialist interests, destroyed the movement toward a genuine independent Argentina. The pay-off, to Amin's way of thinking, is the success or defeat of industrial protection. Countries that protect their own industries when they are underdeveloped, eventually become authentic young capitalist countries. Countries that accept what seems to him the most pernicious ideology of all, the ideology of a free trade, eventually starve their industrial sectors, make their own economies backward, and then perpetuate the poverty of the peasants and of the marginal population in the cities. This, in Amin's view, is what happened in Argentina and is happening in many other countries. One can see that the self-maintaining and relatively deterministic picture both in Galtung's and in Amin's writings leaves only little room for breaking out of the circle and Amin, as does Galtung, turns voluntaristic. What counts in the end is the decision that is made—whether the merchants and the others go with the imperialists or with their own peasantry. Amin thinks that usually they go with the imperialists, and there is very little anybody else can do about it unless the peasantry and the poor begin to raise their consciousness, begin to be active, and essentially make a revolution by a supreme effort of the will.

Conclusion

I have summarized six major theories of imperialism. Each of them neglects the issue of what I would call *emancipatory potentials*. The imperialism theories treat the cultures and peoples of the world as if they were a uniform, grey, homogeneous mass. They are not. If we look at the world in general we find something very striking. Roughly 600 million people live in what we now call highly advanced countries. Another 1400 million or so live in countries that have what I would call *proto-industrial* cultures. By proto-industrial, I mean a culture that has already taught people the value of saving and thrift; the benefit of working for distant goals; the need for accuracy, precision, and reliability; the use of time; and in particular, the maintenance of contracts—both a certain flexibility in making contracts and a certain dependability in keeping them. Chinese or Japanese cultures are typical examples of those that encourage these proto-industrial skills. The Japanese, for instance, had a high understanding of the qualities of steel long before the first factory was built in Japan. If we put together the proto-industrial countries with the highly developed countries of North America and Western Europe, they make up the majority of mankind.

We find, on the other hand, a number of countries with a counter-industrial cultural tradition. Almost all of these countries are Muslim or have had a very prolonged phase of Muslim influence. I count here Spain and Portugal and their offshoots, including all of Latin America. I also count the entire Arab world, as well as Pakistan, Bangladesh, Indonesia, and the Philippines. All of these seem to me to be countries where industry grows more slowly, where industrial habits take a longer time to take root, where there is much trade and little manufacture, and where on the whole there is also much interest in law and little in science. In the Spanish-Muslim complex we find the worst performance records in regard to industrialization. Strikingly enough, this cuts across the social orders. Private enterprise in Uruguay or Morocco is highly uninspiring compared to private enterprise in Connecticut, Sweden, or Scotland; but collective enterprise in Cuba also is not nearly as impressive as collective enterprise in East Germany. We find that in the Spanish-Muslim cultural realm as a whole industrial performance tends to be relatively low either under communism or capitalism, and that in industrial and proto-industrial countries industrial performance is excellent. Communist North Koreans and private-enterprise Japanese for example, both do well in running their economies. One could almost say that with Japanese, Chinese, Germans, or possibly Scotsmen one could run almost any economic system in some form. In Black Africa, too, some tribes, such as the Ibo in Nigeria and the Bamilike in Cameroon, have shown remarkable speed and effectiveness in responding to the challenges and opportunities of modernization and industrialization. This has nothing to do with race, nor even necessarily with that "Protestant Ethic," which Max Weber stressed, but it does seem to be connected with the proto-industrial skills in a wide variety of cultures.

In conclusion, I propose that we could test by reproducible data every one of the propositions in the six major theories I have summarized and in the questions I have just raised concerning emancipatory potentials. For instance, we have the possibility of testing a cultural value through content analysis, through anthropological data from the Human Relations Area Files, and by survey methods such as those of Alex Inkeles and his associates. Suitable methods by now have been worked out to some degree.

When we use them, I surmise that we will find that even the differences between proto-industrial and counter-industrial cultures are not absolute. I have stressed them so heavily, in part because most of the *dependencia* theories of the New Left draw so much of their supporting experiences either from Spanish or Arab countries, and because they seem to argue explicitly, or by implication, that it is not up to the country but to the world system whether a country is backward or not. It seems to me that a Spanish or Muslim country may take a little longer to make an industry succeed than North Korea or Japan but that eventually it, too, will succeed very well, much as Spaniards from Galicia and Colombians from Antioquia are reputed to make successful managers, and just as Lebanese banks by now are probably no less efficient than banks in other countries.

In the end I think we will find that the key to the entire imperialism debate lies in the study of emancipatory capabilities—that is, the study of the abilities of countries to make their way by loosening or modifying their involvement in whatever is left of the imperialist system. Neocolonialism, insofar as it exists, can be overcome by autonomy, by growth. I do believe that the more data-based research we develop in this direction, the more we shall find that indeed men and women are still making their own history.

Notes

1. Though the word allies is often used for imperial relationships, not all allies are satellites of an empire, and not all satellites are allies.

2. Adolf Hitler, *Mein Kampf*, (Munich: Franz Eher Verlag, vol. I, 1925; vol. II, 1927).

3. Karl Lamprecht, *Deutsche Geschichte*, vol. I, (Berlin: Weidmann, 6th ed., 1892); particularly his chapter "Geschichte der Formen des National-bewußtseins," pp. 3-56; see also C. Andler, *Le pangermanisme philosophique, 1800-1914*, (Paris: L. Conard, 1917), p. 139.

4. Oswald Spengler, *Der Untergang des Abendlandes*, 2 volumes, (Munich: Beck, 1918-1922) (England: *The Decline of the West*).

5. On Dostoevsky, see Hans Kohn, *Prophets and Peoples*, (New York: Macmillan, 1946); and E.J. Simmons, *Dostoevsky, the Making of a Novelist*, (New York: Vintage Books, 1962).

6. On Jules Ferry, see *Discourse et opinions de Jules Ferry*, pub. avec commentaires et notes par Paul Robiquet, (Paris: A. Colin, 1893-1898).

7. On Cecil Rhodes see William L. Langer, *Diplomacy of Imperialism, 1890-1902*, (New York: A.A. Knopf, 1935), vol. I, Chapter 3, p. 78 ff.

8. John Atkinson Hobson, *Imperialism; a Study*, (London: J. Nisbet, 1902); Sir Norman Angell, *The Great Illusion*, (Harmondsworth, GB: Penguin Books Ltd., 1939).

9. Clarence E. Streit, *The Essence of Union Now*, (New York: The Union Press, 1940).

10. V.I. Lenin, *Imperialism, the Highest Stage of Capitalism*, (1917), (New York: International Publishers, 1939); Otto Bauer, *Die Nationalitätenfrage und die Sozialdemokratie* (1907), (Vienna: Verlag der Wiener Volksbuchhandlung, 2nd. ed., 1924); Rudolf Hilferding, *Das Finanzkapital*, (1910), (Vienna: Verlag der Wiener Volksbuchhandlung, 2nd. ed., 1923); Rosa Luxemburg, *Die Akkumulation des Kapitals*, (1913), (Leipzig: Frankes Verlag, 1921).

11. Alex Inkeles and David Smith, *Becoming Modern; Individual Change in Six Developing Countries*, (Cambridge: Harvard University Press, 1973).

12. The Netherlands and Argentina by 1965 had far outgrown Spain in per capita income, and the Netherlands had for a time themselves become a substantial imperial power. Portugal's former colony, Brazil, has remained well below even the low per capita income of her former "mother country," but has far outgrown Portugal in aggregate income, population, area, and power. See data in C.L. Taylor and M. Hudson, *World Handbook of Political and Social Indicators: Second Edition*, (New Haven: Yale University Press, 1972).

13. J.A. Schumpeter, "Zur Soziologie der Imperialismen," *Archiev für Sozialwissenschaft*, 46, 1918, pp. 1-36 and pp. 275-310.

14. Thorsten Veblen, *Imperial Germany and the Industrial Revolution*, (New York: The Macmillan Co., 1915).

15. Quincy Wright, *A Study of War*, (Chicago: University of Chicago Press, 1942); J. David Singer, *The Wages of War* (New York: Wiley, 1973); see also Karl W. Deutsch and David Singer, *On Understanding Peace and War*, (forthcoming), particularly chapter 2.

16. J.A. Schumpeter, "Die soziale Struktur Deutschlands," in *Aufsätze zur Soziologie*, (Tübingen: J.C.B. Mohr, 1953).

17. Bruce M. Russett, *What Price Vigilance?*, (New Haven: Yale University Press, 1970).

18. At least this is what I was told by General Andrew Goodpaster who had been Eisenhower's aide at that time. General Goodpaster told me that Eisenhower had been very concerned about the degree of pressure politics and controversy connected with the TFX airplane project and had written his warning about the "complex" in his own hand.

19. Johan Galtung, "A Structural Theory of Imperialism," *Journal of Peace Research*, XIII-2, 1971, 81-118.

20. Stein Rokkan, "Party Preferences and Opinion Patterns in Western Europe: Comparative Analysis," *International Social Science Bulletin*, VII-4, 1955, 575-596.

21. Samir Amin, *Accumulation on a World Scale: A Critique of the Theory of Underdevelopment*, 2 volumes, (New York: Monthly Review Press, 1973). Anouar Abdel Malek, *Sociologie de l'impèrialisme* (Paris: Armand Colin, 1971); *Le développement inegal* (Paris: Éditions Minuit, 1973).

3

Comparing Theories of Economic Imperialism

Andrew Mack
Richardson Institute for Conflict
and Peace Research

Introduction

During the past decade there has been an upsurge of interest in the theories of economic imperialism. This has been evident in the revisionist critique of Cold War historiography, in the renewed interest in political economy in general and in Marxism in particular, and in the now well-known critiques of conventional sociological, political, and economic theories of underdevelopment.

In the United States theories of imperialism still tend to be of interest not for what they explain or attempt to explain, but rather as evidence of the ideological fixations of their proponents. Serious discussion of imperialism has to date been relegated to what Swedish sociologist, Herman Schmid, once described as the "sub-vegetation" of academia—that is, to isolated individuals and to such organizations as the Union of Radical Political Economics, the North American Commission on Latin America (NACLA), and the now defunct Africa Research Group, all of which exist right outside the mainstream of respectable social science.

In Scandinavia, theories of imperialism are taken much more seriously and can be located squarely within the academic mainstream of research on underdevelopment. American critics of theories of imperialism might argue that this is because a greater percentage of Scandanavian academics are "ideologically fixated." However, the fact that U.S. overseas investments form a productive capacity that ranks equivalent to the world's third or fourth largest industrial power, whereas Scandinavian's overseas investments are negligible, may provide a better insight into the American academic reluctance to take the notion of imperialism seriously. There are of course other reasons. The European Marxist tradition is virtually incomprehensible within the paradigmatic frameworks of conventional American social science. The Marxist conception of theory, for example, is totally at odds with the American "positivistic" or "behavioral" tradition and inexplicable within its confines. This clearly poses problems even for many American radicals working in this general area. One only has to compare the work of European Marxists like Louis Althusser with that of American neo-Marxists like Harry Magdoff to get some flavor of the enormous differences in intellectual traditions in the two continents, even where scholars share a common radical outlook.

This chapter attempts an overview of a number of theories of imperialism and is aimed at showing not only that the idea of there being such a thing as *the* theory of economic imperialism is false, but more particularly that different analysts have attempted to explain very different phenomena under the general rubric "imperialism." It is further argued that the level of analysis employed by different writers is also so different as to make comparisons between them—in some instances at least—simply irrelevant. In attempting such an overview, it is necessary firstly to be highly selective (and many will disagree with the selective criteria employed) and secondly to simplify the theories discussed to such a degree that the exposition not only ignores various subtleties of the arguments therein but also ignores some arguments altogether. This is inevitable given the scope of this chapter and may perhaps serve some useful purpose in giving some idea of the very different ways in which imperialism is perceived by different writers, the different levels of analysis at which they work, and the contradictions and complementaries that divide and unite them.

In what follows, I shall briefly refer to the central concerns and the framework of analysis employed by conventional American social science in an attempt to explain underdevelopment and the radical critique of this approach before going on to consider more general theories starting with the classical or "Leninist" theories of imperialism (which are now undergoing stringent re-evaluation by neo-Marxists). Four quite different contemporary attempts at providing *general* theories of imperialism are then considered. The first two examined deal essentially with the economic imperatives that underlie capitalist expansion abroad and as such may be seen as modern counterparts of the Leninist theory. The second two deal with the consequences of this expansion as it affects development—or rather the lack of it—in the Third World.

An underlying political concern of writers using the first approach is the need to explain the various military and non-military interventions carried out by the United States in the Third World—"imperialism" being seen largely in these terms. Interest in this area has without doubt been sharpened by the many barbarities of America's war in Vietnam. Interest in the second approach has been stimulated more by the destruction of liberal optimism regarding the development potential of the Third World that prevailed at the beginning of the first U.N. Decade of Development.

Conventional Theories of Development

It may be remembered that the economic, sociological, psychological, political, and historical theories of development, which formed the conventional social science wisdoms of the late fifties and early sixties, tended to locate the root causes of underdevelopment within the polity, culture, and social and economic structures of the developing countries themselves. Lack of development was thus associated with a lack of "achievement orientation" in the culture of the developing countries, with a lack of entrepreneurial spirit within the economic sector, and with the inflexibility of "traditional" social and political structures. These "theories" in ignoring both past and present linkages between the developing countries and the advanced capitalist countries thus squarely located the causes of underdevelopment in the developing countries themselves. Like the "culture of poverty" arguments borrowed from research into slums of Mexican cities and used to explain the underdog position of blacks in American society, this effectively shifted the responsibility for poverty onto the impoverished. It was of course a perspective that implied not an ounce of criticism of the rich countries or their governments and corporations. Big business could well have been excused for thinking that the "deserving poor" were simply those who deserved to be poor.

The liberal theorists' proposed solution to the problems thus diagnosed was that a diffusion of Western ideas, technology, and capital was necessary to counteract these "internal" obstacles to development. However, the manifest failure of such massive "aid" programs as the Alliance for Progress brought these simplistic ideas increasingly into question—even among their earlier proponents. Various studies in Latin America and elsewhere demonstrated that even such "development" that did take place did little or nothing for the mass of the population in countries where it occurred. The Brazilian economist Celso Furtado argued, for example, that what was called "development" was simply the imitation by a small minority in the poor nations of the consumption patterns of the West.[1] The diffusion of ideas and technology created enclaves of development that, far from benefiting the masses, were often parasitical on their labors. "Industrialization" meant the creation of import substitute industries (typically soft drinks, beer, cigarettes, matches, or the assembly of automobiles). These failed to provide any real infrastructure for development. They were, rather, oriented to the production of goods geared to the demands of the small Westernized elite, and by their very nature were incapable of catering to the basic wants of the masses. The posited benefits of the diffusion of capital were, it was argued, simply a myth. On balance, the net flow of capital was from the poor countries to the rich as Pierre Jalee[2] and many others have demonstrated. Andre Gunder Frank's "The Sociology of Development and the Underdevelopment of Sociology" provides both a summary and polemical critique of much of this literature for those unfamiliar with it.[3]

One critical response to the Western academic development theories was to ignore almost totally the "internal" barriers to progress and concentrate instead on externally imposed barriers to development. This approach shifted—or attempted to shift—the responsibility for underdevelopment from the poor countries to the rich. For fairly obvious reasons, this has tended to be a common response of government economic spokesmen in the Third World itself, especially in such forums as the UNCTAD Conferences. Underdevelopment from this viewpoint arises out of the various trade and tariff restrictions used by the industrialized countries against the developing countries, especially in the case of manufactured or processed goods; by the refusal to aid programs for Third World country industries competitive with overseas subsidiaries of rich country corporations; in the insistence that imports be bought and shipped from aid-donating countries at above world market prices; in rich country attempts to sabotage international commodity agreements and so forth.

However the "external constraints" argument on its own was ultimately no more satisfactory than the "internal constraints" arguments advanced by liberal social scientists. It tended to ignore the active participation of Third World governments themselves in policies that, while providing substantial benefits for the elite, could in no sense be seen as contributing to the development of the country as a whole.

None of these arguments are new; in fact they are now part of a new *radical* conventional wisdom. Evidence for the existence of the externally imposed "blocking mechanisms' described above—and many others—has now been well documented, just as the sociologists and psychologists of development could find evidence that fitted their "internalist" theories of underdevelopment. In fact, there are now literally hundreds of studies showing how particular corporations used particular means to gain advantageous positions for themselves in the developing countries. There are hundreds more showing how the U.S. government, using "persuasion," threats, economic and diplomatic sanctions, and sometimes outright military invasion, intervened on behalf of corporate interests in the Third World or—and this is not necessarily the same thing—*against* various radical movements. The collaboration of various Third World elites with foreign corporate and U.S. "security" interests has also been well documented.[4] What these studies do not provide is anything approaching a *general* theory of imperialism.

We now turn from these essentially descriptive studies that illustrate particular mechanisms of control, to more general theories. Such theories are neither region nor country-specific, nor do they take the form of simply collating together on a global basis examples of control mechanisms used at a national or regional level ("abstracted empiricism"). The best known and most discussed (at least in Europe) general theories are the so-called Leninist or "classical" theories of imperialism.

Classical Theories of Imperialism

The "classical" theories of imperialism include those of Hobson, Bukharin, Kautsky, Rosa Luxemburg, and, above all, Lenin. The immediate issue that all these theories sought to explain was the scramble for overseas territories by the imperial powers in the period roughly from 1870 to 1917. There is general agreement among all these writers that the overseas expansion of capitalism—such that it creates a world economy—goes through three phases: plunder, trade, and finally investment overseas. Crudely trade is associated with competitive capitalism and investment with monopoly or, more correctly, oligopoly capitalism. In a monopoly situation, prices are no longer determined by competition and the market size is, by definition, limited. Thus increased profits cannot be invested internally without driving down the rate of profit. Put another way, the productive capacity of the firm is in excess of the monopolized market. This in turn leads to the search for external investment outlets since the possibilities for profitable investment in other markets at home are limited by the low buying power of the masses. Income redistribution to offset this was seen as politically impossible under capitalism. Thus "surplus capital" seeks overseas outlets and in so doing precludes—or at least postpones—an endemic contradiction in capitalism (arising from underconsumption) from becoming manifest. Lenin additionally suggested that banking and industrial capital merge at the monopoly stage and gain effective control over the state. Thus the competition for external outlets for capital investment becomes a competition between *nations*—in addition to a competition between corporations—which Lenin saw as leading eventually to the First World War. This crude summary grossly oversimplifies the position of other theorists of the period. Kautsky, for example, assumed an identity of interests among capitalist combines seeking *market* outlets and predicted an emergence of a "super-imperialism" that would dominate the world and bring with it an era of peace. Rosa Luxemburg ignored the emergence of monopoly and emphasized (with Hobson and Kautsky) the lack of *markets* for industrial goods as a need for external expansion, while she, Kautsky, and Bukharin also emphasized the need to seek new raw materials.[5] The key theoretical idea that can be drawn from the classical theory (notably the crucial difference between competitive and monopoly capitalism) has retained much of its importance, but in general such theories of imperialism have been subjected to severe criticism both on empirical and theoretical grounds. Some of the main critiques are as follows. First, Lenin incorrectly identified the foreign *assets* of England, France, and Germany with *export* of capital and thus over-emphasized the importance of the latter. Second, in the crucial period of 1870 to 1913 there was a net flow of capital *into* Britain. (As far as can be established, there was probably a net outflow in the early nineteenth century with the break coming around mid-century.) Third, the rate of return abroad was not markedly higher than at home. Fourth, and perhaps most importantly, most of the capital exported went to other capitalist countries that—in terms of the theory—should have been plagued by the same problem of capital surplus. Lastly, the formation of monopolies did not take place in Britain to any significant degree until the end of the "belle-epoque" period—1870 to 1917.[6]

It is important to see that a common theme of the classical theorist was that imperialism was "inevitable," not so much because it is the normal way of life for capitalists to explore all possible avenues of profitable expansion—including expansion overseas—but because without this expansion abroad (expansion at home being ruled out by the allegedly unalterable distribution of income) capitalism would have collapsed.

The classical theorists were thus interested in the *necessary* causes of imperialist expansion. Virtually no attention was paid to the impact of this expansion on the economic, political, and social structures of the colonial possessions. This is of course in marked contrast to the work, briefly discussed earlier, where almost no attention is paid to the internal dynamics of imperialist expansion while much uncoordinated research has been carried out into the effects of this expansion.

Various critics of the classical theorists have, of course, suggested alternative explanations for the imperial scramble of the belle-epoque period. Foremost among these have been "strategic" or power political theories in which economic motives for expansion are relegated to a secondary position—that is, "trade follows the flag." Since there is good evidence for these criticisms, they have required a counter-critique from the Marxist theorists. Paul Sweezy and others have noted that, though English capitalists may have had little to gain through annexation, they had much to lose through annexation by others. The result of an annexation might appear to be a net loss, but what is important is the loss or gain compared to the situation which *would* have prevailed, had a rival succeeded in stepping in ahead. A similar conflict in the contemporary period between geo-political or "power politics" explanations and explanations rooted in global economic relations will be examined later.

As noted above, there are a number of serious difficulties posed by the classical theories even when applied to the so-called belle-epoque period of imperialism. Neo-Marxist explanations of the expansionist imperatives of *contemporary* capitalism have also had to take into account several crucial factors that were not applicable in the classical era. Firstly the buying power of the mass of the population of the advanced industrial countries has increased dramatically—even though the *relative* distribution of income has remained largely unchanged. Secondly there has been a massive increase in "non-productive" state expenditure—particularly military expenditure. Both these factors are seen as tending to "negate" the under-consumptionist/capital investment outlet problem that was the cornerstone of most classical theories. By the same token, this has further weakened the Leninist theory of imperialism as an explanatory framework for the continued foreign expansion in the present era. The third factor is the emergence of the socialist bloc and the consequent development of the Cold War. The inadequacy of the classical theories to deal with the present situation has given rise to a renewed search for the contemporary "driving force of modern capitalism." In the following section two quite different approaches to this problem are described.

The "Institutional Necessity" for
the Overseas Expansion of Capitalism

Both approaches described below argue that capitalism expands overseas not because this is a convenient way to gain extra revenue but rather out of necessity. Both approaches deal with the American experience but the logic of the argument outlined is equally applicable to other advanced capitalist countries. Both attempt to show how and why a foreign investment stake grows, and both argue that this stake will lead corporations to seek state protection for their investments. In other words, both seek to describe a global framework in which foreign interventions of various kinds by the United States can be ultimately explained in economic terms.

Strategic Raw Materials

The thesis that the driving force of U.S. imperialism is the need to acquire and control access to strategic raw materials has been advanced by Heather Dean and Harry Magdoff.[7] The argument runs crudely as follows. The U.S. economy is heavily dependent on imports of such strategic minerals as nickel, chromite, cobalt, bauxite and—most recently and dramatically—oil. Unlike various agricultural commodities—e.g., cocoa—these cannot be produced by Third World countries themselves in view of the huge capital investments and the high levels of sophisticated technology needed to extricate them. In view of the critical strategic nature of these raw materials, it is of the utmost importance that countries in which they are produced should not be allowed to undergo socialist revolutions that could lead them into the Soviet camp and thus place these resources out of reach of the United States and the other advanced industrial powers. Neither can these countries be allowed to industrialize themselves, since if they did so, these resources would be used internally and would, thus also be denied to the United States.[8] Thus, any threat of "subversion" that might lead to a socialist revolution will be met with intervention, corporate and American national interests being equally threatened. Heather Dean further argues that the chief trouble spots around the world are those in which strategically important minerals are to be found—the Middle East, Chile, Congo-Kinshasa, Rhodesia, and so forth. However, while there is no doubt that the recent U.S. diplomatic interventions in the Middle East are inexplicable if not seen in the light of the current energy crisis and the U.S. determination to safeguard future supplies from that area, the strategic resources argument simply will not serve as a *general* explanation for the "institutional necessity" of corporate expansion overseas, nor for the various types of intervention to protect investments. Firstly and most importantly this approach does not deal with the non-extractive industries—investments in manufacturing for example—and secondly it is not wholly convincing on its own terms.

The argument that industrialization in the Third World will mean that these mineral resources are consumed internally simply does not stand up since most of these resources are only required for particular applications at very sophisticated levels of technology. Secondly, it should not be assumed that the "strategic" minerals in question were used because there was simply no substitute. Rather they were employed because they were the cheapest and/or most convenient to use. Thirdly, even if no extant substitutes exist that would fulfill the exact requirements of a particular technology, this does not mean that they cannot be found. Normally, no search for a substitute is made until it is necessary to do so because existing supplies are threatened, as we have seen in the case of oil—the most important of all the Third World's resources. Lastly, even if domestic substitutes, new techniques for low grade extraction, and new methods of recovery and recycling in the consumer nation cannot be found, there is still no ground to assume that Third World countries that undergo some sort of anti-imperialist revolution will necessarily refuse to sell these resources to the West. Guinea is a good example of a country that maintains a militant anti-Western political stance while still allowing Western foreign investment in mineral extraction. In short, while the strategic resources argument may provide an explanation of particular cases of intervention, it cannot provide a framework for a general theory as Dean claims; Vietnam, the Dominican Republic, and the Guatemalan interventions are impossible to explain in these terms, for example. Furthermore, we may note that except for Dean's very weak argument that Third World industrialization must be blocked in order to prevent Third World countries from consuming these mineral resources themselves, there is nothing in this framework that can explain the failure of capitalist development in the Third World. Indeed in both Chile and Zambia the export of copper (one of the listed "strategic" minerals) has provided most of the internal development capital and foreign exchange earnings. _ mono culture

Multinational Corporations

As noted earlier, U.S. foreign investment represents a production equivalent to the third or fourth largest economy in the world. Magdoff estimates that the value of U.S. exports plus overseas production of U.S. companies is equal to around 40 percent of what he calls "the domestic production of goods"—that is, very roughly, GNP minus services and government spending.[9] He further estimates that the Third World absorbs approximately one third of U.S. exports and foreign investment. The accuracy of these estimations is not important in the present context. What is important, as Theodore Moran notes, is that: "Foreign investments are large. They are profitable. They will be defended because they are there."[10] However, as Moran points out, this fact, while it may provide suggestive possibilities for explaining the various types of U.S. intervention overseas, does not explain the dynamics by which such a stake gets built up in the first place. "Indeed, any interpretation of an *accumulated* stake far understates the interest that the most dynamic domestic corporations have in keeping the possibility of foreign expansion open to them in *their future*."[11]

"Institutional Necessity" and the Expansion of Trade and Investment

Theodore Moran in his recent article in *World Politics* rejects both the strategic resources and Leninist attempts to formulate a general theory of capitalist expansion overseas. Drawing extensively on recent research findings from the huge and on-going program of investigation into multinational corporations at Harvard and elsewhere, Moran outlines an argument based on: "Recent studies of U.S. corporate expansion aimed at testing the model of the product cycle and the growth of the firm. . . ."[12] In marked contrast to the Leninist theories in which foreign investment arises from the push of surplus capital seeking an outlet, Moran notes that foreign investment is typically a response to barriers to overseas trade. When, for whatever reason, the possibilities for expansion at home become limited, corporations expand the market for their product by foreign trade with countries with *similar demand structures*—that is, with other advanced industrial countries. However, this process leads to imitation, and imitation to competition. When this occurs, the competing firms abroad pressure their governments into enacting protective legislation—e.g., tariff and quota barriers. In order to maintain the overseas market the corporation must then side-step the trade restrictions by investing directly in that market. According to the research evidence reviewed by Moran, U.S. manufacturing companies do not normally move to invest overseas in local production until threatened by tariff barriers. In one study of the petro-chemical industry, for example, it was found that of 105 direct investment decisions, not one was made until a foreign competitor had commenced production. Moran's thesis thus explains the Leninist paradox of surplus capital—arising supposedly out of lack of investment outlets at home—being invested abroad in other advanced capitalist countries that should have been experiencing precisely the same investment outlet problem. Moran also dismisses the various arguments about rates of profitability often used by neo-Marxists by arguing that stated profitability is not an adequate guide to investment decisions due to the ability of multinational corporations to manipulate profit figures across national boundaries. Rather, "potential loss of export markets, low opportunity cost for capital in the home market, the threat of losing a large part of the global ability to exact oligopoly rent—all indicate high values to be put on foreign investment."[13]

Furthermore, foreign investment may not only be a means of protecting foreign markets, it may also be necessary to protect *domestic* markets indirectly.

This is because U.S. direct foreign investment has increasingly aimed not merely at supplying the local market but also exporting to third countries—most notably back to the United States. In 1969, U.S. foreign manufacturing subsidiaries exported 22 percent of the goods they produced thus becoming an exporting power as large as Germany and twice the size of Japan. The percentage of U.S. owned foreign subsidiaries importing goods back into the U.S. accounted for about one fourth of U.S. imports. According to Moran, "Investment abroad is an option on a potentially very great source of profit and an insurance policy against a potentially very great risk of loss," and he concludes that "As long as American corporations exercise their virtues of inventiveness and aggressiveness, the government will feel intense, even frantic pressures to create and preserve an international system that facilitates foreign economic expansion."[14]

Moran's thesis provides compelling evidence for the "institutional necessity" behind foreign economic expansion and suggests good reasons why it might be considered in the national interest for the U.S. to use various means of economic political and even military intervention to preserve the interests of U.S. capital abroad. What it does not provide is any clue as to the problem of underdevelopment per se. Why, for example, should America's northern neighbor Canada, whose industry is dominated by U.S. capital flourish economically, while to the south, Mexico, a country equally dominated by U.S. capital (albeit in a somewhat disguised manner) remains a clearly underdeveloped country. Various simpliste pseudo-theories of imperialism notwithstanding, the domination of a country by foreign capital is not a sufficient condition to explain capitalist underdevelopment.

In other words in both the Moran-type approach and the strategic raw materials approach, we have an attempt to provide a contemporary answer to the Leninist problem—namely, what is the "driving force" behind the expansion overseas of capitalism. Moran's theory seems to work most powerfully with regard to economic interaction between countries with similar demand structures—i.e., other advanced industrial countries. Furtado's analysis of the generation of Western demand structures in underdeveloped economies (noted earlier) is a useful addition to this approach in helping to explain the spread of capital penetration via trade to the Third World. The strategic raw materials approach of course fails to account for the type of foreign investment (based on manufacturing industries) described by Moran, but by the same token Moran's analysis does not deal with direct investment for mineral extraction—in other words, neither approach is complete. Moran's argument would appear to offer a more compelling case for the "institutional necessity" argument in general, but it complements rather than contradicts the strategic resources argument. Neither approach, however, provides more than a very limited insight into the failure of capitalist development in the Third World. On the other hand both provide suggestive frameworks for the analysis of various types of intervention aimed at blocking the emergence of revolutionary movements whose success could take the nations concerned outside the world capitalist orbit.

General Theories of Underdevelopment

Having examined two approaches that may be seen as contemporary equivalents of the classical theories of imperialism, two more theories of high generality will be examined. These have as their central concern *not* the dynamics of contemporary capitalist expansion, but rather basic mechanisms of underdevelopment. First Galtung's "structural" theory of imperialism is considered and secondly Emmanuel's "unequal exchange" theory. Both writers take the existence of a world capitalist economy as a given and each attempts to show how the economic and political relationships that characterize this world economy, create and perpetuate growth at one of its poles and stagnation at the other.

Galtung's Structural Theory of Imperialism

Galtung describes the world as a "feudal structure," which he takes as one of the defining characteristics of imperialism.[15] By "feudal structure" he means that international relations are characterized by high degrees of interaction between "top-dog" nations, lesser degrees of interaction between "top-dog" and "underdog" nations—e.g., United States/Latin America; France/former French colonies —and very little interaction at all between underdog nations themselves. The relative intensity of these interaction patterns can be measured using a variety of indicators: the flow of people, goods and messages across international boundaries and so forth. The implication is that cooperation between underdog nations—the formation of "producers' unions" for various commodities, for example—is extremely difficult. Secondly, the world is divided schematically into "center" nations and "periphery" nations—i.e., developed/underdeveloped—and nations are themselves divided into centers and peripheries. Cut-off points in these dichotomies are obviously somewhat arbitrary, but the basic message is that there is a harmony of interest between the center of the "center" nations and the center of the "periphery" nation. The elite (center) of the periphery nation acts as the bridge-head for imperialist interests from the center of the "center" nation. In his economic analysis, Galtung concentrates on the implications for development for nations that concentrate on the export sector of their economy and on primary commmodities and raw mineral extraction. The essential mechanism of underdevelopment is located on the international division of labor.[16] The concentration on the production of raw materials for export means that periphery nations, which do the exporting, are denied the added value that comes from processing. Additionally, they are forced to pay both the costs of processing and any profits that are creamed off during this stage *and* transportation costs when they import manufactured goods. More importantly, the processing stages generate positive spin-offs for the developed economy that are denied the underdeveloped nation. Processing, Galtung argues, *necessitates* high levels of skill, education, transportation structures, and other forms of communication. It generates subsidiary industries, loosens up the social structure, encourages a basic psychology of self-reliance and so forth. These benefits are *by definition* denied to the raw material producers. Galtung notes that there are few spin-offs generated by the hole in the ground, which is all the oil rig leaves behind it. Galtung's particular emphasis on the international division of labor differs from other writers but the general emphasis on this feature of the world economy is a very common one among writers on underdevelopment.

There appears to be a great deal of evidence to support Galtung's emphasis on the differential benefits that derive from differing levels of processing between countries. The high correlation between primary commodity production on the one hand, and underdevelopment on the other, for example, is highly suggestive. Furthermore, there are numerous studies describing Western corporate and/or governmental interventions (mostly successful) aimed at blocking the export of processed goods *from* the Third World. Positive sanctions—various bi-lateral and even multilateral commodity agreements, special aid schemes, and so forth—are also used to encourage the export of raw materials. In other words, the developed economies of the West go to some lengths to maintain the existing division of global labor. Even in the case of manufactured goods, it can be argued that the type of import substitute industries, which are typical of Third World programs of industrialization, are mostly characterized by very *low* levels of processing. Automobiles are typically assembled from pre-fabricated parts for example.

Galtung does not argue that there is *no* processing carried out in Third World economies, rather that the industrialized countries are characterized by a far higher *level* of processing and hence greater degree of "intra-actor" spin-off. The higher the rate of spin-off, the higher the rate of economic growth. Galtung further argues that even if raw material prices were raised considerably, this would make no difference in the long run. However if we consider two countries often ignored by writers on underdevelopment—namely, Australia and New Zealand—we find that: (a) the economic relationships that exist between them and the advanced industrial countries are characterized by precisely those features Galtung associates with developed/underdeveloped country relationships and (b) both Australia and New Zealand are highly prosperous. In the case of Australia, the export sector of the economy is heavily dependent on agricultural products—meat, wool, wheat, sugar—and raw minerals. These exports are characterized by low or non-existent degrees of processing. Australian imports, on the other hand, are typically highly processed-electrical and other machinery, motor vehicles, drugs, and chemicals. In the case of New Zealand, the pattern is even more pronounced; frozen meats, butter, and wool are exported while motor vehicles, *refined* petroleum products, light and heavy machinery, and so forth are imported. Since this exchange pattern was even more marked in the early years of these two countries' development, it is

Are they peripheries?

difficult to explain the steady economic growth both have experienced in Galtung's terms. In both cases the posited benefits of "intra-actor spin-off" have been markedly absent since in both cases exports have been very low in processing, while imports have been very high in processing. Today this steady growth has led to *manufacturing* industries assuming a dominant role in both economies. Clearly this pattern of growth cannot be explained in terms of Galtung's processing-level/differential-spin-off model. The international exchange relationships are typical of developed/underdeveloped country relationships; yet the consequences for the two countries in question have been steady growth rather than stagnation. Unless it can be demonstrated how and why Australia and New Zealand form a "special case," then the consequences for Galtung's model are rather serious. Furthermore, if we compare the Australian economy with that of Argentina at around the turn of the century, we find in both cases a heavy orientation towards agricultural production for export. Both countries had strong economic links with Britain, both were settled by Europeans, and both were relatively "empty"—i.e., neither had an indigenous population to exploit economically to any significant degree (contrast South Africa). Despite these marked similarities the developmental progress of the two countries has been markedly different. Again there is little in the structural theory of imperialism to suggest why this should be the case.

This critique does not of course mean that the particular features of the international division of labor to which Galtung refers do not in specific cases act as blocking mechanisms, but rather that this thesis cannot provide the basis for a *general* theory of imperialism/underdevelopment.

The Australia/New Zealand case together with the United States/Canada case are interesting for another reason. In all these countries, capitalist development took place without any significant resistance from pre-capitalist social formations. The indigenous populations were numerically insignificant and did not provide the same type of obstacle to capitalist development as did the quasi-feudal social formations of pre-capitalist Latin America or those of the indigenous peoples of Asia and Africa. Galtung's thesis, like that of Emmanuel discussed below, is curiously ahistorical, but—as with the case of Emmanuel—the "givens," with which the analysis starts, have themselves to be explained. The implication is that a full understanding of imperialism qua underdevelopment would require a historical explanation of the conflict between imperialist/capitalist penetration and indigenous social formations.

You answer yourself

Unequal Exchange Theory

Arghiri Emmanuel's theory of "unequal exchange" is expounded at considerable length in his book of that name, which bears the subtitle *A Study of the Imperialism of Trade*. Here it will only be possible to provide the sketchiest summary of some of the main points in Emmanuel's argument. Like Galtung but unlike the other writers considered previously, Emmanuel takes the existence of a global capitalist economy as a given. The thrust of his thesis is not towards examining the dynamics of capitalist expansion, rather he is interested in explaining the basic underlying processes that give rise to the "development of underdevelopment." He sees imperialism in these terms rather than in a search for the motivations that lead to military or other interventions. Three of the assumptions made in Emmanuel's theory will be dealt with here. 1. Capital is seen as internationally mobile and as shifting around the world in such a way as to cause the rate of profit to tend to equalize. 2. Labor is *not* internationally mobile; there may be some "seepage" across national boundaries—e.g., from North Africa to Europe—but this is unimportant for the purpose of theoretical exposition. Wages therefore tend to equalize within rather than between nations. 3. Wage rates are seen (most controversially) as "independent variables," determined not by prices but rather by social and historical factors.

The theory attempts to demonstrate that there is a hidden or "invisible" transfer of resources from poor to rich countries that engage in trade. This hidden transfer of resources is seen as the *key* mechanism of exploitation, and the much-quoted visible transfer of resources (through repatriated profits and so forth) is relegated to a minor role in explaining underdevelopment. The following interpretation of Emmanuel's theory[17] sketches some of the main arguments in general terms. It is important to note that wage rates in poor countries are assumed to stagnate at a low level. The argument then runs as follows.

When wages in rich countries rise, profits will tend to fall or prices rise. If the latter is true and poor country wages are held constant, the terms of trade between rich and poor countries will deteriorate to the disadvantage of the latter. However, if the wage rise in the rich country causes profits there to fall, then they will tend to fall everywhere, because of the tendency for profit rates to equalize internationally. In other words, poor country profits tend to fall because rich country wages rise. Therefore, because poor country wages are assumed not to change, poor country *prices* must fall. The cost of the wage increases in the rich country is thus shared between the owners of capital in poor as well as rich countries. As a consequence, profits in the rich country will tend to fall less than wages rise and thus again prices in the rich country will again tend to rise. Thus, an increase in wages in the rich country leads to an increase in prices in the rich country and a decrease in prices in the poor country. Thus, the terms of trade can be seen to have deteriorated. Thus again, one can see how an initial gap in wage levels between poor and rich countries will tend to grow in proportion to the increase in wages in the rich country *and* the volume of trade between the two countries.

This very crude summary is presented to give some idea of the framework of Emmanuel's analysis—no more. It should be further pointed out that Emmanuel's theory is based on his reading of Marx and that his interpretation is highly controversial among other Marxists not least for its political implications. For Emmanuel, workers in the rich countries are direct beneficiaries of unequal exchange and they are therefore seen as having a vested interest in imperialism thus defined. In international trade, rich country workers always exchange a smaller amount of their national labor for a larger amount of poor country labor. Note that this is true *even* when productivity of workers (organic composition of capital in Marxist terms) is held to be the same in both countries.[18]

It can immediately be seen that Emmanuel's theory operates at a higher level of generality than do most other theoretical or quasi-theoretical approaches. This has a number of advantages, which should be immediately apparent. First, it comfortably explains the Australia/New Zealand-type anomaly in the Galtung analysis. It can be seen that the international division of labor is simply irrelevant to Emmanuel's analysis. Second, the exploitation of the Third World by the "sucking out" of visible capital is not seen as an essential feature of underdevelopment. Emmanuel sees the flow of visible capital around the world as essentially a regulatory mechanism. It acts to permit the unequal exchange process to take place but is not of itself the essential exploitative mechanism. Unequal exchange would still continue to widen the gap between the rich and the poor countries even if profiteering by corporations with investments in the Third World ceased completely. Third, the *ownership* of capital is irrelevant to this theory. Thus, even capitalist development in the hands of a genuinely commited "national bourgeoisie" will fail to stop the unequal exchange implicit in trade. Fourth, the super-profit argument—i.e., that there is a higher rate of return on Third World investments—is also essentially irrelevant. If true this would appear to run contrary to Emmanuel's postulate that rates of profit tend to equalize internationally. However, the differential, if and when it exists, can be fairly easily explained in terms of the real or supposed risk of investment in these areas. But even if the higher profit argument were accepted *without* making this assumption, it still seems obvious that a theory of imperialism/ underdevelopment that bases itself on differential profit rates (where ratios of 1:1.5 are already high) provides a far less powerful explanatory framework than one that bases itself on differential wage rates (where ratios of 10:1 or even 20:1 are not uncommon). Fifth, unequal exchange theory accounts for the two paradoxes in classic trade theory—namely, the existence of protectionism and the failure of the so-called law of comparative advantage to predict that the prices of primary goods would *fall* relatively, instead of rising.

Finally, we should note that the real difference between Emmanuel's work and that of writers like Dean, Magdoff, and Moran is that they are trying to explain very different phenomena under the common label of imperialism. Imperialism, it should hardly need pointing out, means different things to different theorists. On the one hand, we have an attempt to understand the economic imperatives of capitalist expansion and the various interventions that imperialist states make in order to protect economic interests abroad. On the other hand, we have attempts to understand underdevelopment or, more precisely, the growing gap between the rich and the poor countries. The former group of writers, in common with the classical theorists, do not provide any general theory of underdevelopment. Emmanuel's theory on the other hand shows how the gap between rich and poor countries would continue to grow as a consequence of unequal exchange even in a completely "peaceful" world in which there is no direct Western capitalist stake in the Third World to be defended.

However the most controversial of Emmanuel's assumptions—that wage rates in poor countries are historically and socially determined and stagnate at a low level—poses a real problem. The theory is predicated on this assumption but the facts behind the assumption have themselves to be explained. Low wages are one of the *defining characteristics* of underdevelopment; they are part of what has to be explained. So it might seem that a theory of underdevelopment, which takes low wages as one of its central assumptions for the analysis that follows, must necessarily fail. This is a misreading of Emmanuel. Emmanuel does not attempt to show (in the argument summarized crudely above) why poor nations should be poor in the first place, but rather how and why they get relatively *poorer*. In other words it is a theory that attempts to explain the growing *gap* between rich and poor countries. What remains to be explained is why the "independent variable"—i.e., wages—should be low and stagnant in the poor country in the first place. In one section of his book, Emannuel argues suggestively that the difference in wage rates between North and South America can be explained in terms of the greater proletarian expectations of workers in the United States. This in turn is explained in terms of the religious/cultural differences between the populations of the two regions—Anglo-Saxon Protestantism in the North and Latin Catholicism in the South. This argument of course takes us full circle—back to the much-maligned "internalist" theories of the sociologists and psychologists of development. If this is a correct reading of Emmanuel, then it would seem that unequal exchange exacerbates the "development of underdevelopment," that it provides a genuine theory of the exploitation of the Third World by the rich industrialized powers (which many of the "internalist" theorists have been concerned to deny), but that it does not provide an explanation for the initial low and stagnant wage rates in the developing countries.

The prescriptive implications of Emmanuel's theory are more than somewhat bleak. Political action to raise wage rates in poor countries raises all sorts of obvious problems with respect to the competitiveness of (higher priced) goods on the world market. Cooperation between low wage countries to increase their effective bargaining strength is notoriously difficult. In fact, another area of the literature on imperialism deals with precisely this problem and is manifest in the discussions of "Balkanisation" in Africa, the arguments about the feudal structure of world communications, and so forth. Galtung, who, like Emmanuel, sees exploitation essentially in terms of international economic exchange relationships, advocates cutting the exploitative links as a development strategy. There are many obvious problems (viability of small nations developing in isolation and so forth) involved with this approach, even discounting the political difficulties. But it is worth noting that the one country that provides some idea of the possibilities of development from a predominantly agricultural base and without ties to the Western world—namely China—was totally ignored in the huge debate on development strategies that characterized the inception of the first U.N. Decade of Development. Given the manifest achievements of the People's Republic, it is difficult to see this failure to take the Chinese model seriously in other than political terms.

Imperialism and the Cold War

The third factor noted earlier, which theories of imperialism in the present era have to take into account and which was "inoperative" in Lenin's day, is the emergence of the socialist "bloc" and the consequent development of the Cold War. As noted in the introduction to this chapter, the debate surrounding the "classical" theories of imperialism also included a "power political" or "security" alternative to the theories of imperialism that were rooted in an economic analysis.

In the present era "power political" or "security" explanations for various U.S. interventions in the Third World are commonly put forward as a refutation of theories of economic imperialism of the first type considered (e.g., Moran, Magdoff *et al.*). Thus Vietnam, the Bay of Pigs, the Dominican Republic, Guatemala, and other U.S. interventions are seen as motivated primarily by considerations in which economic interests play a non-existent or subordinate role. Right wing ideologues see such interventions in terms of "the defence of freedom"; "realists" see them in terms of "power politics." Post-Vietnam, a critical liberal voice has been added to this debate and has achieved some prominence, especially in academic circles. Here, U.S. actions of the type described above (and in particular Vietnam) are seen as essentially irrational— that is, obsessed with a fear of Communism that transcends the "objective" needs of national security. This line of reasoning is replete with terms like "paranoia," "fixation," "blunder," "rigid ideology," "quagmire," and so forth. Despite the manifest political differences of their proponents, all these approaches share a common rejection of any attempt to locate the type of interventions noted above within the framework of any theory or theories of economic imperialism. Rather, the use of the term "imperialism" tends to be taken as evidence of the ideological biases of the user. Typically, Vietnam is taken as a refutation of the thesis of economic imperialism. Not only were there no U.S. economic interests at stake there, but the United States was prepared to incur enormous economic, human, and political costs to prevent a "communist takeover." Few radical scholars would dispute the obvious truth of these assertions, but they would argue that this is in no way incompatible with the conception of economic imperialism that is implicit in Moran's work and quite explicit in the work of Magdoff and others. Keeping the world safe *from* "communism" and keeping it safe *for* capitalism are seen as two sides of the same coin. Radical theorists, unlike many liberals, are quite prepared to accept a modified version of the Domino Theory. As they see it—and, as they would argue, the U.S. foreign policy elite sees it—successful anti-imperialist revolutions in one Third World nation encourage the emergence of revolutionary organizations in other Third World nations, while by the same token undermining the confidence of national elites in the ability of the United States to provide them with adequate protection against insurgency. If one revolution succeeds, little is lost. If this sparks a chain of other attempts, the consequences for U.S. overseas *interests* could be catastrophic. Successful revolution implies a strong possibility that the revolutionaries will align themselves with the socialist camp—that is, they will withdraw completely from the world capitalist orbit. Note that in this analysis it is not the direct physical security of the United States that is seen as being at stake but rather America's global interests. In other words, to attempt to disprove the general thrust of the Moran/Magdoff-type of argument by noting that there is no necessary correlation between U.S. intervention and *direct* U.S. economic interests is to miss the point. It should be further noted that to demonstrate that the foreign policy elite were in fact *genuinely* motivated by power political considerations or a militant anti-communist ideology and that they gave little or no thought to the protection—direct or indirect—of U.S. economic interests overseas, *still* does not invalidate this particular conception of economic imperialism. Such an assertion is obviously at odds with much of the political science research on decision-making in foreign policy, and it also requires that the analysis move into the tricky area of "non-decisions." It should not be rejected for these reasons. The key question for the radical researcher in this context becomes: Did the foreign policy elite—*regardless* of their subjective political philosophies—act in the broad general interest of that section of the corporate elite that has a large stake in overseas trade and investment? Since, broadly speaking, "communist takeover" and U.S. capital penetration abroad are inimical processes, the assumption is made that—again broadly speaking—the interests of the two groups *are* congruent. How then could such a theory then be falsified? In this chapter the argument cannot be developed in any detail; it leads rapidly into the confused debate that still surrounds the power-elite/ruling-class versus pluralist theories of democracy in political science. Suffice it to say here that it would seem that the critics of this particular conception of economic imperialism (not that of Emmanuel or Galtung) would have to demonstrate that

(a) the U.S. foreign policy elite *could* implement a foreign policy that ran clearly and consistently contrary to the overseas interests of U.S. corporations and (b) that they in fact did so.

Conclusion

In this chapter I have tried, with reference to the work of four writers, to show that the term "imperialism" is highly ambiguous. One line of search for a general theory (that of Magdoff and Moran) is in the same tradition as the "classical theorists." The other (Galtung and Emmanuel) sees imperialism in very different terms. Since both approaches attempt to explain different phenomena, neither is incompatible. Whether or not a *general* theory, which would transcend both types of theory noted above, is either possible or worth the enormous effort that any attempt to produce it would necessary entail is a moot point. Clearly, the methodological problems raised by the extant work are enormous. Equally clearly, if a fraction of the intellectual and financial resources that have been ploughed into more conventional approaches to international relations research had been devoted to this area, many of these problems would have by now been resolved.

Finally it should be noted that there remains a great wealth of literature on imperialism that has not been considered. I refer specifically to the many in-depth historical studies, most of which have been concerned to study the particular impact of capitalist penetration over a long period in particular Third World countries or regions. Such works include those by Gunder Frank, Michael Kidron, Samir Amin, Giovanni Arrigihi, and many others.[19] Most of their studies are rich in insight and empirical data. However, in common with all individual historical explanations, they provide no hard criteria for distinguishing between universal and contingent features either of capitalist penetration or of the "development of underdevelopment." As a consequence, none provides the basis for a *general* theory of imperialism of either type described above. Furthermore, any attempt to extricate common factors from these studies and to use these as "building blocks" for a general theory ("abstracted empiricism") necessarily fails. Not only does it beg the question of the legitimacy of extricating "events" from the context that give them meaning but at most it leads to trivial "lowest common denominator" generalizations that are of little interest. (This remains a major problem of the "indices" approach to theory building).

At present there is a growing interest in "imperialism" as a legitimate field of scientific enquiry. However, the problems that arise out of incompatible intellectual traditions, different levels of analysis, and different conceptions—of what it is that constitutes imperialism and what it is that constitutes a theory—have created a great deal of confusion. It is hoped that in showing the different problems to which different writers in this general area address themselves and in demonstrating the different levels of analysis at which they work, some small degree of clarification of these issues has been achieved.

Notes

1. See Furtado, "External Dependency and Economic Theory."
2. Jalee, *The Third World in World Economy*, Chapter 6.
3. Frank, *Latin America: Underdevelopment or Revolution*, 1970.
4. See Caspary, *American Economic Imperialism*, for illustrations of the various mechanisms and further references.
5. See Boserup, "Unequal Exchange" and "Notes on the Causes of Imperialist Expansion."
6. For a good summary both of the Leninist theory and critiques and counter-critiques of it, see Owen and Sutcliffe, *Studies in the Theory of Imperialism.*
7. See Dean, *Scarce Resources: The Dynamic of American Imperialism*, and Magdoff, *The Age of Imperialism: The Economics of U.S. Foreign Policy.*
8. Dean, ibid.
9. Magdoff, op. cit.
10. Moran, "Foreign Expansion as an 'Institutional Necessity' for U.S. Corporate Capitalism." p. 371.
11. Ibid., p. 371.
12. Ibid., p. 374.
13. Ibid., p. 384.
14. Ibid., p. 386.
15. See Galtung, "A Structural Theory of Imperialism."
16. See also Jalee, op. cit., and Mandel, *Marxist Economic Theory*, Chapter 13, for an alternate analysis of underdevelopment in terms of the international division of labor.
17. Cf. Boserup, op. cit.
18. For a simple numerical demonstration of the argument using a two-country model, see Emmanuel, *Unequal Exchange*, p. 64.
19. See, for example, Frank, *Capitalism and Underdevelopment in Latin America*; Kidron, *Foreign Investments in India*; Amin, *The Maghreb in the Modern World*; and Arrigihi, "The Political Economy of Rhodesia."

Bibliography

Amin, S. *The Mahgreb in the Modern World*. London: Penguin, 1970.
Arrigihi, G. "The Political Economy of Rhodesia," *New Left Review*, No. 39, 1966.

Boserup, A. "Unequal Exchange" and "Notes on the Causes of Imperialist Expansion." Copenhagen: Mimeographed, 1971.

Caspary, W. *American Economic Imperialism: A Survey of the Literature.* Radical Education Project, Box 561-A, Detroit, Michigan, 48232; 1969 (estimate—no date).

Dean, H. *Scarce Resources: The Dynamic of American Imperialism.* Boston: New England Free Press, 1965.

Emmanuel, A. *Unequal Exchange: A Study of the Imperialism of Trade.* New York: Monthly Review Press, 1972.

Frank, A.G. *Capitalism and Underdevelopment in Latin America.* New York: Monthly Review Press, 1969.

Frank, A.G. "The Sociology of Underdevelopment and the Underdevelopment of Sociology," in Frank, *Latin America: Underdevelopment or Revolution.* London: Monthly Review Press, 1970.

Furtado, C. "External Dependence and Economic Theory," paper presented at International Symposium on *Imperialism: Its Place in Social Science Today.* Elsinore, Denmark, 1971.

Galtung, J. "A Structural Theory of Imperialism," *Journal of Peace Research,* No. 2, 1971.

Jalee, P. *The Third World in World Economy.* New York: Monthly Review Press, 1969.

Kidron, M. *Foreign Investment in India.* London: Oxford University Press, 1965.

Magdoff, H. *The Age of Imperialism: The Economics of U.S. Foreign Policy.* New York: Monthly Review Press, 1969.

Mandel, E. *Marxist Economic Theory.* New York: Monthly Review Press, 1969.

Moran, T. "Foreign Expansion as an 'Institutional Necessity' for U.S. Corporate Capitalism: The Search for a Radical Model," *World Politics,* April 1973.

Owen, R. and Sutcliffe, R. (eds.). *Studies in the Theory of Imperialism.* London: Longman, 1972.

4

Capitalism, Socialism, and the Sources of Imperialism

Thomas E. Weisskopf
University of Michigan

Introduction

"Would a Socialist America pursue a foreign policy fundamentally different from the foreign policy pursued by a Capitalist America?" asks Robert W. Tucker in a critical analysis of the views of the American "radical left."[1] His answer to this rhetorical question is a resounding "no."[2] In this essay I shall seek to demonstrate that the appropriate answer is "yes."

Almost a decade of overt war in Indochina; military interventions in Greece, Iran, Lebanon, the Congo, Cuba, the Dominican Republic, Colombia, Guatemala, Panama, Bolivia, China, Korea and Thailand; military missions throughout most of the "free world"; and American economic dominance of countless Third World countries have combined to impress upon all but the most recalcitrant observer the truth in the assertion that in the postwar period the United States has been a formidably imperialist power. Indeed, a brief review of American history points to a pattern of imperialist behavior that goes back long before the postwar period to the very beginning of the federal republic.[3] That the United States is now and has long been an imperialist power is a proposition that is no longer subject to serious debate. Very much a matter of dispute, however, are the sources of American imperialism.

For Tucker and most of his "orthodox" colleagues, American imperialism is attributable primarily to the international competition that results from the existence of a system of geographically distinct societies claiming independent political sovereignty.[4] The internal socio-economic organization of a society has very little to do with its propensity for imperialist behavior. A putative Socialist America would have just as imperialist a foreign policy as does the existing Capitalist America.

For the "radical left" (and for this author in particular), American imperialism results to a significant extent from the fact that the United States is a capitalist society.[5] Radical theorists argue that the internal socio-economic organization of a society does make a great deal of difference, and that the

The author is particularly grateful to Sam Bowles, Noam Chomsky, Arthur MacEwan, and Harry Magdoff, who, among other friends, provided helpful criticism of two earlier versions of this chapter.

57

replacement of Capitalist America by a Socialist America would significantly reduce the extent of American imperialism.

To argue the radical case,[6] I begin by defining clearly what I mean by the term "imperialism" and by listing as comprehensively as possible various potential motivations for imperialism. In the next section I define the terms "capitalism" and "socialism" and examine some of the significant differences between the two types of social systems. I then go on to consider the extent to which potential motivations for imperialism depend upon whether a society is capitalist or socialist. Finally I conclude in the last section that the radical view of American imperialism is indeed a valid one, and I proceed to examine some of the implications of that conclusion.

Alternative Motivations for Imperialism

The word "imperialism" is notoriously imprecise. So many writers have used it in so many different ways and for so many different purposes that it is incumbent upon anyone intending to discuss the subject to define quite clearly what is to be understood by the term.[7]

In this essay I will use the term imperialism in a non-Marxist sense[8] according to the following definition: imperialism is activity on the part of a national government that involves the use of power (or the threat of its use) to establish or maintain a relationship of domination or control over the government or (some of) the people of another nation or territory over which the imperialist government has no traditional claim to sovereignty. This definition deliberately focuses attention on the activity of government agencies rather than private organizations, thereby ignoring an important but separable component of American imperialism.[9] Included among the imperialist activities of government agencies are not only the most obvious instances of territorial annexation and military occupation but also any use of military, economic, or diplomatic power to establish, maintain, or expand spheres of control over foreigners. In short, imperialism is defined here essentially as an expansionary foreign policy.[10]

Every imperialist activity involves some expenditure of energy and resources by the imperialist government. The expenditure may be trivial—as in the case of diplomatic pressure—or it may be very substantial—as in the case of military intervention. If such expenditure is undertaken by a government, it must be done with the expectation that some kind of benefits will result from it. Accordingly, one can distinguish alternative motivations for imperialism according to the alternative kinds of interests that might be promoted by imperialist activity.

In analyzing alternative interests in imperialism, I will distinguish carefully between a "national interest" and a "class interest." I will say that there is a national interest in an imperialist activity when the activity is expected to benefit the imperialist nation as a whole, in the sense that the aggregate benefits to citizens of the imperialist nation are expected to exceed the aggregate costs. I will say that there is a class interest in an imperialist activity when it is expected to result in net benefits for a particular class of people from among the citizens of the imperialist nation. If there is a national interest in an imperialist activity, there is bound to be also at least one class interest, although there may be other classes for whom the anticipated net benefits are negative. On the other hand, if there is a class interest in an imperialist activity, there may or may not also be a national interest. In the following pages I will review as comprehensively as possible the major national and class interests in imperialism that have been suggested explicitly or implicitly by both radical and orthodox theorists. In so doing, I will attempt to determine which of these interests could conceivably motivate imperialist activity by the government of a modern industrialized society such as the United States.

A major national interest in imperialism that is always cited and most strongly emphasized by orthodox theorists is to enhance *national security*.[11] It is argued that every nation has a collective interest in defending its territory against possible attack by other nations that may be or may become hostile and aggressive. Nations that are sufficiently powerful to engage in imperialist activity will find that efforts to control other nations can contribute significantly to national security by improving the military posture of the imperialist nation vis-à-vis its actual or potential enemies. Although there is good reason to suspect that national security considerations are often invoked to justify an imperialist policy motivated by other concerns, there is no reason to doubt that a modern nation state does have an interest in national security that can independently motivate imperialist activity.

A second possible national interest in imperialism is one that is suggested in the work of many radical theorists: to maintain *macro-economic prosperity*— that is, to avoid economic crises that threaten the viability of the whole economy.[12] A variety of different arguments have been advanced to explain how the pursuit of an imperialist foreign policy can help to maintain the prosperity of an economy. The arguments are usually presented in the context of capitalist economies, although some of them may conceivably apply to non-capitalist economies as well. In the following paragraphs I shall discuss alternative lines of reasoning that have been developed to link imperialism with macro-economic prosperity.

The first line of reasoning is derived from the classical theory of underconsumption and associated with the work of Hobson, Luxemburg, and—apparently erroneously—Lenin.[13] Although various writers have expressed the basic argument in different ways, it can be summarized in a consistent and logically valid form as follows: (1) there is a chronic tendency in a capitalist economy for aggregate demand to be insufficient to absorb all of the output that is produced; (2) there is consequently a continual need to find new outlets for surplus production in order to avoid an economic crisis; (3) foreign countries and territories represent important potential markets for the domestic surplus; and (4) an imperialist foreign policy provides access to these markets for the imperialist country.

Hobson regarded the problem of underconsumption/overproduction as potentially solvable through a redistribution of income, while Luxemburg argued that the problem was inherent in the structure of capitalism. Hobson emphasized the notion of "surplus capital" seeking outlets abroad and the need for capital exports, while Luxemburg stressed overproduction and commodity exports. But the underlying logic of the argument is the same in each case: surplus capital or overproduction at home can be alleviated by net capital exports—that is, by selling more goods abroad than are purchased abroad for home consumption.

A variant of this line of reasoning can be formulated by extending the work of modern Marxists on the problem of surplus absorption in a capitalist economy.[14] This variant begins with the same premise of underconsumption or insufficient aggregate demand. However the solution to the problem is attributed not to net capital exports but to military expenditures. In this case, a motivation for imperialism arises from the need to legitimize such expenditures: an interventionist foreign policy creates a climate in which it is easy to justify the maintenance of a large military establishment and high levels of military spending.

Apart from arguments linking imperialism to macro-economic prosperity via the need to maintain a high level of aggregate demand, there is an alternative line of reasoning that focuses directly on a need to maintain access to foreign economies. Arguments along this line have been advanced by many radical theorists examining contemporary American imperialism,[15] and they are clearly inspired by some aspects of the work of early Marxist theorists of imperialism such as Hilferding, Luxemburg, and Lenin.[16]

One such argument emphasizes a need for opportunities to undertake direct capital investment in foreign countries or territories. It is argued that there tends to be an inadequate supply of profitable investment opportunities at home and that access to more profitable investment opportunities abroad is necessary to maintain overall economic prosperity. Imperialism is motivated by the desire to assure adequate opportunities for such foreign investment.

A second argument focuses on a need for opportunities to export domestically produced commodities to foreign markets. It is argued that exports contribute significantly to economic prosperity—that is, by strengthening the balance of payments—and that imperialism helps to provide the access to foreign markets needed to keep up the flow of exports.

A final argument stresses the importance of imported raw materials for an industrialized economy. This argument begins with the observation that there are a variety of key industrial raw materials whose domestic supply is inadequate to meet the input requirements of the economy. It is then contended that the economy would be severely crippled without access to foreign supplies of these materials and that an imperialist foreign policy can play an important role in maintaining that access.

The first two variants of the macro-economic prosperity interest in imperialism are based on a presumed difficulty in maintaining high levels of aggregate demand. There can be little question that the maintenance of a sufficient level of aggregate demand has been an important policy problem for many industrialized capitalist economies. But in the postwar period there have been no shortfalls in aggregate demand so great as to threaten the very viability of an economy, as was the case with the Great Depression of the 1930s. Modern capitalist governments have managed to apply Keynesian policy techniques rather effectively to maintain a level of domestic demand sufficient to avoid major crises (although they have had great difficulty achieving truly full employment and price stability).[17] As a result, modern capitalist economies have not been dependent on foreign demand arising from net capital exports to absorb a domestic surplus; nor have most of the industrialized capitalist economies depended on high levels of military spending to bolster the level of domestic demand, with the prominent exception of the United States.[18] Even in the case of the United States, however, it appears implausible to suggest that imperialism may be motivated by an interest in keeping up military spending. Granted that imperialist activity does seem to increase the demand for military expenditures, there are surely many other ways in which a high level of military spending can be and has been legitimized by the American government.

The three remaining arguments for a national interest in imperialism to promote macro-economic prosperity focus on a presumed need for foreign investment, exports, and imports, respectively. Two questions must be addressed in an assessment of the relevance of such arguments to modern industrial societies: how important are foreign investment, exports, and imports for the prosperity of the economy, and to what extent does imperialism contribute to sustaining the flow of foreign investment, exports, and imports?

Turning first to foreign investment, there is no doubt that in the postwar period the magnitude and the rate of growth of direct private foreign investment from the industrial capitalist countries have been formidable.[19] In the United States the ratio of direct private foreign assets to the total value of corporate assets is now approximately 10 percent, and the corresponding ratio of after-tax profits is about 20 percent.[20] In Great Britain the percentages are probably somewhat higher; in other industrial capitalist countries somewhat lower.[21]

Should one of these economies suddenly be deprived of access to its foreign investment assets, it is likely that macro-economic prosperity would be threatened. Yet it does not follow that imperialist activity can plausibly be ascribed to an interest in assuring sufficient investment opportunities abroad to preserve macro-economic prosperity, for many of these opportunities are available and will remain available whether or not any imperialist activity is undertaken. More than two thirds of American foreign investment assets and more than one half of the profits therefrom result from investment undertaken in other "developed" capitalist countries[22] whose borders are generally open to foreign investors without serious hindrance.[23] Similar figures apply to other major investing countries.[24] Of the foreign investment assets and profits generated in the "underdeveloped" countries, some might well be dependent on the pursuit of an imperialist policy while others would not. But it is difficult to argue that the overall prosperity of a modern industrial economy would be seriously affected by the loss of investment opportunities that accounted for a small fraction of overall economic activity. The obligation to replace some foreign investments by new domestic alternatives would no doubt inflict some losses on the economy as a whole—and substantial losses on particular firms—but there is every reason to believe that an economy could remain buoyant with a somewhat lower level of direct private investment abroad.

The quantitative significance of exports in contemporary industrial economies varies widely with the size of the economy and the diversity of its resource base. In the United States exports have remained at a level of approximately 5 percent of gross national product throughout the postwar period; in Japan and some of the larger Western European countries the corresponding figure has ranged between roughly 10 percent and 20 percent; and only in the smallest countries, such as Belgium and Holland, has the figure approached 50 percent.[25] The destination of the exports from these countries has primarily been to other "developed" capitalist countries; for no industrialized country has the value of exports to "developing" countries as a proportion of gross national product been much more than 5 percent since the mid-1950s, and the proportion is steadily declining for all industrialized countries.[26] For reasons similar to those suggested in the case of foreign investment, it seems therefore implausible that imperialist activity could be motivated by an interest in maintaining macro-economic prosperity through export promotion.

The case of imports might at first glance appear quite similar to that of exports, for the value of imports as a proportion of GNP is approximately the same as that of exports in all industrial economies. But imports can have a significance far greater than their nominal value if they consist of raw materials required as imports into some production process. For unless the flow of raw materials is maintained, the production of an entire industry may have to be cut back, and this in turn can have significant repercussions throughout an interdependent industrial economy. The extent to which even the large American economy has come to make use of imported raw materials has been extensively documented in a variety of sources.[27] And the dependence of the smaller economies of Western Europe and Japan on imported supplies is all the greater. Moreover, the foreign sources of most of these raw materials are located not in the "developed" capitalist countries but in the "underdeveloped" countries to which access can be unreliable. The current energy crisis has highlighted the extent to which major industrial economies are dependent on an uncertain supply of critical imports.

Granted that industrial economies currently import significant quantities of key raw materials from "underdeveloped" countries, it remains to be determined whether imperialist activity may plausibly be motivated by an interest in keeping up the flow of such imports. Critics of this view[28] have argued (1) that possibilities for substitution in the process of production or in the composition of end products consumed are plentiful enough to provide alternatives to the import of any particular raw material, and/or (2) that imperialism is not necessary to assure access to needed imports because the exporters of key raw materials have nothing to gain (and much to lose) by denying their products to the industrial markets. These arguments may hold in some long-run sense, and they may well support the proposition that some industrial economies are not critically dependent upon imperialism for their ultimate survival. But they do not rule out the possibility that imperialist activity may be intended to contribute to macro-economic prosperity within a shorter time horizon by preventing critical raw material shortages from arising. For in the short run, it is very difficult to change production processes or consumption patterns, and in the short run, it is quite possible that a raw-material-exporting country (or several such countries acting together) might withhold their exports for political reasons. In conclusion, it appears that a national interest in maintaining macro-economic prosperity can be a plausible motivation for imperialism in a modern industrialized society insofar as the imperialist activity is intended to ensure regular and dependable access to foreign sources of key raw materials.

The desire to maintain macro-economic prosperity and avoid major crises is not the only possible national economic interest in imperialism. Most writers would agree that imperialism may be motivated on national economic grounds simply in order to increase the *aggregate economic gains* accruing to the imperialist nation from its economic relations with other nations. The conditions under which private or public enterprises in one nation enter into trade or investment activities with or in other nations are obviously susceptible to the exercise of power. To the extent that one nation can exercise some degree of control over another, there are a variety of ways in which it can secure greater economic gains for its nationals than would be possible under a relationship of equality. The imperialist nation can use its power to improve the terms of trade and thereby lower the effective price of various imported commodities; it can enlarge export markets and increase the country's export earnings; it can secure more favorable conditions for its investors and thereby increase their repatriated profits; and in general it can open up new trade and investment opportunities in areas, which for whatever reasons might otherwise not be receptive to economic intercourse. In all such cases there are of course particular classes of people who have the most to gain from imperialism, and there are others who may have something to lose. But there is always a potential national interest—in addition to a class interest—so long as the overall benefits realized by citizens of the imperialist nation exceed the associated costs.

A fourth kind of national interest in imperialism that has been suggested by some writers is based on a generalized *missionary spirit*.[29] It is argued that the people of a nation can be so imbued with a belief in the desirability of their own institutions and values that they feel morally justified—indeed morally obliged—to extend their system to other parts of the world, even where this requires the use of power to impose the system on recalcitrant foreigners. The gains arising from imperialism of this kind are neither military-strategic nor economic; they are psychic gains involving a sense of satisfaction derived from promoting (what is perceived to be) a better world.

It is certainly true that many governments have sought to represent their imperialist activity as being in the best interest of the people upon whom it is practiced. As in the case of alleged national security interests, one suspects that this kind of argument often serves merely as a legitimizing cover for other interests with less widespread acceptability. But it is nonetheless plausible to suggest that popular belief in the "civilizing mission" of one's country can act as an independent stimulus to imperialist activity.

A final possible national interest in imperialism resembles the missionary spirit in that it involves psychic rather than military-strategic or economic gains: this arises simply from a generalized *urge to dominate*. Proponents of this view often contend that there is inherent in human nature an aggressive instinct that applies both on an individual and a group or national level.[30] People derive satisfaction from domination—from being "number one." Hence nations that can develop and apply the power to dominate other nations will be inclined to do so if only to satisfy the atavistic urge among their people to achieve a position of supremacy over others. Whether or not one considers the urge to dominate a natural human instinct, one can argue that in certain historical periods, it can help to motivate imperialist activity.

Among possible class interests in imperialism one can identify first the interest of the dominant classes of any unequal society in promoting their own *social legitimacy*.[31] There are several ways in which imperialist actions might serve to legitimate the dominance of some classes over others within a nation. By generating or accentuating antagonisms between the nation and other nations on an international level, imperialism can deflect attention and concern away from internal conflicts between dominant and subordinate classes and rally all people behind the leadership of the dominant classes. By maintaining or extending the geographical spread of institutions and values characteristic of the imperialist nation and by limiting the spread of alternative institutions and values, imperialism can discourage the notion that there are any real alternatives to the existing system with its particular class relations. Indeed a national "missionary spirit," as well as excessive concern over "national security," may actually result from the efforts of dominant classes to promote their own social legitimacy on an ideological plane.

A second possible class interest in imperialism may arise from the desire of civilian or military government bureaucracies for *organizational expansion*.[32] Members of virtually any organization have something to gain from an expansion in the volume of activity for which the organization is responsible: it leads to more promotions, more prestige, more power, if not more pay. This general phenomenon is no less true of the civilian and military agencies of government that are directly involved in imperialist activity. Such agencies will have a natural inclination to favor the expansion of imperialism wherever it is at issue.

One last major class interest in imperialism, most frequently stressed by radical writers, arises from opportunities for particular firms, agencies, or classes to increase their *particular economic gains* from international economic relations. Such opportunities are as varied as the opportunities cited earlier for increasing the aggregate economic gains from international economic relations, the only difference being that in this case there may be losses to other groups within the society that outweigh the gains from imperialism. Improving terms of trade, widening export markets, providing privileged access to raw materials, securing better conditions for investors, opening up new areas for trade and investment—any and all of these—can lead to economic gains for particular firms, agencies, or classes. They will therefore be motivated to press for imperialist acts to achieve such results, whether or not the net benefits to the nation as a whole are positive.

The economic interest of private enterprise in imperialist activity is much greater than might appear from current figures on foreign economic involvement. Not only do those firms that have invested abroad, that export to foreign markets, or that import from foreign sources stand to gain by having governmental power exercised on their behalf to help shape the terms and conditions of foreign economic relations, but private firms without any past involvement in foreign economic relations may nonetheless look forward to future opportunities made possible by imperialist actions that help to preserve or to extend the areas open to private enterprise. And even those firms that never trade or invest abroad stand to gain to the extent that imperialism promotes an increasing internationalization of the division of labor, for this places the relatively scarce labor supply of an industrial economy in increasing competition with the relatively abundant labor supply of less industrialized foreign economies.[33]

When there is a national interest in an imperialist activity, there is a *prima facie* motivation for the government to undertake it. The government will refrain from the imperialist activity only if there is a particular class (or combination of classes) that anticipates net losses and also has sufficiently disproportionate power to prevent the government from undertaking the activity, even though the anticipated net gains to other classes in the society exceed the anticipated net losses to the losing classes. But such circumstances are unlikely to arise no matter what the distribution of power in a society. For in the unlikely event that potential losers from an imperialist activity actually have more power than the potential gainers and are prepared to exercise that power, the gainers will be in a position to compensate the losers for their losses while still maintaining some net gains. Hence one would not expect any national government to refrain from imperialism when a national interest is really at stake.

When there is no national interest in a potential imperialist activity, there may nonetheless be a motivation for the government to undertake it if (1) there is a particular class (or combination of classes) with an interest in the activity *and* (2) the power of the interested class(es) is sufficiently disproportionate to induce the government to undertake the activity even though other classes stand to lose more than the particular class(es) stand to gain by it. These class interests in imperialism can but need not necessarily motivate a government to undertake imperialist activity. The extent to which they will do so depends upon the distribution of power among various classes in the society in question.

Capitalism and Socialism

Like "imperialism," "capitalism" and "socialism" are words that mean many different things to many different people; hence it is important to define clearly how I intend to use the terms. I shall begin by juxtaposing definitions for capitalism and socialism and then go on to analyze some important distinctions between the two.

Capitalism is a form of socio-economic organization (or a "mode of production," to use the Marxist term) that is characterized by *all* of the following conditions.[34]

1. *Private ownership of the means of production.* Most of the productive assets of the society are owned by private individuals; private owners of any asset have a special (if not exclusive) claim on any income generated by the asset and on decision-making with respect to the use of the asset.

2. *Proletarianization of the work force.* Most of the population has virtually no source of income other than that resulting from the sale of its labor services in a labor market. It follows that income generated by productive assets (as well as the ownership of such assets) is concentrated among a small proportion of the population.

3. *Hierarchical control of the production process.* Productive activity is carried out by units of enterprise in which decision-making is the prerogative of (at most) a few top owners and managers, while the great majority of workers have no involvement in the decision-making process.

4. *Individual material gain incentives.* Work is motivated primarily by the prospect of material rewards in the form of higher income for the individual worker.

Socialism I shall define as a form of socio-economic organization characterized by four sharply contrasting conditions.[35]

1. *Public ownership of the means of production.* Most of the productive

assets of the society are owned by public agencies accountable to the society as a whole, so that everyone shares in income generated by such assets and in the control of decisions with respect to their use.

2. *Emancipation of the proletariat.* Every member of the society is guaranteed an adequate level of living (given the overall economic constraints and cultural norms of the society), and no person receives a substantial amount of income from privately owned productive assets.

3. *Participatory control of the production process.* All persons working in an enterprise participate in the process of decision-making (within the constraints set by the accountability of the enterprise to the society as a whole).

4. *Collective and/or non-material gain incentives.* Work is motivated primarily by (a) the prospect of material gains for one's whole community or one's whole society rather than for oneself alone; and/or (b) the prospect of non-material gains for oneself (e.g., honor or esteem from one's peers, or satisfaction from the work activity itself).

There can be no doubt that the four conditions associated with my definition of capitalism are satisfied in many parts of the contemporary world, notably in the United States, Canada, Western Europe, Japan, Australia, and New Zealand. It is much more difficult to find any contemporary examples of countries displaying the conditions by which I have characterized socialism. In many of the contemporary countries conventionally labeled "socialist," the means of production are predominantly under public ownership, each person is assured a modest level of living, and no person receives a large amount of income from privately owned productive assets. But even where productive assets are under public ownership and not the source of large private income flows, it is rarely the case that everyone shares in the control of decisions with respect to the use of those assets. Moreover, few "socialist" countries show much evidence of participatory control of the production process or the use of collective and/or non-material gain incentives. In these latter respects, China is probably the country that has progressed furthest toward socialism,[36] but even China is only partially socialist in the sense in which I have defined the term.

The fact that there are no contemporary examples of a fully socialist society makes it difficult to test empirically the hypothesis that a socialist society is significantly less imperialist than a capitalist society. But it remains possible at a theoretical level to reach some relevant conclusions. To develop the argument, I turn now to consider some important consequences of the different conditions defining capitalist and socialist modes of production.

The viability of any social system requires that there be a prevailing set of institutionalized values that encourage patterns of behavior consistent with the smooth functioning of the system.[37] These values are an essential complement to the basic socio-economic institutions that define the system. In the case of capitalism, the successful operation of individual material gain incentives requires that people behave as "homo economicus," the economically rational man.[38] Homo economicus strives for individual gain; he seeks to maximize his money income in order to satisfy his wants; he is concerned about the extrinsic rewards for his productive activity rather than the intrinsic quality of the activity itself. Such behavior must be sustained by a set of values that emphasize the importance of the individual rather than the larger community, that urge competition rather than cooperation, and that stress the primacy of material goods and services (purchasable with money income) for satisfying human needs and promoting human welfare. These capitalist values place a tremendous premium on increasing the supply of marketable goods and services available to the society, while other conceivable social goals—that is, greater equity, development of more meaningful and less fragmented communities, improvement of the quality of the work experience, greater diversification of economic activity at an individual, local or national level—are viewed as subordinate to the primary goal of economic growth.

In the case of socialism a very different set of institutionalized values would be essential to the functioning of the system. For collective incentives to replace individual incentives, the socialist value system would have to emphasize the importance of the community rather than the individual and to urge cooperation rather than competition. The social goal of greater equity would be much more important than under capitalism (and the goal of economic growth would be correspondingly less important) because of the need to sustain a sense of common participation by everyone in both the responsibilities and the privileges of membership in the society. For non-material gains to replace material gains, the socialist value system would have to de-emphasize the significance of money income and the consumption of material goods and services while emphasizing the rewards deriving from the esteem of one's peers and from the intrinsic process of work itself. Such an emphasis would also tend to devalue the goal of economic growth in relation to other social goals such as the development of more meaningful communities, improvement in the quality of work, and diversification of economic activity.

Apart from the significant differences in the value systems associated with the capitalist and the socialist modes of production, there are important differences in both the process and the outcome of income distribution. Private ownership of the means of production and reliance on individual material gain incentives imply that in a capitalist society income distribution is linked directly to the process of production.[39] Property income and labor income are distributed to the owners of productive assets and the sellers of labor essentially according to the market-valued contribution of their assets and their labor to the output of goods and services. Income distribution is therefore not a matter for political determination by the society as a whole; instead, it emerges largely from the process whereby the market mechanism allocates resources to production. This process of income distribution is bound to create great inequalities of income. Not only does the small proportion of the population that owns most of the means of production receive the lion's share of property income, but also labor income is very unequally distributed because of the need to allocate and motivate work through differential economic rewards. Hence, a capitalist society is inherently an economically unequal society.

In a socialist society, by contrast, the process of income distribution is largely divorced from the process of production. Productive assets are mainly under public ownership and the disposition of any income generated by the assets is a matter for political decision-making. And to the extent that work is motivated by collective and/or non-material incentives, the income accruing to workers need not bear any relationship to the quantity or quality of labor provided by the worker. As a result, income can and must be distributed under socialism by a consciously political mechanism. Given the guarantee of a basic level of living for everyone, the absence of large private claims to income generated by productive assets, and the greater importance of equity to the functioning of the system, the outcome of the process of income distribution in a socialist society is bound to be much more equal than in a capitalist society.

A final important distinction between capitalist and socialist societies stems from differences both in the outcome of the process of income distribution and in the nature of control of productive enterprises. Under capitalism, a high degree of economic inequality results from the process of income distribution and a high degree of social inequality results from the hierarchical control of productive activity. Economic and social inequality (which are bound to be highly correlated) imply political inequality. A society that is predicated upon significant economic and social differentials is a society in which there cannot be genuine democracy, in the sense of equal participation in political decision-making by those affected by the decisions. So long as some people have much greater access to economic resources than others, they can have much greater influence on political decision-making;[40] and so long as the structure of decision-making at the workplace is highly authoritarian, one cannot expect the structure of decision-making at the community or national level to be egalitarian.[41] Thus capitalism is fundamentally incompatible with democracy.

Under socialism there is much less economic and social inequality than under capitalism. Both income and the control of productive activity at the enterprise level are shared more equally. It follows that socialist societies can and will be more democratic than capitalist societies at all levels of decision-making.

The Socio-Economic Roots of Imperialism

We may now return to the question posed at the beginning of this essay and consider whether a Socialist America would be significantly less imperialist than a Capitalist America. In the following pages I will examine each of the motivations for imperialism identified in the previous section as potentially relevant to a modern industrialized society in order to determine if and how their significance depends on whether the society is capitalist or socialist. I will first consider the relative strength of national and class interests in imperialism under capitalism and socialism, and I will then turn to differences in the distribution of *power* that affect the extent to which class interests in imperialism are translated into government policy.

Among national interests in imperialism the first potentially relevant one is the interest in *national security*. To the extent that this interest is not merely an ideological cover for other interests, it is one that arises as a result of potential external threats to a nation. The existence and strength of such threats depend upon the disposition of foreign powers towards the nation in question. Whatever the character of the nation's internal socio-economic organization, there is always a possibility that foreign powers will prove hostile. So long as the world is divided into nation-states without an accepted and respected superior authority to maintain world peace, each individual nation-state will have some justifiable concern about its national security. Hence the national security interest in imperialism is one that would not seem to be dependent in any significant sense on whether a society is capitalist or socialist.

The second national interest in imperialism discussed previously is the interest in maintaining macro-economic prosperity. Among various theories explaining how imperialism could serve such an interest, only one has been identified as plausible for a modern industrial economy: that imperialism may be important in ensuring regular and dependable access to foreign sources of key raw materials.

At first glance such an interest would not appear to depend on the internal socio-economic organization of a society. If a capitalist economy is critically dependent upon key raw materials, it is hard to see why such dependence would be any less significant for a socialist economy with the same resources at its disposal. Yet closer examination of the question suggests lines of reasoning that might well link raw-material-oriented imperialism more strongly to capitalism than to socialism.

The demand for raw materials in an economy depends upon both the aggregate level and the sectoral composition of output. The higher the level of output, and the more heavily the sectoral composition of output is weighted toward industries requiring imported raw materials, the greater will be the demand for such imports. Given the emphasis placed on economic growth in a capitalist society, one can argue that capitalism is likely to generate a more rapid rate of growth of output and correspondingly higher levels of demand for imported raw materials than would socialism. Moreover, the very unequal distribution of income associated with capitalism may lead to a sectoral composition of output that is oriented more heavily towards products requiring imported raw material inputs than would be the case with greater equality under socialism. For the kind of products whose production is most dependent upon the import of key raw materials tend to be industrial and technologically sophisticated (e.g. jet engines), and such products cater disproportionately to the demand of rich consumers. The demand of the poor and middle-income classes is more heavily concentrated on agricultural and simpler industrial products whose production is less dependent on scarce raw materials. Assuming that the composition of output reflects to some extent the structure of demand,[42] inequality in the distribution of income will be associated with greater dependence on key raw material imports.

Obviously a socialist society might sometimes have an interest in imperialist activity designed to secure access to foreign sources of raw materials. But the frequency and the strength of such an interest would be considerably higher in a capitalist society by virtue of its emphasis on economic growth and its inherent economic inequality.

A national interest in *aggregate economic gains*—like a national interest in macro-economic prosperity—could serve to motivate imperialist activity both in capitalist and in socialist societies. But again there are good reasons to believe that such an interest would be particularly forceful under capitalism. First of all, the emphasis placed on the desirability of increasing the available supply of goods and services in a capitalist society puts a great premium on the ability of a government to promote economic growth. In a society where there is such pressure to "deliver the goods," the government will be more highly motivated to seek out and exploit opportunities for economic gain through imperialism than it would in a socialist society where other social goals were relatively more important.

Secondly, the opportunities for aggregate economic gain through imperialism are likely to be considerably more extensive for a capitalist than for a socialist society. This is because capitalism encourages a high degree of economic specialization in order to reap the economic gains made possible by a wider international division of labor. Socialist values put less emphasis on such economic gains and more emphasis on alternative goals that involve deliberate diversification rather than specialization of economic activities. Hence a capitalist economy is likely to become more heavily involved in international trade and investment than a socialist economy with the same resource base. As a result, there will be many more situations in which a capitalist government can use its power to affect the terms of international economic relations in favor of its national economy.

The existence of a national *missionary spirit* that motivates imperialism requires that two conditions be satisfied. On the one hand, there must be a strong belief by the people of a society that their own way of life is a superior one. On the other hand, there must be a belief in the acceptability of imposing a way of life on others through the use of dominant power. The first of these conditions cannot be identified more strongly with one form of socio-economic organization than another. For good or bad reasons, people in both capitalist and socialist societies may well come to believe in the superiority of their own system. But whether people will find desirable the use of power to spread a system depends upon the extent to which concern about outcomes overrides concern about the processes whereby those outcomes are achieved. The more highly the values of a society stress genuine democracy—participation in decision-making by those affected by the decisions—the less acceptable will be the imposition of a system on others no matter how "good" for them it may appear to be. Hence the more truly democratic the form of socio-economic organization, the less will be the interest in imperialism based on a *missionary spirit*. And because capitalism precludes true democracy, a capitalist society will be more susceptible to undertake missionary imperialism than a socialist society that is inherently more democratic.

The *urge to dominate* as a source of imperialism is often described as an innate human drive, an element of human nature impervious to the social environment. Yet it seems quite unreasonable to insist that the form of socio-economic organization and the values that complement it have no influence on the attitude of people towards one another. Instead, one would expect rather different attitudes to emerge from (1) a society that stresses the importance of the individual and competition among individuals and (2) a society that stresses the importance of the community and cooperation among its members. The more competitive a society, the more an individual is likely to have an interest in dominating others, and the more the society as a whole may have an interest in dominating other societies. Without question, capitalism is a highly competitive form of social organization, and the urge to dominate is therefore more likely to motivate imperialism in a capitalist society than in a much less competitive socialist society.

The potentially relevant categories of class interest in imperialism identified in section II are associated with the promotion of social legitimacy, organizational expansion, and particular economic gains. A class interest in promoting *social legitimacy* through imperialism becomes significant whenever dominant classes in a society have reason to be concerned about the acceptance of their dominance by the rest of the people. As a very unequal form of socio-economic organization, capitalism obviously generates some dominant classes, and these classes have a potentially greater concern about their social legitimacy than would any identifiable class in a more equal socialist society. But while its basic economic institutions imply profound inequalities, the value system associated with capitalism—with its emphasis on the right (and obligation) of individuals to compete with one another in striving for personal advancement—suggests an ideal of free and fair competition. As people within a capitalist society come to recognize how unfree and unfair the competition often is (because of the inequality inherent in the underlying institutions), they are unlikely to accept the domination of the dominant classes. Thus, under capitalism, a contradiction between the socio-economic base and certain aspects of the ideological superstructure will further intensify the interest of dominant classes in providing some kind of legitimacy for their dominance. No comparable class interest in using imperialism for legitimizing purposes would arise in a socialist society.

A class interest in promoting *organizational expansion* through imperialism would not appear to be significantly more likely under either capitalism or socialism. On the one hand, a socialist system necessarily involves greater use of public administrative organizations than does a capitalist system that relies more heavily on the market mechanism to motivate work and allocate resources. On the other hand, to the extent that the capitalist system of private enterprise limits the role of government organizations in domestic affairs, civilian and military agencies would be all the more enthusiastic about satisfying their growth imperative abroad. In any event, the differences in the demands placed upon public organizations under capitalism and under socialism have been declining over time as the viability of capitalism in a modern industrialized society has become increasingly dependent on involvement by the state in domestic economic and social affairs.[43]

Class interests in *particular economic gains* can be shown to be much more strongly associated with capitalism than with socialism; indeed, such class interests most probably account for a substantial share of the imperialist activity undertaken by capitalist governments. This is not only because of the importance attached to strictly economic objectives in a capitalist society. Nor is it due simply to the fact that under capitalism most of the means of production are privately rather than publicly owned. There is a more fundamental reason why in a capitalist society particular groups should seek to promote imperialism as a means for realizing particular economic gains. This reason has to do with the manner in which income is distributed under capitalism.

To see this, one must recognize that an imperialist activity motivated by a class interest in economic gain involves in effect an anticipated redistribution of economic benefits from the rest of the population to the particular interested class. This redistribution does not involve any direct transfer, but it results indirectly from (1) taxing (or otherwise burdening) the society as a whole for the cost of the activity and (2) benefiting the particular class by bringing about changes in the international economic situation that increase its income-earning opportunities.

It is precisely the *indirect* character of the redistribution that makes it attractive to particular classes in a capitalist society, for under capitalism income is supposed to be distributed to individuals in accordance with their market-valued contribution to production. The only legitimate source of income is the production process itself, as mediated by the market mechanism. Direct transfers of income without any *quid pro quo* are limited to somewhat exceptional circumstances. This means not only that the poor cannot expect substantial relief from poverty through transfers of income from the rich, but also that the rich cannot expect to get the government to transfer income directly from others to themselves—no matter how powerful they may be. Hence any significant redistribution in favor of the rich and powerful can be brought about only indirectly by government activity that affects the *process* by which the market distributes income.

In a socialist society where income is distributed according to explicitly political criteria rather than according to an apparently apolitical economic mechanism, it makes no difference whether redistribution of income is brought about directly or indirectly. The outcome of the income distribution process is the object of concern rather than the process itself. In such a situation, a powerful group would find it no easier to get income redistributed to itself indirectly than directly. Moreover, it would not seek to get income redistributed by an activity that might reduce the size of the aggregate economic pie. Thus, in a socialist society, there would be no class interest in particular economic gains unless there were also a national interest in aggregate economic gains.

However, under capitalism, redistribution in favor of powerful groups can be brought about only indirectly. Hence, in a capitalist society, there are bound to be strong class interests in any goverment activity that indirectly redistributes income in favor of particular classes, even if the activity involves aggregate economic losses. There are a variety of ways in which a government can indirectly redistribute income through domestic as well as foreign programs, but imperialist activity clearly offers many such opportunities. Therefore, a class interest in achieving particular economic gains through imperialism, without any corresponding national interest, is a phenomenon unique to capitalism.

It remains now to consider whether the distribution of power differs systematically as between capitalist and socialist societies in such a way as to result in differential motivations for the government to undertake imperialist activities that serve class interests but no national interest. As a general rule, it is clear that there can be no class-based motivation for imperialism in a genuine democracy. For if everyone in a society participated equally in the political process, the government could not undertake imperialist activities whose anticipated costs to the society as a whole were greater than the anticipated benefits to a particular class. Since socialism is far more conducive to genuine democracy than capitalism, one would expect that any possible class interest in imperialism would be far less likely to motivate imperialist activity in a socialist society than in a capitalist society. To prove the point, however, it is necessary to show that the more unequal distribution of power in a capitalist society favors those classes that stand to gain rather than to lose from imperialism.

Among the classes most likely to lose from imperialism are the taxpaying citizens and firms who ultimately bear the financial burden of imperialism; the soldiers who suffer injury or death in cases of military action; consumers who pay higher prices when the monopolistic position of multinational corporations is protected; workers who lose their jobs because a firm shifts its operations to a more profitable foreign location; businesses that find themselves at a competitive disadvantage because a rival firm secures a privileged position abroad; and so forth. It is quite evident that such possible losers from imperialism have little political strength in a capitalist society. The taxpaying public is a large, amorphous body that is difficult to mobilize politically; soldiers are drawn disproportionately from the poorest and weakest strata of society; consumers, workers and businesses who lose from imperialist activity tend to be isolated and organizationally weak.

On the other hand, the classes that are likely to gain from imperialism tend to be among the most powerful in a capitalist society. The dominant classes with an interest in promoting their own social legitimacy have by definition a dominant position and correspondingly disproportionate power to shape government policy. The civilian and military bureaucracies interested in organizational expansion are close to the levers of power in government. And the capitalist class with its interest in particular economic gains is disproportionately strong in both economic and political terms. Moreover, within the capitalist class, the firms most directly involved in foreign economic operations are typically among the most powerful. For example, in the United States 9 of the largest 10 and at least 18 of the largest 25 corporations (ranked by sales) in 1965 were significantly involved in foreign operations.[44] These 18 corporations alone accounted for almost 20 percent of the total sales and almost 30 percent of the after-tax profits of all American industrial corporations. Hence even when there are conflicts of interest within the capitalist class over particular imperialist activities, the balance of power often tilts in favor of the pro-imperialists.

An important factor that enhances the effective power of the beneficiaries of imperialism is that the gains from an imperialist action tend to be large for the immediate beneficiaries while the losses tend to be spread widely and therefore thinly over the much larger number of losers. Under such circumstances, the gainers are always better motivated and better situated to mobilize themselves as an effective political force. It is not necessary that the beneficiaries of imperialism dominate all policy-making in order that the government be induced to undertake imperialist activities that serve particular class interests; it is only necessary that the beneficiaries exercise disproportionate influence in the sphere of foreign policy, which they can more easily do if the losers have less at stake and hence less interest in foreign policy decisions than the beneficiaries.

In sum, the balance of power is likely to tilt in favor of class-based imperialism in a capitalist society unless the aggregate costs of a given activity become so high as to weigh heavily and obviously on large segments of the population, or unless the activity involves a sharp conflict of interest among powerful classes themselves. Such situations do arise from time to time and they set limits on the extent to which—or the manner in which—a capitalist government is motivated to pursue imperialist policies. The recent history of American imperialism in Indochina is a good case in point. But it is clear that before such a point is reached there is a much greater scope for class-based imperialism under capitalism than under socialism.

Conclusions

The previous discussion leaves no doubt that a capitalist society is significantly more likely to generate imperialist activity than a socialist society. Most of the potential sources of imperialism in a modern industrialized society owe their existence or their strength to characteristics of capitalism, which are either absent or much less significant under socialism. The only relevant source of imperialism that appears to be quite unrelated to the internal socio-economic organization of a society is the one based upon a national interest in national security. Not surprisingly, this is the source that is given the greatest (if not the sole) attention by orthodox theorists. But every other relevant source of imperialism based upon a national interest, as well as every source based upon a class interest, is clearly more forceful in a capitalist than in a socialist society. The radical view of imperialism is thus confirmed.

The analysis of the relationship between capitalism and imperialism in this paper suggests certain directions for anti-imperialist movements in capitalist countries such as the United States. By identifying the specific characteristics of capitalism that contribute most significantly to imperialism, one can gain some understanding of the kinds of reforms that might help to limit the extent of imperialist activity under capitalism and the kinds of radical changes in basic institutions that would be necessary to develop an alternative and much less imperialist society.

Within the context of a capitalist society, the motivations for the government to undertake imperialist activity may be lessened to the extent (1) that the primacy of economic gain as a social objective can be diminished, (2) that the distribution of income can be made a more explicitly political issue; and (3) that income inequality can be reduced and democracy can be made more effective. Progress in these directions depends largely upon the ability of the disenchanted groups and the dominated classes in capitalist society to organize themselves and develop a stronger political force with which to oppose the power of the dominant classes who have the most to gain from the *status quo*. There is some hopeful evidence that the war in Indochina has served to galvanize more effective opposition to American imperialism in particular and to the oppressive aspects of American capitalism in general.

But one must recognize that the very nature of capitalist society places significant limits on the extent to which political reform movements can expect to curtail imperialism under capitalism. So long as the basic institutions of American society remain capitalist, economic gain will remain an important goal, inequality will persist, and genuine democracy will be unattainable. The kinds of institutional changes necessary to make substantial progress in eliminating the imperialist urges of a capitalist society would involve the development of a radically different form of socio-economic organization in which (1) economic activity would be motivated by an incentive system that did not rely primarily on the prospect of individual economic gain in competition with other individuals; (2) income and wealth would be shared in an egalitarian manner; (3) control over the process of production would be exercised by all those involved and the distinction between owner and worker would disappear. For an egalitarian society in which economic activity was based upon collective rather than individual incentives and cooperative rather than competitive behavior would encourage a set of institutionalized values in which social goals other than economic gain were paramount and would facilitate the functioning of a truly effective democracy. In short, the best way to contain imperialism is to build socialism.

The lack of a contemporary example of a fully socialist society has led many critics of the radical view to argue that such a society is an unachievable utopia. Until the allegedly inachievable is achieved, there may be no way to convince the hardened skeptic—or the determined opponent—about its feasibility. But the great variety of historical examples of socio-economic organization, and the extent to which some contemporary "socialist" countries have progressed from capitalist toward socialist institutions and values, suggests that socialism can be a real possibility. Utopian as such a system may appear to some observers, it represents the kind of long-run goal toward which an anti-imperialist movement must be directed if it is to achieve any significant and lasting progress.

Notes

1. The quote is from Tucker (1971), p. 138.

2. The negative answer is not stated explicitly, but it is clearly implied in the discussion in Tucker (1971), p. 138.

3. See, for example, the historical accounts of American imperialism in Zevin (1972), pp. 321-333; in Magdoff (1970); and in Williams (1969).

4. Thus Cohen (1973) states that "the real tap-root of imperialism" is "the anarchic organization of the international system of states. . . . The logic of dominion derives directly from the existence of competing national sovereignties"; and Tucker (1971), p. 73, asks: "Why may we not say simply that the interests of states expand roughly with their power and that America has been no exception to this experience?"

5. It would be impossible to list the names of all radical writers on the subject of American imperialism. For a representative sample of recent radical work, see Magdoff (1969), Kolko (1969), MacEwan (1972), and many of the essays reprinted in Fann and Hodges (1971).

6. There are of course many different varieties of radical theories of imperialism; the radical argument I develop in this paper is a personal one not necessarily shared by other radical theorists.

7. For useful discussions of the problems involved in defining imperialism, see Zevin (1972), pp. 316-321, and Cohen (1973), Chapter 1.

8. For Marxists "imperialism" represents a stage of capitalism associated with the growth of monopolistic firms in the industrialized capitalist nations and the spread of the capitalist mode of production across national borders into previously non-capitalist areas; see, for example, Lenin's definition of imperialism as the "monopoly stage of capitalism" on pp. 88-89 of the 1939 edition of Lenin (1917). For the purposes of this essay, imperialism must be defined in terms that are independent of any particular form of socio-economic organization.

9. By focusing attention on government activity, I am ignoring the variety of means by which private firms or organizations use their own power *directly* to affect conditions abroad. But I do take account of the way in which they do this *indirectly* through their influence on government; see the discussion of motivations for imperialism based on class interests in particular economic gains in the second and fourth sections of this chapter.

10. My definition of imperialism is not equivalent simply to intervention abroad, for it excludes instances of economic or military aid to foreign friends and allies who do not entail any relationship of domination and control.

11. See, for example, Tucker (1971), especially pp. 55-82, and Cohen (1973), Chapter 7.

12. The desire to maintain macro-economic prosperity is often presented by radical theorists in the context of a capitalist society as a class-based rather than a national motivation for imperialism. The reasoning is that only the dominant classes have a real interest in maintaining prosperity because it is primarily they who benefit from the existing economic system, while most of the people would be better off under another system that might replace a crisis-stricken capitalism. But this long-run outcome is problematic: in the short run everyone stands to lose if the economy is in crisis. Thus there is at least a short-run national interest—and possibly also a long-run national interest—in maintaining economic prosperity. This kind of national interest is quite distinct from the kind of class interests discussed later in which the short-run and the long-run benefits accrue only to particular classes.

13. See Hobson (1902), Luxemburg (1913), and Lenin (1917). Although some writers—e.g. Alavi (1964)—associate Lenin with an underconsumption/surplus-capital theory of imperialism, drawing mainly on Lenin (1917), Chapter 4, Harry Magdoff has stressed to me that this is a misrepresentation of Lenin's overall approach to imperialism.

14. Baran and Sweezy (1966), Chapter 7, and Reich and Finkelhor (1970) have developed the argument that military expenditures are an important source of surplus absorption in the American capitalist economy. Although these authors do not suggest that imperialism is necessary in order to sustain such expenditures, Baran and Sweezy do stress the strong compatibility of militarism and imperialism.

15. The work of Magdoff (1969) is probably the best known; other radical

theorists arguing along related lines include Kolko (1969), Julien (1971), O'Connor (1971), and Dean (1971).

16. See Hilferding (1910), Luxemburg (1913), and Lenin (1917).

17. See Shonfield (1965) for a thorough analysis of the manner in which modern capitalist economies have avoided major crises.

18. In the postwar period expenditure on defense as a proportion of gross national product has been of the order of 5 percent or less in all the industrialized capitalist countries except the United States; for representative data see Russett et al. (1964), Table 23. In the United States the rate of military spending as a proportion of GNP has varied between 7 percent and 13 percent since 1950, according to figures displayed in Table C-1 of the *Economic Report of the President* (1973). Moreover, there has been an unmistakable correlation between periods of relatively high military expenditure and periods of relatively high levels of aggregate demand; see the Appendix to Weisskopf (1972b).

19. Hymer (1972) estimates that the value of American direct private investments abroad has grown at a rate of 10 percent per year since 1950, while the corresponding growth rate for other major capitalist nations is somewhat lower but increasing. According to Table 2-7 in Hymer (1972), the United States accounted for approximately 60 percent of all foreign investment in 1966.

20. These percentages are based on an extrapolation of the trend from 1950 to 1969 shown in Weisskopf (1972c), Table 10-B.

21. These estimates are based on a comparison of the relative value of foreign investment assets (given in Hymer (1972), Table 2-7) and the relative size of gross national product (given in the *United Nations Statistical Yearbook* (1972), Table 180) as between the United States and other countries.

22. For documentation see Weisskopf (1972c), Table 10-D.

23. Among the "developed" capitalist countries only Japan places strict limitations on foreign investment in the domestic economy.

24. Country-wise figures on the value of direct investment in underdeveloped countries as compared to the value of direct investment in all foreign countries are given in Hymer (1972), Table 2-7.

25. These figures are documented in the *United Nations Statistical Yearbook*, (1972), Table 181.

26. Data on the value of exports by country of provenance and destination are given in the *United Nations Statistical Yearbook* (1972), Table 147.

27. See Magdoff (1969), especially pp. 45-54; Kolko (1969), Chapter 3; and Brown (1972).

28. See Miller, Bennett and Alapatt (1970), pp. 16-17, and Tucker (1971), pp. 118-126, for criticism of this kind in the context of the needs of the American economy. See also Cohen (1973), pp. 138-141.

29. The notion of a missionary spirit as one among several sources of American imperialism is implicit in the work of Williams (1969), and it is suggested explicitly by Zevin (1972), pp. 357-360.

30. The view that imperialism results from an atavistic human urge to dominate is most prominently associated with Schumpeter (1919), but it is also implied by Landes (1961).

31. Social legitimacy as a class-based source of American imperialism is stressed by MacEwan (1972), especially pp. 49-51.

32. Emphasis on the military bureaucracy as a source of American imperialism is common among contemporary "liberals"; see, for example, Bosch (1968) and Melman (1970).

33. This point follows from the neoclassical theory of international trade and was first emphasized in a classic article by Stolper and Samuelson (1941).

34. For a similar characterization of the capitalist mode of production, see Edwards, Reich, and Weisskopf (1972), introduction to Chapter 3.

35. This definition of socialism is closer to the Marxist notion of pure communism than to either the conventional or the Marxist usage of the word socialism.

36. For evidence on the extent to which China has moved toward the socialist model, see Gurley (1971) and Riskin (1973).

37. This proposition has been elaborated in the work of Gintis (1972), who combines elements of Marxian and Parsonian theories of the structure of social systems.

38. See Edwards, Reich, and Weisskopf (1972), introduction to Chapter 3, as well as Gintis (1972) for discussion of this point.

39. The process and the outcome of income distribution in a capitalist society is analyzed in greater detail by Weisskopf (1972a).

40. Miliband (1969), Chapters 6 and 7, describes many of the means by which economically powerful classes are able to have a vastly disproportionate influence on political decision-making even in a formally "democratic" society.

41. That democracy at the workplace is a prerequisite for democracy in other spheres of life is emphasized by Pateman (1970).

42. In principle foreign trade can break the link between the composition of domestic output and the structure of domestic demand, but in practice trade is never carried out so extensively as to divorce the two entirely.

43. For an illuminating analysis of the growing role of the state in modern capitalist societies, see O'Connor (1970).

44. The figures cited in this paragraph are documented in Weisskopf (1972c), Table 10-E.

Bibliography

Alavi, Hamza. "Imperialism: Old and New," *Socialist Register 1964*. New York: Monthly Review Press, 1964.

Baran, Paul and Paul Sweezy. *Monopoly Capital*. New York: Monthly Review Press, 1966.

Bosch, Juan. *Pentagonism: A Substitute for Imperialism.* New York: Grove Press, 1968.

Brown, Lester R. *World Without Borders.* New York: Random House, 1972.

Cohen, Benjamin J. *The Question of Imperialism.* New York: Basic Books, 1973.

Dean, Heather. "Scarce Resources: The Dynamics of American Imperialism," in Fann and Hodges (eds.), *Readings in U.S. Imperialism.* Boston: Porter Sargent, 1971.

Edwards, Richard C., Michael Reich, and Thomas E. Weisskopf. *The Capitalist System.* Englewood Cliffs, N.J.: Prentice-Hall, 1972.

Fann, K.T. and D.C. Hodges (eds.) *Readings in U.S. Imperialism.* Boston: Porter Sargent, 1971.

Gintis, Herbert. "A Radical Analysis of Welfare Economics and Individual Development," *Quarterly Journal of Economics*, Vol. 86, No. 4 (November 1972).

Gurley, John. "Maoist Economic Development," *Monthly Review*, Vol. 22, No. 9 (February 1971).

Hilferding, Rudolf. *Das Finanzkapital.* Vienna: 1910.

Hobson, J.A. *Imperialism: A Study.* Ann Arbor: University of Michigan Press, 1967; first published in 1902.

Hymer, Stephen. "United States Investment Abroad," in Peter Drysdale (ed.), *Direct Foreign Investment in Asia and the Pacific.* Canberra: Australian National University Press, 1972.

Julien, Claude. *The American Empire.* Boston: Beacon Press, 1971.

Kolko, Gabriel. *The Roots of American Foreign Policy.* Boston: Beacon Press, 1969.

Landes, David S. "Some Thoughts on the Nature of Economic Imperialism," *The Journal of Economic History*, Vol. 31, No. 4 (December 1961).

Lenin, V.I. *Imperialism: The Highest Stage of Capitalism.* New York: International Publishers, 1939; first published in 1917.

Luxemburg, Rosa. *The Accumulation of Capital.* London: Routledge, 1951; first published in 1913.

MacEwan, Arthur. "Capitalist Expansion, Ideology and Intervention," *Review of Radical Political Economics*, Vol. 4, No. 1 (Spring 1972).

Magdoff, Harry. *The Age of Imperialism.* New York: Monthly Review Press, 1969.

_____. "Militarism and Imperialism," *Monthly Review*, Vol. 21, No. 9 (February 1970).

Melman, Seymour, *Pentagon Capitalism: The Political Economy of War.* New York: McGraw-Hill, 1970.

Miliband, Ralph. *The State in Capitalist Society.* New York: Basic Books, 1969.

Miller, S.M., Roy Bennett, and Cyril Alapatt. "Does the U.S. Economy Require Imperialism?" *Social Policy*, Vol. 1, No. 3 (September/October 1970)

O'Connor, James. "The Fiscal Crisis of the State," *Socialist Revolution*, Vol. 1, Nos. 1-2 (January/February-March/April 1970).

O'Connor, James. "The Meaning of Economic Imperialism," in K.T. Fann and D.C. Hodges (eds.), *Readings in U.S. Imperialism*. Boston: Porter Sargent, 1971.

Pateman, Carole. *Participation and Democratic Theory*. Cambridge, England: Cambridge University Press, 1970.

Reich, Michael and David Finkelhor. "The Military Industrial Complex: No Way Out," in Christoffel, Finkelhor and Gilbarg (eds.), *Up Against the American Myth*. New York: Holt, Rinehart and Winston, 1970.

Riskin, Carl. "Maoism and Motivation: Work Incentives in China," *Bulletin of Concerned Asian Scholars*, Vol. 5, No. 1 (July 1973).

Russett, Bruce M. et al. *World Handbook of Political and Social Indicators*. New Haven: Yale University Press, 1964.

Schumpeter, Joseph. *Imperialism*. New York: Meridian Books, 1955; first published in 1919.

Shonfield, Andrew. *Modern Capitalism*. London: Oxford University Press, 1965.

Stolper, Wolfgang F. and Paul A. Samuelson. "Protection and Real Wages," *Review of Economic Studies*, Vol. 9, No. 1 (November 1941).

Tucker, Robert W. *The Radical Left and American Foreign Policy*. Baltimore: Johns Hopkins Press, 1971.

Weisskopf, Thomas E. "Capitalism and Inequality," Section 3.7 in Edwards, Reich, and Weisskopf, *The Capitalist System*. Englewood Cliffs, N.J.: Prentice-Hall, 1972a.

_____. "The Problem of Surplus Absorption in a Capitalist Society," Section 9.1 in Edwards, Reich, and Weisskopf, *The Capitalist System*. Englewood Cliffs, N.J.: Prentice-Hall, 1972b.

_____. "United States Foreign Private Investment: An Empirical Survey," Section 10.3 in Edwards, Reich, and Weisskopf, *The Capitalist System*. Englewood Cliffs, N.J.: Prentice-Hall, 1972c.

Williams, William A. *The Roots of the Modern American Empire*. New York: Vintage Books, 1969.

Zevin, Robert. "An Interpretation of American Imperialism," *Journal of Economic History*, Vol. 42, No. 1 (March 1972).

Comments

Harry Magdoff
Coeditor, *Monthly Review*

Professor Weisskopf has examined in thoughtful and sophisticated fashion the possible and probable reasons for U.S. (and, by extension, all capitalist) imperialism. For this analysis he sorts out two distinct potential sources: (a) those that arise from a national interest, and (b) those that are generated by the self-interest of a class that has disproportionate power to influence government policy. Basic to this approach is the assumption that there is such a thing as U.S. national interest, and that it is an identifiable and measurable objective reality. It is this assumption that I choose to quarrel with.

There are obviously times in the history of nations when national interest supersedes, or exists apart from, divergent class interests. The clearest example is that of a country occupied or controlled by a foreign power. In the absence, however, of similar experiences which unify a people in a common cause (most notably, although not exclusively, in response to actual or threatened economic, social, cultural, or racial exploitation by a foreign power), the so-called national interest of a class society is, and can be, nothing other than the interest of the ruling class (or an alliance of dominating classes).

This identity of the so-called national interest and that of the ruling class is firmly established in the economic structure of capitalist society—an identity that is supplemented and reinforced at every level by political power (executive, legislative, judicial, and military), the reigning culture and ideology, the educational system, and in the United States a long history stretching back to colonial days and marked by slavery, expansionism, and racism. Given the economic structure of this social organism, its success or failure is determined in the final analysis by the success or failure of the production, distribution, and financial enterprises controlled by capitalists. Quite obviously, there is at any given time considerable latitude in choice of government policy—e.g., more or less welfare, and varying degrees of tinkering with money supply, taxing, spending, and subsidies. But the acid test of government policy in a capitalist society must be the ability of private enterprise as a whole to flourish. In this day and age this of course means, above all, the ability of the large corporations, the dynamos of the economy, to prosper: to make as large an amount to profits as feasible, to accumulate capital for further growth of profits, and in further pursuit of these aims to exercise monopolistic-type controls over raw materials sources and markets. If these crucial enterprises are unable to make sufficient profits and to

Editors' note: This commentary was written in response to an earlier version of Weisskopf's chapter. The major theoretical differences between author and critic are, however, sufficiently important and unchanged to merit inclusion of the critique here.

keep on expanding, they reduce output, refrain from new capital investment, and at times close their doors entirely, with the result that the economy goes into a tailspin. That is why the essential needs of giant corporations and their ability to sabotage the economy determine the degrees of freedom of national (and regional) government policy. And in the course of events these business imperatives become either openly identified with, or rationalized behind a smokescreen of, "national interest"—be this "national interest" administered by a conservative, liberal, or even self-styled radical government.

When Weisskopf and others try to quantify what they take to be the national interest and on this basis argue that proportionately foreign trade and other international economic involvement are small relative to the gross national product and hence insignificant, I am reminded of analyses of the chemical composition of the human body. Apparently 93 percent of the human body consists of oxygen, carbon, and hydrogen, with only traces of other chemical elements. If one considered percentages alone, it would be possible to conclude that iodine (only 0.0004 percent), iron (0.004 percent), and magnesium (0.05 percent) are hardly important to the proper function of the human body; no need to fuss over such trifles. True, this may seem a somewhat far-fetched analogy. Yet it can serve as a reminder that when one deals with an organism, one needs to understand much more than the component parts. And a capitalist nation is above everything else a social organism, one that lives and breathes in a world capitalist system in which the struggle among nations for power and control is ever present and is in the nature of the beast. To comprehend this social organism it is important to view the complex whole in historical process, in the course of which some of the small percentages may be of unusual strategic significance.

As an example, and because of limited space, we will refer to only one of these tiny items. Weisskopf points out that "throughout the postwar period net exports from the United States have rarely exceeded one percent of the gross national product, and in recent years have actually become negative." From this fact he draws the plausible conclusion that this component has little effect on the maintenance of aggregate demand, and he therefore dismisses it as a possible matter of national interest. Yet this puny, petty, and picayune percentage of the gross national product has in fact shaken the world of international finance. Against the background of U.S. imperialist activity and the rapid international expansion of U.S. corporations and banks, the shift from positive to negative net exports recently triggered major monetary crises in the leading financial centers, contributed to the downfall of the Bretton Woods system, and has already led to two devaluations of the presumably almighty U.S. dollar. On top of all this, trade wars are sprouting, and currency wars are in the offing, all over this trifling percentage of the gross national product. (For background and further discussion of these developments see "The Dollar Crisis: What Next?" in *Monthly Review*, May 1973.)

It is regrettable that in his essay Weisskopf did not examine the balance-of-payments problems of the advanced capitalist nations and the associated issues of control over the international means of payment, banking, and money markets. The latter are major focal points of the struggle among the leading capitalist countries for power and influence in respect to (a) expansion of exports and foreign investment opportunities (in each other's territory as well as in the underdeveloped areas), (b) control over sources of raw materials, and (c) self-defense against rival powers. Moreover, in the ever present tensions among the leading nations, the countries of the Third World are the pawns. Spheres of influence, or direct control, in the Third World are useful not only as direct objects of exploitation but also as resources which provide added flexibility to the imperialist centers in coping with their balance-of-payments problems and greater room to maneuver for improved strength in the areas of international banking and money markets.

I don't think one can properly understand the history and causes of imperialism, including developments between the two World Wars and since the end of the Second World War, without taking these factors into account. And that is why, in my opinion, when Weisskopf limits his definition, and inquiry, to only the imperialist relations between the metropolitan centers and the periphery, he misses not only the significance of inter-imperialist rivalries but also much that is important in the pressures for control by the imperialist powers in the Third World.

It is important to understand that with the development of capitalism, international trade became ever more political, and that therefore the search for military strength is intimately interrelated with the reaching out for economic power. At times, to be sure, the political and military aspects of international economics are not clearly visible; but they almost invariably surface in periods of crisis. Since there is a time span between crises, however, and each crisis usually has some special features of its own, economists are inclined to think, as apparently Weisskopf also does, that crises are the exception and that normally international trade and investment in the advanced capitalist world are matters of "pure" economics: only in the Third World do military and political pressures play a role in trade and investment processes. Yet one has only to review the attempt by the United States to achieve hegemony in the capitalist world (over other advanced capitalist nations as well as underdeveloped countries) after the Second World War to see how superficial the "pure" economics approach is. Surely the ability of the United States to maintain deficits in its balance of payments over a period of more than twenty years and to use the purchasing power created by the deficits to finance military bases around the globe, wars and invasions, as well as an enormous increase in overseas investment and banking, cannot be separated from the U.S. build-up of worldwide military strength and the military subordination of its allies.

To sum it up, while Weisskopf's well-constructed analysis and thoughtful examination of class interests are appreciated, there is considerable disagreement, especially over (1) the concept of an objective national interest abstracted from the structure and dynamics of a nation's economy, and (2) the separation of the question of metropolitan-periphery relations from that of inter-imperialist rivalries. Further, it seems to me, that the analytical framework he adopts forces him to put into separate compartments key aspects of the imperialist problem that are in fact inseparable. The attempt at clear-cut differentiation of military, political, and economic issues leads to ignoring what is most essential: the interdependence and mutual interaction of these factors. This way of thinking—including the use of the "national interest" abstraction—is quite traditional in orthodox social science, a fact which goes far to account for its historic inability to face up to either the growth and significance of imperialism or to imperialism's roots in monopoly capitalism.

Methodological Issues in the Measurement of Inequality, Dependence, and Exploitation

James Caporaso
Northwestern University

Introduction

The immediate impetus for writing this chapter stemmed from the mounting criticism of the European Economic Community (EEC) by several writers, notably Gunnar Myrdal, Pierre Jalée, and Johan Galtung.[1] While the interest of those who studied the process of regional integration (including my own) was based on the assumption that integration was a "good" thing, these authors persistently called these assumptions into question. Myrdal placed European integration into a global perspective and began to ask troubling questions about the external dimensions of regional integration. Would regional integration lead to local improvements in trade, industrial development, and quality of life at the expense of countries outside of the region? What would be the final impact of an integrated EEC on the global division of labor? Would the less developed countries be permanently relegated to a position of supplier of resources and primary goods for the industrially advanced regional blocs? Jalée in his analysis of the EEC's relationship to Africa explicitly developed the exploitation theme. Finally, Galtung addressed himself to the questions of the symmetry of interactions in Europe, how evenly such valued things as wealth and technology were distributed, and what the strategic impact of a united Europe would be on the East-West balance.

It seemed astonishing to me that two totally opposed interpretations could be drawn from the same set of facts. Regional integration involved voluntary mutual cooperation in joint endeavors, while imperialism involved coercion and subjugation of one people by another. While advocates of regional and global integration have talked about interdependence, joint problem-solving, and mutual sensitivity among partners, scholars of imperialism speak in a different idiom of dependence, inequality, and dominance. While integration theorists talk of commodity exchange, comparative advantage, and the gains flowing from a global division of labor, those with an imperialist focus see unequal exchange, unfair terms of trade, and exploitation. The fact that these two bodies of thought move in different intellectual orbits, utilize different perspectives, and

The author would like to gratefully acknowledge the helpful comments of Mark Levine and Janet Shaw, both of Northwestern University.

express ideas in different conceptual currencies has had the unfortunate consequence of preventing them from coming into contact (and hence conflict) with one another. It is not my attempt in this paper to "resolve" these differences. What I do hope to do is clarify some conceptual and methodological ambiguities in various theories of imperialism. Specifically, I hope to suggest some fruitful ways of measuring several central concepts of imperialism—inequality, dependence, and exploitation—and I hope to provide these suggestions in such a way as to make them acceptable to those whose inclination has been to see integration and cooperation along with those whose ideological and conceptual lenses have encouraged imperialist interpretations.

Development of a Theory of Imperialism:
Specification, Measurement, and Testing

The title of this volume is *Testing Theories of Economic Imperialism*. Let us ask for a moment what such a task entails. Stated in minimal terms, a theory involves (1) a set of concepts, (2) relations among these concepts, and (3) some more or less systematic empirical observations to "test" the validity of these relationships. The concepts are abstract terms (independent and dependent variables) referring to classes of observations. They are linked to observations by "rules of correspondence," such as conceptual and operational definitions. These correspondence rules function as gatekeepers to determine what kinds of observations will be included in a concept and what kinds will be excluded. Thus, when someone says "by inequality I mean observations having the characteristics X, Y, and Z," he is making a firm decision regarding inclusion and exclusion rules for the term. This, of course, has immensely important consequences for testing a theory of imperialism, since the question of the causes of imperialism may (and probably will) differ radically as a consequence of changing these rules. Definitions are certainly not arbitrary at all if by that we mean that they are of no consequence for the validation of our theories.

To state the case more fully, what I am saying is that, before a theory can be tested, there must exist (1) definitional clarity of key concepts and some shared understanding (or conditional acceptance) of these terms; (2) specification of the model, including both the identification of the important variables relevant to imperialism as well as statements concerning the relations among these variables (in the form of hypotheses); and (3) measurement of these concepts. At the simplest level, the process of measurement involves verbal classification— that is, "by international inequality I refer to cases where some nations are systematically inferior to others on certain valued dimensions." Measurement may also lead to quantified scales having properties of "greater than" or "less than" (ordinal scales) or properties of "how much greater than" (interval scales). The advantages of quantified measures are in their flexibility and power of analysis and representation. For example, a set of underdeveloped countries could be described in terms of average levels of national wealth and a distance score between them and a set of more developed countries could be computed. Then, gradual (or not so gradual) changes in the causes of inequality could be used to explain the varying degrees of inequality.

The point of this digression into the components of theory is that some theories are much more advanced (i.e. better specified, relations more clearly defined, variables more precisely measured) and hence in a better position to be tested. The assumption on which this chapter rests is that theories of imperialism are at least only partially testable in their present state. Theories of imperialism suffer from a confusion as to what the dependent variable is, what its causes are, and how one measures both. The result of this three-way confusion is that efforts to test any one theory provide results that are highly equivocal and depend for their cogency on the ideological point of view adopted. Furthermore, what is referred to as "the theory of imperialism" is really an assortment of theories, each with different concepts, different definitions, and different relationships among the variables. These are often not treated as competing models but as different "manifestations of the same underlying phenomenon." A new vocabulary emerges—"new imperialism," "old imperialism," "mercantile imperialism," "imperialism of free trade"—to rescue scholarship from its own confusions, and researchers, satisfied that they have not seen anything differently and content that there is "unity in diversity," proceed to go their separate ways. While this may be an effective way to preserve cherished theories, it is not, in my opinion, a tactic designed to improve our understanding of imperialism.

The Literature of Imperialism

The scholar who is interested in testing theories of imperialism will find no lack of works on the subject. For well over one hundred years, there has been a steady outpouring of books, articles, and political pamphlets on the subject. The diversity of viewpoints expressed, the sheer volume of material, and the antagonistic philosophical underpinnings of these works are enough to humble anyone who may harbor ambitions to synthesize and integrate this material into a coherent statement. Normally, when one tests a theory, it is first appropriate to review the literature with an eye toward identifying some organizing concepts and some central hypotheses. But when the diversity of viewpoints is so pronounced, reviewing what has been accomplished is more likely to invite exegeses of competing viewpoints than it is to produce a coherent propositional inventory. Given this diversity, it would make little sense to argue which definition of imperialism is correct, what "form" the present imperialism is taking, or what factors motivate an expansive foreign policy.

However, this last issue, that of motives, is important enough to warrant some attention. The great majority of work on imperialism focuses on the question of the motives[2] that a country has for being imperialist. Less attention is directed toward understanding the consequences of that behavior for the target of the imperialist policy.[3] Hobson sees the causes of imperialism in underconsumption of goods and accumulation of capital in capitalist countries. Foreign markets and foreign investment thus become the outlets necessary to allow the growth of capitalism.[4] Lenin agrees with the importance of these processes and puts additional emphasis on the transition of capitalism into its monopoly stage.[5] Others see the controlling motives as located more clearly in the political realm.[6] Hans Daalder sees a trend in the literature:

Newer historians have thus found the mainsprings of the movement of European expansion less in the expanding industrial economy and more in the political area of world strategies and ideologies of competing expansive nations. They have strongly emphasized: (a) the unification of Germany and Italy, which formed a new assertive nationalism in these countries; (b) the effects of the Franco-Prussian War of 1870, which tempted France into colonial adventures in order to regain a sense of glory and grandeur. . .; (c) the continued expansion of Russia toward Constantinople, Persia, India, and the Far East, which increasingly threatened long-established British imperial interests; (d) the fact that Britain could not remain aloof from formal annexations when others threatened to move in, thus threatening the foundations of splendid isolation and of traditional balancing policies. . . .[7]

The point is not that motives are unimportant to the understanding or imperialism but rather that a focus on motives shifts our attention to the actor (the imperialist country) rather than the target (the victim of imperialism). It is better suited for an evaluation of the intentions of the actors than the consequences for those acted upon. And while motives (to expand, profit, explore, proselytize, trade, invest) may be a particularly strong part of the explanation of the origin of imperialism, once in existence, it may profitably be analyzed in its own right. As Darwin reminded us, the environment not only prods and pushes, it also selects and reinforces. And there is no guarantee that the forces generating imperialism are the same ones that maintain it.

An analysis of motives fails on two counts. It is both too broad and too narrow. It is too broad because not all attempts to dominate and exploit have resulted in dominance and exploitation. Studies that have attempted to prove the absence of motives for imperialism by pointing to the absence of large profits from foreign investment miss the point. It is too narrow because imperialism as a system of dependence, inequality, and exploitation can result even in the absence of motives designed to bring these conditions about. The conditions under which this occurs are fairly general. The danger is present any time people are not aware of the consequences of their behavior. If you inquire of an official in a trading house of a large firm in an advanced capitalist country whether he is an imperialist he will be quite astonished. Yet he may be engaged in the exchange of manufactured goods for primary goods with the terms of trade systematically working against the latter. Further, this exchange situation may not be due to a natural economic evolution but may be the product of an historically enforced division of labor.

To all those who speak in terms of market principles, the production and exchange of commodities under the forces of supply and demand, and so forth, it seems impossible that the above example can lead to imperialism. To the free trader nourished on the classical economics of Smith and Ricardo, commodity exchanges between countries are based on comparative advantage and cross-national differences in unit costs of production. Similarly, these exchanges result in increases in efficiency, welfare, and factor equalization. But the Marxist sees things differently. He will ask what the respective labor value of each commodity is and whether there is a systematic transfer of labor value from one country to the other.[8] This condition of asymmetric transfer may exist when the price of manufactured commodities increases at a more rapid rate than primary commodities.[9]

Central Concepts of Imperialism

Imperialism will be defined here as a state of inequality and dependence in interstate relations where both the inequality and dependence are maintained by exploitation. Hence there are three central concepts: inequality, dependence, and exploitation. Inequality refers to the manner in which some value (e.g., GNP, profit, industry, security) is distributed; in particular, it refers to the case where some units have more than others. Dependence refers to the condition under which the opportunities and behavior of one actor are affected by another actor. Dependence is a normal part of any social or exchange relationship. When dependence is a two-way street, such that two countries are roughly equally dependent on one another, we speak of interdependence. But when one country is affected strongly by another and the reverse is not true, we have a kind of relational inequality that we call dependence. Exploitation is by far the most difficult of the three terms to define. I will suggest a controversial definition with the hopes that it can be improved. Exploitation is defined as a process of "unfair" exchange with full recognition that the major problem is to come up with reasonable criteria for unfair. Classical economics provided one answer to the question of what constituted a fair exchange for a particular commodity X, namely, whatever the laws of supply and demand under perfect competition dictated. Departures from this in terms of trade distortions—tariffs, quotas, indirect taxes, discriminatory transportation rates, subsidies, cartels, and so forth—result in the imperfect operation of the laws of supply and demand. Marxist theory also provided a criterion—that is, the labor theory of value.[10] To state it simply, the answer to the question "How much is commodity X worth?"

is "It is worth the amount of labor put into it."[11] Thus, if two commodities are being exchanged for one another, e.g., typewriters and cocoa beans, and if over a period of time it takes a greater volume of cocoa beans to buy a constant number of typewriters, and if one adds the further limiting conditions that qualitative and technological improvements are constant, then exploitation is occurring.

It can be seen that the Marxist criterion is much more demanding than that of classical economics. Whereas a classical economist proclaims a gain from trade if each party is better off with trade than without it, a Marxist inquires into the relative gain from the trade and asks who profits more from the labor of the other. An unequal gain, where one actor profits twice as much as another, qualifies for exploitation.

Now I want to turn toward a very complicated point in the literature on imperialism concerning the relationships among our three variables: inequality, dependence, and exploitation. The point is that these three variables must each be present in some degree for imperialism to exist and that if the value of any of the variables goes to zero, no imperialism exists. We could represent this multiplicative relationship very simply as follows:

$$\text{imperialism} = (X)(Y)(Z),$$

where X equals inequality, Y equals dependence, and Z equals exploitation. Then, if $X = 0$, $Y = 5$, and $Z = 9$, imperialism will not exist. Contrast this with the alternative model:

$$\text{imperialism} = X + Y + Z,$$

which is additive and in which X, Y, Z function as main effects. What I am trying to formalize here is the intuitive notion that the variables in question are non-additive.

While this particular way of formulating the model may seem arbitrary and even erratic, I think it approximately reflects the verbal relationships expressed in the literature. When capital investment flows between the United States and Western Europe, it is not described as imperialism, but between the United States and Latin America it is. Similarly when Western Europe *depends* on United States soybean exports, we do not ordinarily characterize that dependence as imperialistic. Even where exploitation exists, but does not either produce or preserve a system of unequal, dependent relationships (as, for example, when a country specializing in high profit, high technology fields, such as electronic circuits, computers, and so forth, trades with a country producing basic steel), we still do not think of imperialism.[12] But when these same activities characterize relationships between weak and strong, superior and inferior, controller and dependent, they become imperialism.

Unless this implicit relationship is fully recognized, confusion will result and, indeed, it is precisely because scholars have proceeded from different implicit understandings of these relationships that they have read and interpreted the same information in such divergent ways. For example, D.K. Fieldhouse rejects Lenin's theory of imperialism by arguing that although a great deal of surplus capital existed in Western Europe, the majority of it went to the United States, Canada, Argentina, Australasia, and South Africa.[13] The implication is that to the extent that surplus capital is exported to developed countries, it does not constitute imperialism. By the same token, both Hobson and Lenin saw the causes of imperialism in the dependence of the advanced capitalist countries on the markets of the Third World. Yet, Pierre Jalée sees these market outlets as becoming decreasingly important.

And trade between the imperialist countries and the Third World amounts to a less and less important factor, in dollar value at least. While sales by the developed countries to the Third World in 1952 represented 32% of their total exports, they did not reach 21% (rounded off on the high side) of these exports in 1967. The Third World is, therefore, becoming a less and less important client of the countries which dominate and exploit it, while those countries remain a very high priority outlet for the Third World: 73% of the total Third World exports in 1952 and 74% in 1967 were sold to the imperialist countries.[14]

At first glance Jalée's conclusions seem puzzling. If part of imperialism is dependence of the advanced countries on the markets of the Third World, then a reduction of exports in this direction seems to augur a decline of imperialism. However, this interpretation overlooks the fact that imperialism rests on a set of relationships between one country and another. One would need to inquire to what extent the Third World depended on the markets of those countries absorbing 74 percent of their exports, whether there were alternate buyers, and so forth. Also, one should ask to what extent the Third World countries depended on the 21 percent exports from developed countries, despite the fact that this figure declined. Unless one begins to uncover this web of dependent relationships between equals and non-equals, he will draw misleading conclusions.

To summarize what I have said up to this point, there are at least three important concepts in the definition of imperialism—inequality, dependence, and exploitation. Inequality refers to differences between countries in desired goods and services, dependence refers to an asymmetric control of one country by another, and exploitation refers to an unequal (or unfair) value transfer. These concepts stand in definite relationships to one another. Inequality by itself need only reflect the luck of the draw—the fickleness of nature in bestowing favor on some nations while depriving others of the basic resources and climate needed for a modicum of development. Likewise, dependence of one nation on another characterizes relations between all patron and client states; yet it is not difficult to produce examples of such relationships that are not thought to be imperialistic (e.g., Israel and the United States). Even when relations of dependency are enforced by force, or the threat of force, we think only of dominance but not necessarily imperialism. It is only when both inequality and dependence are fostered and preserved through the exploitation of the weaker by the stronger that imperialism comes into play. Imperialism, then, might be looked upon as a theory of inequality and dependence where one causal agent is exploitation.

It is true that this definition of imperialism is parsimonious in its representation of key variables. The objections are likely to be that it is simplistic and that it excludes things that are of obvious importance. This list would have to include colonialism, military intervention, coerced tribute, indirect political rule, extraction of taxes from a foreign local population, dependence on foreign markets, and overseas capital investment. It is agreed that all these phenomena have at one time or another entered into the imperialist relationship. The problem here is to allow for this diversity without paralyzing the theory by appending to it a set of singular, unique propositions. I think this can be done by distinguishing between the *form* of imperialism on the one hand, and the *mechanisms* of imperialism on the other.

I will argue that the form of imperialism is constant, that it is fundamentally an exploitative exchange relationship among unequal, dependent countries. The irreducible feature of imperialism, as formulated here, is that of unequal value transfer from one actor to another. However, the particular mechanism (i.e., technique, means, and so forth) through which this value transfer can take place varies greatly. It may involve a direct or indirect colonial rule as in Great Britain's rule of India from the Indian uprisings of 1857 to 1947, the date of Indian independence. Or it may involve nothing more than a free trade relationship in which the terms of trade systematically work against a weaker country. This would occur when the prices of exports for a weak country decrease relative to its import prices from another country. Exploitation may also involve techniques that are not so subtle, e.g., plunder of native lands, or taxing local foreign populations as the British did through the native Indian zamindar. Or, exploitation may involve foreign investment with extremely high profit rates that may be due to the payment of cheap wages or to an artificially enforced price.

These are all different types of exploitation. Which particular mechanism is employed will depend on a variety of factors, including the submissiveness of the exploited country, the degree of competition the imperial country receives with respect to its target country, and how industrially advanced the imperialist country is. Concerning this last point, it is no coincidence that British anti-imperial sentiment arose about the same time as Britain became the supreme industrial power, roughly from 1846, when the Corn Laws were abolished, to the turning of the century, when Germany, Japan, and the United States emerged as serious economic competitors.

My basic thesis here is that exploitation is the regulator of the imperialist relationship in the sense that it is the control device that insures the limits within which inequality and dependence can vary. If a state becomes too strong, it will soon cease to be dependent and the exploitative relationship may soon be brought to an end. Or, conversely, the country may become too weak and impoverished and leave nothing to be gained by the stronger power. Given that there are forces that could upset this unequal relationship (e.g., a policy of autonomy, a native industrialization movement, or local regional integration) a regulator or governor is needed. In some cases, plunder will do; in others, free trade; while in yet others, a policy of formal rule is adopted. These should be seen as differences in technique rather than as fundamentally different processes. From 1600 to 1857 Britain exploited India through the British East India Company, which by the middle of the eighteenth century had established powerful trading centers with quasi-political powers in Bengal, Madras, and Bombay. However, the Indian revolt of 1857-59 led to the dissolution of the East India Company and the initiation of direct British rule. It may be that colonialism and military intervention are "second-best" strategies.

Measurement Strategies for Inequality

In the previous sections I attempted to identify the key components of imperialism and began to integrate these components into a specified model. We are now ready to suggest several possible measures of two of the three main concepts—inequality and dependence. Some ideas on how to measure exploitation will be offered, but at this time I am not ready to advocate formal measurement of this concept.

My intuitive notion of inequality is one in which some value (e.g., GNP, capital investment, employment) is unevenly distributed across several units. Inequality refers to a condition, then, in the dyadic case, where A has more of something than B. At this dyadic level the conceptual and methodological problems are minimal. Dealing with three or more actors opens up many complications. But for the time being let us defer this problem.

Two distinctions are necessary before proceeding. One must distinguish between dyadic and systemic measures on the one hand and attribute and relational properties on the other. "Dyadic" simply refers to pairs of countries, while "systemic" means three or more. An attribute is a property of a unit, in this case a nation-state. Relations are properties of links or bonds between sets of nation-states. The distinction is important because inequality will be thought of in terms of distances between attributes, while dependence is interpreted as relational inequality.

Dyadic Measures of Inequality

There are two dyadic measures of inequality, one based on the idea of simple distance and the other on the notion of absolute distance. Both of these measures are derived from field theory.[15] The central hypothesis of field theory is that the best explanations of behavior are not based on the *levels* occupied by a particular nation on a number of variables but on the *distances* between pairs of nations. In Park's terms, the main proposition of field theory is that ". . . the behavior of one country directed toward another is a linear function of similarities and differences on such attribute dimensions as power, wealth, and political orientation."[16]

Vector of Simple Distance. The simple distance measure, termed the vector of simple difference (VSD), is simply the inequality between two countries expressed as the distance score of A from B and B from A. Thus if A has a GNP per capita of $3000 and B has $1000, the VSD of A from B equals −$2000, while B from A equals +$2000.

Vector of Absolute Distance. The second distance measure, the vector of absolute distances (VAD), looks only at the absolute distance of A and B from one another. This is a symmetric inequality measure that provides only one score. In the above example, the VAD is equal to $2000.

Clearly these two measures provide different information and are, as Park demonstrates, statistically independent from one another.[17] But aside from this, the VAD provides information on only gross equality or inequality between two nations, while the VSD provides some idea of the direction of the inequality. The VSD gives us some handle on the concept of asymmetry and permits us to look at behaviors related to asymmetrical relations. Similarly, as Park notes, the VAD is tied to important theoretical concepts, e.g., "symmetric similarity."[18] What this implies is that ". . . the higher the similarity between two entities, the more a certain kind of interaction takes place."[19] For example, the closer (i.e., the more equal) two nations are in economic development, the more likely they are to trade, and, I might add, the closer two nations are on a number of attributes, the less likely it is that relational inequalities will develop.

Systemic Measures of Inequality

While the logic of measuring systemic inequalities (defined here as three or more units) may be an extension of the bilateral case, there are nevertheless considerable complications of both a practical and conceptual nature in making this transition. When dealing with only two nations, we always know unambiguously what constitutes more or less inequality. The nation with the larger share of some valued commodity is better off than one with less and the magnitude of the inequality is equal to the difference between the two individual magnitudes. However, when three or more actors are under consideration, complicated questions relating to the distribution of values emerge.[20] The following example may illustrate the point more clearly:

I		II	
States	% Shares	States	% Shares
A	90	A	88
B	5	B	8
C	5	C	4

In the first distribution, State A holds more shares than the largest actor in the second distribution. However, States B and C possess equal shares, while B is twice as large as C in the second distribution. Which distribution, then, contains more inequality? By identifying the problems of comparison and interpretation in the minimum case of three actors it gives one a clue as to how complicated the picture gets with five, ten, or twenty nations. However, instead of trying to provide guidelines for dealing with these conceptual ambiguities in the abstract, I will present several systemic measures and attempt to point out their respective properties.

Sum of Squares Indices. As those who have attempted to construct measures of inequality have pointed out, systemic measures of inequality may be based on the sum of the squares of each member's share of the total distribution. One type of sum of squares is based on a simple proportion P_i and the measure is $\sum_{i=1}^{n} P_i^2$. Assume that there is a set of ten countries for which one wants to evaluate the degree of inequality. Once the variables of interest have been specified (e.g., wealth, development, and so forth), it is a simple matter of calculating the proportion of that value held by each of the ten countries. Then square each of the proportions and add them up. If one member possesses all the shares the score is one. The greater the number of actors and the more uniform the distribution among them, the lower the score.

A second type of sum of squares measure is based on the sum of deviations of individual country shares from the "average share." Both the standard deviation and the relative mean deviation intercept fall into this category. The standard deviation is

$$SD = \sqrt{\frac{\Sigma(X - \overline{X})^2}{n}} \quad ,$$

where X equals a particular country's share of a value, $\overline{X}$ equals the average share, and n equals the total number of countries involved. The standard deviation has a lower limit of zero that would occur if each country fell exactly on the mean. The sum of the squared deviations from the mean would then equal zero.

The Lorenz Curve and Gini Coefficient. Most measures of inequality are based on the dispersion of scores in a distribution. The dispersion may be around an empirically observed mean, as with the standard deviation, or around some "ideal" norm, such as perfect equality. The Lorenz Curve is of the latter type. It is a cumulative measure of inequality that is capable of graphically presenting the cumulative shares held by increasing and decreasing proportions of the system.[21]

A Lorenz Curve is constructed in the following way. Along the horizontal axis (see Figure 5-1) the countries who are members of the system under examination are ranked from the lowest to the highest in terms of their respective proportions of the value in question. Along the vertical axis are values of the variable; for this illustration, let us say GWP or gross world product.

Plainly then, if every country possesses an equal share of GWP, each country will fall directly on the line of perfect equality. To the extent that this is not realized, there will be deviations from that line. The Gini Index provides a precise measure of these deviations in that it is based on a summation, for each actor, of the difference between its observed score on the Lorenz Curve and where it would be in the case of pure equality.[22] The values expressed by the Gini coefficient have an intuitively pleasing meaning—these values reflect the proportion of the total area of inequality falling between the Lorenz Curve and the ideal line of perfect equality.

The Concentration Measure. Although the Lorenz Curve and Gini Coefficient provide valuable information about inequality, they contain inherent limitations that, under certain conditions, makes confident interpretations difficult. One problem is that the Gini Index has an upper limit of $1 - 1/N$.[23] In the two-country case the upper limit of maximum inequality would be .50 $(1 - 1/2)$; the three-country case would result in a score of .67 $(1 - 1/3)$ and so on. Thus, even in the event that there were complete inequality among two

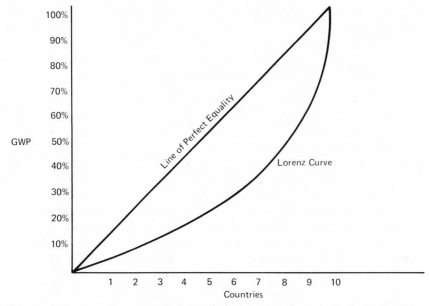

Note: a weighting parameter could be used along the horizontal axis to standardize for the population of each country.

Figure 5-1. The Lorenz Curve

nations, where one country possessed 100 percent of a resource and the others possessed none, the inequality would be .50. However, in what may be a more reasonable size for studies of imperialism, the upper limit for ten countries is .90 and for twenty .95. So in actual practice this limitation may not be so severe.

Unfortunately, this limitation is related to another difficulty that cannot be so easily dismissed, namely the interpretation we attach to two or more Gini indices drawn from systems of different size. This is a serious problem if for no other reason than the fact that imperialism is a phenomenon that occurs through historical stages—that is, it is conceptualized as a process developing over time. And the composition of membership has changed radically over the last century, resulting in the disappearance of some states and the emergence of others. With the number of members varying from one time point to the next a measure whose upper limit fluctuates solely as a function of size can provide no standard temporal interpretation, and hence, no comparability.

To overcome these problems, several scholars have independently developed a measure whose interpretation, in at least one important parameter (the range), is independent of size. Although the particular substantive focus of these scholars

was quite different, the conceptual and methodological similarities (even identities) are striking. Kenneth Janda, in his Comparative Political Parties Project (CPPP), developed a measure of interest articulation that attempted to capture the idea of the evenness of party support that comes from various societal groupings. He suggested the following measure:

$$\text{Articulation} = \sqrt{\frac{\sum_{i=1}^{n} X_i^2 - \frac{1}{N}}{1 - \frac{1}{N}}} \quad ,$$

where X_i equals the proportion of the party's support that is derived from any particular social group and where n equals the number of social groups.[24]

Approaching the problem from a different substantive angle, Ray and Singer suggest the following formula to measure the level of concentration in the international system.

$$\text{Con} = \sqrt{\frac{\sum_{i=1}^{n} P_i^2 - \frac{1}{N}}{1 - \frac{1}{N}}} \quad ,$$

where Con equals concentration, P_i equals the proportion or share of a value of each country in the total of that value and N equals the number of actors involved.[25] This is of course mathematically identical to Janda's measure. A moment's reflection will confirm that the similar structure suits the conceptual interests of both equally well since both are interested in what is essentially the same thing—inequality. Janda is interested in the inequality of support for a political party among different groups in society. Ray and Singer are interested in the inequality of power among sets of states.

I said earlier that the advantage of this measure is that it provides an interpretation of inequality that is invariant with respect to size. More precisely, as Ray and Singer note, this invariance holds for the *range* of values that an inequality measure can assume but not for the scores within that range[26]—that is, the upper and lower limits are one and zero respectively no matter whether there are two or two hundred units in question. This is a desirable property, since if the size of the system changes and this changes the relative distribution, we will want our measure to reflect this.

Measurement Strategies for Dependence

Intuitively, what I have in mind when I speak of dependence is the condition where B's behavior is affected by A, or to reverse the subject and predicate, where A is the *cause* of B's behavior. I speak of "A causing B" and not "A influencing or exerting power over B" since both influence and power signify conscious goals or "ends in view." Uses of the term "power" also bring the opposition of the party being controlled into the picture.[27] A can *cause* or affect B's behavior without willing it and B can be *affected* without opposing A's behavior. A may be ignorant of the consequences of his behavior just as B may be unaware of the causal sources of his.

In addition to this causal connection we add the notion of asymmetry to provide a fuller meaning of dependence. When A and B affect one another in a mutually balanced, equal way, we do not speak of dependence. We then talk about mutual association and integration. But it is precisely when the relations between states become unbalanced and asymmetric that we talk about dependence.

Many scholars of imperialism have felt that asymmetry is important. Richard Wolff sees imperialism as a "network of means of control exercised by one economy (enterprises and government) over another."[28] It may exercise control for the purpose of assuring market outlets, access to essential raw materials, safe spheres of influence for the investment of capital or for military and strategic reasons.[29] Similarly, Dos Santos views the concept of dependence as central to imperialism. Dependence refers to inequalities in the capacity for autonomous growth, with the dominant countries capable of autonomous expansion while the dependent countries are able to grow only as a consequence of this expansion.[30] Dependent countries are thus "dependent" in a quite literal sense.

Both of these definitions, which are very representative of the central idea of imperialism, stress the theme of asymmetric dependence or relational inequality. For what we are talking about with dependence is an inequality—not of attributes of individual units—but an inequality of causal relations. Our measures must attempt to capture this asymmetry.

However, a problem emerges immediately. "Dependence" is much more difficult to measure than "inequality." While "inequality" was conceptualized as an attribute of nations that is directly observable (e.g., GNP, literacy), "dependence" is a dispositional concept that manifests itself only under certain conditions. For example, dependence is observable not at any and all times, but only when the class of things (commodities, relations, services) on which a state depends is withdrawn or curtailed. To depend is to "need," and to say "need" is to hypothesize that there could be adverse consequences if the need were not filled.[31] Statements of the following kind would be needed: "If the United

States could not get Columbium and Chromium from Africa, oil from the Mideast, and so forth, the United States would not be able to build airplanes and U.S. citizens would not be able to drive cars (at least not so cheaply)."

These dispositional statements are virtually impossible to measure and would require such an intricate approach to numerous but fleeting examples (of the above nature) that the measures themselves would become too intractable. Instead, we will try to infer dependency from some more easily observable characteristics. In place of the more volatile behavior of dependency itself, we look at its more stable (hence more easily locatable) structural counterpart.

Dyadic Measures of Dependence

In the remainder of the paper I will suggest various formula and measures for dependence. In the interests of clarity and consistency I have adopted a standard notational system for this even though this means an occasional departure from the letter (but not the meaning) of the original author's notation. The following notations will be used for the remainder of the paper.

Let, E_{ij} = the exports of nation i to nation j (directional),

I_{ij} = the imports of nation i from nation j (directional),

T_{ij} = the total trade of i and j (non-directional),

EC_{ij} = the exports of nation i of commodity j,

TE_i = total exports of nation i to other nations = $\sum\limits_{\substack{j=1 \\ j \neq i}}^{n} E_{ij}$,

TI_i = total imports of nation i from other nations = $\sum\limits_{\substack{j=1 \\ j \neq i}}^{n} I_{ij}$,

TC_i = total consumption of nation i = $\text{GNP}_i + TI_i$,

WC = total world consumption = $\sum\limits_{i=1}^{n} TC_i$,

C_i = nation i's commodity concentration,

G_i = nation i's geographic concentration,

k = the number of commodity classes.

Russett Trade Ratio. The first measure is Russett's "trade to GDP (gross domestic product) ratio." This is provided by T_{ij}/gdp_i and T_{ij}/gdp_j, where T_{ij} equals the total trade between nation i and nation j and gdp_i equals the gross domestic product of nation i. The ratio T_{ij}/gdp_i purports to provide an index of country j's impact on country i, while T_{ij}/gdp_j provides a similar impact measure of i on j.[33] Another way to view these indices is to interpret T_{ij}/gdp_i as actor i's dependence on actor j and T_{ij}/gdp_j as actor j's dependence on actor i.

The distance between these two scores gives one a measure of asymmetric dependence. Notice that these two ratios are not the same. The impact of i on j could be quite different from that of j on i. Imagine that we are dealing with the United States and Chile and that the total trade between both countries totals 100,000 units. Let us assume that Chile's GDP is one million while the United States' is 100 million. Then the impact of the U.S. economy on Chile is 10 percent, while the impact of Chile's trade on the United States is one-tenth of 1 percent. What this measure of dependence provides then is an index modified by the economic size of each of the trading partners. This measurement tactic fits nicely with Russett's theoretical position that "the political effects of trade are subject to decreasing marginal returns."[34]

Share of Trade Ratio. The second dyadic measure is a simple "share of trade" ratio. For example, E_{ij}/TE_i, where E_{ij} equals the exports of country i to country j and TE_i equals the sum of i's exports to all other nations. The trade/GDP ratio is really a ratio of the external to internal marketing and purchasing sources. This measure takes all the trade (imports and exports separately) done with a certain country and asks what proportion of the total is accounted for by this country. Clearly, the principle of asymmetry is again preserved since the exports of i to j divided by i's total exports do not equal the exports from j to i divided by j's total exports.

Systemic Measures of Dependence

Again we are ready to ask how dependence can be measured in the n-country case since it is this which usually interests us. Three measures are proposed; two are from international economics and a third one is a simple measure that I have devised. These three measures of dependence are (1) the index of commodity concentration, (2) the index of geographic concentration, and (3) the economic power ratio.

Commodity Concentration Index. One argument of those who stress the current imperialistic nature of the international system is that during the nineteenth century the advanced industrial nations of Western Europe enforced and then froze a global division of labor that favored them and subjected the less developed countries to a condition of permanent dependence. Michael Barratt Brown sees this historically enforced dependence as the central component of imperialism:

In the nineteenth century, free trade froze the world division of labor between primary producers and manufacturers; but the division had first to be made by the opening-up of the world's markets to European manufacturers. This artificial division of labour was the essence of the unequal relationship between advanced and underdeveloped lands.[35]

The essence of this argument is that the present global division of labor is not the product of a "natural" (read market-determined) evolution but is instead an enforced relationship.

The story of the East India silks and calicoes that were imported into England and caused difficulty for the English textile industry is so well known that it does not need to be told here. It was fortunate for England that no Indian Ricardo arose to convince the English people that, according to the law of comparative costs, it would be advantageous for them to turn into shepherds and to import from India all the textiles that were needed. Instead England passed a series of acts designed to prevent importation of Indian textiles and some 'good results' were achieved.[36]

Part of imperialism today, then, consists of the fact that less developed countries are dependent on a few commodities, usually crops or primary resources. The index of commodity concentration hopes to measure this dependence. In his book *Concentration in International Trade*, Michaely utilizes a concentration index in which country i's commodity concentration in exports, represented by C_i is given by:

$$C_i = 100 \sqrt{\sum_{j=1}^{k} \left(\frac{EC_{ij}}{TE_i} \right)^2} \quad ,$$

where EC_{ij} stands for the value of i's exports of commodity j to the rest of the world, while TE_i represents the total value of country i's exports to the rest of the world, and k equals the number of commodity classes.[37] This measure is a sum of the squared proportions of each commodity class to the totals. The upper limit of the ratio is 100, indicating the highest possible amount of dependence that would exist if all of a country's exports were made up of one commodity. The lower limit is more open-ended and rests essentially on the number of commodity classes dealt with and how evenly trade is distributed over these classes.

Geographic Concentration Index. Just as countries may be dependent on a few basic commodities, they may also be dependent on a few buyers and sellers for their exports and imports. Less developed countries have suffered not only from lack of economic diversification but also because their markets have been limited to buyers in a few metropolitan countries. And again, this has not been an entirely "natural" occurrence. The path from the less developed country was facilitated by lowering transport costs, eliminating tariffs on unprocessed goods and building ports and transportation facilities that favored shipment to the "mother country."

The coefficient of geographic concentration is given by:

$$G_i = 100 \sqrt{\sum_{j=1}^{n} \left(\frac{E_{ij}}{TE_i} \right)^2} \quad ,$$

where G_i stands for the geographic concentration of country i with all other members of the system, E_{ij} equals the exports of country i to j and TE_i represents the total exports of country i.[38] If all of i's trade (e.g. 500 units) is with one country, the following will result:

$$100 \sqrt{ \left(\frac{500}{500} \right)^2 + \left(\frac{0}{500} \right)^2 + \left(\frac{0}{500} \right)^2 + \left(\frac{0}{500} \right)^2 }$$

$$= 100 \sqrt{ (1)^2 + 0 + 0 + 0 } = 100 \times 1 = 100.$$

Therefore the upper limit of this index is 100. Again the lower limit is more open-ended and rests essentially on the number of trading partners in the system and how evenly trade is distributed over these partners.

These two measures of dependency both provide useful information about asymmetric relations among nations. It has long been a hypothesis that large powerful countries have the ability to spread their assets over many different partners while smaller countries must rely more on a few geographic ties for a limited number of products. In addition, it should not be supposed that these two measures are independent from one another. Albert O. Hirschman suggested long ago that the higher the commodity concentration of exports, the greater the geographic concentration.[39] What this means is that LDCs who have undiversified economies are also dependent on a few countries. This lack of a stable base of diversified exports makes them particularly vulnerable to fluctuations in world demand and, in turn, such fluctuations are dependent on shifts in the market situation in a very limited number of countries.

Economic Power Ratio. There are two concepts that this measure hopes to capture and express as a ratio. If I were to interpret the importance of trade in *realpolitik* terms, I would emphasize two things. On the one hand I would want to know the amount of influence a country's trade has on other members of the system and on the other, the degree to which this country is influenced by the trade of these members. The influence of country A on the rest of the system is hypothesized as being equal to its share of the total consumption of every other member of the system. Each country consumes a certain volume of goods and services. Most of the goods and services are produced domestically but not all; some have to be imported from foreign countries. At the same time A is dependent on its imports from the rest of the world since these are responsible for part of its consumption. Let us try to represent this two-way relationship as follows:

$$\frac{TE_i / (WC - TC_i)}{TI_i / TC_i} \quad ,$$

where TE_i = the total exports of i,
           WC = the total world consumption,
           TC_i = the total consumption of nation i,
           TI_i = the total imports of nation i.

Thus, the economic power ratio is really a ratio of two proportions. In the numerator we have the proportion of world consumption provided by the exports of country i and in the denominator we have the proportion of i's imports to its total consumption, indicated by i's GNP plus i's total imports. The entire ratio, i.e. the ratio of the two ratios, attempts to measure the extent to which the world depends on the exports of nation i for its consumption needs in relation to the extent to which nation i depends on imports from the world for its consumption. A large, autonomous country like the United States, which accounts for a substantial amount of world exports, and whose import needs, seen in relation to its own internal production, are small, would probably have a larger ratio.

Exploitation

In an earlier part of this paper, I mentioned that I would not propose formal measures of exploitation in the same way that I did for inequality and dependence. What prevents me from making these suggestions are primarily two factors. First, there is the problem of supplying criteria by which to assess what is "fair" and "equal." The empirical assessment of exploitation depends on the conjecturing of a hypothetical baseline against which to silhouette the observed facts. The solution to this problem is by no means obvious. Should "unequal" refer to any difference in the relative gains from trade—that is, any departure from perfect equality of gain—or should one ask to what degree a commodity price departs from "what the cost would be under conditions of perfect competition," or "whether the price charged exceeds the marginal cost of production," and so forth? Second, there is the problem, perhaps insolvable, of constructing a measure of exploitation that is acceptable both to a Marxian worldview as well as to a philosophy nurtured by classical liberal economic thought. What I am asking here is whether there is a concept (and hence a measure) of exploitation that is trans-paradigmatic in that it retains a common meaning in both perspectives. I have serious doubts at this point whether this difficulty is surmountable. Marxism on the one hand, and classical and neoclassical economics on the other, are different language communities in the most fundamental sense. They are, individually, communities of meaning within which there is a sharing of assumptions, definitions, and meaningful problems but across which there is little in common. If this pessimistic view is correct, it may be impossible to provide a measure of exploitation, and if this is so, it inevitably follows that an empirical test of imperialism is unlikely to satisfy members of these two intellectual traditions.

Exploitation was defined earlier as an exchange process in which one party unfairly acquired most of the value. This definition eliminates outright stealing as exploitation since in stealing the value transfer is unidirectional. It is also involuntary. Exploitation, by contrast, is a two-way relationship that may or may not be voluntary. Exploitation may involve the direct purchase of the labor of another, as in buying slaves. Here all that is given for the life's work of the slave is the initial purchase price and food, shelter, and care sufficient to keep the slave alive and economically productive. There are "softer" forms of exploitation, which, for example, may result when a party receives the product of one's labor without an equivalent product or currency offered as compensation.

Exploitation has received a great deal of attention in recent years, which fact can probably be attributed to its being hypothesized as one of the prime causes of underdevelopment and international inequality. As a hypothesis about international inequality, it competes with a number of other possible causes. Countries may be greatly unequal for a number of reasons aside from the domination of other states. There may be unequal endowment of natural resources, capital may be scarce, land may be barren, and there may be an absence of a cultural ethic favoring work, saving, and investment. The appeal of the concept of exploitation is that it provides an explanation of inequality that looks to foreign sources. It becomes the mechanism providing the chief link between the domestic plight of LDCs and the external environment.

The question now becomes one of identifying the ways in which exploitation manifests itself, or in methodological language, what are the observable indicators of this concept? Several possible indicators are the terms of trade, foreign investment, and the discrimination against processed goods. I will take up the terms-of-trade argument as an illustration.

The terms of trade refers to the ratio of prices that a country receives for its exports over the prices it pays for its imports. Given some arbitrary base year, the terms of trade is said to be improving when this ratio increases and indicates higher relative prices for its exports, and it is said to be worsening when the opposite occurs. During recent years, though not during the nineteenth century, the terms-of-trade argument has been put forward by the less developed countries. Their basic point is that there is a long-term trend in international trade in favor of manufactured goods and against primary goods. Since the less developed countries are exporters of primary foods and raw material, this trend is in effect pauperizing them.

Raúl Prebisch and Gunnar Myrdal have been articulate spokesmen for the less developed countries on this issue. They offer both structural and policy reasons for the LDC's worsening terms of trade. Among the structural reasons Prebisch mentions the slow growth of world demand for agricultural products, development of synthetics to substitute for natural products, the decreasing proportion of raw material going into finished goods (due to higher productivity), and the high pool of unskilled labor in less developed countries.[40] These reasons are taken to be laws of economics that operate in a deleterious manner in a unrestrained free trade environment. In addition to these long-term forces affecting demand and prices, it is also argued that the volume of primary exports has lagged in relation to the volume of manufactured exports. David Wall notes:

Although the total exports of the less developed countries rose some 70.0 percent over the period 1953-65, their share of the total world trade declined from 27.0 percent to 19.9 percent. Over the same period total exports from the industrial areas increased 160.0 percent and their share of total world trade rose from 58.7 percent to 65.5 percent. The change in the relative shares reflects the fact that the trade of the industrial nations is being increasingly carried on among themselves and in mainly manufactured goods.[41]

All of these factors have operated to produce prices for primary products that are consistently lower than prices for manufactured goods. However, not all of the poor terms of trade can be blamed on these anonymous structural features of the international system. Indeed, some of the blame, the argument goes, must be placed on the political forces shaping the commercial policy of the advanced countries. Among the components of this commercial policy are domestic agricultural protectionism in most of the advanced countries, tariff systems that discriminate against semi-processed and manufactured goods, and increase protection against the labor-intensive exports of less developed nations.[42] And because LDCs possess a diminishing share of the world export market, even for primary goods, they exert less leverage over their trading partners for the purpose of changing global commercial policy.

The terms-of-trade argument seems to suggest a ready measure of exploitation. Starting with the exchange prices for imports and exports in some base year, one could interpret departures from this exchange ratio as a worsening or improvement of the terms of trade. From an exploitative standpoint, what is taking place is the progressive accumulation of one country's fruits of productions by another country. The difficulty with proceeding in this direction is that there are several rebuttals to this terms-of-trade argument that have not been adequately answered. These arguments are both empirical and conceptual.

The empirical arguments are very straightforward. They assert that in fact the terms of trade have not persistently worked against exporters of primary products. Michael Barratt Brown details different historical periods when prices of manufactured and primary goods rose faster or declined faster than one another. There were several periods when primary products declined more slowly (e.g., 1800 to 1850) or rose more rapidly (e.g., 1945 to 1952). It is true that recently (i.e., the last twenty years) the terms of trade have been unfavorable to primary products but this should not obscure the fact that over the long haul of history the upper and lower hands have shifted many times.

The shifts in the terms of trade is not a recently discovered phenomenon. In fact the classical economists asserted just the opposite from what defenders of primary exporters are saying today. As Emmanuel points out, John Stuart Mill, David Ricardo, Thomas Malthus, and Robert Torrens all felt that the prices for primary goods would rise more rapidly than those of manufactures. Mill for example, declared:

The exchange values of manufactured articles, compared with the products of agriculture and of mines, have, as population and industry advance, a certain and decided tendency to fall.[43]

In addition to these empirical reasons there are a variety of conceptual counter-arguments. Firstly, there is the argument put forth by Jacob Viner that the worsening terms of trade does not necessarily mean a diminished welfare benefit from trade—that is, it does not deny the "gains from trade" argument. For example, a worsening terms of trade may be accompanied by an increase in the volume of trade or by a decline in the real cost of production.[44] Secondly, there may be improvements in the quality of manufactured goods that outpace qualitative improvements in primary goods. This is not a mere logical possibility. It is much more likely that the efficiency of a typewriter, ball point pen, or automobile will improve more quickly than the quality of primary and unprocessed goods. This is nearly inherent in the definition of what constitutes an unprocessed good. Thirdly, and this is still a relatively new and therefore untried argument, there is the argument developed by Arghiri Emmanuel that, to simplify a complicated presentation, asserts that the type of commodity exchanged has very little to do with the worsening terms of trade. What is crucial is the wage structure of the respective countries who are parties to the trade relationship. While profit margins vary between countries within relatively small ratios, wages may differ by orders of magnitude of ten or twenty. In a paragraph packed with potential for reinterpreting international economic relationships, Emmanuel states:

Underpinning unequal exchange there is a monopoly, all right; not, however, a monopoly of goods . . . but the monopoly position held by the workers in the advanced countries. And this is no structural necessity of the capitalist system.[45]

The power of Emmanuel's argument is not only that he brings our attention to the wage structure rather than the type of commodity exchanged, but also that he shifts the focus from the economic to the political and shows how the two are so intimately related. For it is not the market that determines the wages of labor; rather, the determination of wages is a fact of political organization—that is, the organization of the world into sovereign nation-states and the organization of trade unions within nation-states.

These counter-arguments seem compelling enough at this point to warrant fuller consideration. After a more thorough assessment of the importance of cross-national wages, qualitative improvements in manufactures and so forth, we will be in a better position to devise concrete measures of exploitation.

In this article I have been concerned with setting the foundation for a test of a theory of imperialism. My preoccupation was necessarily with "testability" rather than "testing." This involved the identification of the three concepts of inequality, dependence, and exploitation and the suggestion of observable measures for two of them. When our understanding of exploitation is improved, operationalizations can be provided for terms of trade, investment, capital outflow, and discriminatory tariff structures. When this is accomplished, we will be well on our way toward the specification and measurement of three central concepts of imperialism. Then it will be possible to conduct tests of imperialism that are rigorous, disciplined, and corrigible.

Notes

1. Gunnar Myrdal, *The Challenge of World Poverty* (New York: Vintage Books, 1971), Pierre Jalée, *The Pillage of the Third World* (New York: Monthly Review Press, 1968); and Johan Galtung (ed.) *Cooperation in Europe*, vol. 3 of the International Peace Research Association's Studies in Peace Research (New York: Humanities Press, 1970).

2. There are some important exceptions to this, e.g., V.I. Lenin, *Imperialism, the Highest Stage of Capitalism* (Peking: Foreign Language Press, 1969) and Johan Galtung, "A Structural Theory of Imperialism," *Journal of Peace Research*, 1971.

3. For exceptions to this see Susanne Bodenheimer, "Dependency and Imperialism: The Roots of Latin American Underdevelopment," in K.T. Fann and Donald C. Hodges (eds.) *Readings in U.S. Imperialism* (Boston, Mass.: Porter Sargent Publisher, 1971), Pierre Jalée, *The Pillage of the Third World* (New York: Monthly Review Press, 1968), Pierre Jalée, *The Third World in World Economy* (New York: Monthly Review Press, 1969), and Robert I. Rhodes (ed.) *Imperialism and Underdevelopment* (New York: Monthly Review Press, 1970).

4. J.A. Hobson, *Imperialism. A Study* (London: George Allen and Unwin, Ltd., 1902).

5. Lenin, op. cit.

6. For example, see D.K. Fieldhouse. "Imperialism: An Historiographical Revision," *Economic History Review*, second series, vol. 14, no. 2 (December 1961), pp. 187-209.

7. Hans Daalder, "Imperialism," *International Encyclopedia of the Social Sciences*, vol. 7, edited by David L. Sills (New York: The Macmillan Co. and the Free Press, 1968), pp. 104-105.

8. Karl Marx, *Capital: A Critique of Political Economy* edited by Frederick Engels (New York: The Modern Library, 1906).

9. This is of course the "terms-of-trade" argument, according to which the price curve of manufactured goods is hypothesized to rise more rapidly than the curve for primary goods. One must be careful to qualify this argument by stating that it does not take into account the greater prospect for qualitative improvements and technological refinements in manufactured goods.

10. For Marx's discussion of the concept of labor value see Karl Marx *Capital: A Critique of Political Economy*, op. cit., ch. 7.

11. "Labor" includes not just the work activity itself but also what Marx called the "Subject of that work" and "its instrument." The former seems identical to raw materials and the latter seems fairly close to technology.

12. Servan-Schreiber's *The American Challenge* is an exception to this. He makes an argument that if Europe does not take steps to reverse the present trend in the trans-Atlantic division of labor, Europe will become a technological colony of the United States.

13. Fieldhouse, op. cit., p. 198.

14. Pierre Jalée, *Imperialism in the Seventies*, translated by Raymond and Margaret Sokolov (New York: Joseph Okpaku Publishing Co., Inc., 1972), p. 51.

15. The literature on field theory in international relations has already begun to mushroom. Among the most relevant for present purposes are: (1) R.J. Rummel, "A Field Theory of Social Action with Application to Conflict Within Nations," *General Systems Yearbook*, vol. 10 (1965), pp. 183-211; (2) Tong-

Whan Park, "The Role of Distance in International Relations," *Behavioral Science*, vol. 17, no. 4 (July 1972), pp. 337-348.

16. Tong-Whan Park, "The Role of Distance in International Relations: A New Look at the Social Field Theory," *Behavioral Science*, vol. 17, no. 4 (July 1972), p. 337.

17. By "statistical independence," we of course mean that these two measures are unrelated to one another. Park offers a proof for this from matrix algebra. He also provides the following simple illustration: suppose we have three nations A, B, and C and that they are scored 1, 0, and −1 on some variable, e.g., national wealth. The distance scores for the VSDs and VADs would be: Correlations of column one and two equal zero (see Table 5-1).

18. Ibid., p. 342.

19. Ibid.

20. James Lee Ray and J. David Singer, "Measuring the Concentration of Power in the International System," *Sociological Methods and Research*, vol. 1, no. 4 (May 1973), p. 404.

21. See Hayward R. Alker Jr., "Measuring Inequality," in *The Quantitative Analysis of Social Problems*, edited by Edward R. Tufte (Reading, Mass.: Addison-Wesley Publishing Co., 1970), pp. 191-211 and James Lee Ray and J. David Singer, op. cit.

22. Alker, op. cit., p. 200.

23. Ray and Singer, op. cit., p. 416.

24. Kenneth Janda, "A Conceptual Framework for the Comparative Analysis of Political Parties," Comparative Politics series, vol. 1, edited by Harry Eckstein and Ted Robert Gurr (Beverly Hills, Calif.: Sage Publications, Inc., 1970), p. 94.

25. Ray and Singer, op. cit., p. 422.

26. Ibid.

27. For one of the most quoted and "influential" definitions of power see Robert A. Dahl, "The Concept of Power," *Behavioral Science*, vol. 2 (July

Table 5-1
Illustration of Independence of VSDs and VADs

DYADS	VSD	VAD
A → B	1	1
B → A	−1	1
A → C	2	2
C → A	−2	2
B → C	1	1
C → B	−1	1

Source: Adapted from Tong-Whan Park, "The Role of Distance in International Relations: A New Look at the Social Field Theory," *Behavioral Science*, vol. 17, no. 4 (July 1972), p. 341.

1957), p. 201-218. Dahl defines power as follows: "A has power over B to the extent that he can get B to do something that B would not otherwise do," pp. 202-203.

28. Richard D. Wolff, "Modern Imperialism: The View From the Metropolis," *The American Economic Review*, papers and proceedings of the eighty-second annual meeting of the American Economic Association, vol. 60, no. 2 (May 1970), p. 225.

29. Ibid.

30. Theotonio Dos Santos, "The Structure of Dependence," *The American Economic Review*, papers and proceedings of the eighty-second annual meeting of the American Economic Association, vol. 60, no. 2 (May 1970), p. 231.

31. Incidentally, this is a difficulty that is central to functional analysis. A central proposition of functional analysis is that "social institutions or structures exist because they fulfill certain societal needs." The societal components that presumably benefit are left unspecified. What is needed here of course is not only a positive identification of these societal components but also some predictions as to the degree of harm to these components should a particular social institution atrophy or disappear.

32. For the remainder of the chapter, I will be employing examples from international trade. None of the measures is constructed so as only to be applicable to trade.

33. Bruce M. Russett, *International Regions and the International System* (Chicago, Ill.: Rand McNally and Co., 1967).

34. Bruce M. Russett, "Regional Trading Patterns, 1938-1963," *International Studies Quarterly*, vol. 12, no. 4 (December 1968), p. 362.

35. Michael Barratt Brown, *After Imperialism* (New York: Humanities Press, revised ed., 1970), pp. 159-160.

36. Harry Magdoff, forward to Pierre Jalée, *Imperialism in the Seventies*, translated by Raymond and Margaret Sokolov (New York: Joseph Okpaku Publishing Co., Inc. 1972), p. xvii.

37. Michael Michaely, *Concentration in International Trade* (Amsterdam: North-Holland Publishing Co., 1962), pp. 7-8.

38. Michaely, op. cit., p. 19.

39. Albert O. Hirschman, *National Power and the Structure of Foreign Trade* (Berkeley, California: University of California Press, 1945).

40. Raúl Prebisch, "External Bottlenecks Obstructing Development," from Raúl Prebisch, *Towards a New Trade Policy for Development*, Report by the Secretary-General of UNCTAD, United Nations, 1964, reprinted in Gerald M. Meier *Leading Issues in Economic Development: Studies in International Poverty* (U.S.A.: Oxford Univ. Press, 1970, second ed.), p. 484.

41. David Wall, *The Third World Challenge: Preferences for Development* (Great Britain: Ditchling Press Ltd., 1968), p. 5.

42. Ibid., p. 6.

43. John Stuart Mill, *Principles of Political Economy* (London, 1909), p. 254, quoted from Arghiri Emmanuel, *Unequal Exchange: A Study in the Imperialism of Trade* (New York: Monthly Review Press, 1972), p. xxviii.

44. Jacob Viner, *International Trade and Economic Development* (London, England: Oxford University Press, first ed., 1953), p. 112. See also Paul A. Samuelson, "The Gains from International Trade Once Again," in *International Trade*, edited by Jagdish Bhagwati (Middlesex, England: Penguin Books, 1969), pp. 171-183.

45. Emmanuel, op. cit., p. 169.

Part II
Capitalist Imperialism:
Empirical Theory-Testing

6

The Open Door Imperative and U.S. Foreign Policy

Steven J. Rosen
Brandeis University

Liberal and radical critics of American foreign policy agree in their disapproval of U.S. support for reactionary regimes around the world, but they disagree on the causes and motivations of this behavior. Liberals trace the counter-revolutionary policy of the United States to roots in errors of judgment, exaggerated fears of communism, misperception of other countries, and an excessive confidence in the righteousness of the United States. Radicals, however, reject this "chain of errors" theory and instead trace foreign policy as a logical outgrowth of the capitalist socio-economic system.[1] Neo-Leninist theories of imperialism in particular identify the principal determinant of international relations among capitalist countries and between advanced capitalist countries and less developed countries as the imperative of market security and expansion. "The underlying purpose" of American imperialism, according to Harry Magdoff, "is nothing less than keeping as much as possible of the world open for trade and investment by the giant multinational corporations."[2]

Underlying this theory of the Open Door imperative is an image of political development with concrete empirical referents. The image goes something like this: When political evolution in a developing country shifts to the left, policy alterations tend to occur that reduce opportunities for trade and investment by American firms and imperil the security of existing investments. The U.S. business interests employ an array of positive and negative sanctions and influences under their control to prevent or reverse such adverse changes, but often the multinational firms lack sufficient leverage to affect directly the political evolution of other governments. The firms therefore tend to rely on the support of the U.S. government, over which they have considerable influence in relevant policy issue areas, to take actions against leftward changes in other countries and in support of rightward changes. A shift back to the right tends to reopen the door to U.S. investment and exports, which of course is good for the multinationals.[3]

This image contains two testable assumptions that are the subject of this paper:

The author is grateful to Hrach Gregorian for research assistance and to Raymond Corrado, Roy Grow, and Tom Horst and the Business and Politics seminar at Harvard University for valuable comments.

117

1. General rightward and leftward political changes in other countries specifically affect the degree to which the door is open *de jure* and *de facto* to U.S. private trade and investment; rightward development corresponds to the Open Door and leftward development to the Closed Door.

2. The outputs of American foreign policy correlate with the receptivity of other countries toward private U.S. trade and investment; the U.S. government rewards the Open Door and punishes the Closed Door.

To test these general assumptions, I have selected for analysis five Western-oriented developing countries that have undergone right-to-left and/or left-to-right internal political shifts since 1960 and are regarded as highly salient cases by liberal and radical theorists alike.[4] Included are the change from Sukarno to Suharto in Indonesia; from Quadros and Goulart to the military junta of Generals Castelo Branco, Costa e Silva, and Medici in Brazil; from Frei to Allende to the generals in Chile; from Papandreou to Papadopoulos in Greece; and from Belaunde to Velasco in Peru. In all but the last case, periods of leftward experimentation by civilian governments ended when right-wing military groups seized the instruments of state; in Peru leftward development continues under the aegis of the armed forces themselves.

I will examine several questions in each case. First, was leftward development accompanied by hostility to U.S. business and rightward development characterized by receptivity to foreign investment? This is a critical assumption for the radical theorists.

Second, did actual private investment and commercial export flows from the United States rise and decline with political changes in the predicted directions (i.e., leftward changes reduce U.S. economic penetration while rightward changes increase investment and export)? This is necessary to the Open Door theory to show that receptivity or hostility to American business is not merely rhetorical but has real consequences for the flow of money and goods.

Third, did fluctuations in foreign aid correspond with changes in the flow of private investment and exports and/or with the stated receptivity of government policy in the aid-receiving country to U.S. investment and trade? According to the theory, official foreign policy outputs directed to developing countries, of which aid is a major example, should be used to reward cooperation with private U.S. business and to punish resistance. If so, aid flows should relate positively to the Open Door and negatively to the Closed Door.[5] Non-radical theory would expect a weaker connection between the two private flows and the public flow, since aid would be affected more importantly by other variables (such as United Nations voting, the political importance of the recipient to the donor, the recipient's need for aid, the relationship of the recipient to the USSR, the presence or absence of a Communist insurgency, and so forth).[6]

For compactness of analysis, one indicator will be used for each of the three international economic variables. *Aid* is taken as total bilateral military and economic grants and loans as reported in the United States Agency for International Development (AID), Office of Statistics and Reports, *U.S. Overseas Loans and Grants and Assistance from International Organizations*, various issues. *Investment* comprises total direct private outflows from the United States, plus earnings generated in the host country and reinvested there, minus divestment of assets acquired in earlier years. Portfolio investment is excluded. To simplify the measure, especially for Greece and Indonesia, where detailed data are missing, I will take the net change in accumulated book value of investment at year-end compared to the previous year. Figures for Brazil, Chile, and Peru are published annually in the *Survey of Current Business* by the U.S. Department of Commerce, while figures for Greece and Indonesia (for some years) could be obtained only in unpublished working papers of the Office of Business Economics, U.S. Department of Commerce, with a much lower expectation of reliability. Total U.S. *exports* is taken from *The Statistical Abstract of the United States.*[7]

Linkages of Public Aid with Private Investment and Trade

It is important to note at the outset that official U.S. policy does not deny that aid is used to promote investment and trade, but it does make these connections quite explicitly. Official aid is used to promote American agricultural exports under Public Law 480, originally known as the Agricultural Surplus Export Program and later retitled Food for Peace. This program accounted for 30 percent of agricultural exports in 1970. Industrial sales are subsidized by long-term loans through the Export-Import Bank at less than commercial rates, counted as foreign assistance.[8] External expenditure of aid by recipient countries is, in most categories, tied almost exclusively to purchases from American suppliers.[9] Shipping of AID-financed goods is tied to American-registry vessels under PL 83-664.[10] Imports by the United States from other countries are not substantially affected by AID but are subject to official regulation through tariffs, import quotas, licensing, commodity agreements, and other instruments. Ostensibly the same policy objectives guiding AID allocations can influence legislative and executive controls on imports. Thus, there are substantial and explicit connections between official foreign aid and foreign trade.

American aid is also explicitly linked to the promotion of private foreign *investment* in developing countries. Indeed, "The position to which the United States and other developed countries adhere is that private foreign investment should be considered as development aid."[11] Until January 1971, when the Overseas Private Investment Corporation was established, AID was the principal guarantor of private investment against specific and extended risks of expropriation, war, revolution, insurrection, and inconvertibility of capital and profits. AID programs continue to exist in Housing guarantees (total authority $780 million), pre-investment assistance (especially in Africa), direct loans to industrial development banks leading to sub-loans to United States affiliate firms, and Cooley Loans of PL 480—counterpart local currencies to American subsidiaries to facilitate commerce in agricultural commodities.[12] A much enlarged program of investment insurance and guarantees, direct financial assistance to investors, and pre-investment promotional activities has been undertaken by OPIC since its authorization by foreign assistance legislation in 1969.

Mention should also be made of the Hickenlooper Amendment, which explicitly ties all AID grants and loans to investment by forbidding foreign assistance to governments that nationalize or expropriate American property without effective, prompt, and fair compensation. The amendment has seldom been invoked, but it has been used to pressure recalcitrant governments to treat U.S. business fairly according to American standards. Influence is also used at the World Bank, International Monetary Fund, Asian Development Bank, and other financial institutions to tie official multilateral capital and monetary supports to fair treatment of U.S. firms. Finally, taxation and regulatory powers are used to promote and control foreign investment, such as the Tax Credit method of deducting foreign payments from U.S. obligations.

Clearly, the Agency for International Development and other governmental entities are deeply involved in cooperation with foreign investors. In a typical official statement in 1973, U.S. Secretary of the Treasury George Shultz said:

When [private investment] capital is rejected [by a developing country], we find it difficult to understand that official donors should be asked to fill the gap. . . . Moreover, we do not find it reasonable that a nation taking confiscatory steps toward investment that it has already accepted from abroad should anticipate official assistance, bilateral or multilateral.[13]

On the basis of these policies, covariance of the private investment and official aid curves is to be expected.[14]

Thus, part of Open Door proposition (2) is easily demonstrated and incontrovertible: *de jure* and in principle, the U.S. government is committed to the promotion of trade and investment by private companies in developing countries and is opposed to the erection of barriers to U.S. trade and investment by other governments. What remains to be shown is the empirical connection between this policy and the support of reactionary regimes in actual cases.

Brazil

Brazilian development since 1954 can be divided roughly into three periods: (1) the Open Door of Juscelino Kubitschek, 1955 to 1960; (2) the half-Closed Door of Jânio Quadros and João "Jango" Goulart (1961 to mid-1964); and

(3) the re-opened door of the military junta—Generals Humberto Castelo Branco, Arthur da Costa e Silva, and Emilio G. Medici (1964 to present).

Kubitschek assumed the presidency at a time when Brazil faced a substantial loss of export earnings due to a drop in world coffee prices combined with stiffened competition from new producers. To arrest a growing foreign exchange deficit, the new government sought to promote "a climate favorable for the investment of foreign capital in the country." The policy adopted was a model of the Open Door to foreign investment: (1) funds representing foreign investment could enter and leave the country without restriction; (2) repatriation of profits was unrestricted, and ceilings imposed by the previous Vargas government were cancelled; (3) free admission was guaranteed for plant equipment; and (4) no percentage of Brazilian equity participation was required in companies formed with foreign capital.

The U.S. Department of Commerce reported in 1959 that "the investment climate in Brazil is one of the most favorable in the world."[15] American investors were in fact treated more hospitably than native enterprises. Under Instruction 113 of the Superintendency of Money and Credit, for example, foreign firms imported inputs of capital equipment under preferential tax and tariff terms not available to domestic capitalists.[16] By 1961, foreign money represented well over half of the largest agricultural and industrial business entities.

The short-lived government of Quadros made only small efforts to put restrictions on foreign capital. Quadros submitted to Congress a profits taxation bill that would have raised the effective rate on foreign firms to 50 percent. But the succession of Vice President Goulart, when Quadros resigned on August 25, 1961, raised for the first time the possibility of large scale expropriation and profit restriction. A statute of September 3, 1962 forbade remittances in excess of 10 percent of invested capital and required registration of future investment.[17] Goulart refused rate increases to the American-owned telephone companies, charging poor service, and in January 1962 his brother-in-law, Governor Leonel Brizola of Rio Grande do Sul, expropriated CTN, the ITT telephone subsidiary in that state. The hostility of Goulart to foreign capital reached a climax in a public address on March 13, 1963, during which Goulart signed a decree nationalizing all private oil refineries and distributors, including Standard Oil and Shell.[18] Eighteen days later Goulart was removed by the armed forces, a culmination of the hostility of domestic and foreign business, the state governors, the large landowners, and the military.

The Castelo Branco/Costa e Silva/Medici policy sharply reversed the Goulart policy of hostility to foreign business and eagerly invited foreign capital to invest in heavy industry and utilities. Planning Minister Roberto Campos extended new guarantees to American investors, including a commitment to the U.S. government to reimburse any compensations it might pay to expropriated firms, the amount to be determined by the United States—a policy called by João Quartim "the culmination of Campos' policy of handing over the Brazilian economy to imperialism."[19] Brazil was offered to foreign firms as a production and distribution base from which to penetrate the Latin American Free Trade Association, with a large domestic market to facilitate economies of scale. Small but frequent devaluations compensated for high inflation, subsidized lines of credit offset the high cost of borrowing, and tax rebates were given on exports. The result was an acceleration of already rapid industrialization from 8 to 12 percent growth, and an expansion of the share of exports consisting of industrial goods from 5 to 20 percent.[20] But these gains were achieved at the price of a wide open door to foreign capital. According to Eduardo Galeano, in 1968 foreign firms controlled 80 percent of pharmaceutical production, 62 percent of foreign trade, 48 percent of aluminum, 90 percent of cement, 100 percent of motor vehicles, and 40 percent of the capital market.[21] The intention of the generals was to stimulate new direct investments, but an unintended effect has been the denationalization of existing firms as bankruptcies and receiverships brought on by fiscal austerity and stabilization measures have been bought up by foreign capital.[22]

Roughly, then, we can use this key for the interpretation of Figure 6-1: 1955 to 1960, the Open Door; 1961 to mid-1964, the half-Closed Door; 1965 to

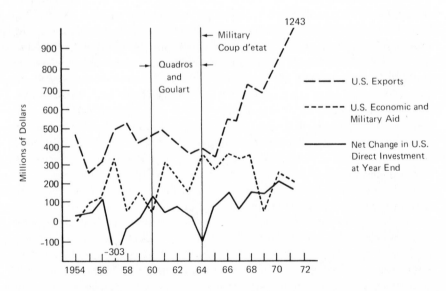

Figure 6-1. U.S. Investment, Exports, and Aid in Brazil

present, the Open Door again.[23] In these terms, the case of Brazil is very nearly consistent with the neo-Leninist predictions. Each leftward and rightward political change has been marked by a proportionate closing or opening of the door to foreign investment and trade. Moreover, the actual flow of private capital and goods from the United States to Brazil has behaved according to the radical predictions. Investment drops steeply after the advent of Quadros and Goulart and rises more sharply after the coup. American exports to Brazil decline under Quadros and Goulart and show a meteoric rise after the coup, with a 300 percent increase from 1965 to 1972. Official foreign aid is, if anything, even more responsive to the political changes; it declines sharply to punish Goulart and is restored sooner than investment and trade to reward the generals.[24]

Whatever objections may be made to the military seizure of power on grounds of democratic principle, it is manifest that the ascent of the generals has been good for American business and that the fluctuations in U.S. government aid have fulfilled the expectations of the radical theorists.

Indonesia

Indonesian development, like that of Brazil, falls roughly into three periods: (1) a period of relative hospitality to investment before the West Irian escalation (late 1957); (2) the militant period of Sukarno and expropriation (1958 to late 1965); and (3) the Suharto period of the re-opened door (especially 1967 to present).

It is estimated that before the second World War only a fifth of non-agricultural capital in Indonesia was indigenously owned, while over half was held by Dutch interests. When the Netherlands conceded independence to all of Indonesia but West Irian in 1949, some effort was made to nationalize the central bank and to increase domestic control over the economy. But when the boom induced by the Korean war collapsed and foreign trade dwindled, elements of the leadership pressed to reopen the country to foreign capital, on the theory that foreign domination is preferable to financial chaos.[25] Throughout this first period, foreign capital operated with a considerable degree of freedom, despite the professed hostility of the nationalist movement.

The period of anti-Western militancy and increased hostility to foreign business begins with the failure of the United Nations in November 1957 to satisfy Indonesia's demand for negotiations with the Netherlands for the transfer of West Irian. Indonesia immediately seized all Dutch properties and estates, and expropriated 3400 of 4000 importers. Additional measures were taken against KMT Chinese properties. But American investors were relatively tolerated until, after the settlement of the West Irian claim in mid-1962, Sukarno turned his guns on the nascent federation of Malaysia and relations with the United States worsened. In July of 1963, the Broomfield Amendment to the foreign aid authorization bill required a presidential determination that continued support of Indonesia was in the American national interest. U.S. Ambassador H.P. Jones argued that "the aid program in Indonesia had never been postulated on shoring up Sukarno. . . . We were attempting, rather, to build up a foundation for Indonesian economic stability and political independence."[26] But Sukarno resisted the pressure of the economic sanctions and said "to hell with your aid." In February 1965, American-owned rubber plantations were formally taken over; in March, Sukarno supervened the three foreign oil companies; in April, all remaining foreign property was expropriated; and in August, Indonesia withdrew from the International Monetary Fund and the World Bank. On the last day of September, Sukarno effectively ceased to rule, and on March 12, 1966, all governmental powers were formally transferred to the junta headed by General Suharto.

Suharto immediately moved to restore foreign estates and plants to their foreign owners and to resume normal relations with the Netherlands and the United States. In the face of mounting debt, runaway inflation, declining exports, and arrested growth,[27] the new regime put a high priority on restoring business confidence and inviting massive foreign capital inputs. The newly Open Door was secured by the Investment Law of January 1967, which (1) prohibits expropriation or obstruction of management except by Act of parliament under a state of emergency; (2) guarantees compensation in case of expropriation in accordance with international law, arbitrated if necessary by the World Bank; (3) permits unrestricted transfer of profits; (4) allows permanent exemption from duties for imported machinery and equipment; (5) extends a variety of tax concessions, including a five-year tax holiday for new investment, accelerated depreciation, reduced rates, and negotiation of other favorable terms; and (6) requires no minimum equity participation by indigenous capital.[28] One illustration of the benefits to foreign investors under the new regime was the acquisition by Freeport Sulphur of an 85 percent equity interest in a $135 million West Irian copper mine for only $22 million of its own capital, with international financing obligations guaranteed by the Suharto government.[29] Truly, Suharto has restored the Open Door.

This is the key for the interpretation of Figure 6-2: 1954 to 1957, the half-Open Door; 1958 to 1965, the progressively closing door; 1967 to present, the wide Open Door. In this case, even more than Brazil, the neo-Leninist predictions are supported. Again, leftward and rightward political changes are marked by a proportionate closing or opening of the door to foreign investment and trade. And the change from Sukarno to Suharto is marked in the statistical trends by a bold upsweep in all three variables, with official foreign aid responding sooner and even more favorably than investment and export flows. The two propositions of the Open Door theory are again generally supported in the case of Indonesia.

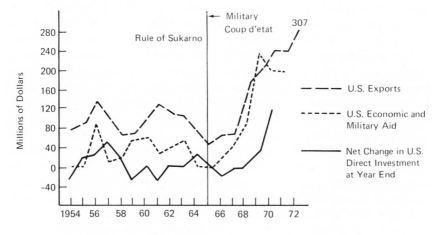

Figure 6-2. U.S. Investment, Exports, and Aid in Indonesia

Chile

In Chile, we can distinguish the wide Open Door before 1964, the 95 percent Open Door of Frei from 1964 to 1968, the closing door of Allende from late 1970 to mid-1973, and the reopened door of the military junta after Allende.

Chile before Allende is often cited as a classic case of the *dependencia* syndrome of export reliance on a single primary product (copper comprising about 80 percent), thorough penetration by foreign firms (e.g., Anaconda, Kennecott, and Cerro de Pasco in copper), decapitalization by the suction pump of repatriated superprofits (American firms remitted $7.2 billion against investments of $1 billion from 1945 to 1972), and co-optation of a national bourgeoisie acting as a bridge-head for foreign interests.[30] Typical of the generosity of the Chilean government to foreign investment during this period was the *Nuevo Trato* of 1954-55, which revised the basic mining law in terms that effectively gave to American firms a gift whose cost has been estimated by Theodore Moran at $34 to $144 million.[31]

Eduardo Frei came to the presidency in 1964 on a platform of "Chileanization" of foreign firms by gradual means—a "revolution in freedom." Agreements were reached with Kennecott in 1964 and Anaconda in 1969 to sell 51 percent of the ownership of the major mines to the Chilean government under terms very favorable to the companies. The Kennecott deal, for example, left that firm with 49 percent of its former assets, but these were increased to 400 percent of their previous worth by the Chilean government in addition to the giving of unconditional guarantees against expropriation under a U.S. AID contract and a special commitment of the Chilean state. Furthermore, a reduction in taxes was given, so Kennecott now received 49 percent of the proceeds from an operation with 64 percent more output at half the former tax rate.[32] Frei's Chileanization program was regarded by other nationalists as pseudo-divestment under terms that unjustifiably rewarded foreign investors with yet increased bounties. Compensation payments under some of the Frei agreements were later stopped by Allende.[33]

Allende assumed the presidency on November 3, 1970 with a well-advertised intention to expropriate the major foreign investors. ITT, as is now well known, had tried to prevent his election and assumption of office in collusion with other businesses through an Ad Hoc Committee on Chile in Washington, and in loose conspiracy with the Latin American division of the CIA. Interestingly, it appears that many firms declined to go along with ITT. The major banks, including Bank of America, First National, Chase Manhattan, and Manufacturers Hanover, did not want to imperil the possibility of recovering large amounts outstanding in loans. Ralston Purina saw a "reasonable prospect of a satisfactory settlement." Here are two comments by W.R. Merriam, ITT Vice President in Washington, from the now "liberated" private memoranda:

Repeated calls to firms such as GM, Ford, and banks in California and New York have drawn no offers of help. All have some sort of excuse. (October 7, 1970)

Practically no progress has been made in trying to get American business to cooperate in some way so as to bring on economic chaos [to force action by the Chilean armed forces against Allende]. GM and Ford, for example, say that they have too much inventory on hand in Chile to take any chances and that they keep hoping that everything will work out all right. Also, the Bank of America had agreed to close its doors in Santiago but each day keeps postponing the inevitable. According to my source, we must continue to keep the pressure on business. (October 9, 1970)[34]

Anaconda may have shared ITT's hard-line approach. Merriam told the Senate investigating committee that strategy coordination efforts of this kind among American businesses happen "all the time,"[35] but the above evidence suggests that no automatic pattern of collusion can be assumed by radical theorists.

Allende's expropriation of the copper firms was unopposed by the other major political parties, and congressional authorization took the form of a unanimous constitutional amendment. But he was restrained in action against other firms by the commanding position of the opposition Christian Democrats and Nationalists in the Congress.[36] However, he was able to move against ITT, GM, DuPont, First National City Bank, and the copper companies, and by mid-1972 had increased government control above 50 percent in fourteen of sixteen industries, according to a *Business Week* tally.[37]

Allende made some effort to negotiate compromise terms of compensation to avoid a full break with the United States and international financial organizations. For example, Chile offered $24 million to ITT for Chitelco, against a company claim of $153 million. Arbitration of this difference was underway in Washington in March 1972 when Jack Anderson disclosed the company's attempted subversion and Chile cancelled the negotiations. In the Kennecott case, Allende agreed to compensation of $80 million—the guaranteed amount of the Frei agreement and more than the net worth of invested capital. But the company wanted the full commercial value of its former equity interest, and sued to confiscate copper shipments in Holland and France. Allende accepted the principle of compensation, but insisted that former excess profits and tax inequities be included in the negotiation of terms.[38]

It is clear from the record that has surfaced that there was extensive collaboration between various official U.S. agencies and private corporate interests to find a way either to overthrow Allende or to force him to be more cooperative with American business. William Broe, director of the Latin American department of the CIA suggested to ITT a strategy to provoke economic collapse that included the following ideas: (1) banks would not renew credits; (2) American firms would obstruct cash flow, spare parts deliveries, and other financial and commodity movements; (3) precarious savings and loans would be permitted to topple to "trigger a run on banks and lead to the closure of some factories resulting in more unemployment"; and (4) technical help would be withdrawn. These ideas were expanded by ITT to an eighteen-point action plan, which included the following specific measures:

Continue loan restrictions in the international banks such as those the Export/Import Bank has already exhibited.
Quietly have large U.S. private banks do the same.
Confer with foreign banking sources with the same thing in mind.
Delay buying from Chile over the next six months. Use U.S. copper stockpile instead of buying from Chile.
Bring about a scarcity of U.S. dollars in Chile.
Discuss with CIA how it can assist the six-month squeeze.
Get to reliable sources within the Chilean Military. Delay fuel delivery to Navy and gasoline to Air Force. (This would have to be carefully handled, otherwise would be dangerous. However, a false delay could build up their planned discontent against Allende, thus, bring about necessity of his removal.)
Help disrupt Allende's UNCTAD plans.
It is noted that Chile's annual exports to the U.S. are valued at $154 million (U.S. dollars). As many U.S. markets as possible should be closed to Chile. Likewise, any U.S. exports of special importance to Allende should be delayed or stopped.[39]

Sanctions against Allende actually imposed by the U.S. government included the following: (1) termination of development assistance through AID; (2) assignment of Chile to the worst-risk category in the Export-Import Bank; and (3) obstruction of Chilean loans and credits in the World Bank, the Inter-American Development Bank, and the International Monetary Fund. Chile was also hurt by a drop in the world market price of copper from 68¢ to about 48¢ per pound—a loss of about $240 million annual. The general squeeze on her economy forced Allende to defer payments on $3 billion in foreign debts, resulting in further pressures from foreign governments and organizations.

The actual scenario of Allende's demise paralleled the ITT/CIA ideas closely. The loss of international borrowing ability and U.S. trade credits led to an exchange crisis that stifled the flow of industrial imports, including critical replacement parts for machinery and trucks. Runaway inflation and opposition to state ownership of business and commerce led to a revolt of the middle classes. Induced economic chaos finally led to the intervention of the armed forces on September 11, 1973. In its first statement of policy, the military junta restored many prerogatives of private business and offered to reopen negotiations with foreign companies with the goal of making Chile once again attractive to foreign capital. The entire policy of the new government is not known at the time of this writing, but the generals appear to favor the Brazilian model of Open Door development for Chile's future.

The key to Figure 6-3, then, is 1954 to 1968, the Open Door; 1970 through 1972, the Closed Door; and late 1973 forward the Open Door again. It is clear

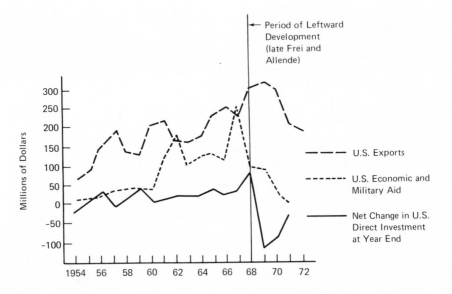

Figure 6-3. U.S. Investment, Exports, and Aid in Chile

that the behavior of the three flows fulfills the radical expectation in the Chilean case, though the decline seems to begin in the latter part of Frei's term for aid and investment, perhaps in anticipation of the worsening situation for American business. Once again, official aid fluctuations agree with the trends in trade and investment, and aid once again leads the field with the earliest response to political changes. One anomaly that is not shown in Figure 6-3 is a slight *increase* of military aid during Allende's term, from about $5 million to $10 million yearly. This might be an attempt to build alliances with the Chilean military in anticipation of future events, or it might be due to external constraints, such as the influence of the U.S. arms export lobby. Another seeming anomaly is the upturn of the investment curve in 1970, which reduces the rate of divestment while remaining in negative balance. This enigma seems to reflect bookkeeping practices in the reporting of divestment and expropriation losses rather than a real increase in investment or decline of divestment. With these small caveats, the data in the case of Chile, amplified by the evidence of the confidential ITT papers, strongly support the radical case.[40]

Greece

The case of Greece falls broadly in three periods: (1) the rule of the parliamentary Right from 1946 through 1963; (2) the Center Union moderate left government of Andreas Papandreou from February 19, 1964 through July 15, 1965; and (3) the Right restoration after the King's coup of July 1965 and especially the Colonel's coup of April 21, 1967 to the present.

The long period of Right parliamentary rule is characterized by a constant expansion of guarantees to foreign business beginning with Article 112 of the Constitution of 1946. Legislative Decree 2687 of 1953 (1) made the terms of investment agreements irrevocable without the consent of the investor; (2) guaranteed the currency convertibility and free repatriation of profits up to 12 percent of imported capital, with the right of carryover across years; and (3) extended a variety of special tax concessions to foreign business. These concessions were supplemented and expanded by Legislative Decree 2176 of 1952, Law 3213 of 1955; and Legislative Decree 4002 of 1959. The rate of improvement of terms for foreign investment accelerated with Law 4171 of 1961, which abolished import duties on capital goods and froze some tax obligations while abolishing others, and Law 4256 of 1962, which raised the ceiling on profit repatriation. The close stewardship of the U.S. armed forces over the Greek government during these years was a further guarantee to foreign investors.[41]

The short reign of Andreas Papandreou and the Center Union (17 months) is more significant for the future line of development implied than for actual steps taken to control foreign business. Papandreou repealed none of the old investment laws, but he did resist the tendency to concede ever more generous terms, a tendency which was immediately resumed by Papadopoulos after the Colonels' coup. No new package agreement with foreign capital was signed by the Center Union government.

A clue to Papandreou's intentions toward foreign capital, had he stayed in power, may be taken from his renegotiation in May of 1964 of an Esso/Pappas agreement originally signed with the previous government in November of 1962. The original agreement had provided for a $25-million oil refinery, a 275-thousand-ton steel mill, ammonia and petrochemical plants, and related facilities, at a package price of $110 million. The consortium was given an array of concessions and monopolies to sweeten the deal. Papandreou, representing a nationalist, anti-foreign segment of the Greek middle class, fought to reduce the servility of the original terms by (1) reducing the number of agreed product monopolies from 29 to 9; (2) raising the price of the package by more than $50 million; (3) increasing the state's royalty share modestly; and (4) increasing slightly the discretionary power of the state over crude oil sources. These relatively moderate revisions aroused a storm of protest, and Papandreou later claimed that pressures from the American embassy were applied "heavily" to "go easy on Pappas." Another sign of international pressure was the refusal of the World Bank to extend to the Papandreou government a small loan in 1964 on very contrived grounds that were quietly forgotten in 1968 when another application was accepted from the colonels.[42]

The indignities suffered by the Esso/Pappas consortium during the reign of Papandreou were speedily ended immediately after the King's coup of 1965. But a full-scale effort to attract massive new foreign investments did not begin until the Colonels' coup in April 1967, which opened an extravaganza of new concessions. Emergency Law 89 of 1967 exempted certain income from income and turnover taxes; Laws 147 and 149 of 1967 extended additional tax concessions; and Emergency Law 378 of 1968 gave an absolute guarantee of security to foreign firms. The culmination of this policy was Article 23, Section 3 of the Greek Constitution of 1968, which enshrined all previous concessions in the protection of the Constitution itself:

Emergency Law 89 of the year 1967 'Concerning Establishment in Greece of Foreign Commercial and Industrial Companies' and Emergency Law 378 of the year 1968 supplementing the above cannot be amended. Subsequent laws to be issued only once and for all may amend them only to confer additional protection.

The *Economist* reported on November 9, 1968 that "The Greek regime . . . since it seized power . . . has leaned over backwards to attract foreign investment." Less than a month after the Colonels' coup, on May 17, 1967, Papadopoulos signed a contract with Litton to attract $840 million in foreign capital by 1978 against an 11 percent profit on development studies and a 2 percent fee on attracted capital.[43] Greece advertised the advantages of its association with the European Economic Community, offering duty-free entry of manufactured goods with the additional advantage of exemption from U.S. restraints on capital exports. Andreas Papandreou, now in exile, reports that U.S. Secretary of Commerce Maurice Stans told the military government during his 1971 visit to Athens that in no country was American investment protected so well, and nowhere were better terms being offered than in Greece.[44]

Once again, an intimate connection between general political trends and the climate for foreign investment is demonstrated in the Greek case. The key for interpretation of Figure 6-4 is as follows: 1954 through 1963, the Open Door; 1964 through 1965, the 25 percent Closed Door; 1966 to present, the wide Open Door. In these terms, the actual data on the flow of investment, U.S. exports, and foreign aid are somewhat inconsistent with the predictions of the radical theory. Exports to Papandreou's Greece rise sharply, and the flow of investment goes up slightly. This would seem to contradict the Center Union's apparent coolness to foreign business. U.S. aid does decline as predicted, but the reduction continues after the King's and Colonels' coups, which suggests that punishment of Papandreou is not the motive. Exports and investment oddly decline with the restoration of the Right after the King's coup, but both recover after the Colonels' coup. The implication here is that the colonels have been good for foreign business but the king was not. Overall, the picture is confused, and the case of Greece seems to defy many of the predictions of the radical theory. Seemingly, other determinants have operated with greater force in

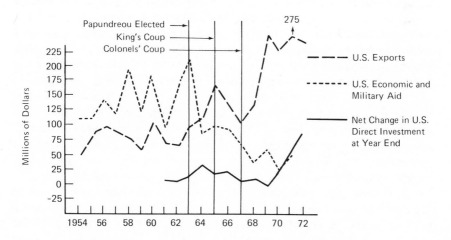

Figure 6-4. U.S. Investment, Exports, and Aid in Greece

Greece than the Open Door imperative. Whether the trends would be clearer if Papandreou had stayed in office longer and had moved further to the left cannot be known.[45]

Peru

The case of Peru is in several respects a counter-example to the four previous cases. While in Brazil, Indonesia, Chile, and Greece leftward experimentation has been ended and an Open Door to American business assured by the armed forces' seizure of power, in Peru controls on foreign business were instituted by a military coup and seem likely to survive. For this reason, some theorists look to Peru for lessons on a viable pattern of controls on the Open Door that might be adopted in other countries.

The Peruvian case falls generally into two periods: (1) the long Open Door period through the end of 1967, including the first four years of the presidency of Fernando Belaunde Terry, and (2) the period of the partly Closed Door, beginning with the final year of Belaunde and the subsequent military regime of General Juan Velasco Alverado, 1968 to the present.

Belaunde was elected in 1963 on a pledge to "vindicate Peru's rights," especially with regard to the notoriously inequitable concessional terms of the International Petroleum Company, an Exxon subsidiary. But the close association of Belaunde with domestic and foreign business and financial interests prevented any real constriction of privileges for foreign firms. Only in June 1968 did the faltering regime finally feel compelled to issue the following modest reforms: (1) institution of the first property tax; (2) subordination of commercial banks to the Central Bank with increased state participation; (3) limitation of foreign control of national banks to 20 percent, plus prohibition of new foreign-controlled branches; and (4) the establishment of mixed Peruvian-foreign ownership in petro-chemical industries. In September, Belaunde finally took action against IPC and nationalized the oil fields at La Brea and Pariñas. But even this policy had the appearance of a "sweetheart" deal. Belaunde agreed to sell 80 percent of the crude oil production to IPC's refinery at Talara and released the company from Peruvian claims of $690 million in back taxes.

Nationalist dissatisfaction with Belaunde's "sellout" was a major element in the coup d'etat three weeks later, on October 3. One of the first acts of the new government under General Juan Velasco Alvarado was the full expropriation of all IPC properties on October 9, 1968—the "Day of National Dignity." The following June, the government expropriated the eight largest agro-industrial firms on the coast, which represented 225,000 irrigated acres and 15,000 workers. Going still further, the Industrial Law of July 27, 1970 declared the intention of the state to control basic industry: steel, copper, oil, basic chemicals, cement, paper, and export marketing of copper, fishmeal, and cotton.

Velasco also moved to nationalize the credit sector, the "key to the export oligarchy's dominance . . . "[46] The Peruvian armed forces, previously the "watchdogs of the oligarchy," became a modernizing, nationalist force.

The Velasco Doctrine is "neither communist nor capitalist," but rather a form of state capitalism.[47] Foreign investment has not been terminated, but "rationalized." Velasco seeks foreign capital in key sectors of the economy, including, for example, $750 million in new financing of copper extraction and refining. But the military government is adamantly opposed to the "enclave" pattern of foreign-oriented development.

Velasco's solution to the control of foreign investment is the *fade-out joint venture*. The Industrial Law requires initial Peruvian equity participation of at least 51 percent—more in some industries—and provides for automatic divestment of foreign partners over time. Ownership reverts entirely to Peruvian private and governmental control "once the total amount of the investment and an acceptable amount of profit has been recovered." The reinvestment of earnings is encouraged through tax, tariff, and other incentives. The Industrial Law also provides for worker participation in ownership, management, and profit-sharing. Peru is also developing the interest of its Andean common market partners in the fade-out joint venture idea.[48]

Velasco has made some effort to encapsulate conflict with American firms by negotiating compromise terms wherever possible. The ITT documents revealed by Jack Anderson indicate that that firm was able to capitalize on Velasco's fear of "international resentment": ". . . on their expropriation of IPC, we were able to capitalize on this and eventually arrive at a deal which allowed them to announce internationally that copper and IPC were special cases and here is an arrangement that we made in a reasonable negotiation with ITT."[49] Peru agreed to pay $150 million in compensation for expropriated U.S. companies. One not compensated, however, is Exxon's International Petroleum Company.

The key to Figure 6-5 is 1954 to 1967, the Open Door; 1968 through 1972, the 25 percent closed door.[50] We can see here that Velasco's solicitous attitude toward foreign business had not by 1972 been successful in attracting enough new capital to offset voluntary and involuntary divestments. In early 1974, however, it appears that a major increase in foreign involvement in oil exploration and development is incipient. In any case, Velasco has managed to remain in power after expropriating American firms, unlike the previous four cases, and he has not as yet found it necessary to associate Peru with the socialist camp as an alternative to participation in the capitalist world economy.

U.S. exports to Peru after 1967 fluctuate in an enigmatic pattern. Export initially drops steeply, but it quickly recovers by 1972. The trend in aid, already reduced to a trickle by 1967, drops slightly after the shift to the left. Thus the case of Peru is generally consistent with the Open Door theory, though with some anomalous movements. Perhaps the hesitation in the data is caused by the ambivalent direction of the Velasco policy itself, "neither capitalist nor Communist."

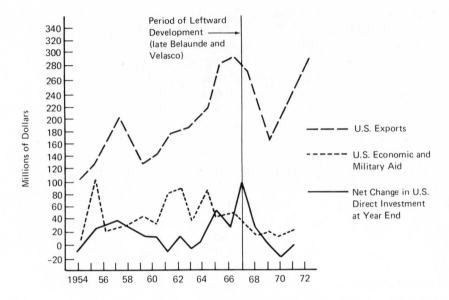

Figure 6-5. U.S. Investment, Exports, and Aid in Peru

Summary of Findings

The historical and quantitative data above can now be compressed into a number of findings.

1. Leftward and rightward political changes in all five cases did substantially affect policies toward foreign investment and trade. Every alteration in the general political environment was accompanied by a proportionate change in receptivity toward foreign business—always in the predicted direction.

2. Actual movements of investment, trade, and aid tended to behave as predicted by the radical theory. Table 6-1 summarizes the results of the case profiles. The investment data is mostly in agreement with expectations and has a tendency toward strong consistency in four of the five cases. Aid scores second best, and exports are in the last, but still supportive, position. The consistency of the aid curves with trade and investment suggests a harmony of policies between private traders and investors and public dispensers of foreign assistance, as predicted by the Open Door theorists.

3. Looking at all three functions by country, we are led to the conclusion that Greece is an exceptional case. In Indonesia and Chile, fluctuations in all

Table 6-1
Condensation of Findings

	Investment	Exports	Aid	Mean Score
Brazil	+ +	+	+	+1.3
Indonesia	+ +	+ +	+ +	+2.0
Chile	+ +	+ +	+ +	+2.0
Greece	0	− −	0	− .7
Peru	+ +	+	+	+1.3
Mean Score	+ 1.6	+ .8	+1.2	+1.2

Key: + + Strongly consistent with Open Door theory
+ Consistent, but some anomalous or equivocal fluctuations
0 Generally equivocal
− Vaguely inconsistent
− − Strongly inconsistent with Open Door theory

three flows were strongly consistent with expectations, and in Brazil and Peru, investment was strongly consistent and exports and aid were consistent, though with some unexplained movements. But in Greece all three functions failed to perform as expected during critical periods, and export fluctuations were the inverse of the radical predictions until 1967—that is, they rose under Papandreou and declined after the King's coup to recover vigor only after the Colonels' coup. An explanation may be a time lag in the response of foreign business activity to Greek political change. Absolute levels of U.S. economic activity are lower in Greece, and American firms may be less sensitive to opportunities in Greece than elsewhere. A study of coverage of Greek economic affairs in the *Wall Street Journal* found few articles before 1967 but a rapid increase in coverage after the Colonels' coup (see Figure 6-6).[51] Figure 6-6 indeed shows a spurt of investment after 1969. Other explanations for different results in Greece include a number of contextual variables: its special strategic importance in relation to the Mediterranean, the Dardanelles, oil transport lanes, and Israel; its association with the European Common Market and NATO; the stewardship of Greek politics by the United States since 1945; and the relatively modest natural resource endowment of the country. But such *a posteriori* explanations must account also for the failure of radical theory to predict *a priori*.

Discussion

Overall, with the partial exception of Greece, the behavioral and empirical predictions of the Open Door theory appear to be amply supported by the data, although the causal and motivational imputations of the theory cannot be confirmed or disconfirmed by these simple tests. What does it mean that U.S.

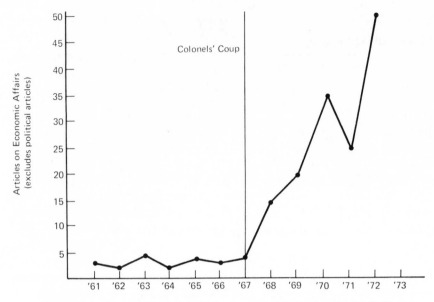

Figure 6-6. Coverage of Greek Economic Affairs in the Wall Street *Journal*

business activity in developing countries is closely associated with right-wing regimes and military juntas, and that U.S. foreign aid allocations tend to correspond with the hospitality of other countries to private American investment and trade?[52]

These findings speak to a number of issues. Liberal critics of U.S. support for reactionary governments, it was noted at the outset, tend to trace the American policy to errors of judgment, false conviction, and exaggerated fears of communism. But this study suggests a structural source of policy: a "natural" hostility to regimes that restrict U.S. business and preference for right-wing, Open Door governments. If this inference is credited, it follows that capitalist economic determinants of foreign policy are more influential than is generally conceded in the liberal theory. Moreover, the Open Door imperative suggests not only opposition to left-wing governments, but also a positive preference for right-wing governments that, as we have seen, are positively associated with high levels of U.S. trade and investment. The shrinkage of U.S. business in countries moving to the left is well known, but the tendency of trade and investment to swell after rightward changes is less often noticed.

It is sometimes asserted that U.S. business is relatively neutral toward the political orientations of other countries, and that multinational investors are able, of necessity, to adjust to a wide variety of ideological expressions. The findings in this study suggest a much lower tolerance and a clear preference for right-wing governments.[53] If we project continued expansion of multinational investment in the future, counter-revolutionary tendencies in U.S. foreign policy may also be expected to increase.

Notes

1. Robert W. Tucker, *The Radical Left and American Foreign Policy* (Baltimore: Johns Hopkins University Press, 1971).

2. Harry Magdoff, *The Age of Imperialism* (New York: Monthly Review Press, 1969), p. 14.

3. A "right"-oriented government is one that favors private ownership of major industries; represents and supports the interests of large landowners and businesses; suppresses labor militancy; and reinforces the stratification of a class society. A "left"-oriented government favors state or collective ownership of major industries; expropriation and redistribution or collectivization of large private landholdings; relative equality of income among all social groups; and egalitarian distribution of resources among the population. These are ideal types on the polar extremities, and most governments of developing states fall somewhere between the two.

4. While the generalizations ostensibly apply to U.S. policy toward all developing countries, this method of validation selects only critical cases for analysis. Most developing countries have not altered their policies toward U.S. investment and trade fundamentally in recent years, nor have they altered their general political orientation from left to right or vice versa. Only by choosing the few cases where there has been such variation in the key dimensions over time can the relationship between variables be seen. Essentially, we are asking what happens to Y when X changes.

5. It is conceded that aid is not the only nor always the most important behavioral output of the United States toward developing countries. But it is a significant and readily quantifiable component of policy to study. No other single policy output is any more representative—that is, military intervention policy and tariff policy also have special determinants and constituencies. See note 52.

6. Eugene Wittkopf, for example, does not include U.S. exports and investments among his eleven independent variables in his study of *Western Bilateral Aid Allocations: A Comparative Study of Recipient State Attributes and Aid Received* (Sage Professional Papers in International Studies, Volume 1, Number 5, 1972).

7. There are numerous inconsistencies between difference sources and between various issues of the same source on all three variables; most of these are relatively minor. Another problem is the danger that some apparent trends in the statistics are actually artifacts of peculiar bookkeeping practices of reporting companies. For example, expropriated properties may be reported as losses in

book value or divestments at the time of confiscation, or their book value may be carried in the official reports for some years until a satisfactory agreement for compensation is achieved. It is also important to note that all four indicators are aggregated at the nation-state level: United States/Brazil, and so forth. Different findings might result from segregating particular industries (e.g., copper in Chile, oil in Peru, rubber in Indonesia), geographic regions (Sao Paulo, Java), or major companies (Goodyear in Indonesia, Litton in Greece, GM in Brazil, Anaconda in Chile). Clearly, decisions are not taken collectively by the entire United States government and industry, as is implied by a state-centric model. But losses in discriminatory power incurred by using aggregate data are, I believe, unavoidable due to missing data and justifiable by the advantages of a parsimonious and comprehensible comparison of five cases. Finally, it will be apparent upon examination of the data that some changes in the three variables are explained outside the Open Door theory. For example, the steep rise in American aid to Brazil in 1961 reflects the Kennedy Alliance for Progress expansion of aid to all Latin American recipients, rather than a response to conditions in Brazil in particular. The present analysis is confined to trends that appear to be related to the political changes under discussion.

8. U.S. Department of Commerce, *Introductory Guide to Exporting* (Washington, 1971), p. 27.

9. Jagdish Bhagwati, "The Tying of Aid," UNCTAD Secretariat, TD/7/ Supplement 4 (United Nations, 1967), pp. 1-57.

10. UNCTAD, *Shipping and the World Economy* (United Nations, 1966).

11. Senate Committee on Foreign Relations, *Alternatives to Bilateral Economic Aid*, a report prepared by the Foreign Affairs Division of the Congressional Research Service, Library of Congress (Washington, 1973), p. 40.

12. OECD, *Investing in Developing Countries* (Organization for Economic Cooperation and Development, Paris, 1972), pp. 96-97.

13. "Low Cost Loans to Poor Lands Backed," *The New York Times*, Sept. 26, 1973.

14. In addition to the expected covariance of trade with aid and investment with aid, we may expect covariance of investment with trade. In the theory of the Open Door imperative, no distinction is drawn between receptivity to trade and to investment. Moreover, multinational investment often means the establishment of co-operant subsidiaries in other countries taking inputs from the American parent or sending semi-finished goods to it. Shipment of high technology capital goods from the United States to affiliates promotes American exports, while production abroad for the U.S. market takes the form of American imports. See G.C. Hufbauer and F.M. Adler, U.S. Treasury Department, *Overseas Manufacturing Investment and the Balance of Payments* (Washington, D.C., 1968). Foreign investment may also result in export generation and import substitution by increasing "the productivity of the factors of the country, whether through scale and agglomeration effects, capital accumulation,

or the upgrading of the labor force." Raymond Vernon, *Sovereignty at Bay* (New York: Basic Books, 1971), p. 176.

15. Department of Commerce, *Investment in Brazil* (Washington, 1959), fact sheet.

16. Andre Gunder Frank, *Capitalism and Underdevelopment in Latin America* (New York: Monthly Review Press, 1969), p. 182.

17. E. Bradford Burns, *A History of Brazil* (New York: Columbia, 1970), p. 362.

18. Thomas E. Skidmore, *Politics in Brazil 1930-1964* (New York: Oxford University Press, 1967), p. 286; Irving Louis Horowitz, "Revolution in Brazil: The Counter-Revolutionary Phase," in *New Politics*, Volume III, Number 2, Spring 1964, pp. 71-77.

19. João Quartim, *Dictatorship and Armed Struggle in Brazil* (New York: Monthly Review Press, 1971), pp. 63-64.

20. *Business Week*, June 12, 1971, p. 46.

21. Eduardo Galeano, "Denationalization and Brazilian Industry," *Monthly Review* (December 1969), p. 13.

22. John Wills Tuthill, "Economic and Political Aspects of Development in Brazil—and U.S. Aid," *Journal of Inter American Studies*, Volume XI, Number 2, April 1969, p. 205.

23. See also Helio Jagauribe, *Economic and Political Development* (Cambridge, Mass.: Harvard University Press, 1968) and Celso Furtado, *Diagnosis of the Brazilian Crisis* (Berkeley: University of California Press, 1965).

24. The decline of aid after 1968 is accountable to a reduction of the total U.S. AID budget combined with a reduction in Brazil's perceived need for aid. Brazil itself becomes an aid donor, giving small sums to Uruguay, Guyana, and Paraguay.

25. Hans O. Schmitt, "Foreign Capital and Social Conflict in Indonesia, 1950-58," in *Economic Development and Cultural Change*, Volume 10, Number 3 (April 1962).

26. Howard Palfrey Jones, *Indonesia: The Possible Dream* (New York: Harcourt, Brace, and Jovanovich, 1971), pp. 321-22.

27. "Indonesia After Sukarno," *Business Week*, July 9, 1966, pp. 159-61.

28. Summer Scott, "The Challenge to American Corporate Investment in Indonesia," *Asian Survey*, May 1972, pp. 399-415; Indonesian Embassy, *Foreign Investment in Indonesia* (Washington, D.C.: January, 1969); M. Clapham, "Difficulties of Foreign Investors in Indonesia," *Bulletin of Indonesian Economic Studies*, Volume VI, Number 1, March 1970; and Roger A. Freeman, *Socialism v Private Enterprise in Equatorial Asia: The Case of Malaysia and Indonesia* (Stanford, California: Hoover Institution, Stanford University, 1968).

29. Cited in Theodore Moran, "Transnational Strategies of Protection and Defense by Multinational Corporations," *International Organization*, Spring-Summer 1973, note 18.

30. Frank, op. cit.; James Petras, *Politics and Social Forces in Chilean Development* (Los Angeles, University of California Press, 1970).

31. Theodore Moran, "A Model of National Interest, Balance of Power, and International Exploitation in Large Natural Resource Investments," in Steven Rosen and James Kurth, editors, *Testing Theories of Economic Imperialism* (Lexington, Massachusetts: D.C. Heath, 1974).

32. Moran, "Transnational Strategies of Protection . . . ," op. cit.

33. The warm climate for American investment under Frei is described by Libert Ehrman, *Opportunities for Investment in Chile* (New York: Holt, Rinehart, and Winston, 1966).

34. Bertrand Russell Peace Foundation, *Subversion in Chile* (a compilation of the ITT internal memoranda and commentary), (London: Spokesman Books, 1972), pp. 51 and 52.

35. *The New York Times*, March 21, 1973, p. 1. See also "The International Telephone and Telegraph Company and Chile, 1970-71," Report to the Senate Committee on Foreign Relations by the Subcommittee on Multinational Corporations, June 21, 1973, (Washington, 1973).

36. "Correspondent," "Chile's Economic Reforms," *World Today* November 1972, Volume 28, number 11, pp. 483-92. Obscure 1932 legislation authorized "the intervention of the central power in all industries producing basic necessities which infringe on norms of functioning freely established by the administrative authorities." Alistair Horne, *Small Earthquake in Chile* (New York: Viking, 1972), p. 122.

37. *Business Week*, August 12, 1972, p. 44.

38. Robert L. Ayres, "Economic Stagnation and the Emergence of the Political Ideology of Chilean Underdevelopment," *World Politics*, October 1972; Luis Corvalan, "Two Years After—What is Happening in Chile?" *World Marxist Review*, Volume 15, Number 11, November 1972, pp. 15-23.

39. *Subversion in Chile*, op. cit.; also, ITT/Chile report to the Senate Committee on Foreign Relations, op. cit., p. 15.

40. Data for the period after Allende are not yet available.

41. I am grateful to Haralambos "Ted" Theodosis for access to his extensive work on foreign investment in Greece.

42. *Economist*, April 18, 1970.

43. Wall Street *Journal*, February 20, 1968. The deal was cancelled in October 1969, by which time only $50 million had been pledged and less than $2 million received.

44. *Monthly Review*, Volume 24, Number 7, December 1972.

45. Sources on Greece: Andreas Papandreou, "The Takeover of Greece," *Monthly Review*, Volume 24, Number 7, December 1972; Richard Closs, ed., *Greece Under Military Rule* (London: Secker and Warburg, 1972); Margaret Papandreou, *Nightmare in Athens* (Englewood Cliffs, New Jersey: Prentice-Hall,

1970); Peter Schwab and George D. Fraugas, eds., *Greece Under the Junta* (New York: Facts on File, 1970); Theodroe A. Couloumbis, *Greek Political Reaction to American and Nato Influences* (New Haven: Yale University Press, 1966); *The Economist*, special supplement on Greek economic and political affairs, July 31, 1971; United States Department of Commerce, *Overseas Business Reports*, April 1967; *International Commerce*, May 12, 1969, June 29, 1969, and May 18, 1970; William Hardy McNeill, *Greece: American Aid in Action 1947-56* (New York: Twentieth Century Fund, 1957); Jean Meynaud, *Rapport sur l'abolition de la démocratie en Grèce*, 2nd edition (Montreal, 1970); George Coutsoumans et al., *Analysis and Assessment of the Economic Affects of the U.S. PL480 Program in Greece* (Athens: Center of Planning and Economic Research, 1965).

46. Jane S. Jacquette, "Revolution by Fiat: The Context of Policy-Making in Peru," *Western Political Quarterly*, Volume 25, Number 4, December 1972, p. 655.

47. Anibal Quijano, "Nationalism and Capitalism in Peru: A Study in Neo-Imperialism," *Monthly Review*, July-August 1971.

48. Guy B. Meeker, "Fade-Out Joint Venture," *Inter-American Economic Affairs*, Volume 24, No. 4, Spring 1971.

49. ITT memorandum of July 9, 1971, in the ITT/Chile report to the Senate Committee on Foreign Relations, op. cit., p. 14.

50. See also Richard Lee Clinton, "The Modernizing Military: The Case of Peru," in *Inter-American Economic Affairs*, Volume 24, Number 4, Spring 1971, pp. 43-46; Francois Bourricaud, *Power and Society in Contemporary Peru* (New York: Praeger, 1970); and James Malloy, "Peru Before and After the Coup of 1968," in *Inter-American Studies and World Affairs*, Volume 14, No. 4, November 1972.

51. This test was conceived and executed by Ted Theodosis, who has given permission to include it here.

52. An argument might be made that foreign aid is more closely associated with business interests than other outputs of U.S. foreign policy. Some non-radicals who doubt the pervasiveness of capitalist influence over foreign policy in general concede it in this one policy domain. Raymond Vernon, for example, says in *Sovereignty at Bay* (p. 212) that "it would be wrong to assume that the aid program was inspired by business interests when it was first created . . . [but] once the programs were well launched, U.S. business interests managed to acquire a major voice in some of the policies governing foreign aid operations." See note 5.

53. One critic suggested another interpretation of the findings in this paper. The "leftward" governments of Sukarno, Goulart, Allende, and Papandreou might have been objectionable to U.S. business, not because of their political orientations, but rather because of their sheer incompetence in managing the national economies. I would argue that the problems of economic disruption, inflation, imbalance of payments, and interrupted growth are characteristic of

the first transitional steps on the "rocky road to socialism" and that they do not necessarily represent incompetence. Socialist regimes that are now regarded as relatively competent, such as the Chinese Communists, also experienced these transformation costs in their early stages. On the other hand, foreign business cannot be expected to favor economic disruption.

7

Correlates of U.S. Military Assistance and Military Intervention

John S. Odell
University of Wisconsin

I

The energy shortages and monetary instabilities of recent years have brought increased public attention to the impact of international economic relations on peoples and their governments and, most dramatically, to the connection between oil and Middle East diplomacy. But well before these developments, some theorists of international relations explained American foreign policy by reference to such economic factors as needs for imported raw materials. The writings of Magdoff, Williams, and Kolko[1] are probably the most widely known. It will be the purpose of this chapter to suggest some steps for the refinement of these "theories of imperialism" and particularly to try in this way to advance the search for "the determinants of foreign policy."[2]

The aim of the empirical theorist is to simplify a complex reality, to uncover regularities, to specify a small number of general factors that account for (changes in) events, relations, or behavior. Of course his general explanatory propositions should be in accord with relevant evidence, and the more rigorous the empirical test a theory has withstood the more convincing the theory. As a preface to the tests and theoretical discussion to come, it will be helpful to sketch briefly the rationale that has guided them. Five steps in particular are especially useful in the process of refining any theory:

1. *Definition.* The concepts that make up the theory must be defined independently. If one were to take literally Lenin's often-quoted definition of imperialism as the monopoly stage of capitalism, one would obviously bypass entirely the empirical question of whether capitalist society is indeed a general cause of expansionary foreign policy. Some adherents of the imperialism school avoid this problem, but others in actual usage seem to make it impossible to classify Soviet or Chinese behavior, for instance, as imperialistic. On that basis the claim that capitalism produces imperialism is at least partly tautological. Tying one's theoretical terms to operational indicators helps to keep those terms distinct.

The author is grateful to Earl Brubaker, Edward Friedman, Scott Harris, Victor Johnson, David Kay, and Margaret Odell for reading and commenting on an earlier version of this chapter.

2. *Formalization.* Stating the empirical claims of a theory in explicit, formal propositions makes it possible to recognize more readily which evidence is most relevant and which hypothesis is most strongly supported by evidence. Formalizing the theory in this sense forces us to specify more clearly which aspects of the subject matter are related to which other aspects. If possible, these propositions should state which of two given factors is the cause, which the effect, and whether causation is reciprocal.[3] For example, in general does overseas economic involvement lead to official action on behalf of businessmen, or does trade follow the flag, or both? Formalization is virtually unknown in imperialism studies.

3. *Falsification.* Theories must be falsifiable in principle—that is, they must avoid tautology. But in addition they can be strengthened and refined if concepts and the relations between them are specified more precisely and applied more uniformly. To take a single illustration, Kolko writes: "The relationship between the objectives of foreign economic policy and direct political and military intervention therefore has been a continuous and intimate one—indeed, very often identical."[4] He gives these general terms more specific meanings, but as he takes one case at a time, the meanings shift. In Indonesia in 1963 the economic objective was "effective control of the [oil] industry" in the face of a takeover threat, and the intervention was a threat to discontinue foreign aid. But in the case of Vietnam, his explanation of a different type of intervention does not refer to protecting American investments.[5] Of course, other propositions can be added to make the argument more complex, but after reading this literature, one is left wondering whether any general relationships between concepts that have fixed, agreed meanings do indeed hold across many cases. I propose to specify operational definitions or indicators for concepts that will then stand as the evidentiary standard for judging the empirical worth of hypotheses. Hypotheses that have survived efforts to falsify them in this manner are more persuasive than those that have not. The question of which indicator is most reasonable is certainly debatable, but such debates are likely to advance theory development more than those in which each proponent cites a different handful of events to illustrate his position without specifying the evidence that would constitute falsification.

It is never possible to falsify any hypothesis in an absolute sense, let alone to falsify all competing hypotheses but one. But we can hope to judge from the evidence which hypotheses fit best under which specified conditions, or in which time periods. Further, theories by their nature will always contain terms too ambiguous to allow us to reduce them to simple measures. This "openness of meaning"—for example, in the term "American economic interests"—has important scientific uses; it can prevent the premature closure of our ideas and convey insights we are as yet unable to make more precise.[6] I do not argue that imperialism theorists should have met an ideal standard unmet by social scientists studying any other subject, nor do I make the naive claim that quantitative data are the only useful kind of evidence. I do argue that the imperialism literature has weaknesses that can be fruitfully treated by means of the research strategy used below.

4. *Comparison.* The study of a single case or the use of isolated cases as illustrations is less persuasive evidence than that provided by a systematic comparative analysis. The more cases to which the theory could apply that are included simultaneously in the test, the more discriminating and convincing is the test. An impartial rule for selecting the cases enhances the test. Typically a study of U.S. military intervention will examine the interventions in Cuba, Vietnam, and so on, to find the reasons for the action, but will fail to look then at the many cases where no interventions took place to see whether the postulated causal conditions in fact did not obtain there. Further, it typically does not introduce systematic comparisons with other nations to show why they did not or do not intervene. Comparative analysis not only casts light on the validity of a particular general hypothesis, but it can also reveal the need to reformulate the conceptual framework and suggest causal factors that had been overlooked.

5. *Variation.* To put this point in a slightly different way, a theory should be able to account for the variations in behavior as well as its central tendencies. The actions of capitalist nations do differ in important respects. American behavior varies from nation to nation and changes over time. Imperialism theorists recognize some variation, but in general they emphasize the continuity and constancy in the behavior they study, and they tend to rely on the single factor—economic expansionism—to account for the whole.[7] Any theory, which is in the position of discounting the relevance of interesting differences, could be made stronger and more comprehensive by research that focuses directly on variation. This study is designed to do that.[8]

II

Any theory can be refined and tested, in sum, by identifying hypotheses that account for variation, making them explicit and formal, providing independent definitions and reliable measures of the variables to allow "falsification," and performing comparative analysis. What hypotheses can be formulated, then, from imperialism studies? That literature is large and diverse, different studies taking different faces of the subject as the matter to be explained.[9] It is broader than the study of the determinants of foreign policy, but this investigation will be confined to the thread of ideas related to U.S. military intervention and military assistance, two types of foreign policy behavior.

Magdoff's *The Age of Imperialism* and Kolko's *The Roots of American Foreign Policy* are concerned with these two types of government action. Magdoff provides a compressed statement of the main thesis:

... there is a close parallel between, on the one hand, the aggressive United States foreign policy aimed at controlling (directly and indirectly) as much of the globe as possible, and on the other hand, an energetic international expansionist policy of U.S. business. The demonstration of this parallel of course does not prove that one is the cause of the other. What it does suggest is that ... the spread of U.S. international economic affairs has to be introduced as an important consideration in any hypotheses attempting to explain what goes on in the world today.[10]

In the imperialism perspective capitalism has always been a global system, and the present is understood in terms of the past:

... a substantial portion of the huge military machine, including that of the Western European nations, is the price being paid to maintain the imperialist network of trade and investment in the absence of colonialism.[11]

Washington's general interest is to continue the economic dependence of the new nations and also to expand the economic empire where possible.

Various theorists agree that this American economic system has three important dimensions. First, the domestic economy is highly dependent on raw materials that must be imported, many of them from the new nations. Second, many of the largest corporations look to overseas divisions for sizeable proportions of their sales and earnings, and for several reasons they and other firms feel great pressure to expand foreign investments. Third, with the search for certainty and continued growth "the dependence on export markets becomes a permanent feature" of many industries. In brief, they argue that "the entire mechanism of a market economy ... force(s) a restless drive of capital to expand,"[12] with the result that foreign countries have economic value for the United States as sources of raw materials, opportunities for investment, and export markets. They disagree on the mechanism through which these economic interests work their way into foreign policy. For some, aggregate economic forces determine an expansionist policy regardless of who the leaders are; for others, only certain groups in the society have an interest in imperialism but they dominate domestic politics; for others, certain misconceptions on the part of leaders have been necessary for expansionism. For all, it is these global economic interests that cause American officials and firms to oppose leftist governments and revolutions and to favor stability in the new nations.

The techniques of control used to protect and advance these economic interests will vary with the situation. The financial power and technological edge of American firms have enabled them to dominate in some areas simply by virtue of market forces. The U.S. government can influence the economic and political climate abroad by means of tariffs on imported manufactures, embargoes, attaching conditions to loans, and manipulation of commodity prices. From this perspective economic development loans and the threat to halt foreign aid are additional levers of control.

However, even if many leaders prefer these less direct methods, [economic] "imperialism necessarily involves militarism. Indeed, they are twins that have fed on each other in the past, as they do now."[13] The donation or sale of arms and the use of economic aid funds to train local police can help equip client regimes to defend free-enterprise societies against socialist armies or rebels. By befriending local military elites and bringing them to the United States for training and social interaction, the military assistance program can affect the "internal power balance" in Third World nations in the direction of greater hospitality to multinational corporations than would be the case otherwise.[14] In certain cases where all these methods fail, the same economic logic can lead to direct intervention by American forces. One of the contradictions of global imperialism, this approach argues, is that it spawns opposing "people's wars." Interventions to suppress such rebellions even in places like Vietnam are explained in terms of a "domino thesis" similar to that of the U.S. State Department: intervention is necessary to safeguard access to raw materials and economic opportunities in adjacent territories because these would be jeopardized by a victorious revolution.[15]

III

If this brief summary is a fair statement of the arguments dealing with the central tendency of American military activity, what can we say about the variations? In one of the rare general claims that can be considered applicable to this question, Kolko argues:

... However high [the cost of political and strategic intervention] may appear today, in the history of United States diplomacy specific American economic interests in a country or region have often defined the national interest on the assumption that the nation can identify its welfare with the profits of some of its citizens.[16]

Apparently no theorist has ventured claims with specific reference to the distribution of military assistance. But keeping in mind the Kolko argument, the foregoing analysis, and the great attention given to raw materials, foreign investments, and exports, let us propose to test the proposition that *the amount of U.S. military assistance given to a government is positively related to the level of American economic interest in the country, specifically to the value of the country as a source of raw materials imports, the amount of U.S. investment in the country, and the proportion of U.S. trade that is conducted with the country.* From the imperialism perspective the more valuable country would receive military aid or more of it for either or both of two reasons: its conquest by a socialist power would mean greater loss (thinking of Western Europe), or the collapse of the government or the business climate due to internal uprising or instability would mean greater loss. Granting more military aid might in turn affect the political climate in the nation, which might then affect the subsequent level of U.S. investment and trading.[17]

As noted in the first section, the claims of imperialism theorists are not normally expressed in this form, and so at least some of them would almost surely disavow this proposition and the others suggested for testing. The methods used to generate indicators corresponding to these variables are detailed in an Appendix. The units of observation are 119 nations independent as of 1965, and the design compares those having higher and lower economic value for the United States to see whether U.S. military action responds to (or conceivably contributes to) these differences. All the measures should be considered only rough approximations to theoretical terms, particularly so with "Raw Materials Value." This score indicates the number of critical raw materials imported from the nation in 1958 and is modified to take account of the proportion of U.S. imports of an item the nation supplied. "Military Assistance" refers to the total deliveries to the nation for the years 1950 through 1965.

Table 7-1 displays the first test of this proposition. Moving across the table from the countries that supplied no critical raw materials to those that did supply some, a tendency toward larger military aid receipts is clearly apparent, in keeping with the hypothesis. Goodman-Kruskal's Gamma and Kendall's Tau provide alternative summary indices of the strength of this association.

According to Table 7-2, the association of military aid with private investment is also in the expected direction and is slightly stronger. Countries with low investment and low military aid (the upper/left cell of the table) include Nigeria, Czechoslovakia, and Burma. India and Spain fall in the medium/medium cell. Peru and Brazil are among those with high investment amounts and medium military aid levels. Great Britain, France, and West Germany show high levels on

Table 7-1

Relation Between U.S. Military Assistance Given to and Raw Materials Value of Nations

Military Assistance	Raw Materials Value			
	0	1–3	4+	n
0–8	71%	52%	21%	71
8–656	26	24	43	33
656+	3	24	36	15
Total	100%	100%	100%	
n	72	33	14	119

Gamma = .55   Tau–b = .34

Entries show percent of nations. Military assistance refers to total deliveries from 1950 to 1965 in million dollars. The raw materials value of the nation, 1957, is given in terms of a special scale (see Appendix).

Table 7-2

Relation Between U.S. Military Assistance Given to and U.S. Private Investment in Nations

Military Assistance	Private Investment			
	0-25	25-300	300+	n
0-8	79%	43%	19%	71
8-656	14	38	63	33
656+	8	19	19	15
Total	101%*	100%	101%*	
n	66	37	16	119

Gamma = .60   tau–b = .50   *Rounding error

Entries show percent of nations. Total U.S. Military assistance, 1950-1965, and U.S. Private Direct Investment, 1957, both given in million dollars.

both variables. South Korea is a counter-example for this hypothesis, having little U.S. investment but receiving much military aid during this period (the lower/left cell), but the result of this analysis is to show that South Korea is not typical of nations at that investment level.

For reasons of space, only the summary figures will be reported for the tests to follow. The relation between military assistance and the proportion of U.S. trade accounted for by the country is similar to the first two. The strength of association is .81/.57 (Gamma/Tau). Again in this third sense, it seems that grants of U.S. military aid vary with the level of economic interest in the recipient.

It may be, however, that this covariation is spurious—that is, it merely reflects a third variable that is related to each of the two involved in a test. In particular, larger countries may account for more of U.S. exports, raw materials imports, and investment opportunities than smaller ones, simply because of their size, and leaders may give more military aid to larger nations in recognition of their political and strategic importance. Let us then try to remove the effects of size (indicated by Gross National Product) to see whether economic interests have effects in their own right.[18] Using Table 7-3 we can compare each of the three relationships defined over the complete sample with the same relationship measured over subsets of nations grouped roughly according to economic size. For nations of moderate size American dependence on a nation for raw materials supplies has virtually nothing to do with the level of military aid allocated. But in no other condition is the "controlled" relationship trivial. The materials effect is weaker among the smallest nations; the investment effect, among the middle powers; and the trade effect, among the smallest and medium groups. But all three relationships are *stronger* among the largest economies than they are in the sample as a whole.[19] So the covariation of military aid with economic interests

Table 7-3

Relation Between U.S. Military Assistance Given to and Economic Value of Nations, Controlling for Gross National Product

	Complete Sample	GNP		
		Low	Medium	High
Raw Materials Value	54/29	47/18	05/02	75/42
Private Investment	78/48	79/45	48/25	94/63
Trade Proportion	76/46	71/34	54/29	100/59
n	119	44	41	34

Entries show strength of association, Gamma/Tau, decimals omitted. Total U.S. Military Assistance, 1950-1965, and 1957 U.S. private direct investment in million dollars; proportion of U.S. trade, 1964-1965, in percent; 1965 GNP cutpoints in million dollars: 935 and 6391. The indices for the complete sample differ slightly from those reported previously because four-cell rather than nine-cell classifications were used for this test.

is not simply spurious. A similar test controlling for population supports this conclusion with minor variations. In summary, we have evidence that imperialism theories are suggestive of testable hypotheses that do make a contribution to the explanation of variations in one type of American external behavior.

IV

With reference to a different type of behavior, direct military intervention, explicit statements of the factors that account in general for the variations are also rare. Typically analysts argue that "only when indirect policies fail are the older instruments of coercion and force brought into play, and the principle of continuity in change applies."[20] But why at some times and in some places rather than others? As a basis for his "theory of United States global role" Kolko suggests an analysis of British imperialism by Gallagher and Robinson. Their subject is the British shift toward greater formal annexation of colonies in the latter nineteenth century, which is to "free-trade imperialism" as U.S. military intervention is to less drastic U.S. policy instruments. Their formulation is the most explicit and appropriate one I have seen for present purposes:

Imperialism, perhaps, may be defined as a sufficient political function of this process of integrating new regions into the expanding economy.... Two qualifications must be made. First, imperialism may be only indirectly connected with economic integration in that it sometimes extends beyond areas of economic development, but acts for their strategic protection. Secondly, although imperialism is a function of economic expansion, it is not a necessary function.... It is only when the polities of these new regions fail to provide satisfactory conditions for commercial or strategic integration and when their relative weakness allows, that power is used imperialistically to adjust those conditions. Economic expansion, it is true, will tend to flow into the regions of maximum opportunity, but maximum opportunity depends as much upon political considerations of security as upon questions of profit. . . . Conversely, in proportion as satisfactory political frameworks are brought into being in this way, the frequency of imperialist intervention lessens and imperialist control is correspondingly relaxed.[21]

If we can understand these references to "imperialist intervention" as applicable to post-World War II American military interventions, perhaps we can also find a way to confront these ideas with comparative data. This theory seems to consist of four causes or conditions that, in some combination, produce intervention: (a) an overseas economic interest, "opportunity" or need; (b) a need for "strategic protection" of some foreign economic interest; (c) some "political insecurity" or challenge to economic empire or its expansion; (d) relative weakness of the target nation. At least the latter two are clearly necessary conditions.

The Yale World Data Analysis Program has provided the best available record of military interventions, which they define as "any attempt to engage in military activity within the borders of another country with the intent of influencing the authority structure of that country." This definition excludes "wars" and actions like the Kennedy blockade of Cuba, and the record covers 1948 to 1967. Based on this source, I have constructed a rough measure of the "extent of U.S. military intervention" during that period for each country (see the Appendix). At the top of the scale are Laos, Cuba, Zaire, Dominican Republic, and South Vietnam. I have found no way to measure "profit opportunity" or anticipated economic involvement for a large number of cases, but it would seem worthwhile to ask whether *the extent of U.S. military intervention in a country is positively related to the (existing) level of American economic interest in the country*, as defined by our three indicators. A quick scanning of the most familiar interventions does not call to mind America's largest investments or markets, and intuition may lead us to doubt this proposition; the data will allow a general test. The second idea, acting in one area to protect economic development in another, resembles the "domino thesis." It may be that the greatest intervention takes place in the regions of greatest economic value. The hypothesis that *the extent of U.S. military intervention in a region is positively related to the (existing) level of American economic interest in the region* will be matched with the country data aggregated into four regions. The immediate occasion for some of the interventions has been a disorder or insurrection, or they have occurred in nations noted for histories of political instability (one kind of "insecurity"). Let us represent this third idea with the hypothesis that *the extent of U.S. military intervention in a country is positively related to the level of political instability in the country*, measuring the latter by the number (per capita) of domestic organized "armed attacks" recorded for the nation during 1948 through 1967 by the Yale Program. Clearly, these theories do not predict American military intervention in powerful nations under any circumstances, and we can represent this fourth "weakness" condition in these tests by excluding from the sample the 28 "strongest" nations, by using a combination of economic and military criteria.

Intuition would have served us well in the case of the first hypothesis. Among the weaker 91 nations, those representing greater American economic interest are no more or less likely as candidates for intervention than others. Table 7-4 shows the U.S. trade variable. The ordinal relation is .14/.06 (Gamma/Tau) for raw materials value and .11/.05 for private investment. Of course, many of the largest concentrations of U.S. investment and trade are located in the advanced industrial nations that have been excluded here; Table 7-4 is thus one way to display our inability to explain Third World interventions by simple reference to the distribution of economic interests. But the instability hypothesis finds support even among data restricted to the middle and lesser powers (Table 7-5). Thirteen of the 16 nations that experienced interventions are within the least-stable subgroup, and the strength of this association must be considered fairly high when the marginal distributions are taken into account. We are not able to tell from this analysis how much the results are due to a tendency of intervention to produce or increase domestic conflict (as in Guatemala, for instance) and how much to the reverse process—instability causing intervention. While these results are consistent with the theoretical clues provided by Gallagher and Robinson, they are also consistent with other theories. The official explanations for the Dominican and Vietnam interventions emphasized insurrection inspired by outside Communist agents. Where these and imperialism theories diverge sharply, of course, is in identifying which outside forces are responsible for the unrest.

Since an imperialism theory can plausibly argue that an American economic

Table 7-4

Relation Between Extent of U.S. Military Intervention, 1948-1967, and Proportion of U.S. Trade, 1964-1965, with Nations

Military Intervention	Proportion of U.S. Trade			
	0-.3%	.3-1.5%	1.5%+	n
None	86%	68%	100%	75
Lesser	10	23	0	11
Greater	5	9	0	5
Total	101%*	100%	100%	
n	63	22	6	91

Gamma = .23   Tau–b = .09   *Rounding error

Entries show percent of nations. The "Lesser" row includes nations having non-zero intervention scores less than 50; "Greater" includes those with 50 or higher. Nations judged "stronger" on military and economic criteria are excluded. See Appendix for further detail.

Table 7-5

Relation Between Extent of U.S. Military Intervention and Political Stability of Nations, 1948-1967

Military Intervention	Most Stable	Medium	Least Stable	n
		Political Stability		
None	94%	96%	61%	75
Lesser	6	4	24	11
Greater	0	0	15	5
Total	100%	100%	100%	
n	34	24	33	91

Gamma = .76   Tau−b = .35

Entries show percent of nations. The "Lesser" row includes nations having non-zero intervention scores less than 50; "Greater" includes those with 50 or higher. Stability categories are determined by the number of domestic "armed attacks" per capita, using .003 and .022 as cutpoints. Nations judged "stronger" on military and economic criteria are excluded. See Appendix for further detail.

interest and political instability (the failure of less drastic means of control) are both necessary to produce a military intervention, we should ask what the data show when these two conditions overlap. (The answers must be cautious because of the small number of cases under analysis.) First, if we look only at the least-stable subgroup, do we find that the likelihood of intervention is more strongly related to economic interests than in the ("weaker") sample as a whole? The raw materials value and the private investment value of the nation are no more useful under this condition, but the trade effect is noticeably stronger (Gamma = .68, Tau-b = .38). Among these 33 least-stable societies, 60 percent of those of greater trade importance experienced interventions, while 78 percent of those of lesser trade value experienced none. Conversely, if we look only at the areas of greater economic involvement, do we find that the likelihood of intervention is more strongly related to instability than in the larger sample? This stronger stability relationship is not greatly affected by controlling for the economic conditions. It is slightly stronger within the larger-investment and larger-trade-proportion subgroups. These data are consistent with the tentative conclusions, then, that instability is a more important correlate of military intervention than is American economic interest, that bringing economic interests into the analysis adds only slightly to our explanatory ability, and that economic interests are not a necessary condition for intervention.

It seems desirable to ask what these data can tell us about the "domino" hypotheses, even if compressing all the country data from a region into a single figure involves a considerable loss of information and runs the risk of concealing relationships visible at other levels of analysis. After eliminating the "stronger" nations (and thus the European region), we have four regions, and for each we can measure the total extent of military intervention, total amount of investment, and so on. In recognition of the crudity of the measures let us base the analysis only on the rankings of the regions and summarize each relationship with the ordinal "correlation" Tau.[22] The results are mixed. The typical argument about the Vietnam intervention points to raw materials supplies elsewhere in that region. Comparison of regions reveals a discernible but almost trivially slight tendency of military intervention to increase with the measurable materials value of the region to the United States (Tau = .18). The relation between intervention and investment is also in the expected direction but not much stronger (Tau = .33). But the extent of intervention in a region does vary fairly strongly with the region's proportion of U.S. trade (Tau = .67); if East Asia had surpassed Latin America as the leading Third World trading partner, the trade ordering would be identical to the intervention ordering. Could this be pure coincidence? Possibly; it might also be that the meaning of a region like East Asia to high American officials is (consciously or otherwise) colored by their realization of its importance as an American market and source of imports compared with the Near East-South Asia, for example, and that these meanings become manifest in their behavior. (Why one region is more important as a trade partner than another is a different question, which might be answered without a theory of economic imperialism.) It is unfortunate that these data do not allow us to control for political instability or some other measure for "challenge to empire," for it is under that condition that an imperialism theory would predict a military intervention rather than some other form of action. In any case, the bivariate relation we discovered between intervention and political instability at the nation level is not visible at this high level of aggregation (Tau = 0). If the "domino" thesis is extended to take in the entire world—as in arguing that the Vietnam intervention was undertaken in order to protect the global economic empire—then other kinds of analysis are required to evaluate it.

Finally, we have evidence for testing one complementary hypothesis. Yarmolinsky argues that "the Military Assistance Program and the Military Sales Program make the use of American military power somewhat more likely for two reasons."[23] They create ties to the recipient regime that can lead to greater involvement, as in Vietnam where American leaders felt their own credibility was at stake because of earlier commitments. And the military assistance mission provides a target for attack and challenge to the regime by the domestic opposition. As Yarmolinsky might have predicted, we find a mild positive relation between the amount of military assistance granted to a nation and the extent of military intervention, as defined here, among the weaker nations (Gamma = .56, Tau-b = .27). The relation is slightly higher among the least stable nations.

V

To summarize, using familiar social science methods of inference, we have found that the level of American military assistance given to a nation during the Cold War years varied with the importance of the nation to the United States as a supplier of critical raw materials, as a field for private investment, and as a trade partner. We found that the extent of U.S. military intervention in a Third World nation was greater the less stable the nation, but we found very little support for the hypotheses that variations in intervention could be accounted for by raw materials value or private investment amounts, either among nations or regions. Among the least-stable nations, those that provided a larger proportion of U.S. trade experienced greater intervention, and trade and intervention were also associated at the regional level. Military intervention was associated with receiving military assistance.

These results do not seem to point toward a simple, unambiguous deduction about the utility of imperialism theories for explaining foreign policies. None of the authors we consulted has proposed the formal hypotheses tested here, or any other formal hypotheses. Some of the ideas formulated from their work were useful for generalization and some not so useful. The implications will become clearer as investigation expands in two directions. First, we need better testing of imperialism theories, which requires sharpening and broadening our ideas as well as improving our data. The imperialism approach may find its strongest empirical support when it seeks to explain economic conditions and non-military types of government action. A single measure of expansionism might reveal a closer association with economic factors than does any type of action considered apart from the others. A design that includes both official and non-governmental actors would be a richer one. We need studies that compare the behavior of several major powers, including the Soviet Union.[24] We especially need longitudinal data that would provide more discriminating tests than are possible with a cross-sectional design and aggregated data. For example, it may be that the presence of economic interests leads to military aid, but that under some conditions military aid programs can arouse domestic opposition and embolden military leaders to intervene in politics, such that the increased political instability discourages further foreign investment. Reciprocal effects working against each other in this manner would reduce correlations of the type reported here, but these effects could be separated in a time-series analysis. Finally, this approach to theory development can also profit from intensive studies of particular incidents seeking to determine the set of factors that were most salient in the minds of the individuals who made the decisions.

Second, we can better assess the utility of the imperialism approach by comparing its evidence with that gathered to test different conceptions and hypotheses. Indeed, there is no reason why we must confine ourselves to any single theory. Keohane's and Nye's "world politics paradigm"[25] shows promise as the beginning of an effort to ask different questions of some of the same phenomena. It helps one avoid both the assumption that the corporations can be overlooked and the assumption that they are never in conflict with the American government. It highlights not only dependence but complex interdependence in a manner that evokes Kautsky's idea that advanced capitalist development may bring less rather than more war. And this paradigm is not the only competing approach. The distribution of military aid may reflect recipient governments' access to resources from other sources[26] and perceived "Communist" military plans[27] as much as it reflects American economic interests. The Vietnam intervention has been interpreted as an outgrowth of domestic politics rather than economics.[28] The prediction that expansionary behavior will vary with a nation's power resources should be evaluated alongside the prediction based on its type of economic system. My speculation, consistent with the findings reported here, is that economic hypotheses for explaining actual uses of force will find relatively weak support in comparative tests. At any rate, it is fair to conclude generally that economic factors must not be overlooked, but that the conditions for their effects and the phenomena to be explained must be specified carefully.

Notes

1. Harry Madgoff, *The Age of Imperialism: The Economics of U.S. Foreign Policy* (New York: Monthly Review Press, 1969); William A. Williams, *The Tragedy of American Diplomacy*, Revised and enlarged edition (New York: Dell, 1962); Gabriel Kolko, *The Roots of American Foreign Policy: An Analysis of Power and Purpose* (Boston: Beacon Press, 1969) and other books.

2. Arnold Wolfers, *Discord and Collaboration: Essays on International Politics* (Baltimore: Johns Hopkins Press, 1962).

3. Hubert M. Blalock, Jr., *Theory Construction: From Verbal to Mathematical Formulations* (Englewood Cliffs, N.J.: Prentice-Hall, 1969), Chapters 1-3.

4. Kolko, op. cit., p. 81.

5. Ibid., Chapter 4.

6. Abraham Kaplan, *The Conduct of Inquiry: Methodology for Behavioral Science* (Scranton, Pa.: Chandler, 1964), Chapter II.

7. Kolko, op. cit., p. 86, notes one type of variation—the extent to which U.S. interventions succeed—but he fails to offer an explanation for the differences.

8. For an example of a related study that embodies most of the elements of the method suggested here, see F.L. Pryor, *Public Expenditures in Communist and Capitalist Nations* (Homewood, Ill.: Richard D. Irwin, Inc., 1968), Chapter

III. Pryor compares defense spending (in proportion to GNP and to per capita income) in seven centrally planned economies of Eastern Europe with seven market economies and finds no significant difference. Comparison of Warsaw Pact nations as a group with NATO nations yields the same result.

9. For more extensive reviews and elaborations of these theories, see chapters in this volume such as those by Deutsch, Mack, and Weisskopf; Hans Daalder, "Imperialism," *International Encyclopedia of the Social Sciences* (New York: Crowell, Collier & Macmillan, 1968); James O'Connor, "The Meaning of Economic Imperialism," in K.T. Fann and Donald C. Hodges (eds.), *Readings in U.S. Imperialism* (Boston: Porter Sargent, 1971), pp. 23-68; Robert W. Tucker, *The Radical Left and American Foreign Policy* (Baltimore: Johns Hopkins Press, 1971); Richard J. Barnet, *Roots of War: The Men and Institutions Behind U.S. Foreign Policy* (Baltimore: Penguin Books, 1972), Part II.

10. Magdoff, op. cit., pp. 12-13.

11. Harry Magdoff, "Militarism and Imperialism," *American Economic Review* Papers and Proceedings (May 1970), p. 240.

12. Magdoff, 1969, pp. 36 and 24.

13. Magdoff, 1970, p. 240.

14. Miles D. Wolpin, *Military Aid and Counterrevolution in the Third World* (Lexington, Mass.: Lexington Books, D.C. Heath and Co., 1972).

15. Kolko, op. cit., pp. 85 and 89. Paul Baran and Paul Sweezy, *Monopoly Capital: An Essay on the American Economic and Social Order* (New York: Monthly Review Press, 1966), Chapter 6, interpret the hostile U.S. reaction to the Cuban revolution, as contrasted to that of other capitalist powers, in terms of the alleged need of "monopolists" like Exxon not only to compete for business abroad but to maintain paramount control and privileged arrangements in many countries. If little Cuba could defect to the socialist camp successfully, so could any country in the "free world."

16. Kolko, op. cit., pp. 84-85.

17. For testing such claims time-series data are preferable; they allow the analyst to observe two variables at separate time points and then to look for a change in the second produced by a change in the first. Such data are difficult to obtain for these variables, especially an accurate value for U.S. investments in particular countries. For present purposes we rely on a cross-sectional design and data aggregated for each country over a twenty-year period. For this reason the propositions suggest only association, not causal direction.

18. For this set of nations the strengths of association (Gamma/Tau, decimals omitted) are:

	GNP	Population
Raw Materials Value	70/46	66/43
Private Investment	63/42	36/23
Proportion of Trade	85/58	67/43
Military Assistance	69/42	59/35
Military Intervention	−21/−05	06/02

19. Within this High GNP group the (only) countries that had no U.S. investment during this period were identically the countries that had Communist governments. Of those, only Yugoslavia received military aid, while only 5 of the 25 non-Communist nations failed to receive aid. At this highly simplified level, one could say that for this group both the distribution of investment and the government action are accounted for by the presence or absence of a Communist coup or revolution. The question of why Communist government and GNP level appear to be associated is germane but beyond the scope of this paper.

20. O'Connor, p. 59. See Kolko, p. 86.

21. John Gallagher and Ronald Robinson, "The Imperialism of Free Trade," *Economic History Review*, 2d Series, VI, 1, 1953, pp. 5-6. Quotation reproduced with the permission of The Broadwater Press Ltd.

22. Each variable is the simple regional sum, except that intervention scores are divided by the number of nations in the region, and the stability indicator is "armed attacks" per capita. See the Appendix for details. Information from 92 nations is used, including China for substantive reasons. The only possible values for Tau here are 0, ±.33, ±.67, and ±1.0, except where there are ties. The rankings are as follows, where 1 = Latin America, 2 = Europe (excluded), 3 = Africa, 4 = Near East and South Asia, 5 = Far East and South-east Asia:

Rank	Inter-vention	Materials value	Invest-ment	Trade prop.	Attacks/capita
Highest	5	1	1	1	3
Second	1	3, 5	4	5	5
Third	4		5	4	1
Lowest	3	4	3	3	4

23. Adam Yarmolinsky, *The Military Establishment: Its Impacts on American Society* (New York: Harper & Row, 1971), pp. 144-7.

24. See Wynfred Joshua and Stephen P. Gibert, *Arms for the Third World: Soviet Military Aid Diplomacy* (Baltimore: Johns Hopkins Press, 1969), pp. 104 and 118, for arguments that the Soviet military loan program has been continued despite counter-revolutionary effects and that in some cases it may have even yielded a net profit for the USSR.

25. Robert O. Keohane and Joseph S. Nye, Jr. (eds.), *Transnational Relations and World Politics* (Cambridge, Mass.: Harvard University Press, 1971).

26. See Joan M. Nelson, *Aid, Influence, and Foreign Policy* (New York: Macmillan, 1968), pp. 31-35.

27. Edgar S. Furniss, Jr., *Some Perspectives on American Military Assistance* (Memorandum No. 13), Center of International Studies, Princeton University, June 1957.

28. Daniel Ellsberg, "The Quagmire Myth and the Stalemate Machine," *Public Policy* (Spring 1971).

Appendix 7A

Analysis

The set of nations is a standard set of 136 entities from which 17 were excluded for lack of independence or missing data. Unlike some previous studies of aid allocations, this one includes in the analysis nations receiving zero aid. To exclude them would allow us to apply more powerful statistical models but would prevent us from answering what seems to be the most important question: Why aid is given at all? The result is that the marginal distributions of the variables are in most cases highly skewed and require caution in interpretation.

Measurement and Data Sources

1. U.S. Military Assistance: total deliveries of equipment, training and related support for fiscal years 1950 through 1965. Main source: U.S. Department of Defense, *Military Assistance and Foreign Military Sales Facts* (March 1971). Missing data for 11 nations were estimated using *World Handbook of Political and Social Indicators* (2nd ed.; machine version supplied by InterUniversity Consortium for Political Research); Stockholm International Peace Research Institute, *Yearbook of World Armaments and Disarmament* 1969/70 (New York: Humanities Press, 1970), and *The Arms Trade with the Third World* (New York: Humanities Press, 1971); George Thayer, *The War Business: The International Trade in Armaments* (New York: Simon and Shuster, 1969); Joshua and Gibert (fn. 24), p. 130.

2. Extent of U.S. Military Intervention, 1948 through 1967. The daily event file from the *World Handbook* (machine version) was first reduced by eliminating reports of additional troop arrivals or air actions during an on-going intervention. The final score reflects a count of interventions weighted for "length of intervenor presence in country" (1 for less than one week; 4, less than one month; 24, less than six months; and 50 for greater than six months). Because of the imprecision of the last category, we must regard the scores as indicators only of rough differences: the Laos score exceeds the Vietnam score because two separate interventions are recorded for Laos whereas an even longer presence in Vietnam was continuous. Interventions carried out by irregular forces like Cuban exiles based in Florida rather than official forces are weighted one-half. Oddly, the Yale file does not record an intervention in Vietnam. For this study, U.S. activity there shifted from advisory to military intervention by the Yale definition as of October 1962. See George McT. Kahin and John W. Lewis, *The United States in Vietnam* (Delta, 1967), pp. 137ff. Scores: Greater

intervention—Laos 151, China 106, Cuba 78, Zaire 54, Dominican Republic 50, South Vietnam 50; Lesser—Greece 29, Lebanon 25, Thailand 25, Panama 5, Taiwan 5, Guatemala 2, Haiti 2, Costa Rica 1, Tanzania 1, Jordan 1, Indonesia 1; None—all others.

3. Raw Materials Value, 1958. Critical materials were defined as those stockpiled by the federal government (Group I items) plus petroleum, iron ore, and pig iron, excluding any item for which less than 20 percent of the 1958 new supply came from imports. A score was assigned to each nation according to the number of items that were imported from the nation in 1958, weighting items double where the nation supplied more than 50 percent of U.S. imports. Most scores are between 0 and 5 with Canada having the upper extreme of 21. U.S. Office of Civil and Defense Mobilization, *Stockpile Report to the Congress, January-June 1958* (1958); U.S. Bureau of Foreign Commerce, *Contribution of Imports to U.S. Raw Materials Supplies, 1958* (World Trade Information Service, Part 3, No. 59-51, 1959).

4. Amount of U.S. Private Investment, 1957. Values are national totals of the book values of direct private investments owned by American residents or organizations, taken from U.S. Office of Business Economics, *U.S. Business Investments in Foreign Countries* (Supplement to the *Survey of Current Business*, 1960). Book values clearly understate the true worth of the enterprise to its owners, but better figures over such a large range are not available. Because values for the Middle East are not reported by country, the total was allocated according to the total amount of energy consumed in each country. The margin for error is probably not sufficient to affect our conclusions.

5. Proportion of U.S. Trade, based on import and export figures for 1964 and 1965 combined. International Monetary Fund, *Direction of Trade: A Supplement to International Financial Statistics Annual 1962-1966* (Washington: I.M.F., 1967), pp. 348-350.

6. Region. Countries were grouped according to the five-region classification by the U.S. Department of State, *United States Foreign Policy 1972: A Report of the Secretary of State* (Department of State Publication 8699, April 1973).

7. Political Stability, 1948 to 1967. The indicator is the total number of "armed attacks" recorded for the period, defined as "an act of violent political conflict carried out by an organized group with the object of weakening or destroying the power exercised by another organized group." Government forces, including metropolitan forces in a colony, may be either actor or target. Excluded are attacks by foreign groups and non-violent protest. Original sources are the *New York Times Index* supplemented by area-specific periodicals. Charles L. Taylor and Michael C. Hudson, *World Handbook of Political and Social Indicators* (2nd ed.; New Haven: Yale University Press, 1972), Table 3.3.

8. 1965 Gross National Product, 1965 Population, and "Strength" were all taken from *World Handbook* (machine version). The 28 stronger nations include the Soviet Union and its Warsaw Pact allies, Mongolia, and every other nation

whose total 1965 defense expenditure was greater than $1 billion or whose 1965 GNP per capita exceeded $1,000. Thus they include most of northern and western Europe, Canada, Australia, New Zealand, Israel, Kuwait, and China. An intervention was recorded for China, which under these arrangements must be explained by special conditions.

8

The Theory of International Exploitation in Large Natural Resource Investments

Theodore H. Moran
The Brookings Institution

The performance of a foreign-dominated primary export sector has frequently determined the possibilities for broad national development in Third World countries. One might assume, therefore, that host governments in developing countries would want to have that sector generate as many returns as possible to be used for domestic growth and welfare.

Most natural resource industries—such as copper, petroleum, natural gas, bauxite, iron ore—are oligopolies with large barriers to the entry of competition, a wide spread between selling price and marginal cost, and an ability to generate substantial (quasi-)rents. The bargaining efforts of the host government will determine the absolute level of industry operations within the country and also how the rents are divided between the host country and the foreign investor.

Why would a government not use all the bargaining strength it had—pulling, pushing, and shoving—to get as much as possible from the foreign-dominated sector?

One reason could be because of ignorance and error. A government might not know what range of strategies might be appropriate in the game of mutual dependence played by foreigner and host. Consequently, it might choose a strategy that was not at all effective in the effort to maximize the absolute level of returns to the country in the long or the short run.

A second reason could be that the government is trading favorable treatment for the foreign companies for something else clearly in the national interest. Thus benefits potentially derivable from the foreign-dominated primary export sector would show up instead in the form of some other obvious public good. (Certainly there could be disagreement about whether the "something else" were in fact a public good, or merely a payoff to particular interests within the country. As will become clear, however, I do not think that in the case of negotiating or renegotiating large concession agreements at periodic intervals this presents a serious analytical problem.)

In other cases there could be a third explanation. Domestic groups that have a large influence on the determination of policy toward foreign investors in the natural resource sector might want to use payoffs to the foreigners—i.e., not pushing as hard as they know they could, or pulling more generously than they have to—in order to receive some side benefit that serves their own individual interests.

What is to be explained, then, are deviations that are not attributable to ignorance or error but that are nonetheless deviations from the way a host government would behave if it used its available strength in an attempt to maximize the direct or indirect benefits to the country from a foreign-controlled primary export sector. To arrive at such an explanation in any particular case, it is necessary to go beneath the state-centric model of a "host country" and look at policy toward foreign companies as the outcome of the interplay of domestic groups trying to maximize their own particular interests as well as the larger national interest.

This chapter will define "exploitation" as an outcome in which the national interest is not being maximized because actors crucial to the decision-making process are using payoffs to foreign investors to advance their own private good.[1] Exploitation in this model, then, does not exist without "complicity" on the part of domestic elites. Exploitation may include specific pressures or bribes from foreign groups, but it need not. This model explicitly does not identify asymmetry of power *per se* between host countries and foreign investors as a basis for "exploitation," but rather only the refusal of domestic elites to act in the national interest to the extent that they have the power to do so. As will be seen, the history of the evolution of large natural resource concession agreements suggests that there are abrupt shifts in the relative balance of power between host countries and foreign companies and that both can take advantage of the asymmetries of power.

How does one reconstruct how much strength a host country could exercise at a point in time? How does one test for "deviations" from the use of power?

Most analysts who try to estimate how the economic rent from a primary export sector might be generated and divided between investor and government use a model of bilateral monopoly and/or game theory. If not used carefully, however, these have dangerous static assumptions when made to represent the relations between a host country and foreign investors. This chapter will argue that the balance of power between host governments and large natural resource investors goes along a thoroughly predictable course—that is to say, there is a clear evolution in the strength of the host country's position that it could use in pulling, pushing, and shoving against the foreign companies if it wanted to try to maximize its returns from the industry.

This chapter will develop a framework for tracing the evolution of the balance of power between host countries and foreign investors in large natural resource concessions in general and then illustrate its use as a tool in identifying, measuring, and examining the causes of exploitation in the history of the copper industry in Chile.

On the one hand, since this model is based on recreating the options open to policy-makers within the horizons of domestic knowledge and experience available at each stage of their relations with foreign companies, it should best not be used to suggest that "exploitation," even when rigorously defined, has a unique value. Rather, it can be shown to have a range of more and less probable values.

But, on the other hand, the evidence of "complicity" and "exploitation" turns out in the Chilean case—and, I suspect, would turn out in other histories of large natural resource investment—to be clearly identifiable and measurable.

I

To test for deviations from the pursuit of maximum gains from a foreign-dominated primary export sector, one must begin from some model of what powers the host government could exercise if it were so inclined. The most familiar frameworks for conceptualizing how foreign investors and host countries could pursue their interests in their relations with each other rely on game theory and bargaining models (especially bilateral monopoly models).[2]

The foreign investor has resources, skills, experience, access to markets and finance that the country needs to develop its resource base. The country has the ore bodies, the labor force, and control over taxation that can be mixed in some proportion to produce an attractive opportunity to the investor. The terms under which a foreign investor will be allowed to enter the country, then, constitute a problem in joint-maximization.

As both the foreign investor and the host government try to increase their returns from the industry, each side has threats to make and benefits to offer. This is not a zero-sum game since the absolute level of returns is a function of the relative shares. Some kinds of collaborative strategies can increase the size of the pie to be divided and increase the absolute returns to all parties.

In the Chilean case, this kind of explicit bargaining did characterize relations between Anaconda and Kennecott and the host government in each of three times that major new corporate commitments were sought after 1945—just after the Second World War in 1947-48, with the passage of the country's basic mining legislation (the *Nuevo Trato*) in 1955, and at the time of Chileanization beginning in 1964. In each instance, however, the foreign companies were at a temporary peak point in a steadily declining balance of power vis-à-vis the host country.

The use of the bilateral monopoly model or the game theory approach is not dynamic enough to show underlying trends or cycles in bargaining strength.[3] To understand how a host government or a foreign investor can use its strength to pursue its own advantage over time, one must first add considerations about the role of uncertainty in the investment process.[4]

Uncertainty plays a large role in determining the terms for development of the first large natural resource projects in an underdeveloped country. Despite costly surveys and feasibilities studies, the initial foreign investors are faced with a decision to sink a large amount of capital with substantial risk of failure before they can gain much reliable information about the structure of production costs. The host government is typically even less qualified to judge the risk of failure than the foreign investors and must accept the worst estimates. The foreigners enjoy near-monopoly control over the capacity to find a potential orebody and bring it on-line. Since the host government cannot itself duplicate the foreigners' skills, its only alternative would be to try to replace one set of foreigners with others from the same industry at broadly similar costs. Thus the conditions under which the first foreign companies will agree to invest will reflect both their monopoly control of skills and a heavy premium for uncertainty. They can credibly threaten not to invest at all unless they are allowed to bring the full power of their position to bear on the initial terms, and they generally try to freeze those terms to reflect their moment of peak strength vis-à-vis the host country for 20, 40, or even 99 years. If an investment is made and the operation is not a success, other ventures will require the same or greater enticements.

But once an investment is made and the operation is a success, the whole atmosphere that surrounds the bargaining situation begins to change. The old doubts can be forgotten. A gamble with large risks has been won, and a host government that is looking out for its own interests is unlikely to want to keep paying a premium that reflects those risks for long. An uncertain investment in a natural resource industry has frequently been turned into a bonanza. With the investment sunk and successful, the host government is in a position to bring pressure for renegotiation.

At the same time that the first mines are successfully opened, uncertainty about the existence of orebodies and about the structure of production costs has been reduced for subsequent investors. The government can drive a tougher bargain with later entrants, and this in turn increases the leverage in demanding revision of the original concessions to be in line with the later agreements.

In short, with the reduction of uncertainty the bargaining strength inevitably shifts from the foreigners toward the host government. The latter finds itself with the power to force "renegotiations," "adjustments," "surtaxes," "back taxes," "recomputations," and so forth to reflect this shift in the balance of power. One test of the shift in bargain power is provided by examining the extreme counter-examples: those governments such as Iran, after the overthrow of Mossadeq in 1951, and Venezuela, after the overthrow of Betancourt in 1950, that were most effectively manipulated by foreign corporations.

After Mossadeq was ousted, a new agreement was negotiated with the Anglo-Iranian Oil Consortium. But state revenues from the petroleum sector have not stopped rising, nor have domestic pressures allowed them even to remain level, for any two-year period since the beginning of the new agreement in 1954—no matter what was happening to final demand! The profit split between the Iranian government and the Consortium climbed from 68 to 32 percent in 1954 to about 80 to 20 percent by 1970.

In Venezuela, even the dictator Pérez Jiménez, who overthrew the more nationalistic Rómulo Betancourt with the promise of helping the foreign oil companies, found that he needed ever more revenues to finance urban construction and industrial growth. He provoked a major crisis in the international petroleum industry in 1956 by recalling options and auctioning off large concessions to new companies more willing than the old ones to expand production. He and successor governments pushed the host country share of petroleum revenues from about 51 percent in 1950 to more than 70 percent in the 1960s with a national commitment to "sow the petroleum" for development.[5]

Empirically, since the end of the Second World War, few successful concession agreements in developing countries—in ferrous and non-ferrous metals, petroleum, sulphur, and natural gas—have remained long unaltered.[6] In mining and drilling industries where investment for new production or processing facilities must come in large discrete lumps, the shifts in bargaining power are repeated before and after each new major corporate commitment. Before the investment for new production capacity, a new smelter, or a new refinery is made, the relative weight of bargaining strength tilts in favor of the foreign investor; after the operation has proven successful, it begins to tilt back toward the host country. A schematic representation of this changing balance of power between foreign investors and the host government can be seen in Figure 8-1.

II

A model of the balance of power between the host country and foreign natural resource investors would be incomplete, however, if uncertainty were the only independent variable. The experience of most developing countries with rich natural resource endowments requires introducing the idea of a learning curve for the host country.[7]

A country with no history of mineral or petroleum exports has had no occasion to build up a bureaucracy with skill in analyzing proposals made by such industries. In many cases, host governments are not initially familiar enough with transnational corporate accounting, with international tax provisions, or with terms of concessions in other countries to make a negotiation process very meaningful. The possibility of earning foreign revenues from unknown mineral deposits may appear as a windfall, and primitive forms of tax collection—often royalty payments—have frequently been the reward collected by governments ill-equipped to monitor an income tax.

Successful ventures, however, provide an incentive for a host country to develop a bureaucracy with skills and expertise appropriate to the industry. From a very low position, a country moves up a learning curve, often by trial and error, in analyzing proposals, overseeing corporate behavior, acquiring knowledge about the dynamics of the industry.

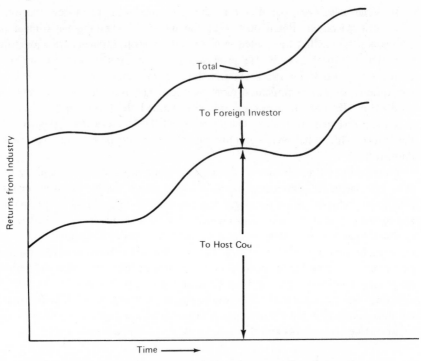

Note: since returns are a function of final market prices, the curves will not be smooth.

Figure 8-1. The Sharing of Benefits of Foreign Investment: The Basic Model

In Chile, the great risks that Anaconda and Kennecott took in the early twentieth century to develop huge mines in the midst of the Atacama desert and the Andes mountains were combined with the ignorance and inexperience of Chile to produce concessions that entailed almost no taxes or other obligations from the companies.[8] From 1913 to 1924, for example, Kennecott's subsidiary, Braden, paid less than 1 percent of the value of gross sales in taxes, and many Chilean argued that the provision of employment alone was sufficient contribution to expect from the foreigner. Chilean governments had no clear idea of how profitable the early operations of the U.S. corporations were or how much additional tax burden they might be made to bear. Consequently the first readjustments of the original concession agreements were very slow and cautious. With Anaconda's and Kennecott's two great mines (Chuquicamata and

El Teniente) successfully on-line in the 1920s and a third (Anaconda's Potreril-los) about to come into production, the reformist government of Arturo Alessandri made the first movement in 1925 to increase the country's share of copper earnings through a daring income tax of 6 percent and the imposition of social legislation covering copper workers.

Further attempts to tighten the original treatment of the foreign companies came in response to domestic crises in Chile that required additional revenues; such measures included a jump in tax rate during the depression, another after the terrible earthquake of 1938, and an excess profits tax during World War II. Chilean legislators felt that the foreign investors with their huge operations should be forced to share more of their income with the host country. They tried imposing more taxes and found, by trial and error, that the companies stayed and bore the heavier burden quite easily. Until well after the Second World War, however, no Chilean administration, no Chilean legislator, or no Chilean state agency had any sure idea how high the companies' profit rates were on Chilean operations, nor did they have more than the vaguest notions of how the country's agreements with Anaconda and Kennecott compared with alternative mining opportunities in Latin America, Africa, or the United States.

With the hopes and demands generated by social mobilization, urbanization, and industrialization during the war, however, Chile, like other countries in Latin America and post-colonial Africa and Asia, realized the need to try to maximize returns from the primary export sector. Relations with the foreign copper companies began to take on a character of explicit confrontation and negotiations with a national resolve to build up a bargaining capacity vis-à-vis the foreigners. A domestic bureaucracy was created to oversee behavior in the industry. Experts were trained in transnational accounting and international tax. Finally, more and more Chileans were required in the ranks of management, and government representatives were required to be invited to observe arrangements for international purchasing, international marketing, and international finance. As a host country like Chile chips away at ignorance and secrecy, the esoteric value of the foreigners' services decline. There is a cumulative shift in power away from the international corporations toward the host country. (In most natural resource industries the increase in domestic skills has coincided since the end of the Second World War with an increased capacity to hire independent consultants and technicians to strengthen the host country position.)

Consequently, as the host country moves up a learning curve of bargaining skills and operating experience, its relations with foreign investors in the industry do not merely swing back and forth. Rather, the balance of power looks more like the schematic representation in Figure 8-2.

Without the introduction of the idea of short-run swings in the balance of power between foreign investors and the host country and a long-run cumulative shift in the balance of power toward the latter, the conventional use of game theory and bargaining models misrepresents the behavior of the host country

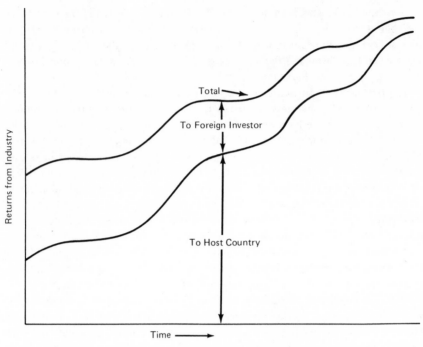

Note: since returns are a function of final market prices, the curves will not be smooth.

Figure 8-2. The Sharing of Benefits of Foreign Investment: The Revised Model

and largely conceals the possibility of testing for exploitation. It freezes examination of host country-foreign investor relations at only those points where the foreign investor is in the strongest bargaining position—namely, where large explicit new commitments are made and formal bargains are struck. But the instances where host governments give full and formal consent to the terms of a new bargain are precisely at the points where the country is yielding, of necessity, to the terms of an adversary at his strongest—just as the instances of "readjustment" in formal agreements and the cumulative tightening of all agreements reflect a process in which foreign investors have to yield, of necessity, to terms of an adversary gaining strength.

Within the conventional joint-maximizing framework, only the foreign corporations are portrayed as acting "rationally" (and "morally") with proper respect for sanctity of contract, while host countries suffer from "spurts" or "waves" of economic nationalism in which they act irrationally, emotionally, and "irresponsibly"—that is, they break contract.

In fact, joint-maximization is a process of on-going mutual adjustments in which foreign investors act in accord with their best interests when they are in the strongest position and accede to necessity when they are weak and exposed, while host governments accede to necessity when they are weak and act in accord with their best interests as they gain strength.

There is no mystery why foreign investors respect contracts that are invariably written heavily in their favor. There should be no mystery why host governments may try to "readjust" contracts, when possible, in their own favor. The so-called bursts or waves of emotion and economic nationalism are no less "rational" ways of testing the strength of the country's bargaining position than the formal contract with the ritual 20-40-99-year guarantee of "inviolability" are a way of celebrating the foreign investors' moments of strength.

What does demand explanation is why a host country diverges from this path reflecting its accumulated bargaining power. Why does a government deviate from acting in its own rational self-interest, if such deviation is clearly not attributable to ignorance or error? Obviously there is no single strategy that an objective observer could say, even in retrospect, a host country should have adopted at any particular point in time. What needs to be explained, however, is the behavior of governments that refuse to test their changing strengths at all, either after a new investment has turned out to be highly successful or in the process of negotiating the new investment itself.

To attempt such a task, it is necessary to discard the abstraction called the "host country" or "host government" and look at the interplay of domestic political and economic interests in the determination of policy toward the foreign investors.

There were three major renegotiations of policy toward the large U.S. copper companies in Chile from the end of the Second World War until their nationalization. The most important of these occurred in 1954-55 when the country's basic mining legislation, called the *Nuevo Trato*, was written.[9]

The examination of the creation of the *Nuevo Trato* shows that in Chile, as elsewhere, one can make clear tests for "exploitation," show that it is empirically identifiable, and make quantified measurements of its cost to the country.

III

From the beginning of the Second World War through the end of the Korean War, successive Chilean administrations, headed by non-Communist, center-left, radical presidents, pushed hard against Anaconda and Kennecott by raising the effective tax rate to near 80 percent and finally establishing a national sales monopoly for all domestic copper output to be sold at prices determined by the Chilean Central Bank.[10]

In contrast to other areas of the world, however, Chilean output was not expanded during the Korean War and the Chilean share of the world market declined from 16 percent in 1951 to 14.6 percent in 1954. Domestic attempts to hold up the price of copper after the Korean War were not successful, and national inventories were growing. To top off these problems, Anaconda announced that its second largest mine, Potrerillos, was becoming depleted and would have to be shut down in the near future. Chilean sources, public or private, could not replace the output.

The balance of power between the copper companies and the host country which since the last major expansion by Anaconda in 1947-48 had been rising steadily in the country's favor, had shifted. All sectors of Chilean society, including Marxist and non-Marxist left, conceded that some sort of new bargain would have to be struck.[11]

What did both sides want? Chile wanted a flood of new investment—to increase production by a substantial amount and to regain and maintain its former share of the world market. The country needed to entice the foreign companies to develop a new mine, or new mines, to replace the almost exhausted Potrerillos. Chile wanted refining capacity, especially electrolytic refining capacity, to serve the growing needs of the European market. To achieve these goals, the government was willing to dissolve the state sales monopoly, and Congress was prepared to rewrite the country's basic mining code to make it more attractive.

The companies, for their part, wanted the elimination of implicit taxation through an artificial exchange rate and the consolidation of all taxes into an income tax—in order to gain the full benefit of the U.S. Foreign Tax Credit. (The U.S. Foreign Tax Credit relieves a U.S. corporation of its U.S. tax liability on earnings remitted from abroad for foreign taxes up to the U.S. rate [then 47 percent].) They wanted the total tax burden to be lowered. They wanted a special accelerated depreciation rate for new investments, plus liberal expensing regulations for mine development in the accounting procedures. And the companies wanted to be given back control of sales and prices from the Chilean state monopoly.

But the atmosphere that surrounded the writing of the *Nuevo Trato* hardly gave the impression of hard bargaining. The country's behavior departed clearly and significantly from any reasonable interpretation of the national interest, from any reasonable approximation of the curve of relative power with the companies that had been sketched before the Second World War or would be continued after the repudiation of the *Nuevo Trato* in the early 1960s.

The key to the 1954-55 Chilean legislation was the "automatic stimulus" of the "good investment climate"—that is, private enterprise by nature seeks profit, it was argued,[12] and if profit rates could be made higher than alternatives elsewhere, the companies would automatically invest to expand operation and increase production: if tax rates could be made attractive enough, depreciation rapid enough, importation and expensing rights generous enough, the foreign corporations would naturally respond to these stimuli with higher output, new mines, and new refineries.

In accord with this philosophy of laissez-faire—and against the objections of many economists, *técnicos*, and business experts—the new mining legislation was written to give Anaconda and Kennecott literally all the concessions on their shopping list and demand no specific commitments in return. The final legislation let go unchallenged Anaconda's suggestion that it be allowed to depreciate its major new copper mine, El Salvador, in the first five years. This made the new mine show losses (which were allowed to be carried forward) and not begin to pay substantial income taxes until 1966.

The result was that Anaconda did build a new mine (although not a new refinery) to replace Potrerillos. But the company did not expand capacity at its largest mine, Chuquicamata. And Kennecott did not expand mining capacity nor build refining capacity at all. In fact, Kennecott used its substantially higher profit remittances from Chile to build a refinery precisely to refine Chilean copper for export to Europe—in Maryland![13] The practical effect of the *Nuevo Trato* mining legislation was to turn Chile into a capital exporter to finance the vertical integration and diversification of the multinational copper companies outside of Chile.[14]

What is to be explained, then, is why Chile gave away so much and asked so little in return? Why did the *Nuevo Trato* depart so clearly from the "normal" pattern of negotiation and renegotiation?

The answer is not to be sought in ignorance; although the legislators probably would not have written the *Nuevo Trato* exactly as they did if they had known just how disastrous the results would be. Many of the most influential leaders in the Congress agreed with the *técnicos* and economists that the philosophy of "automatic stimulus" was largely rhetoric.[15] They had learned, since the Second World War, that they had to work closely and precisely with the foreign companies if they wanted to achieve their goals in pricing, marketing, and investment.

The answer lies in the specific interests of center and right wing political and business groups—that is, the conviction that the *Nuevo Trato* was crucial as a model in their counterattack against state intervention in the Chilean economy. The industrial base built up during and after the Second World War was threatened by increasing controls as the "structuralist" viewpoint on inflation and domestic development gained prominence.[16] There was a threat of agrarian reform because landholding groups, which included most of the prominent families in Chile, allegedly did not respond to profit incentives.

In reaction to this, the liberal and conservative parties, and many non-political business interest groups, were mounting a campaign to move the new

President (General) Carlos Ibáñez to the right, away from his agrarian-labor Peronist predilections, away from the structuralist position, and away from selective credit controls, selective price controls, land reform, and the creation of state enterprises.

Jorge Alessandri, president of the Confederation of Production and Commerce (Chile's largest business organization) and later conservative President of Chile, and Senator Hernan Videla Lira, powerful figure in the liberal party, were leaders in establishing the theme of the domestic debates—that is, Chilean businessmen and landowners should support the *Nuevo Trato* for the foreign copper companies as part of their own struggle in national politics and should identify their interest in higher profits and fewer controls with the dynamics that would best serve Chile in its relations with Anaconda and Kennecott.[17] *El Diario Ilustrado*, the influential newspaper representing the views of the conservative party, supported the *Nuevo Trato* with the same line of argument: the new mining legislation certainly would help Chile, the editors claimed, by giving guarantees to the foreign copper companies with the idea that they would expand production. But even more important than this, the editors concluded, the mining law would be a good model (*"buena orientación"*) for public opinion. The emphasis that the *Nuevo Trato* gave to freedom and security for private enterprise pointed a true path to the solution of Chile's major domestic problems.[18]

Similar reflections on the profit motive as an incentive and the value of the *Nuevo Trato* as an example for domestic policy were expressed by presidents of the Chilean Chamber of Commerce, the National Association of Manufacturers, and the Institute of Mining Engineers.[19] Popular conservative associations like the Rotary Club de Santiago were treated to special speeches of support for the principle of the *Nuevo Trato* legislation.

The use of policy toward the foreign copper companies to serve their particular domestic interests rather than the broader national interest meant that the liberal and conservative parties, and major segments of the Confederation of Production and Commerce, acted with complicity in the exploitation of their own country.

IV

Just as an impartial analyst can look at any point on a curve representing the balance of power between the host country and foreign investors and ask if there is a clear deviation from the range of strategies that the government might be pursuing if it were using its full bargaining power in the national interest, so he can also reconstruct hypothetical alternatives to the host country's behavior and estimate the amount or the cost of the deviation. The result is a measurement of the "exploitation."

In explaining such a deviation, the idea of a learning curve helped the analyst to separate ignorance and error from complicity. In measuring the extent of the "exploitation," the idea of a learning curve helps the analyst to use the country's accumulated experience from the past to estimate what kinds of bargains might realistically have been struck.[20]

Let us say, for example—as seems clear from the evidence[21]—that the most important leaders of the Chilean Senate, the most important *técnicos* in the Ministry of Mining of the Ibáñez administration, and the most important directors of the National Mining Society did learn from the experience of 1950-53 that the national interest was best served by returning control over pricing and marketing back to the copper companies, that the national interest was best served by eliminating the implicit tax and consolidating it into a single income tax (to allow the companies the benefit of the U.S. Foreign Tax Credit while costing Chile nothing), and that the national interest would require making some real concessions in tax burden in a bargain for new mining and refinery capacity.

Let us also hypothesize, however, that the men who were crucial to the direct determination of copper policy in 1954-55 were not yet as sophisticated in accounting as their counterparts would become by 1964 and could be hoodwinked about allowing expensing rather than capitalizing mine development and about allowing a super-accelerated depreciation schedule. The evidence supports this assumption as well.[22]

Then let us bracket the campaign of the liberal and conservative parties and the Confederation of Production and Commerce to make the *Nuevo Trato* into a model for their own interests, and reconstruct what the negotiations might have looked like without it.

First, we must ignore the rhetoric in Congress about increasing production to 1 million metric tons annually or about boosting the Chilean share of the world market to 23 percent (its 1945 level) as a result of these negotiations. There is no realistic set of assumptions about corporate behavior that would justify such expectations.

Second, we should make a cautious reconstruction of what the companies would have required to make new commitments. It appears that return of control over sales and pricing and reconstitution of the tax structure were *sine qua non* for beginning any negotiations. Then, with regard to the exchange of tax benefits for new investments, the most conservative assumptions would be the following: that Anaconda could under no conditions have been persuaded to do more than replace the depleted Potrerillos mine with El Salvador—due to pressure from its stockholders and creditors—and that neither Anaconda nor Kennecott could have been persuaded to build any new electrolytic refining capacity in Chile. (These assumptions are probably too pessimistic.)

There follow then three possible bargains, all involving Kennecott, that might have been struck.

1. A doubling of production capacity at El Teniente (from 160 to 320

thousand metric tons per year), or the development of a new mine, in return for a tax reduction from 80 percent to the lowest possible level feasible under the U.S. Foreign Tax Credit, namely 47 percent. This would have produced $324 million in tax revenue for Chile from 1955 to 1960 instead of the $225 actually paid, meaning that the cost of not pursuing this alternative amounted to $99 million in the first five years.[23] It does not appear in retrospect that this was a very likely negotiating outcome, however, simply because there were never any concrete indications that Kennecott could double capacity—although the possibility was talked about in the Congressional hearings on the *Nuevo Trato* as if it existed.

2. An increase of production capacity at El Teniente from 160 thousand metric tons to 280 thousand metric tons per year in return for cutting the tax rate from 80 percent to 65 percent. Kennecott in fact developed plans in the latter part of the 1950s for just such a project (the Codegua Project).[24] This hypothetical outcome is quite reasonable and would have produced $369 million in taxes in the first five years and given a value of $144 million to this alternative.

3. An increase of production capacity at El Teniente to 280 thousand tons per year in return for cutting the tax rate to the lowest possible level feasible under the U.S. Foreign Tax Credit (47 percent). This would have produced $266 million in total revenues from 1955 to 1960 and given it a value of $41 million. This appears to be the very least Chile could have gotten from Kennecott if the company had been willing to negotiate at all.

What if Kennecott had simply refused to bring any new corporate resources to Chile?

1. Chile simply could have left the tax level on Kennecott where it was (about 80 percent). This would have produced $259 million over the first five years, or a gain of $34 million.

2. Chile could have raised the tax level on Kennecott to 90 percent as a punishment to the company for refusing to enter into any negotiations. This would have produced $292 in tax revenues, or a gain of $67 million.

It is hard to see how these two actions would have hurt Chile. Even at a 90 percent tax rate, Kennecott would still have been earning about 7 percent on the capital invested in Chile. And the alternative to collecting this 7 percent was zero, which meant that the company would be unlikely simply to shut down and leave.

Thus, in a period when Chile badly needed foreign exchange revenues for its own growth and welfare, the country lost at least $34 million to $44 million (and probably much more) in a five-year period alone due to the complicity of some of its conservative business groups in the exploitation of their own country.

V

This chapter has offered a model of the evolution of the balance of power between host countries and foreign investors in large natural resource concessions. The model predicts changing tilts in the balance of power as a function of shifts in the perception of uncertainty and predicts a cumulative shift in the balance of power toward the host country as the country moves up a learning curve of negotiating skills and operating experience in the industry. This provides a dynamic underpinning for conventional joint-maximization approaches to analyzing foreign investor-host country relations.

The chapter then offered a definition of exploitation—the trading of a policy that advances the national interest for a policy that advances the interests only (or primarily) of specific domestic groups—based on this balance of power model. The Chilean case showed that such a definition of exploitation can be clearly operationalized, unambiguously identified, and quantitatively measured.

The explanation for complicity in exploitation in any specific instance must be discovered from examining the struggle of domestic groups over the formulation of policy toward foreign investors in that historical setting. Perhaps, after studies have been made of many such instances, a pattern or sequence will emerge. But, in any case, this study suggests that economic nationalism must be seen not as an "emotional wave" or "outburst of sentiment," but rather as a movement that rationally seeks to turn a prominent foreign investment into a genuine transfer of technology, to chip away at the foreigners' monopoly of skills and experience, and to right the initial asymmetries of power that exist between the foreign investor and the host country.

Notes

1. Preliminary suggestions in favor of this definition of "exploitation" were developed by Edith Penrose, "Profit Sharing Between Producing Countries and Oil Companies in the Middle East," *Economic Journal*, June 1958, pp. 238-254, and *New Orientations: Essays in International Relations* (New York: Humanities Press, 1970).

For other attempts to pierce beneath a state-centric model to study the politics of policy formation, see Graham Allison, *Essence of Decision* (New York: Little, Brown, 1971).

2. Cf. George Stigler, *The Theory of Price* (New York: Macmillan, 1961); Thomas Shelling, *The Strategy of Conflict* (London: Oxford University Press, 1963); Charles Kindleberger, *Economic Development* (New York: McGraw-Hill, 1965, second edition) and *American Business Abroad* (New Haven: Yale

University Press, 1969); and Raymond Mikesell, ed., *Foreign Investment in the Petroleum and Mineral Industries: Case Studies in Investor-Host Country Relations* (Baltimore: The Johns Hopkins Press, Resources for the Future, 1971).

3. Also, to the static tendencies of most bargaining models are frequently added, without justification, the implicit moral and legal assumptions of contract theory: once a bargain is struck, it must be honored because it represents a contract between freely consenting individuals. Contract theory has traditionally been criticized because it overlooks inequalities of power at the moment of making the bargain—as long as one of the parties has not been put under obvious physical duress by the other—and refuses to recognize subsequent changes in the balance of power as justification for invalidation or renegotiation. In many cases the same argument must be made about the uses to which bargaining models are put.

The so-called *"clausula rebus sic stantibus"* doctrine (this agreement is binding only so long as all surrounding conditions remained unchanged) has so far been applied only to international treaties.

On contract theory and the problems of foreign investor-host country relations, see Henry Steiner and Detlev Vagts, *Transnational Legal Problems: Materials and Text* (Mineola, New York: The Foundation Press, 1968); Kenneth Carlston, "Concession Agreements and Nationalization," *American Journal of International Law*, vol. 52, 1958, pp. 260-79; Simon Sikek, *The Legal Framework for Oil Concessions in the Arab World* (Beirut: Middle East Research and Publishing Center, 1960); and Oliver J. Lissitzyn, "Treaties and Changed Circumstances (Rebus Sic Stantibus)," *American Journal of International Law*, October, 1967, Vol. 61, No. 4, pp. 895-922.

4. Studies that incorporate the role of uncertainty in the evolution of bargaining relations include: Raymond Vernon, "Long-Run Trends in Concession Contracts," *Proceedings of the American Society for International Law*, April 1967, pp. 81-90, and *Sovereignty at Bay: The Multinational Spread of U.S. Enterprises* (New York: Basic Books, 1971); Louis T. Wells, Jr., "The Evolution of Concession Agreements in Developing Countries," Harvard Development Advisory Service, mimeo., March 29, 1971. This particular model of the evolution of the balance of power between foreign investors and host countries in large natural resource concessions has been developed in my "Politics of Economic Nationalism and the Evolution of Concession Agreements," *Proceedings of the American Society for International Law*, September 1972, and in "The Evolution of Concession Agreements in Underdeveloped Countries and the U.S. National Interest," study and testimony presented to the Senate Foreign Relations Committee subcommittee on multinational corporations, July 1973.

5. Cf. Raymond Mikesell, ed., *Foreign Investment in the Petroleum and Mineral Industries: Case Studies in Investor-Host Country Relations*, op. cit.; Edwin Lieuwen, *Petroleum in Venezuela: A History* (Berkeley: University of

California Press, 1954), and *Venezuela* (London: Oxford University Press, 1965); and Harvey O'Connor, *World Crisis in Oil* (New York: Monthly Review Press, 1962).

6. For case studies in these industries, see Edith Penrose, *The Large International Firm in Developing Countries* (London: Allen & Unwin, 1969); Michael Tanzer, *The Political Economy of International Oil and the Underdeveloped Countries* (Boston: Beacon Press, 1969); Raymond Mikesell, ed., *Foreign Investment in the Petroleum and Mineral Industries: Case Studies in Investor-Host Country Relations*, op. cit.; Robert Barnes, "International Oil Companies Confront Governments: A Half Century of Experience," *International Studies Quarterly*, Vol. 16, No. 4, December 1972, pp. 454-72; Miguel Wionczek, *El Nacionalismo Mexicano y la Inversión Extranjera* (Mexico: Siglo veintiuno editores, 1967); Zuhayr Mikdashi, *The Community of Oil Exporting Countries* (London: George Allen & Unwin, Resources for the Future, 1972); Raymond Vernon, "Long-Run Trends in Concession Contracts," op. cit., and *Sovereignty at Bay: The Multinational Spread of U.S. Enterprises*, op. cit.; and Louis T. Wells, Jr., "The Evolution of Concession Agreements in Developing Countries," op. cit.; and Theodore H. Moran, *Economic Nationalism and the Politics of International Dependence: The Case of Copper in Chile 1945-1973*, (Princeton: Princeton University Press, forthcoming, 1974).

7. For evidence from the petroleum, copper, tin, iron ore, bauxite, and sulphur industries, see the sources cited in footnote 6.

8. For the history of the copper industry in Chile, see Julio Kaulen, *Las Empresas Mineras Extranjeras en Chile y la Economía Nacional* (Santiago: 1916); Machiavello Varas, *El problema de la industria del cobre*, (Santiago: 1923); Aníbal Pinto, *Hacia nuestra independencia económica* (Santiago: Editorial del Pacífico, 1953) and *Chile: un caso de desarrollo frustrado* (Santiago: Editorial Universitaria, 1959); Marcos Mamalakis and Clark Reynolds, *Essays on the Chilean Economy* (Homewood, Illinois: Richard D. Irwin, 1965); Raymond Mikesell, ed., *Foreign Investment in the Petroleum and Mineral Industries: Case Studies in Investor-Host Country Relations*, op. cit.; and Theodore H. Moran, *Economic Nationalism and the Politics of International Dependence: The Case of Copper in Chile 1945-1973*, op. cit.

9. For background to the *Nuevo Trato*, see *Historia de la ley 11.828*, 1954-55 (three volumes of Chilean Congressional hearings on the revision of the basic mining legislation); Aníbal Pinto, *Hacia nuestra independencia económica*, op. cit., and *Chile: un caso de desarrollo frustrado*, op. cit.; Mario Vera Valenzuela, *La política económica del cobre en Chile* (Santiago: Universidad de Chile, 1961).

10. Kennecott's return on investment in 1950 with an effective tax rate of 78 percent was still 29.7 percent. Anaconda's return with an effective tax rate above 70 percent in 1950 was between 8 percent and 24 percent depending upon whether one accepts the Chilean government figures on net worth, or various versions claimed by the company.

All figures come from the official statistics of the Corporación del Cobre de Chile but do not differ significantly from the statistics recorded in the annual reports of the Chilean subsidiaries of the U.S. companies, unless specified otherwise.

11. Interviews with leaders of the Chilean Socialist party confirmed that, despite the rhetoric of nationalization in the mid-1950s, the most important Socialist officials concerned with mining realized that a deal with the foreign companies was the only way to increase production and keep the industry running. For an analysis of the positions of domestic groups across the Chilean political spectrum, see Moran, *Economic Nationalism and the Politics of International Dependence: The Case of Copper in Chile 1945-1973*, op. cit.

12. *Historia de la ley 11.828*, op. cit.; analyses of the strategy for constructing the new basic mining legislation were also contained in the journal of business and economics, *Panorama Económico*, September 24, 1954, May 27, 1955, August 5, 1955, October 8, 1955, October 27, 1955, and November 25, 1955.

13. *Annual Report*, Kennecott, 1956.

14. In brief, there were three reasons why the model of *estímulos autmáticos* did not work when applied to the international copper companies. First, for large natural resource companies sitting on reserves far greater than needed to service projected demand, it was unlikely that a reduction of income taxes alone would automatically bring forth an increase in production, especially if that might bring oligopolistic retaliation. Second, stock holders and creditors were putting pressure on Anaconda and Kennecott to make any production increases that were planned take place outside of Chile, to create a more diversified geographical base for the companies. Third, most of the members of the international copper producers' oligopoly had strong internal pressures to use available funds for vertical integration and diversification (especially into aluminum, where the cross-elasticity of substitution was very high). Cf. James L. McCarthy, "The American Copper Industry, 1947-1955," *Yale Economic Essays*, IV (Spring 1964); and Moran, *Economic Nationalism and the Politics of International Dependence: The Case of Copper in Chile 1945-1973*, op. cit., Chapter 3.

15. *Historia de la ley 11.828*, op. cit., passim; *Panorama Económico*, op. cit.

16. For a summary of the structuralist position in Chile, see (in addition to the works already cited by Aníbal Pinto): Albert Hirschman, *Journeys Toward Progress* (New York: Doubleday & Company, 1965); and Robert L. Ayres, "Economic Stagnation and the Emergence of the Political Ideology of Chilean Underdevelopment," *World Politics*, October 1972.

17. *Industria* (official publication of the National Manufacturers' Society), 1954-55; *Boletín Minero* (official publication of the National Mining Society), 1954-55; *Historia de la ley 11.828*, op. cit.

18. *El Diario Ilustrado*, May 4, 1955.

19. *Memoria* (official publication of the Santiago Chamber of Commerce), 1954; exposition of the new acting president of the *Sociedad de Fomento Fabril* (National Manufacturers' Society), Domingo Arteaga, *Industria*, July 1955; Hernán Elgueta Guerin, president of the National Association of Importers, *El Diario Ilustrado*, May 5, 1955; Institute of Mining Engineers, statement in *Industria*, February 1954. The speech of César Fuenzalida Correa to the Santiago Rotary Club was reported in *Boletín Minero*, January-June 1955.

20. On the testing of counterfactual propositions on historical data, see John R. Meyer and Alfred H. Conrad, "Economic Theory, Statistical Inference, and Economic History," *Journal of Economic History*, No. 17, December 1957; Robert W. Fogel, *The Railroad in American Economic Growth* (Baltimore: Johns Hopkins Press, 1964); Douglas C. North, *Growth and Welfare in the American Past* (Englewood Cliffs, New Jersey: Prentice Hall, 1966). On the simulation of alternative futures and alternative pasts, see William Greenberg and Hayward Alker, "The UN Charter: Alternate Pasts, Alternate Futures," in E.H. Fedder, ed., *The United Nations: Problems and Prospects* (St. Louis: University of Missouri, Center for International Studies, 1971).

21. *Historia de la ley 11.828*, op. cit.; *Boletín Minero*, op. cit.

22. *Historia de la ley 11.828*, op. cit.; *Historia de la ley 16.425* (three volumes of hearings by the Chilean Congress on the Chileanization program of President Eduardo Frei, 1964-66); Rául Sáez, *Chile y el Cobre* (Santiago: Departamento del Cobre, January, 1965).

23. For simplicity of presentation, these calculations assume that new production comes on-line immediately and that there is no discount rate on future earnings. Also, these calculations are based on an estimation of constant costs and no effect on final prices. There was actually some indication that average costs would fall with the Codegua Project. And a production increase the size of one mine for one company in a highly oligopolistic industry such as copper probably would not have a great effect on final prices.

24. Braden Copper Company (Chilean subsidiary of Kennecott), *Annual Reports*, 1958-1960.

9

Trade in Raw Materials: The Benefits of Capitalist Alliances

Stephen D. Krasner
Harvard University

Introduction

In a world governed by socialist principles and practices, things would not be what they are. Miners in Chile would be paid at the same rate as those in Sweden. The per capita distribution of income among states would be equalized. Even with conventional pricing mechanisms, patterns of demand would be radically altered. The international movement of goods would follow very different paths. This is not, however, a world we are likely to see. The leaders of less developed countries (LDCs) must deal with things as they are. They cannot change the basic structure of the world economy.

Less developed states are highly dependent on primary commodity exports. Table 9-1 summarizes the situation for sixty-nine countries in Africa, Asia, and Latin America in 1970.

The leaders of producing countries have three basic objectives in international commodity markets—higher returns, more stable prices, and greater market control. Higher international earnings provide resources to build support for the regime and satisfy popular demands for higher living standards. Stable prices make economic planning easier and eliminate political dissatisfaction generated by domestic income fluctuations. Greater market control satisfies desires to escape dependence on forces they cannot alter.

Given the parameters established by extant tastes, wealth, and resources the leaders of Third World countries are faced with difficult choices. They have not in the past been able to form effective producer-nation cartels, the institutional arrangement through which they can achieve all of their basic aims. If they do establish durable independent control, a step some petroleum exporting countries have begun to take, it will be because alliances with capitalist states or multinational corporations (MNCs) have given them the resources that make cooperative behavior possible. Consuming industrial nation governments have joined and enforced international commodity agreements that have compelled exporting states to cooperate with each other, as well as giving them higher and

Completion of this chapter was made possible by grants from the Center for International Affairs, Harvard University, and the Washington Center of Foreign Policy Research, Johns Hopkins University School of Advanced International Studies.

Table 9-1
Percentage of Export Earnings from Leading Commodity Export

	75-100%	50-74%	25-49%	0-24%
Number of Countries	13	18	29	9
Cumulative Percentage	19	45	87	100

Source: International Monetary Fund, *International Financial Statistics*, September 1970, (Washington, D.C.: 1970)

more stable prices. MNCs have erected oligopolistic structures that have provided a substantial revenue base that can be tapped by host country governments. Tacit or explicit ties, however, with companies or advanced states inevitably involve some loss of autonomy. Leaders of poorer states must sacrifice their symbolic aspirations to secure their economic ones.

Impediments to Cooperation among LDCs

Attempts to establish cartels are rarely successful. There is an inherent tension in any market restriction scheme between cheating and cooperation. With prices above competitive levels, any individual member of a collusive agreement can secure windfall profits, because some period of time will elapse before price cutting is discovered, and other members of the coalition abandon restrictive practices, or attempt to punish a miscreant. For exporting states, the short term benefits of competitive behavior have proven more attractive than the long term benefits of cooperation unless MNCs or consuming states have helped restrict the market. No group of producing countries has ever controlled an important raw material for more than a few months without the assistance of capitalist institutions.[1]

Collusion is facilitated by market concentration, inelastic demand, government support, shared values and experiences, and the ability to take a long run perspective. International commodity markets are characterized by some of these conditions. As Table 9-2 shows, the level of market concentration is substantial for several commodities. The price elasticity of demand for most raw materials is low. Collusion among exporting states has, however, been impeded by three fundamental problems—the inherent absence of a political enforcement mechanism, the lack of shared values and experiences, and most importantly, the inability to take a long term perspective.

Absence of Political Authority

The most effective way to guarantee adherence to a scheme for market restriction is to invoke the power of the state. When levels of production are

Table 9-2
Market Shares of the Four Largest LDC Producers

	Tin	Coffee	Cocoa	Sugar	Rubber	Tea	Petroleum	Iron Ore	Copper
Percent of World Production	70	49	58	14	30	36	32	11	25
Percent of World Exports	82	55	73	45	60	66	52	30	61

Sources and Explanation: Figures for sugar cocoa, tea, coffee and rubber from Food and Agriculture Organization of the United Nations, *Trade Yearbook, 1971* and Food and Agriculture Organization of the United Nations, *FAO Commodity Review and Outlook, 1971-72*; for petroleum from British Petroleum Corporation, *BP Statistical Review of the World Oil Industry, 1971* (London); for copper, tin and iron ore, Metal Bulletin Books Ltd., *Metal Bulletin Handbook, 1972* (London: 1972). All figures are for 1970. Values for rubber include synthetic rubber.

fixed by law, violators face confiscation, fine, or imprisonment. When they are not every member of a coalition will continually weigh the benefits of cheating against the costs.

Within national markets states have often intervened to limit the free movement of goods, but there is no political authority governing international trade. Exporting countries can agree upon production restrictions, but they have no legal or military instruments to enforce them. The durability of an arrangement depends upon economic judgments continually made by each member state.

Lack of Shared Values and Experiences

In making these judgments producing nation governments have in the past chosen policies that preclude durable collusion, first, because they have not had shared values and experiences and, second, because of their need to maximize short-term earnings. Shared experience increases perceived interdependence among potential members of a collusive arrangement. It increases the level of communication within an industry. Greater communication facilitates cooperation. Shared values provide a basis for agreement on what constitutes reasonable market shares and levels of return.[2]

The most significant arenas for increasing shared experience among exporting states have been created by capitalist states or multinational corporations.

Through international commodity agreements such as those for coffee, cocoa, and tin, representatives from less developed states have been brought together at regular intervals over an extended period. They have been forced to agree among themselves on allocating the burden of market control. The collusive practices of petroleum companies have provided an institutional structure within which oil exporting states have bargained jointly through the Organization of Petroleum Exporting Countries (OPEC). States producing commodities such as rubber whose markets have not been effectively organized by MNCs or consuming area governments have been able to do little more than share information.

None of these experiences exposes Third World states to all of the rigors of the mixed-sum game played by producers restricting the market without help from third party intermediaries. In commodity agreements, participation of consuming states mutes conflict because a disgruntled seller does not have the option of cheating. Corporations have assumed most of the burden of market control in extractive industries. The extensive interaction precipitated, however, through ties with MNCs or capitalist states may give exporting country governments the kind of shared experience they need to successfully intervene on their own in the future.

The absence of a set of shared values has also hindered cooperation in most commodity markets. Collusion requires agreement on individual market shares. Quotas can be based on existing levels of production or sales, economic need, population size, production costs or rates of growth.[3] If states do not weigh these criteria in the same way, satisfactory export allocations will elude them. The spill-over of political rivalries into commodity markets may also obstruct cooperation. Leaders who distrust each other for ideological or strategic reasons may find economic cooperation difficult.

Petroleum is the one raw material market in which these difficulties have at least temporarily been overcome. The anti-Israeli policy of Arab producers has facilitated the formulation of joint market restrictions. There is no equally compelling value shared by any other group of countries exporting the same commodity.

Inability to Take a Long Run Perspective

The most serious constraint on Third World countries attempting to control international markets is their inability to work with an extended time horizon. Cartels maximize returns for individual members only over the long term. Any coalition member can increase present returns by cheating. A producer that does not have the resources, either political or financial, to adopt an extended perspective will be an unreliable coalition member. If political survival requires maximizing short-run receipts, long-run income is meaningless.

Political underdevelopment is characterized by a level of resources inadequate to meet political demands. These resources take several forms of which wealth is not the least important. Third World countries have a smaller tax base than industrial nations, and their governments procure relatively less of this base than do those of wealthier areas. The percentage of national product accounted for by public expenditure is highly correlated with per capita income. While direct taxes are the most important source of income for rich states, poor ones are heavily dependent on levies on foreign commerce.[4]

As Table 9-3 indicates, the only group of producing countries to accumulate the kind of wealth that makes it possible to work with an extended time horizon are the petroleum exporters. The massive reserves held by several oil-rich states have left them in a position to virtually ignore current earnings. States producing other commodities do not enjoy a level of monetary resources that would free their leaders from concern about meeting short run demands.

With pressing demands and few resources decision-makers must place a high discount on future earnings. This increases the temptation to cheat on oligopolistic agreements. When the market is restricted a state can secure increases in its own receipts by shading prices. Political leaders may not be able to maximize gains over the long run because failure to satisfy immediate needs can result in their removal from office or even radical transformation of the state. Governments with pressing short-run needs for material resources will not be reliable participants in an oligopolistic agreement.

In summary, lack of shared values and experiences makes agreement difficult in the first place. The inability to take a long-run perspective makes cheating likely even if agreement is reached. The absence of political authority makes it difficult to detect and punish a cheater. Third World states are likely to secure the resources to overcome these impediments only through. alliances with corporations or industrial states. Even if independent market control proves illusive such alliances can raise and stabilize the earnings of exporting countries.

Table 9-3
Reserve Holdings of Primary Producers

	Tin	Coffee	Cocoa	Sugar	Rubber	Tea	Petroleum	Iron Ore	Copper
Number of Countries	5	12	6	5	4	2	10	6	4
Ratio of Reserves to Annual Imports	.48	.32	.29	.20	.44	.38	1.33	.16	.39

Sources and Explanation: All values are averages of the scores for major exporters of the designated commodity weighted by their level of production. Levels of production were taken from the United Nations, *Statistical Yearbook, 1971.* Whenever available 1970 figures were used. The ratio of reserves to imports for groups of commodity producing countries was derived from figures in International Monetary Fund, *International Financial Statistics, 1972 Supplement.*

Three Examples

Recent events in three international markets—coffee, cocoa, and petroleum—illustrate not only the difficulties exporting states have had when acting alone but also the benefits procured from alliances with capitalist institutions. Coffee-producing countries secured higher revenues from an international commodity agreement after having failed to organize the market through producer arrangements. The cocoa exporting states' attempt to control the market on their own ended in disaster. Multinational corporations have played a vital role in maintaining the oligopolistic structure of the world petroleum market and have provided Arab exporting states with resources that have made it possible for them to exercise independent market control.

Coffee

In terms of value, coffee has been the second or third most important commodity in international trade. It is the most important source of foreign exchange for fourteen states in Africa and Latin America. Coffee prices, which reached record levels in 1954, steadily declined until the early 1960s.

In December 1962, delegates from over fifty consuming and producing countries signed the International Coffee Agreement that established export quotas for the world market. These restrictions were enforced by consuming states that agreed not to accept coffee that did not have proper certification. Imports from non-member states were limited in 1965. These arrangements governed the world coffee market until 1972 when the economic provisions of the agreement lapsed.

The agreement was beneficial for producing countries. It raised prices and returns. Any quota system is biased toward increasing prices. Limiting exports can place an effective floor on prices but cannot establish a ceiling if supplies are not available. The Coffee Agreement prescribed exports in excess of quotas, but did not obligate producing members to meet their allocations even if they had stocks available. Brazil often did not export to permissible limits. During 1963, coffee prices rose for the first time in six years, although the level of production remained relatively stable and the level of stocks increased.[5] While coffee prices under the agreement did not return to the record levels of the mid-1950s, they have never fallen below the average price prevailing around 1960. Estimates of the value of transfers to producing states as a result of the agreement have ranged as high as $600 million per year.[6]

The effect of the agreement on price stability is more ambiguous. If the standard deviation for monthly coffee prices is taken as an indicator, then prices were more stable under the agreement than during the previous decade.[7] If changes in annual prices are used, then fluctuations were higher from 1962 to

1972.[8] Any increase in instability was, however, more than overshadowed by the benefits producing states derived from higher returns.

Coffee-producing states had been unable to regulate the market without consumer enforcement. In 1955, Brazil and Colombia signed a short lived "Gentlemen's Agreement." By 1960, twenty-eight states in Latin America and Africa had joined a producer agreement calling for various levels of stock retention. Only Brazil and Colombia, however, actually withheld coffee from the market.[9] African and Central American producers lacked the financial and storage facilities needed to carry coffee from one season to the next, or even to spread sales more evenly over the year. African exporters did not want to inhibit their rapidly growing share of the world market. The producer arrangements that preceded the Coffee Agreement were widely ignored and there were no sanctions against cheaters.

Effective market control was made possibly only by the consuming states that joined and enforced the agreement for political reasons. The United States saw the Coffee Agreement as an economic device to further political aims. American officials believed democratic political development was intimately related to stable economic growth.[10] The Coffee Agreement was identified with foreign assistance and the Alliance for Progress.[11]

The coffee market now offers an indication of the importance of shared experience provided by ties with consuming countries. The quota provisions of the agreement lapsed in 1973 because the membership was unable to agree on prices. Four major producing states—Brazil, Colombia, Ivory Coast, and Portugal (Angola)—have formed a marketing company. Other producers have pledged stock retention. If exporting countries, having failed before 1962, succeed in 1973, their success must be attributed primarily to experience gained through an international agreement that brought them together on a regular basis and forced them to establish a common front in bargaining over general quota levels with consuming countries. This experience was made possible only by accepting ties with capitalist states.

Cocoa

Cocoa accounts for about $500 million in international trade. In the 1960s it was the leading source of foreign exchange earnings for three countries—Togo, Nigeria, and Ghana. It was an important secondary export for several others including the Ivory Coast, the Cameroons, and Ecuador. Prices declined from a record high average level of 58¢ per pound in 1954 to a low of 11¢ in 1965. Except for rubber, cocoa has had larger price fluctuations than any other major primary export.[12]

Confronted with declining prices and an inability to reach agreement with consuming states, the cocoa producing countries attempted to regulate the market on their own.[13] In January of 1962, Ghana, Nigeria, Brazil, the Ivory Coast, and the Cameroons formed the Cocoa Producers Alliance (COPAL). They were later joined by Togo. The primary objective of COPAL was to coordinate stock retention when world prices fell below an indicator level set by the organization's executive board. This level was not to be lower than the average price for the preceding twelve months.[14]

The Alliance intervened in the market at the beginning of the 1964-65 cocoa marketing season. In October, the executive board set the indicator at 23.75¢ per pound, about a cent above the market price. Buyers refused to purchase. In mid-October, COPAL ordered its members to limit sales. Export quotas were set at 90 percent of the Alliance's basic quota of 1,066,000 tons. Prices did not rally. In November, the executive board ordered exports cut to 80 percent of the basic quota. Allowable sales to the end of 1964 were reduced from 50 to 40 percent of quotas and shipments from 30 to 25 percent. There was still no market response.[15]

At the end of November, the Alliance announced that its members would begin destroying stocks. On December 11, Ghana burned 500 tons of cocoa. The government said it would burn 2 percent of Ghanaian supplies or some 8,780 tons of cocoa. Other members were asked to adopt the same policy. Cocoa futures responded with a healthy advance but the rally was short.[16] Only Ghana actually destroyed any cocoa and then not in amounts approaching those to which the government had committed itself.[17]

At the January meeting of COPAL, producers made their last effort. They announced that 250,000 tons of cocoa would be diverted to non-conventional uses at prices that barely covered costs. This had no effect on the market that continued to weaken.[18]

Late in January, the members of COPAL abandoned their attempt to raise prices. Future deliveries for March had sunk to 18.61¢ per pound. This low was not the end, however. By June 1965, prices had fallen to 11¢ per pound in response to the selling off of the 1964-65 crop and prospects of a large harvest.

Foreign exchange earnings declined, which reduced government revenues. In Ghana, an already difficult economic situation was further exacerbated. The COPAL effort was particularly costly for its primary instigator, the Ghanaian regime. The drastic decline in cocoa prices was one of the causes of the coup that led to Nkrumah's overthrow.[19]

COPAL's market intervention failed because some of its members cheated and the rest lacked the political and financial resources needed to maintain quotas until cocoa buyers exhausted inventories. The Ivory Coast and the Cameroons, which accounted for some 21 percent of production nominally under COPAL's control, did not abide by the agreement. By the middle of January, both countries had sold almost all of their crop.[20] With a substantial part of the market left uncontrolled, it would have been impossible for COPAL to secure an increase in prices during the beginning of the 1964-65 crop year.[21]

Why did the Ivory Coast and the Cameroons break the agreement? In the first place, they may not have trusted their major partner. Ghana, the world's largest producer, was highly dependent on cocoa, which provided nearly 70 percent of her foreign receipts. By the fall of 1964, her economy was in desperate straits. Foreign exchange reserves had dropped from $272 million to $128 million in six years.[22] In a test of will with consumers, Ghana did not look reliable. The leaders of the Ivory Coast and the Cameroons, foreseeing failure, might simply have decided to cash in before the fall.

Furthermore, Ghana and the Ivory Coast had been rivals since independence. In economic matters, the Ivory Coast had adopted a strategy of gradualism and Ghana one of structural transformation.[23] The Ivory Coast had maintained close relations with France. Nkrumah had opened relations with the East, and sought to make his nation a leader of the Third World. Houphuet-Boigny did not share with Nkrumah values that might have offset doubts about Ghana's ability to continue to withhold cocoa stocks from the market.

The defection of the Ivory Coast and the Cameroons does not alone explain COPAL's failure. By January, those two countries had sold most of their crop. Despite reports of large stocks being held by cocoa processing companies the *Financial Times* of London was predicting a rise in prices. Nigeria, Brazil, and Ghana now controlled the only sizeable amounts of cocoa available. Some companies would have to replenish inventories, and short sales would have to be covered. Speculators who paid attention to the *Times* lost a good deal of money.

Ghana was unable to keep its stock off the market. The government was in dire need of foreign exchange reserves. Its time horizon was short. Nkrumah's tenure in office was in fact to end in less than a year. The Ghanaian leadership could not take a long-term perspective because its short-term needs were so pressing. When Ghana began selling in February, the cocoa market collapsed. Thus COPAL's market intervention failed because some members of the agreement cheated, the organization had no means of enforcing its provisions, and Ghanaian leaders lacked the resources needed to take a long-run perspective.

Petroleum

Petroleum is by far the most important raw material in international trade. Its value is several times that of any other commodity. It is the largest source of foreign exchange for ten developing countries and is vital to the economic well-being of industrial and industrializing states.

The present world petroleum market is the most spectacular case of oligopoly control the world has ever known. The major architects of this structure have been the seven major international oil companies—Exxon, Mobil, Shell, Gulf, Texaco, Standard of California, and British Petroleum. The oil-exporting countries have become the major beneficiaries.

The problem for the oil industry has always been one of potential oversupply. The danger of glutting the market has been minimized by a high level of coordination within and between firms. All the major companies are vertically integrated from production to end product. They are horizontally linked by joint ventures particularly in production.

Explicit accords such as the Red Line Agreement of 1928 in which the major companies agreed to limited development in what had been the Ottoman Empire have also helped control output. Prices were coordinated for many years by a system that based all crude, regardless of its production cost, on the price prevailing at U.S. Gulf of Mexico ports modified by differences in transportation costs.

When the corporations have been unable to control the market on their own, they have procured official support. The first petroleum law in the United States were state statutes limiting output to amounts that could be sold at a specified price. In the 1920s, the U.S. Federal Oil Conservation Board recommended that state agencies be empowered to set monthly allowable production levels and allocate them among wells. State action and later federal intervention supported a market structure that the companies themselves in the face of new discoveries and independent producers were unable to sustain.[24]

Limitations on production and administered prices created a huge pie from which the producing states have been able to take an increasingly larger share. During the early years of the century, returns to host country governments were extremely modest. They first received payment in the form of royalties—a fixed sum for each barrel of oil exported. Despite some adjustments, payments remained low until after the Second World War. In 1946, Venezuela achieved a major victory when concessionaires agreed to a tax equal to 50 percent of the profit of crude oil. This arrangement quickly spread to the Middle East. Since the Treasury Department allowed these payments to be written off against U.S. tax liabilities, the companies were virtually unaffected. For the next two decades the situation remained stable. As production increased particularly in the Middle East, government receipts grew, but the price paid per barrel remained more or less the same. Since 1969, however, in a dizzying series of negotiations, agreements, new demands, re-negotiations, and unilateral action, the producing countries have secured massive increases in their receipts from petroleum exports. The posted price for petroleum, on which taxes are based, no longer bears the slightest relationship to the cost of getting oil out of the ground any place in the world.

These changes have resulted in huge revenue increases for producing countries. In 1963, earnings from petroleum exported by Third World countries amounted to a little over $3 billion. By 1972 they were over $12 billion.[25] For the Middle East alone, estimates of 1980 revenues have been placed at over $100 billion, largely the result of projected price increases rather than greater production.[26] The oil-exporting states have not done badly through their association with the major petroleum companies.

The necessary condition for these massive increases in earnings is the oligopolistic pricing structure of the international petroleum industry. In a competitive market, oil would sell at a fraction of its present price. Collusion could not have been created and sustained without the major corporations. Managers enlisted the support of their home country governments in restricting the market. They have willingly participated in a tax structure that enables producing countries to coordinate their behavior and discourages them from cheating.[27]

While OPEC members have been successful in securing higher prices, an area where they all share the same interest, they have been unable to agree on *general* production restrictions, an area where one country's gain can be another's loss. Several resolutions of OPEC calling for greater government control over national production levels have been without effect. In 1968, the membership failed to reach any agreement on quotas because Saudi Arabia, Iran, and other Middle East countries resisted arrangements that would reduce the market advantage they derive from their low production costs.[28] The reluctance of the major oil-producing states, in particular Saudi Arabia, to nationalize the corporations indicates that their leaders are aware of the dangers of competition. The concept of participation—acquisition of majority ownership—was devised by the oil minister of Saudi Arabia as an alternative to nationalization.

While the OPEC membership as a whole has been unable to act a subset of producing states—Libya and the countries on the Persian Gulf—have cut back production. The 1973 Middle East war triggered joint output controls. Three independent conditions converged to make this possible: the lack of alternative sources of supply, anti-Israeli sentiment, and surfeit wealth. Had any of these conditions been absent, effective market intervention would have been unlikely. If shortfalls from Arab areas could be made up from other sources, restrictions would have been ineffectual. The Arab cause against Israel—a highly salient shared value—helped to overcome ideological and political differences. Surfeit wealth, which allowed political leaders to take an extended time horizon, removed the fear that production cut-backs would lead to bankruptcy, and bankruptcy to domestic instability.

The accumulation of immense wealth would not have taken place without the collusive practices of the major oil companies. Even now, if the companies became buyers rather than sellers of crude, the kinds of monetary flows that have made limited, if not general, export restrictions possible, might dry up. Countries without surfeit funds, which account for more than half of OPEC's exports, might then act more competitively by shading prices to secure more revenue. Libya and the Persian Gulf producers might see their market share erode while prices stabilized or declined, which situation would force them to reconsider their policy of production controls. What the outcome of such a reconsideration would be is not clear. Restrictions might continue because individual states would still have more than they could spend and because anti-Israeli sentiment would continue to coordinate behavior. At the present moment, however, the companies continue to play an important role. Producing states have not yet demonstrated that they can restrict trade in a market where corporations are competitive buyers rather than oligopolistic sellers of crude oil.

In summary, recent experiences in world commodity markets indicate that it is difficult for producing countries to assert independent control. They can, however, secure higher and more stable prices by joining with consuming capitalist states in international commodity agreements, or by tapping the tax base provided by the restrictive practices of multinational corporations. By generating revenue and increasing shared experiences, such alliances may provide the resources needed by Third World states to establish durable international cartels. The road to independence lies through alliances with capitalist institutions.

Implications for the Theory of
Economic Imperialism

There is no general theory of economic imperialism but rather a group of loosely related propositions concerned with two distinct issues—the motivation of advanced capitalist states and the impact of the world economy on backward areas. In both areas arguments have been made at aggregate and disaggregate levels.[29] With respect to the behavior of advanced states, radical analysts argue at the aggregate level that foreign policy reflects national economic necessity— the need for raw materials, foreign markets or capital outlets. At a disaggregate level, they suggest that policy-makers seek to protect the interests of particular corporations.[30] With respect to poorer areas, writers associated with the concept of economic imperialism maintain that international economic relations exploit the national wealth of backward areas. At a disaggregate level they contend that imperialist relationships benefit a small native elite at the expense of the masses.[31] Recent experience in international commodity markets does not support the proposition that capitalist states act to satisfy aggregate economic needs, or that backward areas are plundered, but does indicate that corporate interests are supported. The empirical examples presented in this chapter shed no direct light on the disaggregated effect of commodity exchange on particular classes in less developed countries.

American policy-makers have protected corporate interests. The consequence of this policy, however, has been to jeopardize aggregate economic objectives. The failure of the United States to undermine the position of the oil companies, by adopting measures that could increase competition, has made it easier for producing states to secure oligopoly prices. Collusion has generated more revenue than some exporting states can spend. Surfeit reserves have made it possible to cut back production without affecting domestic expenditures. By tacitly supporting the oil oligopoly the U.S. government has raised prices and threatened supplies. With large revenues, producing states do not need foreign investment. American behavior cannot be interpreted as an effort to secure raw materials, foreign markets, or capital outlets, for all of these aims would be better served if oil exporting states used all of their revenue to meet current needs.

Political objectives have led consuming states to participate in commodity agreements that have raised prices, and decreased the commodity and trade dependence of exporting states. The Coffee Agreement, the most important international arrangement in terms of value and number of countries affected, discouraged additional coffee production. The Coffee Diversification Fund, which was strongly supported by the United States, was established to finance projects that shifted resources out of the coffee sector. During the agreement, almost all exporting countries reduced the percentage of their export earnings derived from coffee, and the relative amount of coffee sent to their major trading partners.[32] The Coffee Agreement cannot be interpreted as a device for keeping Third World states dependent on a single commodity or importing state, the ideal situation for assuring supplies and maintaining a dependent relationship. Both the effect of the agreement and the behavior of American officials support the proposition that political, not economic, aims were of paramount concern.

The evidence presented in this chapter is much less relevant for evaluating assertions about the impact of the world economy on backward areas. Judgments can only be made at the national level and then only by comparison with competitive conditions rather than a socialist international system. In these terms, however, LDCs have not fared badly. Despite their inability to organize markets on their own they have been the beneficiaries of restrictive schemes imposed by consuming states or multinational corporations. For most primary commodities, actual prices are higher than those that would prevail in a free market. In terms of neoclassical concepts of value, consuming states have been exploited by producing areas.[33]

There is implicit in these findings support for a dialectical process that has been ignored by radical writers. By supporting corporate interests and commodity agreements, advanced capitalist states have given the governments of less developed areas the opportunity to decrease their dependence. Over time host countries have been able to increase their technical skills and knowledge of the market. Capital is more and more generated out of internal operations rather than foreign investment.[34] Commodity agreements widen the shared experience of exporting states. These processes increase the possibility for successful collusion among commodity exporting states and enable them to deal with corporations and consuming states on a more equal footing. Foreign control may be self-liquidating.

Most writers associated with the notion of economic imperialism have, however, been primarily concerned with the disaggregated impact of the world economy on backward areas. They argue that the capitalist system has created a chain of exploitation that stretches across national boundaries from the peripheral areas of backward states to the bourgeois centers of industrial societies. The evidence presented here sheds no light on the accuracy of this contention. While the governments of LDCs have procured higher returns than under competitive conditions and increased possibilities for collusion through ties with capitalist institutions, the internal impact of these receipts has not been investigated.

In summary, recent events in several important commodity markets challenge the assertion that the leaders of capitalist states act primarily to secure raw materials, markets, or investment outlets. By protecting their corporations and joining commodity agreements, they have increased aggregate returns and made durable collusion among exporting states more likely. These conclusions do not constitute a general refutation of the theory of economic imperialism, for many critical issues have not been touched upon. Given, however, the diffuseness of the theory as it now stands, all that can be done is to examine piecemeal specific arguments. The analysis and examples presented do not support assertions associated with the concept of economic imperialism.

Notes

1. There have been cases of *single* exporting states holding a dominant share of the world market and successfully controlling trade. Before the development of artificial fertilizers, by Germany during the First World War, Chilean policies affected the world nitrate market. During the first four decades of this century, Brazil successfully intervened on the world coffee market. Recent sky-rocketing petroleum costs indicate that at least in the short run Saudi Arabia holds a monopolistic position in the world oil market, i.e., it can raise its revenues by cutting back production. Whether the Saudis can maintain market control in the long run without corporate assistance is at this writing a moot point.

2. Mancur Olson, *The Logic of Collective Action* (Cambridge: Harvard University Press, 1965), p. 47; and William Fellner, *Competition Among the Few* (New York: Augustus M. Kelley, 1965), pp. 33 ff.

3. See Zuhayr Mikdashi, *The Community of Oil Exporting Countries: A Study in Governmental Cooperation* (London: George Allen and Unwin Ltd., 1972) for an attempt to develop a set of characteristics that could be used to allocate quotas among oil-producing states.

4. Harley Hinrichs, *A General Theory of Tax Structure Change during Economic Development* (Cambridge: The Law School of Harvard University, 1966), passim.

5. Figures on levels of production and prices can be found in Pan American Coffee Bureau, *Annual Coffee Statistics*, various years.

6. Bart S. Fisher, *The International Coffee Agreement: a Study in Coffee Diplomacy* (New York: Praeger, 1972), p. 153.

7. Stephen D. Krasner, "Business-Government Relations: The Case of the International Coffee Agreement," *International Organization*, Vol. 27, No. 4 (Autumn 1973), p. 501.

8. Alton D. Law, "Coffee: Structure, Control and Development: A Review Article," *Journal of Inter-American Economic Affairs*, Vol. 27, No. 1 (Summer 1973), p. 79.

9. Estimates of coffee stocks in producing countries are given in Blair Eugene Rourke, *Causes and Predictability of Annual Changes in Supplies and Prices of Coffee*, Unpub. Ph.D Dissertation, Stanford University, 1969, pp. 307-310.

10. Robert A. Packenham, "Political Development Doctrines in the American Foreign Aid Program," *World Politics*, Vol. 18, No. 2 (January 1966).

11. For typical statements by American officials, see United States, Congress, Senate, Committee on Foreign Relations, 88th Cong., 1st Sess., *International Coffee Agreement, 1962, 1963*, p. 3 and United States, Congress, Senate, Committee on Foreign Relations, 90th Cong., 2nd Sess., *International Coffee Agreement 1968*, pp. 5, 44, and 58.

12. Walter Birmingham, I. Neustadt, E.N. Omabe, directors and editors, *A Study of Contemporary Ghana, Vol. I, The Economy of Ghana* (Evanston: Northwestern University Press, 1966), p. 379. Price data can be found in Gill and Duffus, *Cocoa Statistics* (London: 1968), p. 35.

13. After a decade of negotiation, an international agreement for cocoa was finally concluded in the fall of 1972. The United States, however, did not join.

14. S. Lee Seaton, *The Failure of Development: The Political Economy of Ghana under Nkrumah*, Unpub. Ph.D Dissertation, University of Hawaii, 1971, pp. 346 ff. and Henri Bazin, *Cooperation among Developing Countries with Regard to Commodity Exports*, United Nations Conference on Trade and Development, TD/B/293, 29 December 1969, pp. 15-24.

15. *Wall Street Journal*, November 9, 1964, p. 24.

16. *Wall Street Journal*, December 14, 1965, p. 9.

17. *The New York Times*, January 25, 1965, p. 49.

18. *Financial Times* (London), January 29, 1965, p. 2.

19. David Apter, "Nkrumah, Charisma and the Coup," *Daedalus*, Vol. 97, No. 3 (Summer 1968), p. 786.

20. *Financial Times* (London), January 19, 1965, p. 2; *Journal of Commerce* (New York) December 7, 1964, p. 7; *The New York Times*, January 1, 1965, p. 47. Since these sales were illegal or at least in violation of treaty obligations undertaken by the Ivory Coast and the Cameroons, there are no public fully reliable sources on their magnitude and timing. Major newspapers in New York and London, however, did report the same story.

21. Ghana, Nigeria, and Brazil, members of COPAL obeying the agreement, accounted for 54 percent of world production in 1964-65.

22. International Monetary Fund, *International Financial Statistics, Supplement 1965-66*, p. 98.

23. See Eliot J. Berg, "Structural Transformation Versus Gradualism: Recent Economic Development in Ghana and the Ivory Coast," in Philip Foster and Aristide Zolberg, eds., *Ghana and the Ivory Coast* (Chicago: University of Chicago Press, 1971) for a trenchant comparison of the two countries.

24. Robert Engler, *The Politics of Oil* (Chicago: University of Chicago Press, 1961), pp. 135-141.

25. *Petroleum Press Service*, Vol. 40, No. 11 (November 1973), p. 416.

26. *The New York Times*, November 14, 1973, p. 63.

27. M.A. Adelman, "Is the Oil Shortage Real?" *Foreign Policy* 9 (Winter 1972-73) explicates the critical role played by the tax structure in maintaining the oligopoly.

28. Donald A. Wells, "Aramco: The Evolution of an Oil Concession," in Raymond F. Mikesell et al., *Foreign Investment in Petroleum and Mineral Industries* (Baltimore: The Johns Hopkins Press, 1971), p. 225.

29. See the papers by Andrew Mack and Roy Grow in this volume.

30. This was the primary concern of early analysts of European expansion such as Hobson and Lenin. More recently a number of writers associated with the *Monthly Review*, such as Harry Magdoff, Paul Baran, and Paul Sweezy, have directed their attention to the same problem.

31. Works by Andre Gunder Frank, Pierre Jalee, Paul Baran, Johan Galtung, and Arrighi Emmanuel have elaborated this aspect of economic imperialism.

32. Figures can be found in Krasner, op. cit., p. 505, n. 20.

33. Exploitation in a neoclassical sense can be identified as a level of prices above those that would prevail under free market conditions. If, however, a labor theory of value is taken as a standard the level of wages in most Third World raw materials industries would suggest that consumers exploit producers.

34. This argument has been developed by Raymond Vernon. See in particular his *Sovereignty at Bay* (New York: Basic Books, 1971), Chapter II.

10 Exploitation in Ocean Resource Development

Donald E. Milsten
University of Maryland Baltimore County

The traditional uses of the oceans have expanded immensely during the past twenty-five years. In addition to fishing, transportation, and strategic uses, nations now look to the oceans for mineral resources that are becoming scarce or difficult to recover on land. The ownership of these ocean resources is imprecisely defined in international law, and the leaders of developing nations wish to secure control over them before they are exploited and consumed by industrialized nations. Already both developed and developing nations have moved to obtain jurisdiction over certain ocean resources by extending territorial waters far out to sea. Others have held back and have argued that ocean resources should be available for use by all and be placed under some form of international control.

While nations prepare for another Law of the Sea conference (to be held in 1974), leaders of many developing nations have questioned the intentions and roles of the industrial nations in ocean affairs.[1] They point to past acts of imperialism and fear that such acts will continue as oceans are tapped for additional wealth. Their anxiety leads us to examine this issue as part of our interest in theories of imperialism. The central task of this chapter is to examine the basis for the developing nations' fears about ocean imperialism. Put another way, does exploitation by industrial nations take place in ocean development?

In order to answer this question, we shall focus upon three ocean resource development areas. Two areas—petroleum and fishing—have been discussed in the Law of the Sea preparatory meetings. The third area—shipping—is not generally identified as a resource to be developed. In this case, however, the surface of the ocean can be seen as a resource to be developed. Developing and using this resource means to obtain and/or use the proper vehicle—ships. It should be noted that there are also mining operations in the seabed for minerals such as copper, cobalt, manganese, zinc, and various salts; however, this industry is relatively small in comparison with the others and is still in its infancy.

The Webster's Dictionary defines exploitation as selfish or unfair utilization. This definition may be refined as it applies to ocean resource development. As different industries operate in each of the three areas, they not only encounter but create different types of problems. Consequently the definition for exploitation in each area must also vary. In the oil resource area, the oil industry exploits when it returns a very low royalty or tax while it makes a very high profit. Here the oil industry exploits because it does not pay the original owners an adequate return in view of the high market value of the resource. This is a relative judgment, of course; but, in the case of oil, the judgment has been made by those who claim to be exploited. This chapter will examine their claims as they apply to ocean development.

Exploitation in fishing occurs when a modern fishing fleet moves into an area ordinarily fished by a less modernized coastal fleet and monopolizes the catch. In this way, coastal commercial fishermen are denied fish nurtured in and near their national waters. Instead of sharing the catch with the coastal fishermen, the exploitative fleet removes most of a particular fish from the sea; this disrupts the feeding grounds and destroys additional species as well.

In the area of shipping, exploitation takes place when some shippers must consistently pay higher rates, or enjoy fewer advantages, than other shippers do for the same services. In this case, one group receives the services for lower rates than they would pay if the rates were applied evenly to all.

With these definitions of exploitation in mind, we can examine the three basic ocean industries that operate in the resource areas under discussion.

The Petroleum Industry and
Offshore Oil

The petroleum industry dominates ocean mineral development, and its critics have linked it to international economic exploitation. While oil company behavior in land operations has been well established and widely discussed, large-scale activity over the seabed is a more recent phenomenon. It would be helpful, therefore, to present figures about offshore drilling activity as they apply to developing countries.

Until the mid-1960s, the bulk of offshore oil exploration and production was concentrated near the coasts of the United States and Venezuela.[2] The depletion of easily tapped land sources, coupled with the tremendous increase in demand, encouraged an upsurge in offshore exploration. This offshore drilling has expanded to global proportions and non-industrialized nations have begun to account for a large share of this oil. For example, from 1960 to 1971, 52 percent of all world offshore oil production occurred near the shores of developing nations.[3]

Exploration has been widespread too. In 1971, oil companies drilled 693 exploratory wells near the shores of 120 nations. Of these wells, 345 were in U.S. waters. Of the remaining wells, 243 were off the shores of developing nations. Exploration is a sign of expected gain. Relative to exploration on land, offshore activity accounted for just over 27 percent of all exploratory wells drilled in developing nations in 1971. Those developing countries, for which figures are available, that have five or more exploratory wells are Angola, Gabon, Malagasy Republic, Nigeria, Senegal, Indonesia, Malaysia, United Arab Emirates, Argentina, Brazil, Ecuador, and Trinidad and Tobago.

To examine the question of exploitation in offshore oil development, it will be useful to see who is sinking exploratory wells. An example can be found in recent offshore drilling near Indonesia in the South China Sea, the Java Sea, and the Makassar and Karimata Straits. In 1972, twenty-four oil companies were operating in these waters. Of these, one was British, one Dutch, one French, one Japanese, one Canadian, and one was an Indonesian national company. There was one French-American company, one American-Japanese combine, one Dutch-Japanese combine, and one American-Indonesian combine. The remaining sixteen were American owned.[4] Five of the seven largest international oil companies (known as the seven majors) were directly involved in these operations.[5]

While these figures show that the major oil companies are active near the shores of developing nations, they do not demonstrate exploitation. The best way to do this would be to present concrete data relating to production costs and pricing policy in the designated areas. However, because this data is not available, the case for exploitation in offshore oil development will have to be examined with less direct evidence.

First, there is some doubt about the popular notion, fostered by oil company advertising, that offshore exploration is exceedingly more expensive than onshore exploration. One economist has pointed out that offshore wells are operated twenty-four hours a day in contrast to onshore wells that operate only during daylight hours. The location of offshore wells near tidewater ports may also lower the overall transportation cost per barrel of oil. Development costs may also be lowered because offshore sediments are often softer and newer than onshore sediments and thus are easier to work.[6]

The idea that oil companies exploit in offshore oil development was reinforced by the industry's early position in Law of the Sea discussions. The suspicions of leaders from developing countries were raised when the major oil companies opposed the creation of any international ocean mineral regulatory agency over which developing nations would exercise a majority vote. The companies feared that such an agency would impose unacceptable restrictions on their offshore activity and thus reduce their profits.[7] Oil lobbyists worked to encourage a minimum of international control, and there is evidence that their efforts were successful. This is seen in Law of the Sea proposals made by developed nations. These nations favor an international agency with minimum regulatory jurisdiction, some kind of licensing procedure, and weighted representation for the industrialized nations. United States Law of the Sea proposals, for example, are in line with this.

International oil executives also opposed any extension of international authority over the continental margins.[8] They viewed this as a threat to their operating authority and an encroachment on vital national oil reserves. Developing nations divided on this issue, however. On one hand, leaders of land-locked developing states wished to restrict national authority over offshore areas so that the profits from offshore oil could be distributed to all developing countries. On the other hand, leaders of coastal developing nations sided with the oil companies and opted for a wide national margin.[9]

This latter position indicates a shift in the attitudes of leaders from developing nations, the majority of whom are from coastal developing countries. The international generosity of these states appears to diminish when the oil companies begin to sink exploratory wells near their shores. In the meantime, there is increasing evidence that offshore oil reserves near the industrial nations will not be sufficient to satisfy their energy needs. The tables have turned with the developed nations now in need of some international agency to ease their problems in obtaining oil from new offshore producing areas. This explains why the oil companies have refrained recently from public opposition to an international seabed agency.

The change in the attitudes of many developing nations raises further questions. The case for exploitation rests on the notion that offshore oil production is, after all, an extension of onshore production. One can argue by analogy that behavior patterns established in one sector of activity will follow into another. There is no question that the major oil companies at one time took immense profits from underdeveloped oil-producing states. In 1946, they were reaping from 90¢ to $1.75 per barrel on Middle East oil, while production costs including royalties were only 10¢ to 25¢ per barrel, and in 1955 they were making a similar amount.[10] But of course this profit-making picture has greatly changed. As early as 1949, Saudi Arabia demanded and received increased royalties and taxes for its oil. This trend has continued, and it received significant impetus when the Organization of Petroleum Exporting Countries (OPEC) was formed in 1960. M.A. Adelman argues that the trend has moved so far that by the early 1970s the oil companies and the U.S. government were acting as tax collectors for the Arab sheiks.[11]

To sum up this section, it is well to reiterate that offshore oil production is an expanding enterprise. Many nations are being introduced to oil exploration, and while they have neither long-range experience with the oil companies nor the local expertise to deal with petroleum executives, they may very well join with the experienced developing nation producers to protect themselves from exploitation. OPEC is a militant organization and is gathering new members. The attitudes of leaders from developing states have already begun to change as they perceive the potential for offshore oil wealth. If they join with the OPEC countries, they are most unlikely to become objects of exploitation by major oil companies and developed states.

**International Shipping and the
Developing Nations**

The second area of ocean development to be examined in this chapter is international shipping. Most states require access to international shipping in order to participate widely in international commerce. The key to ocean transport is the availability of sufficient low-cost service to move goods. But often this service is not available to shippers from developing countries. Their political leaders believe that many elements of the shipping industry act to restrict their access to this service and thus "constitute a barrier to their development."[12] Developing nation leaders have worked through such organizations as the United Nations Conference on Trade and Development and the General Agreement on Trade and Tariffs to remove some of the barriers, but their success has been limited.[13]

There is no question that shipping by companies based in developed states dominates the industry. In 1970, the net gross tonnage controlled by nationals and firms located in the United States amounted to 32.2 million gross registered tons (g.r.t.). Behind the Americans were the British with 29.5 million g.r.t. Japanese owners controlled 22.2 million g.r.t. followed by Scandinavian owners with 26.5 million g.r.t. The remaining Western European nations accounted for 46.4 million g.r.t. together. But the total gross tonnage for all developing states in the same year was only 13.9 million g.r.t.[14]

Three areas of interest will serve to illustrate the way in which economic practices in shipping affect ocean development; these areas are preference, the type of ship used, and rate-making conferences. Each of these touches upon aspects of shipping in which developing countries find their producers at a competitive disadvantage.

Preference means that some shippers receive financial advantages not readily available to others. Such things as the availability of cargo space, movement schedules, liability provisions and costs, opportunities to negotiate cost-reducing contracts and choice of shipping line can affect cost. Because preference is given to shippers from industrial nations, a producer from a developing state is often at a competitive disadvantage. This reduces sales and income and increases the nation's balance-of-payments deficit.[15] In turn, the value of the country's currency is weakened, and it becomes increasingly difficult to obtain the capital necessary for industrialization.

Goods move in ocean commerce by three basic ship types—bulk carriers (including tankers), tramp steamers, and liners. Each type presents problems for developing states. The greatest volume of cargo moved is crude oil. The majority of the tankers used to move this resource are owned and controlled by the major oil companies. Some tanker tonnage is owned by independent shipping firms,

but these ships are generally leased to the oil companies on long-term contracts.[16] Similar patterns hold for dry bulk cargo carriers. While a few
developing nations export huge quantities of raw material, these quantities
usually go aboard bulk ships based in developed nations.

Tramp steamers are available for charter and can be engaged by anyone. They
do not steam on regular schedules or over designated routes as do the liners.
Although they are more flexible than liners or tankers, they still present a
problem for developing nations because they usually require the charter of a full
ship. Aside from a few bulk raw material cargoes, developing nation shippers
have difficulty filling a steamer. This is especially true for the finished products
they export.

Because of the limited quantity of cargo they ship, producers from developing nations find it most convenient to ship by established liner service. These
ships will accept partial cargoes and move along established routes. Because of
their importance in moving a wide variety of materials and goods, liners are the
primary shipping links of communications between nations. If developing
countries wish to establish their own merchant fleets, they find the liner service
the "logical" place to begin because their partial cargoes can be accommodated
most easily by liners.[17]

Finally, developing nations encounter their greatest difficulties in shipping
because of rate-making practices in the liner trade. Liner rates are set arbitrarily
and governed by regional groups called conferences.[18] Membership in the
conferences is limited to existing, established companies—that is, companies that
are headquartered in developed nations. It has been very difficult for newly
established liner companies to gain admittance to existing conferences; only a
few such firms have been accepted. Members of the conferences are able to
enforce their rate structures by refusing to carry for shippers who use
non-conference liners. These practices make it especially difficult for developing
nations to open up their own services—something many of them wish to do in
the light of disadvantageous preference treatment from the established liners.

To summarize this section, it can be stated that developing nations are at a
disadvantage relative to industrialized countries in the use of the oceans for
trade. This is not simply a function of their underdevelopment, but is also a
result of economic discrimination. Shippers from developing nations do not
receive the special advantages that reduce costs, they cannot exercise much
control over the type of ships they use most often, and their efforts to establish
competing lines have been resisted by existing companies' action through liner
conferences. These patterns of discrimination in shipping increase the cost of
industrialization and the leaders of developing countries conclude that their
economic progress is being retarded by policies of imperialism.

Fishing and Ocean Development

Conflict over fishing rights has created serious problems in ocean affairs. Several
nations claim territorial waters extending two hundred miles from shore, while

others deny the validity of these unilateral extensions. For example, Chile, Ecuador, and Peru argue that the wider limits are just compensation for mineral potential denied by very narrow continental shelves. Fish in their offshore waters are fed, in part, by nutrients washed down from the Andes Mountains and so are claimed as national resources.

To understand better the problem of the fishing industry in ocean development, it will be helpful to illustrate three points. First, the fishing industry has been characterized as fragmented and localized[19] and is not comparable to petroleum or shipping in the magnitude of capital investment. Although there are elements of fishing that involve sophisticated ships, modern factories, and heavy capital outlay, much of the world's fishing is done with old-fashioned methods and outdated equipment. One might expect to find poorly equipped fishing fleets in non-industrial nations; however, a large portion of the coastal fishing business in developed countries is also out of date. In the United States, coastal commercial fishermen often demand, and usually get, legal protection for their traditional techniques at the expense of modern organization and efficient operation.[20]

Secondly, the leading fishing industries are not concentrated in developed countries as are the leading petroleum and shipping companies. From 1966 to 1972, the top five fishing nations in terms of tonnage caught were, in order: Peru, Japan, the USSR, China, and Norway (which replaced the United States on the list at that time).[21] In terms of the highest cash value of catch in millions of U.S. dollars, Japan, China, and the USSR lead the rest of the world by a wide margin.[22]

Finally, in terms of modernization the industrial nations that have spent the most to develop modern, distant-water fishing fleets are the USSR and Japan. Such fleets promise the greatest return on investment. Other industrial fishing nations such as the United States, Great Britain, Canada, and Norway have concentrated on improving their coastal fishing industries. This means that they are building up fleets that cannot exploit foreign fishing grounds. The U.S. tuna fleet does fish off the coast of South America and does have some modern vessels, but it is small relative to the larger Japanese and Russian fleets.

Peru presents a special case and should be noted because it has had the largest world catch. Nevertheless, the cash value of that catch leaves Peru ranking only nineteenth among fishing nations. This does not indicate exploitation, however, because over 90 percent of Peru's harvest is in anchoveta, a herring species that is turned into the relatively inexpensive product of fish meal.

Fishing differs from the other industries in another important way too. More than oil or shipping, fishing has been subject to international political adjustment. This takes the form of international agreements pertaining to fisheries; there are three basic types. First, there are bilateral treaties that arrange reciprocal fishing privileges for specific areas. Beyond these are multilateral research treaties and stock regulatory treaties; the latter set up agencies for managing particular species. Finally, there are regional regulatory treaties that attempt to eliminate conflicts in wide areas of the oceans.

These treaties present two possible problems. One is the question of stock quotas, and the other is the problem of entry into existing agreements. Stock quotas are the agreed upon amount of fish that participating nations may take. These quantities may or may not be based on sound conservation considerations, but some attempt is usually made to limit the size of the catch. Thus, if a nation wished to join an existing stock regulatory treaty, there would be a problem reallocating shares of the permitted catch.

Where treaties confirm the historical use of fishing grounds, developing nations in particular may find it difficult to gain access. In all likelihood they will not have had distant-water fleets that can claim to have fished certain foreign areas over many years. Agreements designed to confirm such traditional fishing rights will be viewed by developing nations with the same impatience they often display for other Law of the Sea provisions. They hold that these laws were written by older, usually developed, nations to confirm their advantage in international affairs. If developing nations expand their interest in international fishing, they are very likely to challenge existing agreements among previous users.

To summarize, it should be noted that there are great differences between the fishing industry and the other major industries discussed in this chapter. Most of the developed nations do not have large, modern, distant-water fleets capable of exploiting fish near the coasts of other countries. Further, coastal fishermen from developing countries face the same problem with distant-water fleets as do the developed nations. In this industry the burden of exploitation appears to follow the fish and not the type of country.

Much of the difficulty faced by coastal commercial fishermen is caused because they do not have modern equipment with which to compete effectively against distant-water fleets. Several governments are moving to remedy this problem, and here the developed nations will be better able to assist their fishermen than the developing nations. Such action will encourage more economically sound local fishing industries but will not contribute to the exploitation of fish off foreign shores.

Conclusion

We must now return to the main question raised in this chapter: Does exploitation occur in ocean development? To provide the answer, each ocean development area and its main industry will be considered in turn.

From the viewpoint of developing states, past exploitation by oil companies in onshore oil production is an historical fact. All things being equal, they could assume that company behavior in offshore production would follow a similar pattern. But while oil companies have exploited in the past and would probably like to do so in the future, the prospects for exploitation in offshore oil are hardly assured. There are several reasons for this. First, massive exploration for offshore oil may not result in significant production. Second, pressure for a new legal regime in the Law of the Sea may obligate the governments of developed nations to place offshore oil production under international scrutiny. Third, experience with OPEC since 1971 demonstrates that producing countries can obtain price concessions from the companies and that the home governments of these companies are not effective in mitigating or preventing this. If OPEC coverage widens to include new producing areas, or if these areas come under international jurisdiction, it will be very difficult for the oil companies to exploit offshore oil to their advantage.

In international shipping, it is apparent that the companies, through conferences and other rate-setting organs, make it very costly for developing nation producers to ship goods. In effect, the companies overcharge developing nations for services sold to developed country businessmen at cheaper rates. This amounts to exploiting the poor to subsidize the rich. Price and service discrimination not only make it more costly for developing nations to utilize the oceans as a transportation resource but place an added burden on their development as well.

The prospects for future exploitation in shipping may be dimming, however. The move to containerized cargo in the Atlantic trade during the late 1960s brought about sharp changes in the carrying capacity of ships and thus disrupted traditional rate-making policies. This has undercut the financial power of the conferences with consequent strains showing up in both the Atlantic and Pacific shipping industries.[23]

The fishing industry is localized and the bulk of industry politics are directed toward protecting local fishing grounds for native fishermen. The problems created by modern, subsidized fishing fleets are not confined to the developing nations. American coastal fishermen, for example, face the same problem. Consequently, it is very difficult to describe the fishing industry as one in which the developing countries are subject to imperialism. It is ironic that the leading South American proponents of a broad territorial sea base their argument on the fishing issue. In their case, at least, other reasons may also be found. Figures on oil development near South American coasts show that 16 percent of Peruvian oil production took place offshore from 1960 to 1971 and that offshore oil exploration in 1971 accounted for 18 percent of the total in Columbia, 32 percent in Brazil, and 40 percent in Ecuador.[24]

Finally, the entire question of exploitation in ocean affairs must be considered in the light of recent events. It is just possible that many traditional complaints and considerations about imperialism will change as a result of the 1973-74 Arab oil embargo and what it implies. At least three lessons can be drawn from the embargo. First, the unity of Arab oil producers demonstrates that developing nations can join together to affect international commerce and politics. Secondly, the oil-exporting states not directly involved in the embargo moved easily to take advantage of scarcity. Prices for their resources skyrocketed. Thirdly, and most important, the industrial nations rejected "gun-boat" diplomacy in the crisis. Most tried to work around it or make political concessions to relieve their shortages. The point here reinforces the first two; without effective resistance, the antagonists were encouraged to increase their demands.

The embargo should be a lesson for other developing nations—particularly those with an interest in ocean resources. They now know that they too can unite and make successful demands concerning the valuable resources near their shores. They can neutralize the superior technology of the industrialized nations and demand concessions and guarantees for granting the privilege of exploration and extraction. If the developed nations are deterred from, or eschew, the use of force, the traditional roles of dominator and exploited may be reversed. The act of crying imperialism will be but an excuse for demanding further concessions from the developed nations.

Notes

1. United States, Congress, Senate, Committee on Interior and Insular Affairs, *The Law of the Sea Crisis*, 92nd. Cong., 1st Sess., December 1971 (Washington: GPO, 1972), pp. 2-3; Terese Sulikowski, "The International Seabed: Prospects and Proposals," *SAIS Review* 17 (Fall 1972), pp. 14-16; and Robert L. Friedheim and Joseph B. Kadane, "Ocean Science in the UN Political Arena," *Journal of Maritime Law and Commerce* 3 (April 1972), pp. 487-91.

2. Richard J. Howe, "Petroleum Operations in the Sea—1980 and Beyond," reprinted from *Ocean Industry*, August 1968, in George A. Doumani, *Exploiting the Resources of the Seabed*, Subcommittee on National Security Policy and Scientific Developments of the Committee on Foreign Affairs, House of Representatives (Washington: July 1971), pp. 134-45.

3. These percentages were extracted from data in John P. Albers, et al., *Summary Petroleum and Selected Mineral Statistics for 120 Countries, Including Offshore Areas*, Geological Survey Professional Paper 817 (Washington: GPO, 1973), pp. 130-4.

4. Robert E. King, "Offshore Interest Centers on North Sea, Far East," *World Oil* 174 (May 1972), p. 65.

5. These seven, major, vertically integrated, multinational oil enterprises are Exxon, Gulf, Mobil Oil Corporation, Standard Oil of California (Chevron), Texaco, British Petroleum, and Royal Dutch/Shell Group. All but the last two are owned and controlled by Americans. There are also many "lesser" companies that have significant holdings in developing countries. Examples are Cities Service, Atlantic-Richfield, Getty, and Phillips Petroleum.

The five majors involved in the Indonesian offshore operations are Gulf, Texaco, Royal Dutch/Shell Group, Exxon and AGIP, a subsidiary of British

Petroleum. There may also be much indirect participation in this field (including the two additional majors) through stock holdings and other arrangements. Together, the seven major companies account for about three-quarters of all crude oil production in the world. Edith T. Penrose, *The Large International Firm in Developing Countries* (Cambridge: MIT Press, 1968), p. 88. While it is common to assume that these major companies conspire to fix prices and limit competition, the nature of their relationship is not as simple as this. They do, for example, belong to common production organizations such as the Iranian Oil Consortium, and they have joined to control many foreign companies such as Aramco in Saudi Arabia. However, definitive proof of collusion is difficult to produce so such assumptions must be qualified. For examination of this problem, see M.A. Adelman, *The World Petroleum Market* (Baltimore: The Johns Hopkins University Press, 1972), pp. 2, 3, 145-8. See also, Peter R. Odell, *Oil and World Power* (New York: Taplinger, 1971), pp. 14-16.

6. Adelman, p. 205.

7. Ann L. Hollick, "Seabeds Make Strange Politics," *Foreign Policy* 9 (Winter 1972-1973), p. 157.

8. The continental margin includes the continental shelf, slope, and rise as they drop toward the deep ocean floor. For the early position taken by the oil industry see "American Petroleum Institute Statement of Policy—Jurisdiction Over the Natural Resources of the Ocean Floor," United States, Congress, Senate, Subcommittee on the Outer Continental Shelf of the Committee on Interior and Insular Affairs, *Outer Continental Shelf*, 91st Cong., 2nd Sess. (Washington: GPO, 1970), pp. 285-7.

9. United States Senate, *Law of the Sea Crisis . . .* , p. 5.

10. Robert Engler, *The Politics of Oil* (Chicago: Chicago University Press, 1961), p. 67.

11. M.A. Adelman, "Is the Oil Shortage Real? Oil Companies as OPEC Tax Collectors," *Foreign Policy* 9 (Winter 1972-73).

12. S.A. Lawrence, *International Sea Transport: The Years Ahead* (Lexington, Mass.: D.C. Heath, 1972), p. 202. For essays written by analysts from several developing countries see the special issue #582 of *International Conciliation* (March 1971), *Shipping and Developing Countries*.

13. Olav Knudsen identifies a major West-South conflict dimension in international shipping affairs. Developing states want access to Western markets for finished goods and they want more favorable rates and concessions for the raw materials they supply. *The Politics of International Shipping* (Lexington: Lexington Books, D.C. Heath, 1973), pp. 158-9.

14. Figures are drawn from Lawrence, p. 16. It should be noted that these figures are for ownership and control, not registry. Registry means nothing in terms of locating those who control shipping. Many developing states have set up "flag-of-convenience" registry for the convenience of owners who wish to avoid high taxes and strictly enforced rules; that is why Panama and Liberia have such

large fleets. See Boleslaw A. Boczek, *Flags-of-Convenience, An International Legal Study* (Cambridge: Harvard University Press, 1962).

15. Laurence Whitehead has demonstrated how costs of all kinds, including rates and insurance, cut into developing nations' balance-of-payments. From 1960 to 1967, nineteen Latin American countries (excluding ex-British territories and Cuba) enjoyed a favorable merchandise balance of $11.5 billion. Shipping costs for the same period ran $6 billion, reducing this balance to $5.5 billion. "The Trade and Aid Relationship in Latin America," in Barbara Ward, et al., eds., *The Widening Gap* (New York: Columbia University Press, 1971), pp. 216-7.

16. Critics of the oil industry hold that use of a rating formula such as the "average freight rate assessment" (AFRA) in tanker shipping unduly inflated shipping costs for developing countries. Michael Tanzer, *The Political Economy of International Oil and the Underdeveloped Countries* (Boston: Beacon Press, 1969). Adelman argues, however, that since 1969 tanker rates have declined and that, at its height, AFRA was only one of several rate formulas in use. He holds that AFRA may have a limited impact on a few countries but that it "is not a market factor." *The World Petroleum Market . . .*, p. 114.

17. Knudsen, p. 64. See also L.M.S. Rajwar, "Trade and Shipping Needs of Developing Countries," in *International Conciliation . . .*, p. 9.

18. Liner rates are not dependent upon volume and weight because these ships move on regular schedules whether or not they are full. Thus the addition of cargo does not increase the cost of operating the vessel.

19. Lawrence, p. 236, and Edward Miles, "Transnationalism in Space: Inner and Outer," in Joseph S. Nye, Jr. and Robert O. Keohane, eds., *Transnational Relations and World Politics* (Cambridge: Harvard University Press, 1973), p. 257-8.

20. Francis T. Christy, Jr. and Anthony Scott, *The Common Wealth in Ocean Fisheries* (Baltimore: The Johns Hopkins University Press, 1965), p. 208.

21. U.S. Department of Commerce, National Maritime Fisheries Service of the National Oceanic and Atmospheric Administration, Current Fishery Statistics No. 6100, *Fisheries of the United States, 1972* (Washington, March 1973), p. 29.

22. Ibid., p. 30. Values for 1971 were: Japan, $2708 million; China, $1955 million; and USSR, $1480 million. The next highest in dollar value of catch was the Philippines with $651 million. The United States followed with $643 million.

23. Two American lines withdrew from Pacific Conferences in 1973 and rejoined only after special rate-making concessions were reached. These companies had difficulty obtaining freight in competition with non-conference container ships. Baltimore *Sun*, December 17, 1973, col. 7, and January 11, 1974, C7.

24. Percentages derived from Albers et al., pp. 131-3.

11 U.S. Economic Penetration of Western Europe

Walter Goldstein
State University of New York at Albany

Sufficient data is now available to demonstrate that the American economic presence in Europe is of great industrial and political significance both to the European and to the U.S. economies. $27 billion worth of direct investment (in book value, or $50 to $75 billion, if priced at market value) investment in Western Europe is controlled by multinational corporations (MNCs) domiciled in the United States; and nearly ten thousand affiliates owned by these MNCs operate within the dozen economies of Western Europe.[1] Previous studies have noted three important points about these American industrial bridge-heads.

1. The investments and affiliates of the MNC are tightly concentrated in only a few industrial sectors. They are to be found neither in the primary nor in the labor-intensive sectors of the "host" economies. They congregate thickly where capital or expensive technologies are required in large aggregations. The American MNC plays a prominent role in those key industries that contribute a relatively small but a disproportionately important strength to the growth capabilities and to the competitive standing of various European economies.[2]
2. The American-based MNCs have made their deepest incursion into those industries that are subject to oligopoly control. These include capital-intensive industries (e.g., automobiles, petro-chemicals and oil), science-based industries (e.g., computers, electronics and nuclear engineering) and giant chains in the service sector (e.g., hotels, banking and food processing). Each of these industries manifest some form of oligopoly structure. Entry into their markets is severely limited; or prices are effectively stabilized and administered; or a small number of big firms operate under the marketing characteristics of imperfect competition.[3]
3. The factor of organizational "size" bears further proof of the oligopoly interests of the MNC in general and of the American MNCs in particular. The companies that play a mammoth role in the home market are those that also exert the largest influence in the host economies of Europe. The firms that appear at the top of the *Fortune* listing of the Top 500 corporations in America are the same as those (with a few remarkable exceptions) that set the pace in many of the strategic growth sectors of European industry.[4]

The motives that have driven American companies to penetrate European industry have been investigated by Marxist scholars (such as Ernest Mandel and André Gorz), by economic nationalists looking to Europe as an industrial "third

211

force" (such as Servan-Schreiber and Christopher Layton), and by innumerable professors of business or economics (Raymond Vernon, Jack Behrman, and Charles Kindleberger, to name only three).[5] The Marxists aside, their conclusions may be summarized as follows: The cause is not the pressure of American capital for investment outlets abroad; nine-tenths of American investment in Europe is financed out of European resources. Nor is the motive a conspiratorial design for political dominion. These theories as well as the theory of sheer technological superiority are rejected by Arthur Schlesinger and M. Servan-Schreiber in the popular polemic, *Le Défi Américain.* The critical disparity lies instead in the "art of organization"—in the mobilization of intelligence and talent in the fields of invention, development, production, and marketing. American industry expands out across the world primarily because of the energy released by the American system.[6]

The alarm raised in 1967 by *Le Défi Américain* has quieted down in the wake of new developments in the last five years. MNCs of European origin have successfully emulated and competed with the expansion strategies of their American rivals.[7] The dollar has weakened considerably on the world's money markets; as a result, the American practice of cheaply taking over European companies or of implanting local subsidiaries has appreciably slowed down. In some cases, the American penetration has been blocked by new controls legislated by host governments or by the rulings of the European Economic Community (EEC).[8] No longer can it be said, as M. Servan-Schreiber once predicted:

Fifteen years from now it is quite possible that the world's third greatest industrial power, just after the United States and Russia, will not be Europe, but *American industry in Europe.* Already, in the ninth year [1967] of the Common Market, this European market is basically American in organization.[9]

The list of American MNCs that have established their position in the key markets of Europe today is, nevertheless, awesome in dimension and in promise. To name only a few: IBM and Honeywell enjoy a larger share of the European computer market than *all* of their European rivals (e.g., ICL, CII, Philips, and Siemens) combined. The seven "major" oil companies, five of which are American, exercise a distribution and price leadership over local "independents" or "national" competitors (e.g., DEA in Germany, ENI in Italy, or ELF-Erap in France) that will be hard to break. Admittedly, DuPont, Dow, and Union Carbide have had to counter strong competition (from ICI, Bayer, or Rhone-Poulenc), but they have held their markets by creating a maze of joint-ventures and cross-licensing agreements in man-made fibers, pharmaceuticals, and naptha or ethylene derivatives. The giant auto facilities of GM and Ford in Britain and Germany have integrated vertically into France and the Low Countries; strikingly, U.S. electronics companies (Fairchild, Motorola, Texas Instruments) have seized a major share of the European market for micro- and integrated circuits. The most visible successes remain, however, in the service sector. Hilton, Sheraton, Avis, and J. Walter Thompson (advertising) are especially well known. The Morgan Guaranty bank, Chase Manhattan and First National City have not only opened hundreds of branches across Europe; their activity in the Euro-dollar market and in the trans-national consortia of banks (most of them located in London) has enlarged the leading role that American finance plays in Europe's "mature" stage of capitalism.[10]

One last point must be noted in this *tour d'horizon*. The political resentment generated by the presence of giant American oligopolies in Europe has greatly subsided. Ten years ago, President deGaulle denounced the technological imperialism of America and vetoed the entry of the United Kingdom (as America's "Trojan Horse") into EEC. At the same time, Harold Wilson warned that Britain must not become "a helot to the sophisticated apparatus of American business," and the EEC sought for common oil, transport, and computer plans in order to defeat the border-crossing expansion of American MNCs. Though parties and labor unions on the Left have attacked the profit-seeking growth of the MNC—warning that the ITT/CIA links in Chile would reappear in Bonn or Paris—it is evident that the American industrial thrust in recent years has not provoked the great outcry that had been anticipated. In many (though not all) cases, productivity has improved and strikes have decreased at plants taken over by American firms. To a great extent, consumer manipulation through TV advertising has been denounced in the elite press as a latter-day form of Coco-colonization. And yet, European firms have copied the slick packaging of food, tourism, and even bank marketing invented in New York. America's military intervention in Vietnam, it is true, was fiercely criticized, but its economic assault in Europe has been accepted as something of a *fait accompli*.[11]

The Tests of Imperialism

Two difficult questions need to be asked about the selective but powerful expansion of American capital in the economies of Europe. First, was it really imperative that the U.S. corporate economy should expand in this manner? Second, did the benefits of expansion reward the entrepreneurs who planned the "imperialist" expansion of American MNC activity in Europe?

A considerable amount of data would have to be marshalled to provide a definitive answer to either of these questions. Unfortunately, neither is the data sufficiently available (as the recent *U.N. Report* illustrates), nor are the confines of this chapter adequate to provide the full-scale confirmation that is required.[12] An attempt can be made, however, to formulate a set of relevant hypotheses. These must stand, *faute de mieux*, in place of a detailed and precise formulation of proof.

The first hypotheses to be noted are those suggested by the "classic" works on monopoly capital, economic determinism, and industrial imperialism. Baran and Sweezy, Hobson, Lenin, Kautsky, Kolko, and Magdoff have asserted that an advanced form of capitalism must (for different reasons) expand aggressively into new markets overseas to widen its monopolist influence. They argued that the inevitable decline in profits at home would compel companies to venture overseas to escape the inadequacies or contradictions of the home economy. Thus monopoly capital would *necessarily* drive outwards to colonize foreign markets. Not only were opportunities for the exploitation of surplus labor or capital outlets overseas indispensable to growth, but these distant markets also provided the raw materials or the security arrangements that American capitalism required to preserve its industrial base.

To these assertions of "free trade imperialism" were added another set of explanations. These focussed upon power-elite or class-interest explanations of economic behavior. C. Wright Mills, Richard Barnet, Gabriel Kolko, David Horowitz and other writers of the New Left emphasized that the managers of America's expansionist economy were driven by their class perspectives to fashion an imperial foreign policy; this helped both to enrich giant corporations with defense contracts and to safeguard the global interests of the corporate economy. In their view, the Cold War was to be understood largely as an economic thrust concealed beneath the facade of an ideological confrontation.[13]

Unfortunately, these hypotheses are not particularly helpful. Most of them are either too sweeping to be verified or too abstract to serve our present purposes. The older theories, of Lenin or Hobson, are in many ways no longer relevant to contemporary conditions of world trade. Contrary to earlier belief, the United States has neither been forced to export surplus capital to capture foreign markets nor to colonize its overseas sources of supply. Previously, emphasis had been placed upon three basic factors: foreign investments, foreign markets, and foreign sourcing. Today it is evident that these are not critical to the survival of the corporate economy. Of course, the giant MNCs would be hurt, but they would not be irreparably crippled if the capital "rent" or the dividend income flowing from these three sources were gradually terminated. At the very worst, if many of the MNCs' operations were truncated, the U.S. domestic economy would not grind to a halt, nor, in all probability, would a revolutionary movement emerge to sweep the "technostructure" elites from the Wall Street eyries of corporate power. Obviously, GM, GE, ITT, Exxon, and Ford would bitterly contest the expropriation of their assets, markets, and supplies overseas since many of them do 50 percent or more of their business outside the home economy. But the case remains to be proven that these leviathans of capital and technology would cave in—and bring the social structure down with them—if they were compelled to withdraw to their home market.[14]

Given the information that we now have about the functioning of advanced capitalism, a more useful set of hypotheses must be employed than those stressing the need to export surplus capital from the home market or to exploit the raw material sources of the developing world. As much as 90 percent of the MNCs' expansion overseas has been financed with host rather than home country capital. Moreover, European MNCs entering the United States have found that there is a shortage (rather than a surplus) of capital on Wall Street; and they have profited enormously by bringing funds into the United States via the Euro-dollar market or Swiss tax havens. Not much more credence can be given to the assertion that markets in the developed or developing world are indispensable to the U.S. economy as sources of raw material, surplus labor, or untapped purchasing power. As Theodore Moran has put it, these market explanations demonstrate the "convenience" rather than the "necessity" or the "institutional need" of the MNC to expand abroad.[15]

A different set of hypotheses must be sought, therefore, to answer the first question: Was it imperative for the American MNC to penetrate so far into the industrial structure of Europe? These new hypotheses must attend to the specific characteristics of the MNC rather than to classical models and generalizations (e.g., micro-level theories of the firm or macro-level suppositions) about the capitalist system. Prominent among these hypotheses must be propositions that seek to explain the behavior, motives, and rewards of the MNC. Attention must focus on the MNC's use of transfer pricing to re-allocate cash reserves and credit loans across national borders; its optimization of economies of scale through specializing component production in one country, sub-assembly work and vertical integration in a second, and R & D in a third; or its fulfillment of the "product life-cycle" that governs the MNC's expensive R & D and its patented, tightly controlled, and firm-specific technology.

The literature on the MNC is rich with such hypotheses. Many of them have been tested to determine whether the MNC is truly as unique in its strategic deployments, as effective in establishing an "oligopoly equilibrium" in its markets, and as consistent in global planning as its critics and advocates believe. Though the advocates view the MNC as an unprecedented engine of progress— and the critics as an unmitigated threat to the nation-state—there is enough hard data and tough reasoning in the literature to generate a dozen fresh hypotheses. The advocates argue, often persuasively, that the "cosmocorp" will bring peace to the world and affluence to the United States by competing with Japanese or German MNCs, where they are most vulnerable, on their home ground. The critics respond, as in their support for the Burke-Hartke bill before the U.S. Senate, that the MNC can indeed compete effectively overseas but that it will do so by exporting jobs, investment capital, and patented technology in order to return profits to the parent company from the various host economies that it has penetrated.[16]

Studies have been made of such notable MNCs as International Harvester,

Ford, Singer, and Westinghouse.[17] They have described how the factor-mobility or the oligopoly advantages of the MNC were exploited in the markets of the capitalist world. By taking advantage of differential tariff barriers, interest rates, factor costs, and currency exchange rates, the MNC has learned how to cope with competition abroad and how to defend its home base against the global penetration strategies of rival MNCs. In building its plants overseas, it has been guided by the laws of comparative advantage and by calculated economies of scale. In pursuing (as economists put it) the "international equalization of factor costs," the MNC has shipped labor-intensive work to cheap wage economies; or it has amortized expensive R & D against expanded sales overseas; or it has taken profits where taxes were low and borrowed money where interest rates were depressed. More important, the MNCs' standardizing of product lines and its administering of prices has succeeded, by and large, in extending its market power and stabilizing its profit schedules. Given the "technostructure" management and the conglomerate interests of the MNC, these techniques of market control have helped promote its extraordinary growth and profit.

Who Gains and How?

The hypotheses that explain MNC motives and behavior are strongly supported with micro-level (case studies and company reports) or aggregate data. They can be summarized as follows:

1. Most of the prominent MNCs are giant companies; and most of the giant companies of the United States (and Europe) operating across the European continent are MNCs.[18]
2. Of these companies, a large number earn 50 percent or more of their profits through host country affiliates; wholly owned by the parent company, in most cases, these affiliates extend the product life cycle, the marketing strategies and the transfer pricing devised by the parent company as part of a global strategy. Thus they create and thrive in oligopoly conditions.[19]
3. The MNC tends to take profits where taxes are low and repatriate dividends where they are high; to charge stiff royalty fees where competition is weak and lend money to affiliates where it is strong; or to respect "arms length" regulations where host governments are strict but transfer credits and goods below par where scrutiny is lax. Thus the MNC tends to record a better return on investment and to grow at a faster pace than many non-MNCs in the same industry.[20]
4. In the capital-intensive or science-based industries where MNCs settle thickly, the parent company enjoys the market power to choose between strategic options. It can either increase its return on investment by developing new product innovations at home or extending existing lines overseas; it can retain earnings abroad to finance subsidiary expansions or it can repatriate dividends and licensing fees to finance home-based R & D; or it can decrease its profit margin in its biggest markets (as the oil "majors" do in Europe) in order to

enlarge the global scale of its operation. Thus the MNC can spread its risk, optimize its opportunities and exact oligopoly rents within one, worldwide calculus.[21]

The record of American MNCs in fulfilling some or all of these options is quite impressive. Some notable failures have occurred, of course, and a few MNCs have fumbled badly (like the Frigidaire plant of GM in France, or the Celanese Corporation in Sicily) through their ignorance of local market conditions. Overall, however, the big MNCs have grown bigger, their profit margins better, and their strategic planning more effective. The fastest growing and the most technologically advanced have capitalized on the dynamics of host country growth rates, especially in Europe, where imperfect competition provides a favorable environment for oligopoly expansion. This has been spectacularly shown in the European automobile, chemical engineering, and metal industries. In these sectors are to be found the leviathans of corporate industry. There are 127 American MNCs that do from $1 to $10 billion worth of business overseas—as against 84 non-American companies recording an equal turnover. Obviously, they would be severely hurt if they were severed from their profitable affiliates in Europe. But they would not be demolished even by so draconian a cut as they are too soundly established at home to be ruined by amputation. Though their profits depend to a great extent on foreign operations, their long-term survivability—Marxist theorists notwithstanding—does not (see Table 11-1).

This tentative answer to the first question, regarding the *compulsion* of American MNCs to expand across Europe, can help to answer the second query: Who gains from their operations overseas?

This question can be answered at several different levels. First, at an aggregate level of national accounts, the balance of payments and the American position in world trade have benefitted from the cash flows generated by MNCs. Between 1968 and 1970, the inward flow of direct investment flowing into the United States (as an annual average) was $727 million and the outward flow $3,621 million. Despite this imbalance, or perhaps because of it, $7,241 billion more was received as income on these investments than was paid out to foreign investors ($8,107 million received and $866 million paid out).[22] In 1971, the United States received $2,569 million in royalties, fees, and payments ($1,874 from affiliate firms and $695 million from non-affiliates), while it paid out only $216 million to foreign investors.[23] One cause of these asymmetric payment flows is to be found in the $7,598 million spent on manufacturing R & D, 94 percent of which was kept at home while only $526 million was spent overseas.[24]

Second, it should be noted that though American-made exports declined, in relative terms, in the tough competition of the developed world's trade, the U.S. balance of payments position hinged to an ever greater extent upon the strength

Table 11-1
The Top Ten MNCs, 1971

Rank	Company	Total Sales ($ millions)	Foreign Content as Percentage of				
			Sales	Production	Assets	Earnings	Employment
1	General Motors	28,264	19	–	15	19	27
2	Standard Oil (N.J.)	18,701	50	81	52	52	–
3	Ford Motors	16,433	26	36	40	24	48
4	Royal Dutch/Shell	12,734	79	–	–	–	70
5	General Electric	9,429	16	–	15	20	–
6	IBM	8,274	39	–	27	50	36
7	Mobil Oil	8,243	45	–	46	51	51
8	Chrysler	7,999	24	22	31	–	24
9	Texaco	7,529	40	65	–	25	–
10	Unilever	7,483	80	–	60	–	70

Note: *The U.N. Report* listing is amended.
Source: *The U.N. Report*, 1973, Tables I and III.

of the MNCs' operations overseas. At a conservative estimate, American MNCs generated $172 billion in international production (though most of this sum was retained overseas), while its conventional export trade realized only $43.5 billion in 1971 sales.[25] This four-to-one ratio is of enormous significance to the role played by the United States in the world economy.

The third country sales effected by U.S. affiliates abroad have allowed the MNCs to penetrate markets that might otherwise have been closed to them for political and tariff reasons, or too tough to crack with home-made exports. Indeed, U.S. affiliates overseas have exported more than Germany and twice as much as Japan. (In addition, 8 percent of their product has been imported back into the United States and thus accounts for nearly 25 percent of all U.S. import bills; a considerable portion of these re-exports came from U.S. affiliates in Canada, especially in the aftermath of the United States-Canadian automotive agreement.)[26] Ranging the lucrative markets of the world in order to rationalize their investment and R & D deployments, the MNC has created ever wider options for itself in world trade. This global deployment has also allowed the MNC to counter the threat posed by low-cost imports or oligopoly competition entering its prized markets at home and overseas.[27]

Two severe criticisms have been levelled against the MNC. Both must be noted in answering the last question: Who gains from their operations?

First, it has been claimed that the MNC is uniquely responsible for exporting low-paid or unskilled jobs to cheap wage economies. Incensed by the U.S. government estimate that 700,000 jobs had been exported, largely to the 10-cents-an-hour plants built by electronics MNCs in South East Asia, the AFL-CIO threw its backing behind the Burke-Hartke bill in an attempt to curb the MNCs' freedom to maneuver. In response, various business groups and MNCs have published their own statistics and estimates in order to demonstrate: (a) that U.S. employment had increased rather than decreased as a result of their expansion abroad; and (b) that the adoption of protectionist legislation would cripple the investment plans of the MNC without helping the American worker. These claims and counter-claims must be examined carefully. Though they both appear to be correct at an aggregate level, they both distort the evidence on a firm-by-firm analysis. GE and Ford have both increased their activity in Europe and maintained high employment levels at home. But they have also managed— like many other MNCs—to increase the insecurity perceived by labor unions at home. The unions have realized that the MNC could rapidly relocate work out of an economy where wage rates, inflation, or interest rates are soaring or where productivity and labor "discipline" are falling away.[28]

The second criticism relates to the powerful options and insurance strategems that the MNC can create for itself. These can be achieved, as in a zero-sum game, at the expense of either the home or host government. So long as the MNC can choose whether to relocate its cash balances, production components, work schedules, or R & D, it can also degrade the economic autonomy of the nation-state. Willingly or not, the capitalist state remains responsible for the regulation of the nation's balance of payments, inflation controls, export subsidies, and long-term growth plans. Thus many governments have been sorely troubled by the growing power and size of the MNC. Equally important, many of these firms have settled in the key, strategic sectors—such as petroleum, automobiles, banking or computers—that are vital to the host country's growth. Logically, therefore, the increase in the MNC's discretionary power has threatened the regulatory economic authority of the state as well as the survival of its political sovereignty.[29]

The dimensions of the threat can be gauged from the data appearing in Table 11-2. The inroads made by American MNCs into the advanced economies of Europe have been enormous. Britain, in particular, faces the prospect of moving toward the situation recorded in Canada, where 63 percent of industrial and petroleum assets now lie in the control of foreign firms; or of Australia, which is nearing the 35 percent mark. Though this penetration has been beneficial in many ways to the host economy, and certainly to the directors and share-holders of the parent company, it is questionable whether the consequences will always be advantageous. So far the U.S. penetration has occurred during a fast-rising period in world trade. Should a major recession set in, American firms will have to decide whether to lay off workers in one country, transfer assets out of another, anticipate currency devaluation in a third, or to flee before political upheaval in a fourth.

Table 11-2
American Investments in Europe, 1970

Industry	Belgium and Luxembourg	Canada	France	German Fed. Republic	United Kingdom
All manufacturing:	14.1	32.2	5.8	12.3	20.9
Of which:					
Food	–	23.5	0.9	2.0	4.4
Chemicals	24.9	68.1	2.1	10.4	17.9
Primary & pre-fabricated metals	–	–	1.0	8.4	21.1
Non-electrical machinery	12.0	57.8	23.3	27.8	29.0
Electrical machinery Transportation equipment	–	–	9.8	27.8	45.5
All other manufacturing	10.8	13.6	2.8	2.7	18.2

Note: Percentage of manufacturing industries: share of U.S. plant and equipment expenditures in gross fixed capital formation of industry.
Source: *The U.N. Report*, 1973, Table XXIV.

The recent movements of American MNCs toward the authoritarian regimes of Europe (Spain, Greece, Portugal, and Turkey) reveals that some forms of pre-emptive action have already been taken. Were many more MNCs to relocate to the fascist fringe of Europe, however, political criticism and protest would surely intensify. Labor unions and European parties, both on the Left and on the nationalist Right, might begin to question whether it was their own economy or the American managers and share-holders who should profit from the MNCs' expansion. The 1973 oil crisis re-opened the issue with great force. Loyal and defecting allies, alike, asked what were the industrial benefits that their citizens had gained by surrendering so much of their industry and capital to foreign control? Might they not have survived better in the political confrontation with the Arab oil suppliers if the "international equalization of factor costs" had been programmed by agencies less concerned with profit-taking or global deployments than the MNCs?

The future answer to these questions cannot be foreseen. The oil crisis of 1973 re-awakened the fears of both home and host governments across the Atlantic. The U.S. corporate economy had clearly gained from the lucrative share that MNC oil giants shared in the European market and their earnings suddenly increased by 50 to 80 percent. Though the MNCs had brought about an influx of new capital, technology, and management to the petro-chemical industries, the political costs were well-nigh exorbitant. Were Mobil, Texaco, or Exxon to order it, no power in Europe (or in the Middle East) could stop them from rerouting their tankers from Rotterdam to New York or from converting their sterling balances into yen or dollars.

It can be seen that the costs and risks of the MNCs' expansion in Europe might one day prove to be hurtful to the United States, too. The American balance of payments, the purchasing power of the dollar, the employment prospects of the work force and the "technology gap" (which supposedly runs in America's favor) could be gravely impaired if world trade flows were subject to a grave recession. Workers, consumers, and government economists might find themselves, indeed, in a position that few of them had foreseen. Though many benefits might have been generated by the MNCs' dominance of the most promising, science-based and capital-intensive industries in times of prosperity, its degrading of the control mechanisms of nation-states in times of crisis might verge, realistically, toward a condition of catastrophe.

Should this extreme condition materialize, the political repercussions might well be of awesome consequence. Home and host governments might have to break the GATT and IMF agreements in order to protect their currencies or to shore up their faltering terms of trade. Though most nations now recognize that the thrust toward a greater interdependence in world trade is irreversible, they might come to dispute whether the MNC is the best arbiter of the pace and the direction in which interdependence should develop. MNCs are accountable neither to home governments nor to its overseas workers and clients. Their search for an optimum allocation of resources or profits could generate serious and destabilizing outcomes.

In a post-industrial society, Daniel Bell tells us, the resentment of economically disfranchised workers and voters poses a severe threat. Elite management, skilled in the trans-national control of technology, might find themselves caught in a fierce political crossfire. MNC bankers on one side and surging populist movements on the other might call into question both the source of their authority and the direction of their loyalties. To be stateless and economically detached, in a period of decline, would neither help the MNC nor the cosmopolitan constituencies that it claims to serve. Thomas Jefferson, observing the business practices of 1800 noted that "merchants have no country. The mere spot they stand on does not constitute as strong an attachment as that from which they draw their gains."[30]

That this crisis scenario might never materialize is, of course, a reasonable proposition. Indeed, in place of turmoil might come that World Peace through World Trade (as the chairman of IBM often asserted) that Robert Heilbroner has identified as the businessman's Utopia. However, even were the rich to get richer as a result of the wealth-building extensions of the trans-Atlantic MNCs, the problems of the Third World would still remain to be resolved. Furthermore, it does not require a pessimistic analysis to suggest that these problems will become more acute if the American presence in Europe should become more affluent.

Unless the present oil and dollar crises should call for drastic policy changes, the strength of the MNC will surely grow and—to the same degree—the regulatory instruments of government will lose strength. The MNC will not be the only agent to assault the economic sovereignty and defense works of the nation-state. But insofar as it accelerates the internationalization of economic growth and interdependence, it will do more than any other agency to dramatize the fundamental conflict of our times. Mass electorates cling for political and psychological purposes to a political organization, the nation-state, even though its economic viability is now in question. The MNC can not replace the state, nor can it submit to its constraining force. At the present time it seems more likely that the MNC will divide state against state—or against its own mass electorates—than that it will bring about a businessman's Utopia of peace and harmony.[31]

Notes

1. The most complete listings of data on MNC assets, operations and growth rates are to be found in the *Survey of Current Business* published by the U.S. Department of Commerce (see Vol. 52, No. 11, Nov. 1972 for the latest figures); and in the U.N. Report of *MNC in World Development* (hereafter referred to as the *U.N. Report*) published by the Department of Economic and Social Affairs

(New York: United Nations, 1973, ST/ECA/190). The latter collates and abridges statistical data derived from many international sources, both in the private and public sectors. NB: It is conventionally assumed that the market value or the sales turnover of the MNC's holdings overseas are two or three times greater than the indicated book value of their direct investments. A listing of American investments in Europe appears in Table 11-2.

2. The heavy concentration of MNC investment in manufacturing and petroleum industries is emphasized throughout the *U.N. Report* (pp. 10-15 and Tables XIII-XVIII); these industries absorb 75 percent of U.S. direct investments in the developed or "mature" economies of Western Europe.

Rarely do the combined investments of the incoming MNCs surpass 5 percent of the host country's GDP. The careful selection in the location and concentration of this venture capital, as the data in Table 11-2 lists, has allowed foreign affiliates to play a prominent role in British automobile, French engineering, German chemical and Belgian petroleum industries. The motives of the MNC in pursuing this pattern of concentration is investigated at length in the theoretical chapters of Raymond Vernon, *Sovereignty at Bay* (New York: Basic Books, 1971). The *U.N. Report* reveals (Table XV) that in 1970, 41 percent of direct U.S. foreign investments outside the developing world were in manufacturing and 28 percent in petroleum.

3. A valuable criticism of the literature on oligopoly theory and MNC expansion appears in Theodore H. Moran, "Foreign Expansion as an 'Institutional Necessity,' for U.S. Corporate Capitalism: The Search for a Radical Model," *World Politics*, Vol. 25, No. 3 (April 1973), pp. 369-86. The emphasis upon economies of scale, market control, and extensions of the "product life cycle" theory in Moran's view explains the new form of industrial imperialism practiced by the MNC.

4. Many attempts have been made to explain why giant companies at home are quick to expand their operations overseas. Among the more interesting are Robin Murray, "The Internationalization of Capital and the Nation-State," *New Left Review*, No. 67 (May-June 1971), pp. 84-109; and Stephen Hymer and Robert Rowthorn, "MNCs and International Oligopoly: The Non-American Challenge," in Charles P. Kindleberger (ed.), *The International Corporation* (Cambridge: M.I.T. Press, 1970).

5. Ernest Mandel, *Europe versus America? Contradictions of Imperialism* (London: New Left Books, 1970); André Gorz, *Strategy for Labor: A Radical Proposal* (Boston: Beacon, 1964); Jean-Jacques Servan-Schreiber, *The American Challenge* (New York: Atheneum, 1968); Christopher Layton, *Industry and Europe* (London: Political and Economic Planning, No. 531, October 1971); Raymond Vernon, op. cit.; Jack N. Behrman, *National Interests and the Multinational Enterprise* (New Jersey: Prentice-Hall, 1970); and Kindleberger, op. cit.

6. Servan-Schreiber, op. cit., p. ix.

7. Non-American MNCs have begun to expand at a faster rate than their U.S. counterparts in recent years. The devaluation of the dollar and the development of cross-national commerce in EEC have provided powerful stimuli to their further growth. In 1971, U.S. direct foreign investments (at book value) were $86 billion; those of Britain were $24, France $9.5, Germany $7.3, Switzerland $6.8, Canada $6 and Japan $4.9 billion. (*The U.N. Report*, Table V.) Using the conservative formula, that turnover is only two—not three—times greater than book values, it now appears that the total sales of all MNCs combined ($320 billion p.a.) is slightly larger than the cumulative worth of *all* export and import trading. Fifty-two percent of these sales were made by American MNCs; but U.S. firms are expanding at 9.2 percent p.a. while Japan's MNCs record a 28.3 percent and Germany's a 22.8 percent annual rate of growth. (Ibid., Table X.)

8. A start has been made by EEC to curb MNC activities by imposing anti-trust constraints against the chemical dye giants, against Continental Can and against various joint venture and marketing arrangements. The limited effectiveness of these constraints is surveyed in Leon N. Lindberg and Stuart A. Scheingold, *Europe's Would-Be Polity* (New Jersey: Prentice-Hall, 1970).

9. Servan-Schreiber, op. cit., p. 9, (his italics). A critical review of this best selling polemic appears in the present author's "Europe Faces the Technology Gap," *Yale Review*, Vol. 59, No. 2 (December 1969), pp. 161-78; and in Rainer Hellmann, *The Challenge to U.S. Domination of the International Corporation* (New York: Dunellen, 1970; translated by Peter Ruof).

10. A useful European perspective on the expansion of MNC industry and banking in Europe can be gained from various contributions to John H. Dunning (ed.), *The Multinational Enterprise* (London: Allen and Unwin, 1971). Listings of the leading MNCs and of their market positions appear in such European business journals as *Expansion, The Economist, Vision, Management Today* and *Sucesso*; and in Heinz Aszkenazy, *Les Grándes Societes Européennes*, and Michel De Vroey, *Propriété et Pouvoir dans les Grandes Enterprises*, both published in Brussels by C.R.I.S.P. (1971 and 1973).

11. Parties on the Left have been critical of the MNC and have even issued a few, subdued threats to nationalize their property. However, the Labour Party in Britain or the Social Democrats in Scandinavia and Germany (and in Canada) have not shown any ardor for such action; neither have their trade unions. The confusion on the Left is illustrated in the remarks made by the Communist leaders from fifteen European parties, collected in *The International Firms and the European Working Class* (London: Communist Party of Great Britain, n.d.). The representatives from Austria went so far as to insist that:

The interlocking of capital and the establishment of co-operation with foreign organizations must not be tied to conditions which endanger either the property or the independence of Austrian factories. (Ibid., p. 8.)

12. The scarcity of data on MNC activities is so acute that *The U.N. Report*

(p. 100) calls on the U.N. Secretariat to put every effort into the collecting and disseminating of specialized information on MNCs. This recommendation concludes a Report that summarizes 43 Tables of data in 72 closely filled pages.

13. A dozen critiques have been written recently on the need to bring the 'classic' literature on imperialism up-to-date or to redefine its differing thrusts in the light of the new challenges brought by the MNC. To cite only two efforts: James O'Connor, "The Meaning of Economic Imperialism" in K.T. Fann and D.C. Hodges (eds.), *Readings in U.S. Imperialism* (Boston: Porter Sargent, 1971); and Thomas Weisskopf, "U.S. Foreign Private Investment: An Empirical Survey," in R.C. Edwards, M. Reich and T.E. Weisskopf (eds.), *The Capitalist System* (New Jersey: Prentice-Hall, 1972).

14. The retreat home would not be easily made, of course, and the process of adjustment might bring grave turmoil. The U.S. economy relies upon the MNC to an enormous extent to secure its balance of payments and to maintain a high level of employment. MNC sales overseas realize $165 billion or more each year while exports bring only $50 billion in foreign payments. Moreover, nearly one-third of export payments come from the intra-company transfers from home-based American MNCs; and Stateside companies, such as Ford and GE, calculate that 10 to 20 percent of their domestic employment derives from the servicing of overseas operations. Nevertheless, a forcible substitution for U.S. imports and a redeployment of the American work force could be programmed if world conditions cut off "the American economy abroad"; it contributes less than 20 percent of our $1.3 trillion GNP and it accounts for less than 10 percent of the work positions in a highly flexible and mobile economy.

15. Moran, op. cit. (p. 371), sensibly warns that the giant size of the MNC and of its overseas operations should not mislead us. Though the combined worth of MNC sales might equal the size of Japan's GNP and its annual rate of growth, there is no need to explain this new economic phenomena by resorting to neo-classical or neo-Marxist formulae. The outward expansion of the MNC can be explained in terms of its own dynamics without resorting to needs that supposedly remain to be fulfilled in the capitalist system.

16. The academic literature (that passes as non-partisan inquiry) is proliferating at an accelerating rate. A review of recent inquiries in the literature—and of the arguments before Congressional and business groups appears in Hugh Stephenson, *The Coming Clash: the Impact of MNCs on National States* (New York: Saturday Review Press, 1972). However, the author fails to note Prof. Kindleberger's awesome conclusion that "the nation-state is just about through as an economic unit," in *American Business Abroad* (New Haven: Yale University Press, 1969), p. 207.

17. The early history and the expansionist motives of many American MNCs are investigated at length in Mirra Wilkins, *The Emergence of Multinational Enterprise* (Cambridge: Harvard Universtiy Press, 1970); in Vernon, op. cit.; and in Edith T. Penrose, *The Theory of the Growth of the Firm* (Oxford: University

Press, 1966). Empirical studies of the chemical, electronics and other manufacturing MNCs are summarized in Moran, op. cit. The emphasis placed by "the technostructure" on growth and oligopoly control, rather than on the maximization of profit, is best associated with J.K. Galbraith, *The New Industrial State* (Boston: Houghton Mifflin, 1967).

18. The concentration of giant firms in direct foreign investment is revealed in many different industries in *The MNC: Studies on U.S. Foreign Investmeht*, Volume 2, (Washington: U.S. Department of Commerce, April 1973).

About 250 to 300 U.S.-based MNCs account for over 70 percent of all foreign investments. If the *Fortune* list of the 500 largest U.S. companies is used for comparison, almost the entire direct investment universe would be included. (Ibid., p. 5.)

19. Of the 76 MNCs sampled in the Department of Commerce *Studies*, Ibid., p. 6, 33 sought to "maintain or increase market shares locally," 25 reported that they would otherwise be "unable to reach markets from the United States because of tariffs transportation costs, or nationalistic purchasing policies"; 20 went overseas to "meet competition" and 15 because of "faster sales growth than in the United States."

20. The same report (Ibid., p. 9) notes "that foreign investments [i.e., worldwide] were regarded as more risky than domestic ones; consequently, it was necessary to have foreign projects earn a higher rate of return before investment would be made overseas." By 1970 profit margins were higher abroad than in the United States, and MNCs in Europe averaged a return of 10 percent p.a. (or 7 percent if petroleum companies were included). (*The U.N. Report*, Table XXXVII.)

21. The success of the MNC in fulfilling these objectives was measured in a special study issued by the Business International Corp. (New York, November 1972), *The Effects of U.S. Corporate Foreign Investment, 1960-1970*. The 125 manufacturing MNCs in the sample accounted for $133 billion of worldwide sales, of which $36 billion or about 27 percent were to non-U.S. customers; their exports ($9.4 billion) represented 25 percent of all U.S. non-agricultural exports, with over 50 percent of them going to their own foreign affiliates. These 125 firms accounted for 40 percent of the book value of all U.S. foreign manufacturing investment and 70 percent of investment outflows in 1970.

22. *The U.N. Report*, Table XX.

23. Ibid., Table XXXVIII.

24. Ibid., Table XLIX.

25. Ibid., Table XIX.

26. Moran, op. cit., pp. 384-85. The strength of these third country sales are borne out by the data sampled in the "Department of Commerce" and "Business International" studies (footnotes 18 and 21 above).

27. The "Business International" study (fn. 21) reports that between 1960

and 1970 its sample of 125 MNCs increased their exports by 205 percent (while U.S. non-agricultural exports grew by only 128 percent); and that their inter-affiliate exports grew by 302 percent. Sales to U.S. customers increased by 104 percent and to non-U.S. clients by 306 percent. As a result, the 125 companies' contribution to the balance of U.S. trade doubled (to nearly $5 billion) while the overall U.S. trade surplus during the decade was halved (from $5.4 to $2.6 billion). Though $20 billion had been invested overseas by 1970, only 6.7 percent of this sample had been financed by a financial outflow from the United States. The rest came from foreign depreciation, reserves, earnings and borrowings. 1970 remittances of dividends, fees, earnings, interest and royalties totalled $2.2 billion, five times more than they had been in 1960.

28. The "Business International" study, op. cit., argued that its 125 sample companies increased their net employment at a rate about 2.5 times faster than the average U.S. company. In the last five years of the 1960 to 1970 period, the rate was four times faster. At the same time, their net investment within the United States grew by 178 percent, as compared to a rise of 121 percent for all manufacturers. The strongest arguments against the Burke-Hartke bill appear in many of the studies issued by the National Foreign Trade Council, such as *The Impact of U.S. Foreign Direct Investment on U.S. Employment and Trade* (New York, November 1971). This asserts in 34 pages of data and anecdote that "Not to invest abroad would lose more jobs" (p. 7). A contrary set of facts and narrative appear in Steve Babson, "The MNC and Labor," *Review of Radical Political Economics*, Vol. 5, No. 1 (Spring 1973), pp. 19-36. He surveys the job skills of the work that was or that might be relocated at the discretion of the MNC management; he finds considerable reason to support organized labor's fear that relocation threats will be used to break strikes, to speed up assembly lines and to evade government regulations.

29. The contradictions and conflicts emerging between global MNCs and territorial-based governments are likely to become acute in the next decade or more. (See Murray, op. cit., fn 4.) The economic logic of the MNC requires the fullest mobility for its transfer operations and the least feasible respect for political frontiers. By contrast, the political imperative of the nation-state is to conserve the autonomy of its economy, the authority of its government and the sovereignty of its citizens. For example, the decision taken by Ford to build the Pinto engine in Britain, and then to cancel it, was made without consulting the British government or work force. Ford, obviously could relocate a major project out of the United Kingdom without trouble; but the British could not go to Detroit to protest.

30. Cited in the statement of Leonard Woodcock, the president of the UAW, in the *MNC Hearings* of the U.S. Senate Subcommittee on International Trade (93rd Congress, 1st Session, March 1, 1973, p. 293). He also cites (p. 276) the conclusion of Professor Vernon (Ibid., fn. 2) that:

Men with power have an extraordinary capacity to convince themselves that what they want to do happens to coincide with what society needs done for its own good. This comfortable illusion is shared as much by strong leaders of enterprise as by strong leaders of government.

31. Professor Vernon concludes his careful study of the MNC (Ibid., p. 284) on a similar note by questioning how nation-states will "convert issues they had once thought domestic into issues of international concern." He assumes that the "basic asymmetry between multinational enterprises and national governments" might be redressed by some new world body to which the MNC would remain accountable. Since there is little evidence for the belief that such a world body can be built it is relevant to quote his ultimate finding:

If this does not happen, some of the apocalyptic projections of the future of the multinational enterprise will grow more plausible.

A more radical projection of the conflict between the MNC and the nation-state appears in David Calleo and Benjamin Rowland, *America and the World Political Economy* (Bloomington: University of Indiana Press, 1973). They conclude that only the national state can provide a semblance of popular control over the surge of market forces and oligopoly capital. But they are not sure, either, that it will succeed in its task much longer.

Part III
Soviet Imperialism:
Empirical Theory-Testing

12

The Political Economy of Soviet Relations with Eastern Europe

Paul Marer
Indiana University

Introduction

The purpose of this chapter is to discuss three economic issues that must be considered in testing the hypothesis that the USSR has been an imperialist power in East Europe since World War II. Economic imperialism is defined as political domination for the purpose of economic extraction. The three issues are (1) the size of unrequited capital transfers during the period of 1945 to 1960, (2) the terms of trade, and (3) the commodity composition of exports and imports. No claim is made that these topics exhaust the relevant issues, only that these are among the principal ones that are important. Unless otherwise specified, East Europe refers to the six smaller European members of the Council for Mutual Economic Assistance (CEMA); these are Bulgaria, Czechoslovakia, East Germany, Hungary, Poland, and Rumania.

On each issue, the approach is to state the problem, discuss its background and the considerations involved, summarize the evidence, in quantitative terms whenever possible, offer alternative interpretations of the evidence, and arrive at tentative conclusions. An attempt is made in the concluding section to place the findings into a theoretical framework that shows economic extraction is only one of several economic instruments at the disposal of dominant power pursuing "imperial" objectives in its relations with smaller nations.

This theoretical framework was developed by Albert Hirschman *before* the Soviet Union became the dominating power in Eastern Europe.[1] It stresses the political benefits that accrue to a big power from nurturing economic dependency and that political considerations might even require a big power to forego economic gains.

The principal findings of this study show that:

1. Until after Stalin's death in 1953, the Soviet Union's political domination of Eastern Europe was accompanied by conventional kinds of economic extraction from the region, with the size of the unrequited flow of resources from East Europe to the Soviet Union being approximately of the same order of

The author is grateful to the International Development Research Center of Indiana University for support and facilities and to Professors Robert Farlow and Walter Jones for valuable comments on an earlier draft.

231

magnitude as the flow of resources from the United States to Western Europe under the Marshall Plan.

2. Since the mid-1950s, there is no clear evidence that the Soviet Union obtains unrequited resource transfers from Eastern Europe; in fact, evidence suggests that the USSR might be paying an increasingly steep price for the political benefit it derives from the continued economic dependence of the East European countries on the Soviet Union.

The first section presents a cumulative balance sheet of reparations and other forms of subvention transfers from East Europe to the USSR and Soviet foreign aid to these countries. The year 1960 was chosen as a dividing line, mainly because it might be the last year in which transfers related to the war had been settled.[2] While during the first postwar decade resources flowed primarily from East Europe to the USSR, during the second half of the 1950s there was a reverse flow that may be viewed as partial compensation for earlier excessive extractions. Therefore, it seems fair to discuss both these flows in the same context. The frequency and relative importance of subvention- and aid-type transfers have diminished considerably since 1960.

In drawing up the balance sheet, no account was taken of several types of potentially important actual or foregone capital transfers, such as the sacrifice to East Europe of not being permitted to participate in the Marshall Plan, the aid that East Europe has been obliged to provide to other socialist countries and to the Third World, the net value of blueprints and licenses provided to each other free of charge, the subsidies that might be involved in a cumulative trade surplus, or the implicit subsidies that may result from discriminatory non-commercial exchange rates used in settling invisible transactions.

The first part of the next section presents empirical evidence on the terms of trade that is based on work I have recently completed. It is introduced by a discussion on why terms of trade indices between state-trading countries do not lend themselves to the same interpretation as those calculated for market economies. This section also discusses the commodity composition and presents several viewpoints on the question: Were exports to the Soviet Union during the first postwar decade and the internal development strategy with which trade was closely interconnected imposed on East Europe from without or were they decided voluntarily by the countries themselves? It also describes how the economic interest of the USSR has undergone a full transformation during the postwar period.

The last section offers some conclusions and attempts to show the continuity and coherence in Soviet policy toward Eastern Europe in spite of significant changes in the type of economic instruments it employs in the pursuit of its objectives.

Every alleged fact or controversial statement is documented. It is hoped that it will be possible to improve on the estimates presented as more information becomes available and also to quantify those variables it was not possible to do so in the context of this chapter.

**Capital Transfers Between East
Europe and the USSR**

The probable Soviet objectives in East Europe during the first postwar decade were (1) *military*: to deny the area to Germany (whose reemergence was a potential long-term threat) and, later, to potentially hostile Western powers; (2) *political*: to ensure that individual countries would not be controlled by governments hostile to the USSR; and (3) *economic*: to use the resources of the area for Soviet reconstruction and industrialization via reparations and other forms of economic extraction. To be sure, reparations-type deliveries by the ex-enemy countries of East Germany, Hungary, Bulgaria, and Rumania must be viewed in the light of the destruction inflicted on the Soviet Union during the war.

Reparations-Type Transfers

East Germany. The Soviet Union demanded $10 billion of reparations at *prewar prices*. In the absence of an agreement with the Allies, it proceeded unilaterally to collect from the Eastern zone. Reparations took the form of (1) "official" dismantling of industrial installations (as well as conscription of much timber and livestock in six waves from 1945 until the spring of 1948), whose rough order of magnitude is estimated at $4 billion in 1955 prices and which represent one quarter or more of East Germany's postwar industrial capacity;[3] (2) reparation deliveries to the Soviet Union from current production until the end of 1953 which, though reduced twice, are estimated as over $6 billion in current prices; (3) deliveries to the Red Army stationed in Germany until the end of 1958, estimated at about $4 billion in current prices; and (4) other deliveries, such as uranium (1946 to 1960) as well as inventory depletion of expropriated German companies just before they were returned in 1952-53, for an estimated combined total of more than $4 billion in current prices.[4]

East Germany's total reparation-type deliveries to the Soviet Union are thus estimated to have amounted to about $19 billion (most estimates range between $10 and $25 billion), which represented from one-fifth to one-third of East German GNP during the first eight years after the war.[5] According to one calculation, East German reparation deliveries in 1950 amounted to about 3 percent of Soviet national income,[6] although the percentages were probably higher during the early postwar years. East Germany of course lost much more than the Soviet Union gained because of wasteful dismantling of installations.

Poland. Although not an ex-enemy country, Poland made two kinds of transfers to the USSR in connection with German reparations. First, even though, according to an agreement signed in Moscow on August 16, 1945, the Soviets renounced all claims to German property in Poland, including those located on former German territory, much industrial and transport equipment and livestock was removed from the new Polish territories both before and after the signing of the agreement, as revealed by a Polish publication in 1957.[7] Second, according to the agreement, German reparations to Poland were to be handled by the Soviet Union and were to amount to 15 percent of total German reparations to the USSR. In return, Poland agreed to deliver to the USSR each year, for the duration of the reparations, large quantities of coal at a special low price of $1.25/ton, which was somewhere in the neighborhood of one-tenth of the world market price. (Why the USSR should have been compensated by Poland for German reparations to Poland is not clear.) According to estimates, however, even during the early years Soviet deliveries of German reparations to Poland amounted to much less than the agreed 15 percent,[8] and deliveries stopped altogether in 1948. At the same time, Polish coal deliveries at below world market prices continued, apparently until the mid-1950s. After the autumn 1956 upheavals in Poland, the Soviet government recognized "past relations of inequality among socialist states" and in November 1956 agreed to a $626 million reimbursement, in the form of cancelling Poland's debt to the Soviet Union.[9] This amount, however, reportedly represented less than half of Poland's claim on the USSR on the reparations account.[10] Perhaps more important than the precise equity of the settlement is that by 1956 coal was no longer in short supply in the world market so that whatever chance Poland had earlier to earn hard currency with which to buy investment goods on favorable terms had passed.[11]

Hungary, Rumania, and Bulgaria. The Soviet Union also required reparations from Hungary and Rumania[12] as follows:

1. Deliveries from current production. $200 million was required from Hungary (mainly metallurgical products) and $300 million from Rumania (mainly crude oil and derivatives), with actual deliveries subsequently reduced to $134 and 226 millions, respectively.[13] The amounts were fixed in gold dollars, i.e., in goods valued at 1938 prices. Because of this fact, plus especially low accounting prices during the early years, the value of deliveries at current prices was perhaps double the nominal amount.[14]
2. Payments to the Soviet Union of debts incurred by these states to Germany during the war (while their claims on Germany were cancelled). $200 million was claimed from Hungary alone, of which $45 million was delivered.[15]
3. Additional deliveries to compensate for equipment and objects removed from Soviet territory and for supplies consumed by troops in their zone of occupation during the war. More than $500 million was originally claimed from Rumania alone, of which almost $200 million was delivered.[16]
4. Until at least the latter half of the 1950s, supply the Soviet Army stationed in these countries. In addition, during the early years there was considerable

dismantling of industrial property (as well as the usual "trophy campaign" by troops). A very rough estimate would place the value at $1 billion in Rumania and Hungary each.[17]

No formal reparations were requested by the Soviet Union from Bulgaria, and no industrial equipment was removed from that country. According to one source, however, Soviet transfers took the form of forced exports of foodstuffs and the profits of Soviet-Bulgarian joint companies[18] which are discussed next.

Soviet-East European Joint Enterprises

Background. Before and during the war one aspect of Germany's strong economic penetration eastward was its acquisition of substantial financial and operating assets in East Central Europe. At the end of the war the Allied countries—Czechoslovakia, Poland, and Yugoslavia—recovered these assets, while the German assets in the ex-enemy countries were transferred to the Soviet Union and became the basis for joint Soviet-Hungarian, Soviet-Rumanian, and Soviet-Bulgarian enterprises. The Soviets contributed the assets formerly owned by German interests and subsequently some investment goods; the bloc partner delivered additional capital and most of the labor and material inputs (although each party supposedly contributed half of current outlays), with *de facto* management firmly in Soviet hands. In 1946-47, Yugoslavia voluntarily agreed to participate in two joint companies with the Soviets in river navigation and civil aviation.

These joint companies gave controlling positions at some key economic points in the four countries to the USSR, with the relative importance of these enterprises being the greatest in Rumania, somewhat less in Hungary, and smaller in Bulgaria and Yugoslovia.[19] In East Germany, 213 enterprises, originally earmarked under reparations—mostly in basic and metal-working industries—to be shipped to the Soviet Union, were transferred to Soviet ownership and operated in Germany as Soviet enterprises[20] in many respects similarly to the joint enterprises in other bloc countries.

The Special Case of Uranium. An important special case is Soviet exploitation of the uranium resources of East Germany, Czechoslovakia, and Hungary. In East Germany the prospecting and mining of uranium was started by a Soviet company, Wismut, in 1945. Until the end of 1953, all ore deliveries were credited (at what price?) to the reparations account. In 1954, Wismut became a joint Soviet-German enterprise (as far as it is known to me it still is) with total output being shipped to the Soviet Union.[21]

In Hungary, as well as in Czechoslovakia (which is not an ex-enemy country!), the uranium mines have been operating as joint companies.[22] We obtain some insight about how the Soviet Union handled these transactions, at least under Stalin, from the testimony of Czechoslovakia's Deputy Minister of Foreign Trade, who was frequently in charge of his country's trade negotiations with the Soviet Union until 1949. He relates that, even though the general principle was to conduct intra-bloc trade at world market prices, for uranium the Soviets were willing to pay only the much lower price of cost plus 10 percent. Of the November 1947 negotiations he writes:

My argument was that we paid world market prices for wheat and for [iron] ore from Kriwaj Rog [USSR] and that I could not see why we should accept other than the world market prices for what was practically our only natural wealth. After the war the price of uranium was very high and thus considerable sums were involved. Price was all the more important at this juncture, as we were being expected to increase the amount we mined. . . . [After February 1948] the whole uranium question was taken over by Gottwald's presidential chancellery and . . . after that the subject of uranium ore became taboo and even the cause of criminal action.[23]

Operation and Dissolution. From all available evidence, the exclusively Soviet-owned and mixed companies were run to provide maximum benefit to the Soviet economy at the expense of local interests. The Soviet advantage derived from arbitrary high valuation of its contribution, the enterprises' preferential legal, tax, foreign exchange, and material supply status, and discriminatory pricing in favor of Soviet customers.[24] These enterprises thus represented a visible burden imposed on these countries by the USSR, although the resulting resource transfer is very difficult to quantify.

After Stalin's death the Soviets made the political decision to relinquish these highly profitable enterprises (except uranium) by selling their share to the respective countries—a decision no doubt designed to reduce the pent-up popular dissatisfaction throughout the bloc that had erupted in the June 1953 East German riots. Most of the agreements were signed in 1953-54, and in many cases the resulting financial obligation was converted into loans payable with goods in installments over a period of years.[25] After the Polish and Hungarian revolts of 1956 the Soviets cancelled unpaid debt obligations; such largesse, along with successive reductions of the amount of reparations levied, constituting a significant part of Soviet foreign aid to the bloc, as discussed next.

Soviet Aid to East Europe

Under economic assistance provided by the Soviet Union, CEMA sources include (a) loans; (b) cancellation of debts; (c) cancellation of reparations; and (d) release of joint stock companies. Of these, (a), (b), and (d) represent a real transfer of resources, while (c) can be considered either a gesture or a real sacrifice, depending upon how just and realistic were the initial demands, about which opinions are likely to differ. The timing and composition of USSR assistance to individual East European countries have been recently compiled from Western and CEMA sources.[26]

With respect to timing and purpose, USSR aid can be divided into (1) immediate postwar loans to provide relief of troubled situations of one kind or another (about $50 million, plus food loans, plus debt and reparations cancellations of about $260 million); (2) consolation loans in 1947-48 to countries pressured into rejecting the Marshall Plan ($450 million to Poland and smaller loans to Czechoslovakia, Rumania, and Bulgaria); (3) loans and concessions following the death of Stalin and the Berlin eruption thereafter, mainly to East Germany (a loan of $125 million and other concessions); and (4) the comprehensive aid program of 1956-58 following the Polish and Hungarian revolts. This last stands apart with respect to size and composition from previous aid programs—that is, item (4) amounted to about $3.6 billion, comprised of $1.4 billion of loans, close to $1 billion of debt cancellations, and more than $1 billion (claimed value) of free transfer of joint stock companies, whereas the big-ticket items earlier had been reparations cancellations.

Toward a Balance Sheet of East European
Subventions and Soviet Aid

To arrive at some tentative conclusions about the direction and size of uncompensated resource transfers during the period of 1945 to 1960, East European subventions and Soviet aid flows are brought to a common denominator by calculating their grant equivalent, which measures the unilateral transfer component of each transaction. The application of this approach to intra-bloc transactions was pioneered by Horvath,[27] here we attempt to fill in the details with documented estimates and assumptions that in some cases differ from those of Horvath. Because reliable information is scarce, no more can be attempted than to estimate rough orders of magnitudes, subject to corrections as more accurate information becomes available.

The balance sheet excludes Albania and Yugoslavia, the former because information on Soviet aid is not available and because the benefits it received from the USSR under Stalin would have to be balanced against losses due to Soviet economic pressure after 1960,[28] which is outside the scope of this analysis, and Yugoslavia because we would have to quantify the cost of Stalin's economic blockade and other pressures, which is again outside our scope.

Subvention. The grant equivalent of East European countries' subventions to the USSR is calculated in Table 12-1. For some subvention items, the donor's sacrifice is not identical to the recipient's gain: in the case of reparations

Table 12-1

Subvention Transfers to the USSR from East European Countries, Cumulative 1945-1960 (Millions of Current Dollars)

Conveyor Country	Plant Dismantlement		Reparations-Type Payments			Favorable Prices on Commercial Exports (6)
	Sacrific (1)	Gain[2] to USSR (2)	Direct to USSR (3)	To Red Army (4)	Uranium and Other (5)	
E. Germany*	4,000[1]	1,333	6,471[6]	4,210[7]	4,382[8]	n.a.
Bulgaria	–	–	–	–	–	n.a.
Czechoslovakia	–	–	–	–	n.a.[11]	n.a.
Hungary	1,000[3]	333	269[9]	n.a.	n.a.[12]	n.a.
Poland[4]	–	–	–	–	–	626[14]
Rumania	1,000[5]	333	453[10]	n.a.	187[13]	n.a.
Total	6,000	2,000	7,193	4,210	4,569	626

Conveyor Country	Joint Stock Companies				Grant Equivalent	
	Assets		Profits			
	Sacrifice (7)	Gain (8)	Sacrifice (9)	Gain (10)	Sacrifice (11)	Gain (12)
E. Germany*	453[15]	453[15]	–[20]	–[20]	19,516	16,849
Bulgaria	–[16]	6[17]	n.a.	n.a.	–	6
Czechoslovakia	–	–	–	–	–	–
Hungary	–[16]	150[18]	60[21]	180[21]	1,329	977[22]
Poland[4]	–	–	–	–	626	626
Rumania	–[16]	200[19]	80[21]	240[21]	1,720	1,413
Total	453	809	140	420	23,191	19,871

*The value of all reparations-type payments was calculated by Kohler *Economic Integration in the Soviet Bloc*, Table 1, pp. 25-28, based mostly on East and West German documents, in domestic currency which cannot be translated into dollars at the official exchange rate. Dollar values shown here were estimated on the basis of implicit devisa-ruble/DM exchange rates calculated by Kohler, Table 28, p. 272, since 1950, with devisa-ruble values converted to dollars at the official pre-1961 rate of $1.00 = 4 rubles. Dollar values for 1945 to 49 were obtained on the basis of index numbers constructed for values shown in Kohler, Table 1, linked to 1950 dollar values as obtained above.

[1] Harper and Snell, "Postwar Economic Growth in East Germany," p. 566.

[2] Following Horvath, "Grant Elements in Intra-Bloc Aid Programs," p. 14, assumed to be one-third of the sacrifice, due to very large waste during the transfer.

[3] Estimate cited in Wszelaki, *Communist Economic Strategy*, p. 69.

[4] Even though industrial and transport equipment was removed from the newly acquired Western parts, these may be viewed as affecting Germany's lost territories rather than Poland. Bierut estimated the value of plant dismantlement up to the Potsdam Agreement as $500 million; *Rzeczpospolita*, August 24, 1945, as cited in Zauberman, *Economic Imperialism*, p. 11.

[5] Author's estimate: same as Hungary. The order of magnitude is supported by Montias, *Economic Development in Communist Rumania*, pp. 17-18, fns. 40 and 41, and Wszelaki, p. 69; the estimates cited by both sources are higher than this author's. Speaking of economic disruption after the war, Ceausescu, *The Rumanian Communist Party*, without directly

Table 12-1 (cont.)

mentioning the Soviets, stated: "The war reparations Romania had to pay and the other material losses totalled $1 billion dollars" [p. 65].

[6] 1945-53; Kohler, Table 1.

[7] Including direct and indirect deliveries, 1945-1958; Kohler, Table 1.

[8] Estimated uranium ore deliveries 1946-60 ($4.1 billion) and inventory depletion of SAG firms 1952-53 ($260 million); Kohler, Table 1.

[9] 1945-52: $134.3 "gold" dollars (Spulber, *The Economics of Communist Eastern Europe*, p. 167), multiplied by a factor of two to take account of price increases since 1938 and especially low accounting prices (noted in Spulber, p. 170) during the early years.

[10] 1945-52: $226.5 "gold" dollars (Spulber, p. 167), multiplied by a factor of two (see note above and Spulber, p. 173).

[11] Should include loss on uranium ore exports to USSR (see text).

[12] Should include (a) uranium ore deliveries on reparation account and possible loss on commercial uranium exports, as is known to have been the case for East Germany and Czechoslovakia, and (b) payment, if any, for objects removed from Soviet territory during the war; Spulber, pp. 39-40.

[13] Restitution for goods and materials taken by Rumanian troops from the USSR during the war (Spulber, pp. 175-6).

[14] Amount of Polish debts cancelled as compensation for low prices paid for coal during 1946-56; Spulber, pp. 176-7 and Goldman, *Soviet Foreign Aid*, p. 7.

[15] In the case of East Germany, enterprises were expropriated and subsequently returned, first against payment and later free of charge. From East Germany's point of view, subvention was involved (other than operating profits foregone shown in the next columns) only when the firms were repurchased. The amounts are shown by Kohler, p. 47, here converted to dollars through the implicit devisa-ruble/DM exchange rates calculated by Kohler, Table 28, p. 272, and the official pre-1961 rate of $1.00 = 4 rubles.

[16] For Bulgaria, Hungary, and Rumania no subvention is assigned because to the extent that they made partial payment (mostly during 1954-56 until the debt was cancelled) they were acquiring assets previously owned by foreigners.

[17] Spulber, p. 194.

[18] Spulber, p. 205.

[19] Spulber, p. 204.

[20] Operating profits were included under reparations-type payments. See Kohler, pp. 46-47, fn. 22.

[21] Since evidence detailed in the text suggests that joint companies yielded maximum benefit to the USSR, it is assumed that the division of total profits gave a 15 percent return to the USSR and a 5 percent return to the bloc partner annually on investment, which is assumed to have been shared 50-50. If so, the profit sacrifice to the bloc partner is 5 percent of its invested capital annually for eight years, 1946-53.

[22] Includes $45 million paid by Hungary to the USSR on a $200 million commercial debt to Germany, subsequently claimed by the USSR; Dewar, *Soviet Trade with Eastern Europe*, pp. 68-70. The remaining $155 million cancelled debt appears as a component of the $197 million entry for Hungary in column (3) of Table 2.

dismantlings, the wastefulness of the operation made the donor's sacrifice considerably greater than the eventual gain realized by the USSR; in the case of joint stock company assets transferred to the USSR, these were previously owned by foreigners (except in East Germany) so the Soviet's gain cannot be considered a loss to the bloc countries; and in the case of profits from these companies, the Soviet gain is assumed here to be a sacrifice only to the extent that the earnings were unfairly distributed.

On balance, we find that the cumulative grant equivalent of East Europe's estimated sacrifice during the 1945 to 1960 period was $23.2 billion and the corresponding gain to the USSR, $19.2 billion. These figures do not include uranium shipped by Czechoslovakia and Hungary and the maintenance of Soviet troops in Hungary and Rumania, for which no estimates are known to the author, and do not take account of unfavorable prices on commercial exports during the early postwar years, except on Polish coal. The largest burden by far was shouldered by East Germany: its $19.5 billion sacrifice represents almost seven-eighths of the East Europe total, although its share would be reduced somewhat if estimates of comparable completeness were available also for the other countries. The next largest burden was on Rumania ($1.7 billion), then Hungary ($1.3 billion), followed by Poland ($626 million). Among the ex-enemy countries, Bulgaria apparently received preferential treatment, at least relative to that of other countries.

Soviet Aid. The grant equivalent of Soviet economic assistance to East Europe is estimated in Table 12-2 in two versions: one which excludes, realistically we believe, reparations cancellations, and the other which includes this item at full value (the approach followed by CEMA sources). The grant equivalent of loans to East Europe has been calculated by assuming, following Horvath,[29] that all Soviet loans were for 12 years, at 2.5 percent interest, with a two-year grace period, a 10 percent opportunity rate of discount, fully delivered,[30] and that aid tying represented a 10 percent cost to the recipient as compared to aid that could have been spent freely on the world market. The calculation is based on Horvath's formula, which yields a grant ratio of .26 to the face value of the loan.[31]

On balance, we find that the cumulative grant equivalent of Soviet aid from 1945 to 1960 was $2.6 billion, excluding reparations cancellations, and $9.4 billion including this item. According to the first version, all countries benefited, in amounts ranging from $16 million for Czechoslovakia to $842 million for Poland, with the composition of aid varying from country to country. According to the second version, more than two-thirds of the aid benefited East Germany because the Soviet Union claims to have lightened the country's reparations burden by almost $7 billion.

Balance of Aid and Subvention. The net balance of the foregoing estimates is shown in the last four columns of Table 12-2. If reparations cancellations are excluded, the six East European countries have provided, on balance, approximately $20 billion subvention to the USSR (corresponding gain to the Soviet Union about $17 billion). If reparations cancellations are also included, the net subvention estimate declines to below $14 billion (with the corresponding gain about $3 billion less). The size of this flow of resources from East Europe to the USSR is of the same order of magnitude as the flow of resources from the

Table 12-2

USSR Economic Assistance to East European Countries and Balance[1] of the Grant Equivalent of Aid and Subvention Transfers, Cumulative 1945-1960 (Millions of Current Dollars)

Recipient Country	Loans (A) Face Value (1)	Grant Equivalent (2)	Debt Cancellations (B) (3)	Reparations Cancellations (C) (4)	Release of Joint Stock Companies (D) (5)
E. Germany	238	62	–	6,612	200
Bulgaria	343	89	45	10	–
Czechoslovakia	62	16	–	–	–
Hungary	379	99	197	78	250
Poland	831	216	626	–	–
Rumania	222	58	–	147	710[2]
Total	2,075	540	868	6,847	1,160

Recipient Country	Grant Equivalent of Aid Excluding Rep. Cancel. (6)	Including Rep. Cancel. (7)	Balance of Aid and Subvention Excl. Rep. Cancel. Sacrifice (8)	Gain (9)	Incl. Rep. Cancel. Sacrifice (10)	Gain (11)
E. Germany	262	6,874	(19,254)	(16,587)	(12,642)	(9,975
Bulgaria	134	144	128	134	138	144
Czechoslovakia	16	16	16	16	16	16
Hungary	546	624	(783)	(431)	(705)	(353)
Poland	842	842	216	216	216	216
Rumania	768	915	(952)	(645)	(805)	(498)
Total	2,568	9,415	(20,629)	(17,297)	(13,782)	(10,450)

[1] Net transfers to USSR in parentheses.

[2] Goldman, *Soviet Foreign Aid*, p. 19. The range of $700-1,100 million shown for this item in Goldman, Table 11-1, and the $900 million average shown by Horvath, "Grant Elements . . . ," Table 1, probably includes the value of delivered Soviet investments in joint stock companies which was repaid by the Rumanians, as discussed in Montias, *Economic Development in Communist Rumania*, pp. 146-7.

Source: Columns (1)–(7) are based on Horvath, Table 1, except as noted; Columns (8)–(11): Columns (6) or (7) less Table 1, Columns (11) or (12).

United States to West Europe under the Marshall Plan, which amounted to about $14 billion. The distribution of this large subvention (or what may be called coerced grant) has been most uneven, however, because East Germany accounted for more than nine-tenths of the total. Significant amounts were also provided by Rumania and Hungary, whereas Bulgaria, Czechoslovakia, and Poland are shown to have been net beneficiaries in small amounts.

It cannot be emphasized enough that these figures should be interpreted with a great deal of caution, not only because of the roughness of the component estimates but also because the above calculations take account of only some of the most highly visible capital transfer items. Other important considerations are the terms of trade and the commodity composition, issues to which we turn next.

Terms of Trade and Commodity Composition

Terms of Trade

Background and Methodology. The technique of intra-CEMA price determination has been shrouded in secrecy. Prices are said to be based on those on the world market because such prices represent alternative opportunities to CEMA buyers and sellers and also because, given arbitrary domestic prices, CEMA countries have not been able to come up with an alternative to world prices acceptable to all members. There is no question, however, that considerable bargaining does take place on prices, if for no other reason than that of "world market price" being too ambiguous a concept to serve even as a starting point. Furthermore, world prices are said to be adjusted to delete the influence of speculation and monopoly and to take into account CEMA demand and supply.

CEMA literature offers only limited insight on how world prices are translated into CEMA prices. The only aspect that is clear is that certain formal principles have been agreed upon as to which historical period's prices should be used by negotiators as a base.

During the period of 1945 to 1950, prices were reportedly based, at least formally, on current capitalist world market prices. The period of 1951 to 1953 was the era of "stop prices," when negotiators used prices agreed upon prior to this period in order to avoid the distorting influence of inflation due to the Korean War. From 1954 to 1957, selected "stop prices" were adjusted to eliminate the greatest discrepancies between these and current world prices. A situation existed whereby "stop prices," their adjusted version, and current world market prices for newly traded products existed side by side, thereby causing frictions that came more and more to the open rather than remaining repressed, as under Stalin.

A major landmark, the ninth session of CEMA (Bucharest, June 1958) adopted comprehensive new rules to the effect that (1) average 1957-58 world market prices would be introduced (with exceptions that were not clearly defined); (2) prices would remain fixed for several years, except for new and improved products whose prices would be currently negotiated; (3) certain specific documents would become acceptable documentation of world prices in bilateral negotiations; and (4) the principle of "half-freight" charge would be introduced, adding one-half of the hypothetical transport cost between the main

Western market and the importing CEMA country to the world market price to arrive at a price that would serve as the documented negotiating base. Prices continued to be determined bilaterally; the new element was the multilateral agreement on rules to be followed in bilateral negotiations.

Because by the early 1960s CEMA prices were recognized as having deviated from current world market prices, an agreement introducing a new 1960-64 world market price base was reached during the mid-1960s and implemented during the period of 1965 to 1967 in several stages. At the beginning of the current (1971-75) five-year plan, a new, average 1968-69 world market price base was introduced.

It is important to note in connection with interpreting empirical studies on CEMA prices that individual commodity prices are determined not by single buyers and sellers in relative isolation from the prices of other commodities, as in the West, but by government agencies that bargain over a whole range of export and import prices at once. Thus, if a Western observer finds the price of a particular commodity high or low relative to current world prices, this *may be* because the CEMA price has remained fixed, while the world price has changed or, alternatively, because the price that is "out of line" *may be* compensated by offsetting deviations in the prices of other export and import items. Of great importance also is the fact that not only prices but quantities too may be at disequilibrium levels—that is, a country may agree to sell a commodity to a particular buyer below the world price, but it then might withhold from this purchaser much of the volume it could supply. Thus, one centrally planned economy may discriminate against another not only through prices but also through quantities: the stronger partner may supply little of the scarce or favorably-priced commodity or may pressure the weaker partner into supplying larger quantities or a different assortment than it would do of its own volition.

Another important point, stressed by both Holzman and Campbell, is that the preferential treatment CEMA trading partners give to each other means that members voluntarily channel a portion of their trade to bloc partners even when more profitable opportunities are available on the world market.[32] But even though on some deals the seller might obtain a better price than he could get on the world market and on some transactions he might pay a lower price than he would have to pay in the West, it is possible that all CEMA countries lose from such preferential agreements. On the one hand, this might happen if a CEMA country foregoes opportunities to earn convertible currency with which it could acquire goods that are available (or in adequate quantities) only on the world market—a dilemma that appears to be facing the Soviet Union. On the other hand, this might also happen if the preferential or "sheltered" CEMA market absorbs for a long time poor quality goods and obsolete equipment, thereby reducing the incentive to innovate and produce "for the market" and causing the exporter to fall more and more behind its competitors. This is a dilemma that appears to be facing some of the smaller and relatively more advanced CEMA countries like East Germany, Czechoslovakia, and Hungary.[33] Furthermore, the importer of shoddy goods and equipment loses potential productivity gains; yet it might not be able to resist buying such goods if its own producers are dependent upon the same CEMA suppliers for their export market. This is why in a bilateral, state-trading framework terms of trade considerations cannot be divorced from the commodity composition of trade, discussed briefly in the last section of this chapter. But now let us summarize some of the principal findings on prices and the terms of trade.

Empirical Evidence. Statistical information on CEMA prices before 1955 is scarce and episodic. Whatever there is suggests strongly that the Soviet Union under Stalin used every chicanery in the book to obtain favorable prices. We have already mentioned the case of low prices for Hungarian and Rumanian reparations goods, Polish coal, and Czech uranium. Circumstantial evidence is offered also by the Stalinist purges of senior Communist leaders in Bulgaria (Kostov in 1949) and in Czechoslovakia (Slansky and Loebl in 1952), who during their trial were charged with having asked too high and offered too low prices in trade negotiations with the USSR and trying to maintain commercial secrecy during the negotiations.

Numerous other cases and episodes are also listed in the specialized literature.[34] It would be very difficult, however, to quantify the extent of price discrimination by the Soviet Union during this early period. Until additional systematic evidence becomes available, we must stay with the vague conclusion that, until 1953 at least, prices were most probably slanted heavily in favor of the Soviet Union.

The period of 1954 to 1958 was one of upheavals, retrenchment by the Soviet Union, and a movement toward putting all aspects of intra-bloc commercial relations on a more stable and equitable basis. Covering the period since the mid-1950s, statistical evidence and interpretive studies suggest the following:[35]

1. Foreign trade prices in trade among socialist countries are substantially higher than world market prices. During the period 1958 to 1964, the price-level gap between CEMA and world prices is estimated to have been about 20 percent, ranging between 20 to 40 percent for major groups of manufactures and between 0 to 20 percent for groups of primary products. Since 1965, the price-level gap narrowed to about 10 percent, but the just-noted differences between manufactures and primary products persisted. Contributing to the emergence and persistence of high CEMA prices have been: (a) the sellers' market at CEMA that, combined with shortages of hard currency, places the CEMA supplier in a favorable position; (b) exchange rates that overvalue domestic currencies of CEMA countries and result in high prices whenever prices charged are determined partly or fully on the basis of domestic costs; (c) the hypothetical freight charge that is added to the basic contract price in addition to actual freight costs; and (d) bilateralism, under which it is the easiest to

obtain compensation for high import prices in the form of high export prices. Except for (c), the enumerated causal factors affected manufactures more than primary products.

2. Price fluctuations were much greater before 1959 than afterwards, which underscores the importance of the first CEMA-wide revision of prices in 1958. Prices tended to fluctuate narrowly from 1959 to 1964, until the second all-CEMA price revision of 1965-67. The two price-adjustments of 1958 and 1965-67 reduced CEMA prices on balance, particularly the prices of raw materials and industrial consumer goods. Since the USSR is the largest supplier of raw materials to the rest of CEMA (absolutely as well as in terms of percentage of trade volume), these adjustments have led to a deterioration (roughly 20 percent) in Soviet (net barter) terms of trade with CEMA between 1957 and 1970. During the same period, the terms of trade of Czechoslovakia, East Germany, and Hungary with all socialist countries as a group improved. This finding does not imply anything about the level or equity of Soviet-CEMA prices during the mid-1950s (although according to my calculations, in trade with Hungary Soviet prices in 1955 were reasonably close to estimated world market prices,[36] except that the Soviet Union's export prices have fallen relative to import prices so that the Soviet gains from trade are now relatively lower than they were during the mid-1950s.[37]

Commodity Composition

The First Postwar Decade. It is almost a cliche to state that after postwar reconstruction had been completed by 1948-49 (later in East Germany), the development strategy of all East European countries appears to have followed the Soviet model—that is, concentrating on industry, and within industry, on machine-building and metallurgy, and increasing the share of investment in national income to very high levels, mostly at the expense of consumption. As a result, these countries have achieved good-to-spectacular growth rates, with fluctuations, and at the same time created serious imbalances, inefficiency, and a host of other problems.[38]

Each East European country's development strategy determined the changes in the economic structure, which in turn was reflected in the new geographic and commodity composition of trade. The question we would like to pose, therefore: Was the adoption of the extreme version of the "Soviet model" by national Communist leaders voluntary or was it imposed on them from without? If the latter, did this serve Soviet economic interests? If yes, did it represent economic extraction by the Soviet Union, and if so, in what form and for how long? We do not as yet have complete enough factual information to provide unqualified answers; below some viewpoints are presented and a tentative interpretation is offered.

Much of the Western literature would answer the above series of questions by indicting the Soviet Union. To quote from one that is well documented:

The direction and structure of [postwar] East European trade has been designed primarily to accord with Soviet economic and strategic priorities, at considerable cost to East Europe's own economic development.... The Soviet-dictated policy of broad industrial diversification fell more heavily on the more developed Czechoslovak and East German economies than on the other East European economies.[39]

Yet this conclusion has not been found fully convincing by all because of an apparent contradiction between presumed Soviet economic interests on the one hand and the parallel industrialization patterns and the structure of Soviet-East European trade on the other. For example, Granick observes that East Europe as a whole after the war was a relatively underdeveloped area that gave prime attention to developing its heavy industry.[40] Elsewhere in the world, including in the USSR during its First Five-Year Plan, such a pattern has been supported by exporting primary products in exchange for investment goods. Postwar East Europe, however, followed this pattern by becoming almost immediately a net exporter of investment goods and a net importer of primary products, particularly in trade with the Soviet Union. Why? According to Granick:

We shall for the sake of argument make two underlying assumptions: that the USSR determines the pattern of development of Eastern Europe, and that it determines this pattern solely in terms of its own national interest [defined as strengthening the USSR alone or the bloc as a whole].[41]

He then argues:

Desire for increased availability within the USSR of industrial equipment and other products of heavy industry would not explain why such production has been pushed in Eastern Europe. The Bloc's resources might just as well have been allocated in such a fashion as to concentrate such production in the USSR and to develop primary consumer goods industries in Eastern Europe.... Furtherance of military security of the USSR would also not appear to require a program of rapid expansion of heavy industry in Eastern Europe. On the contrary, one could make a strong case—on grounds of relative susceptibility to attack—for the concentration of the Soviet Bloc's expansion of producer goods production within the borders of the USSR.... The hypothesis is that Eastern European development is dictated by narrow Soviet interests cannot explain the observed development pattern. For while it may be correct in positing that the criterion of development is the production of the greatest "surplus" for the Soviet Union to "milk," it begs the question of why one pattern is superior to another in this regard.[42]

While Granick's argument is logical, his conclusions appear to be contradicted by countless eyewitness accounts testifying to the decisive role Soviet "advisors" and "shopping lists" played in choosing development strategies in East Europe from 1948 to 1953, and perhaps beyond. The nature of the problem is such that considerably more "digging" remains to be done before a final verdict can be rendered. But a useful approach might be to examine Soviet-East European relations on a country-by-country, case-by-case basis rather than to deal with all of heterogeneous East Europe combined.

To understand the role of indigenous versus foreign influences in postwar development strategies, Czechoslovakia is very important. After the war it was already a relatively highly developed country whose industrial base had not been destroyed; the country had an influential indigenous Communist party as well as alternative economic development programs. Postwar economic events in Czechoslovakia have been reconstructed in meticulous detail by Holesovky, a source on which the following account is based.[43]

During 1947-48, a significant debate about development strategy took place between proponents of what Holesovsky calls the "Swiss strategy" that stressed balanced growth, diversification, and specialization in products with low import content and high domestic value added, and the Communist-advocated "machine shop" strategy that emphasized specialization in heavy industrial machinery and metallurgical products, with trade gradually oriented toward the Soviet bloc. (Some elements of this debate are reminiscent of the industrialization debates in the USSR during the 1920s.) Advocates of the "machine shop" strategy foresaw a stable, long-term demand for investment goods from industrializing East Europe and expressed confidence that regional cooperation and central planning would prevent trade-induced fluctuations, which had been one of the main worries of Czech economists remembering the Great Depression. The crucial points, carefully documented by Holesovky, are, first, that the "machine shop" strategy as originally advocated contained elements of the "Swiss strategy" and, second, that it posited a realistic rate of growth so that rising investment would not be at the expense of consumption. But then came the double *coup d'etat*: that of the Communist party over parliamentary democracy and that of the Moscovite faction over the rest of the party, which was immediately followed by two successive, very large, and crucially important revisions in the draft of the original First Five-Year Plan (1950-55). To explain what prompted these revisions, Holesovsky invokes the testimony of an economics text by Olsovsky and Prucha, published in Prague in 1969:

[The first revision] arose to a large extent from the content of long-term contracts with member states of the CEMA. . . . For Czechoslovakia, the treaty with the Soviet Union for 1950-55 was the most important one. These agreements raised the demands upon Czechoslovak heavy industry, in particular upon the production of heavy machinery and equipment. . . . These articles were highly material-intensive and required the construction of new capacities, or a reconstruction of existing ones.[44]

As to the second revision in 1951:

Demands addressed to Czechoslovakia, which had a developed armaments industry in the past, were considerable, and the entire economy was subordinated to them. However, these tasks were no longer integrated into a modified plan but represented a plan of their own.[45]

Citing the same source, Holesovsky finds that the planned growth of industrial output was changed from 10 to 20-25 percent per annum, total requirements of the military with respect to industry quadrupled from 1950 to 1952, and armaments production increased sevenfold from 1948 to 1953.

We now turn to postwar foreign trade data released by the USSR in 1967 to gain another perspective on the events reconstructed by Holesovsky.[46] Table 12-3 shows the growth of USSR imports from Czechoslovakia and East Germany for the period 1948 to 1955; the figures probably do *not* include defense items. We find that between 1948 and 1953 not only did total imports increase rapidly (particularly from East Germany where many goods supplied under reparations until 1948 became commercial exports), but that the share of machinery and metallurgical products increased steadily until it reached more than four-fifths of total exports to the USSR. The data therefore, are consistent with the hypothesis that at least in Czechoslovakia and East Germany, postwar development strategies were significantly influenced by Soviet strategic priorities. A Hungarian economist arrives at a similar conclusion:

Decisions which shaped the economic structure of individual countries were based on bilateral economic relations, primarily the relations with the Soviet Union. This was so not only because the Soviet Union had a decisive share in each country's foreign trade but also because only Soviet industry was able to produce or to share the technical documentation of large metallurgical and machine-building projects and to supply the basic raw materials; and also because its prestige and experience served as an example of every socialist country. However, given the known distortions of Stalinist policy, this [approach] frequently resulted in one-sided decisions even in questions of detail.[47]

We tentatively conclude that during the first postwar decade the USSR was instrumental in forcing the development of high-cost industrial branches in East Europe, and probably for several interrelated reasons. First, the Soviets probably did believe that their own pattern of industrialization was ideologically correct and did have universal applicability for the new socialist states. Second, this model also had beneficial political ramification of placing limits on the East European states' interaction with one another, at least more so than specialization would have, and thereby heightened each state's dependence on the Soviet Union. Third, this dependence was beneficial to the Soviet Union as a

Table 12-3

USSR Imports from Czechoslovakia and East Germany, 1948-1955 (Millions of Current Dollars or Percent)

Year	Value (Mill. $) (1)	Growth Previous Year = 100 (2)	Total (%) (3)	Machinery (CTN 1)* (4)	Metallurgy (CTN 24-27, 29) (5)
			Czechoslovakia		
1948	136	348%	48%	18%	30%
1949	205	151	41	18	23
1950	201	98	68	29	39
1951	253	126	71	31	40
1952	299	118	78	36	42
1953	312	104	84	36	48
1954	318	102	83	46	37
1955	386	122	73	41	32
			East Germany		
1948	62	283	6	4	2
1949	146	237	18	15	3
1950	160	109	41	38	3
1951	328	205	52	44	8
1952	365	111	61	54	7
1953	483	132	78	73	5
1954	618	128	79	75	4
1955	506	82	84	78	6

Columns span: Total Imports (1,2); Share of Machinery and Metallurgical Products (3,4,5).

*CTN = CEMA Trade Nomenclature (cf. *Compendium*, Appendix A).

Source: *Vneshnaia torgovlia SSRS; staticheskii sbornik, 1918-1966* [Foreign Trade of the USSR; statistical volume, 1918-1966].

means of supplementing its requirements for investment goods from the more advanced, and for other products from the less industrialized East European countries, during the Western embargo. For example, each year between 1949 and 1953, Soviet imports of machinery from CEMA increased faster than its exports of machinery to CEMA so that East Europe's share in total USSR machinery imports climbed from 43 to 85 percent during this period.[48] The main suppliers were East Germany and Czechoslovakia, and, to a lesser extent, Hungary. By the mid-1950s, however, the specific USSR objectives and the nature of Soviet-East European relations had been radically transformed, as outlined next.

Developments Since the Mid-Fifties. During the second postwar period (approximately 1956 to 1965), the USSR must have realized that the political cost of economic extraction probably exceeded the economic benefits gained, hence extraction was discontinued in most cases. Also, as the embargo was relaxed and as the more developed East European trade partners gradually fell behind Western technological standards, the USSR probably attached less and less importance to imports from East Europe. It is conceivable that during this period the USSR had no definite policy on what commodity composition could provide maximum benefits from intra-bloc trade. To be sure, large and very useful bloc-wide projects had been completed. Much discussion was also heard of the need for improved bloc-wide specialization and integration, but, as far as it is known to me, the USSR has not specified the economic content of these broad objectives.

As a consequence of East Europe's development strategy, poor endowment of natural resources, and wasteful use of materials, the USSR became the sole net supplier of raw materials and energy to CEMA during the 1960s, to the extent of about $2.5 billion by 1970, as other CEMA countries absorbed an increasing share of their total output of primary products domestically and redirected some raw material exports to the West.[49] Today, the Soviet import mainly machinery and equipment and consumer goods but complain that these are not up to world standards.

Since the beginning of the third postwar decade (since 1966), the USSR has come to the conclusion (judging from its position in CEMA debates) that the exchange of raw materials for manufactures is disadvantageous because it limits its ability to import technology and other goods from the West for which it pays predominantly with primary products, chiefly raw materials and fuels. To be sure, the argument is phrased in terms of issues such as that its exports to East Europe are more capital intensive than its import substitutes and it does not wish to export capital and that its terms of trade with CEMA are unfavorable. The real issue is, however, that the Soviet economy would clearly benefit by reorienting trade to the West, particularly as the worldwide energy crisis is boosting the value of Soviet exports by substantial margins.[50]

Since a drastic reduction of fuel and raw material exports to East Europe is precluded by the serious adverse economic and ultimately political consequences such a step would have in the importing countries, Soviet options have been limited. The Soviet response to this dilemma can be seen as gradually implementing a new trade policy *vis-à-vis* East Europe since the mid-1960s. First, as a *quid pro quo* for unfavorable prices and as compensation for the high capital intensity of fuels and raw materials, it now ties the export of some of these products to interest-free loans from importing CEMA countries. Loans are granted in the form of machinery, equipment, pipes, and consumer goods. Second, a few years ago it, too, began to practice "commodity bilateralism"—a network of tied exports and imports—under which machinery imports are increasingly linked to machinery exports.[51] (This bargaining strategy has been practiced heretofore primarily by Bulgaria, Rumania, and Poland in their trade with Czechoslovakia,

East Germany, and Hungary.) Thus, according to plan figures for the 1971-75 Five-Year Plan, while USSR total exports to CEMA will increase by 50 percent and fuel and raw materials by only 27 percent, machinery exports will jump by 100 percent.[52] Third, it now encourages these countries not only to rely more on high-cost domestic sources and to cooperate more closely with each other in exploration, but also to turn gradually to non-socialist sources to meet their increasing needs.[53] Fourth, it now pays much more attention than before to the quality and composition of imports:

We shall under no circumstances be customers for an assortment of goods which we cannot sell on other markets. The goods [supplied to us] must be of first quality, and must meet the needs of the Soviet Union. A proportion of them must consist of products made from import materials or under foreign licence. If Czechoslovakia saves an enormous sum through its purchases of raw materials in the USSR, it is only right, in my opinion, that it investigate the possibility of spending some of this profit on the purchase of goods or licences useful to the Soviet Union.[54]

Conclusions

On the basis of political and economic considerations, one might suggest that since World War II the principal economic objectives of the USSR in East Europe have been the desire to place and maintain these countries economically dependent on the USSR (first priority), followed by the need to derive maximum economic benefit from the relationship, subject to certain political constraints. The economic dependence of these countries is probably seen as the ingredient that helps to cement the political cohesiveness of the bloc, an objective obviously prized highly by the Soviet Union. The pursuit of this objective gives a degree of continuity and coherence to Soviet policy and appears to be consistent with the described trends.

The framework in which a power-minded policy (call it imperialism, domination, or whatever) can use commercial policy to achieve its ends was developed three decades ago by Hirschman; we find that his theoretical insights can help to illuminate the political economy of Soviet-East European relations. Hirschman argues that foreign trade has two main effects upon the power position of an "imperialist" country. First, by providing gains from trade it increases economic power, or what Hirschman calls the *supply effect*. Second, foreign trade may become a direct source of power if other countries become economically dependent on trade with the dominant country, or what Hirschman calls the *influence effect*.

During the first postwar decade, the evidence strongly suggests that the *supply effect* had dominated Soviet-East European relations. The economic gains from trade were obtained by outright domination and economic extraction, which included the dismantling of machinery and equipment in some countries, reparations, enforced shopping lists, "advisors," joint stock companies, and unfavorable terms of trade.

Since the mid-1950s, it appears that the *influence effect* has become much more important. A prerequisite of the influence effect is that dependence must be greater for the trade partners of the dominant power than for the latter country itself. In such a situation the small and dependent countries might and very likely will consent to grant the dominant country certain economic, political, and military advantages in order to maintain stable trade relations. Such a dependency and the resulting influence effect is greater the more difficult it is for the smaller countries to dispense entirely with trade with the dominant country or to replace it as a market and source of supply. In the case of CEMA, it is clear that it is much more difficult for the smaller East European countries to dispense with trade with the USSR than it is for the Soviet Union to do so.

But there is more to dependence than just the volume of trade and the relative importance of a given volume to the national economy. Hirschman argues:

A specific policy by country A to prevent its trading partners from diverting trade to other countries is by creating monopolistic or monopsonistic trading conditions. Country A may try to change the structure of country B's economy so as to make it highly and artificially complementary to A's own economy . . . [creating] what might be called "exclusive complementarity."[55]

For the more developed East European countries, this dependence was created during the early postwar period primarily on the export side, for the less developed East European countries primarily on the import side.

In addition to creating "exclusive complementarities," there are also price considerations. Hirschman argues:

If by some preferential treatment A induces B to produce a commodity for export, A becomes B's only market, and the dependence of B upon A thus created may be well worth to A the economic cost involved in not buying in the cheapest market. In general, any attempt to drive the prices of exports from trading partners above world prices . . . will fit in with the policy of increasing their dependence.[56]

The argument, which seems to be applicable to Soviet-East European relations after the mid-1950s, is that there may be a conflict between securing maximum economic gain from trade and the policy of securing the greatest influence through trade partner dependence, because such dependence can be increased by enlarging the gain to the partner. Thus, the deterioration in the Soviet terms of trade with East Europe is not necessarily inconsistent with the Soviet Union's political interest.

And one final point, again citing Hirschman:

> Is there any means of extending [export dependence] to imports as well? The policy of bilateralism is perfectly fitted to take care of the problem. Indeed, a real impossibility of switching exports induces a technical impossibility of switching imports. In this way the device of bilateralism is seen to be an important link in the policies by which the aim of maximum power through foreign trade may be attained.[57]

We find that bilateralism is a principal feature of intrabloc trade. This trading framework is continued to be supported by the Soviet Union, whereas some East European countries are actively searching for the possibility of multilateral arrangements.

I am foregoing the temptation to offer some grand conclusion at the end of this study. The purpose was to identify some of the main considerations involved in testing the theory of economic imperialism and to provide, hopefully, concrete facts and diverse but informed points of view. The evidence leads to some definite conclusions about the nature and magnitude of Soviet imperialism in East Europe during the first postwar decade; since then, one would be hard put to establish beyond controversy which side benefits or loses the most economically. The possibility that there are no net beneficiaries but only substantial net costs to all partners certainly cannot be excluded. The USSR of course derives substantial benefits in political terms because of the leverage provided by East Europe's strong economic dependence. But if the Cold War will continue to thaw, so that security conditions for the USSR will become less important, this will make possible the surfacing of real commercial conflicts within the Soviet alliance structure, just as this has also been the case in the West.

Notes

1. See Hirschman, *National Power and the Structure of Foreign Trade*, 1945.

2. The year 1960 is the last year in which the USSR cancelled debts incurred right after the war; 1959, the last year in which it cancelled reparations obligations; 1958, the last year in which "joint" companies in East Europe were released and perhaps the last year in which ex-enemy countries contributed significantly to the support of Soviet troops on their territory.

3. See Kohler, *Economic Integration of the Soviet Bloc*, 1965, pp. 11-17 and Harper and Snell, "Postwar Economic Growth in East Germany," 1970, pp. 565-6. These figures do not include the so-called "trophy campaign," i.e., the gathering of war booty, estimated as between $.5 and 2 billion [Kohler, p. 11].

4. Kohler, ibid., Table 1.

5. Ibid., pp. 33-35.

6. Wiles, *Communist International Economics*, 1969, p. 397.

7. Cited in Wszelaki, *Communist Economic Strategy*, 1959, p. 69.

8. Ibid., p. 70.

9. Goldman, *Soviet Foreign Aid*, 1967, p. 7.

10. Wszelaki, op. cit., p. 70.

11. According to Goldman, op. cit., p. 7, "... whatever the ultimate compensation, the effect from 1947 to 1953, and to some extent to 1956, was as if Poland was paying reparations to the USSR with the one internationally accepted currency it had, coal."

12. Reparations were also levied on Hungary payable to Czechoslovakia and Yugoslavia ($50 million each) and on Bulgaria payable to Yugoslavia and Greece ($25 and $50 million), stated in 1938 gold dollars. See Spulber, *The Economics of Communist Eastern Europe*, 1957, p. 39.

13. Ibid., p. 167.

14. Ibid., p. 179. Reparations deliveries, representing a substantial portion of budget expenditures in the early postwar years, absorbed 26.4 percent of the Hungarian and 37.5 percent of the Rumanian budgets in 1946-47 and 17.8 percent and 46.6 percent, respectively, in the following year.

15. Ibid., p. 172.

16. Ibid., p. 176.

17. Wszelaki, op. cit., p. 69.

18. Ibid., p. 71.

19. In Rumania, about 400 commercial and industrial enterprises (mainly in oil prospecting, drilling and processing, coal mining, air and river transport, metalworking, and banking and insurance) were taken over and consolidated into approximately 15 joint companies. In Hungary, about 200 companies (mainly in bauxite mining, processing and related operations, oil and other minerals, and air and river transport) were organized into half a dozen joint companies. In Bulgaria joint partnerships were established in mining, civil aviation, shipbuilding, and construction. See Spulber, op. cit. pp. 185-94. In 1948, exclusively Soviet and Soviet-Hungarian firms employed just under 4 percent of Hungary's total gainfully employed in manufacturing [Spulber, p. 189].

20. Kohler, op. cit., p. 17.

21. Ibid., p. 23.

22. Goldman, op. cit., p. 19.

23. Loebl, *Sentenced & Tried*, 1969, p. 31.

24. Spulber, op. cit., pp. 182-223; and Goldman, op. cit., pp. 10-22.

25. In East Germany, nearly half of the plants, but apparently not including the most important ones, were returned in 1947; the rest were returned in stages by 1953. Those returned before 1952 were paid for by East Germany in cash or

equivalent; the remaining ones were turned over free of charge after the 1953 riots. See Kohler, op. cit., p. 47. The Soviet-Yugoslav companies were liquidated on Yugoslav initiative in 1949. Yugoslav charges concerning Soviet exploitation through these companies contributed significantly to the conflict between the two countries during the late 1940s. See Freedman, *Economic Warfare in the Communist Bloc*, 1970, Chapter 2.

26. Horvath, "Grant Elements in Intra-Bloc Aid Programs," 1971, Table 1.

27. Ibid.

28. Freedman, op. cit., Chapter 3.

29. Horvath, op. cit., pp. 2-6.

30. The largest known exception is the $200-million loan granted by the USSR to Yugoslavia after the war that remained largely undelivered, but Yugoslavia is not included in the analysis.

$$31. \, g = \left[1 - \frac{i}{q} \right] \left[1 - \frac{e^{-qM} - e^{-qT}}{q \, (T - M)} \right] - g_1 \, ,$$

where

g = ratio of grant equivalent to the face value of the loan;
i = interest rate charged;
q = opportunity rate of discount;
T = maturity in years;
M = grace period in years;
e = base of natural logarithm; 2.718;
g_1 = grant element of aid tying.

32. See Holzman, "Soviet Foreign Trade Pricing and the Question of Discrimination," 1962, p. 146, and Campbell, "Some Issues in Soviet Energy Policy for the Seventies," 1973, pp. 15-16.

33. Thus, an important objective of Hungary's comprehensive economic reforms introduced in 1968 is to expose the country gradually to genuine international competition, as discussed in Brown and Marer, "Foreign Trade in East European Reform," 1972.

34. See Loebl, passim; Pryor, *The Communist Foreign Trade System*, 1963, pp. 136-9; Wiles, op. cit., Chapter 9; and Wszelaki, op. cit., Chapter 7.

35. In addition to my own calculations, these findings are based on studies by CEMA economists; the most informative ones are Ausch, *CEMA Cooperation: Situations, Mechanism, and Perspectives*, 1969, and Marton, "Price Developments in Hungary's Foreign Trade: 1949-1970," 1972. On Western calculations, the most comprehensive one is Hewett, "Foreign Trade Prices in the Council for Mutual Economic Assistance," 1971. All are discussed in Marer, *Postwar Pricing and Price Patterns in Socialist Foreign Trade*, 1972a, whose summary exposition is followed closely in this text.

36. Marer, "Foreign Trade Prices in the Soviet Bloc," 1968.

37. Gains from trade must also take into account productivity changes in the export and import-competing industries and changes in the commodity composition of trade, but these factors are not likely to alter the conclusions, as is shown in Hewett, op. cit., pp. 115-18.

38. See Brown and Neuberger, *International Trade and Central Planning,* 1968, Appendix, for a succinct abstract of the development strategy, institutions, and results under a typical centrally planned "command" economy.

39. See Hardt, "East European Economic Development, 1970, pp. 7 and 13. Many of the other indictments unfortunately are based on sweeping generalizations or one-sided presentation of fragmentary evidence. Among the many works that fall into this category, two recent ones are Mieczkowski, "Patterns of Soviet Exploitation in Eastern Europe in the 1970s," 1972; and Whitney, "Russian Imperialism Today," 1972.

40. Granick, "The Pattern of Foreign Trade in Eastern Europe and Its Relation to Economic Development Policy," 1954.

41. Ibid., p. 392.

42. Ibid., p. 393. Granick's hypothesis is that East European governments were aiming for a "balanced" national economy under which each country would produce not the precise composition but the *value* of primary products, consumer goods, and industrial investment goods needed domestically, and then enter into trade with other bloc countries *within* each of these major groupings [pp. 397-8].

43. Holesovsky, *The Czechoslovak Economy in Transition*, forthcoming.

44. As quoted in Holesovsky, ibid., p. 32, from Rudolph Olsovsky and Vaclav Prucha, eds., *Strucny Hospodarsky Vyroj Ceskoslovenska Do Roku 1955.*

45. Ibid.

46. No systematic information is available on the commodity composition of Czechoslovak-Soviet trade from Czechoslovak sources prior to 1958.

47. Ausch, op. cit., pp. 42-43. Another dimension, which perhaps partly explains why the less developed East European countries also followed the same pattern, is noted by Brzezinski,

... it is quite impossible to discuss the pattern of Communist interstate relations ... without specifically referring to Stalin's role. Stalin as a symbol, Stalin as a victorious leader, Stalin as the builder of socialism in the USSR, contributed to these relations an intangible yet crucial psychological dimension which introduced devotion, fear, and hatred into the policy-making process and made him present in any important discussion ... it is no exaggeration to say, and this has been confirmed by many former East European Communists, that between 1949 and 1953 many (but certainly not all) of the most radical decisions were made not on the basis of direct orders from Stalin but through the application of the principle of "anticipated reaction"—by attempting to do what Stalin might wish done [pp. 111-2].

48. Marer, *Soviet and East European Foreign Trade, 1946-1969,* 1972b, Series III.

49. Ibid., Series II and III.

50. A prime case in point is oil, one of the main earners of hard currency for the USSR. Until 1971, the nominal price to East Europe was much higher than to the West (close to $20/ton until 1964 and about $15/ton since then versus $9-11/ton to the West, as calculated from Soviet foreign trade yearbooks). More recently, the Soviet price to the West has risen along with the world price to about $16/ton (1972 data; including some oil products besides crude), and it continues to charge approximately the old price to East Europe (now about the same as to West Europe), where the real purchasing power of its earnings is much lower. As Campbell, op. cit., 1973, shows in an excellent analysis of Soviet fuel policy during the 1970s, the Soviets deliver one-third of their energy exports to CEMA but they bitterly complain about its high opportunity cost. Their present and future commitments to East Europe, however, only allow these countries to meet urgent current demands but not to undertake the much-needed large-scale conversion of their antiquated fuel consumption structure from solids to hydrocarbons.

51. A counselor at the Soviet Embassy in Prague, Semynov writes in a 1972 Czecholsovak publication (cited in Radio Free Europe Research, Nov. 7, 1972, New York):

We want our partners in the socialist countries to understand that if their markets are not opened to Soviet machinery and equipment, the Soviet Union will not be in a position to expand economic relations, because our ability to supply fuel and raw materials is limited. The continuation of this rising trend is impossible if the present structure and pace are maintained.

52. Loshakov, "Epoch-Making Success, Good Prospects," 1971, pp. 3-6.

53. Semyonov, op. cit., writes: "In my view we cannot meet the whole demand for fuel arising out of the present rate of growth in Czechoslovakia and the Socialist countries. It serves no purpose to make unrealistic demands."

The deputy chairman of the Planning Commission of Czechoslovakia writes in November, 1972: "As far as oil is concerned, the USSR will continue to be our chief supplier, although it will also be both expedient and necessary to import oil from the countries of the Near and Middle East in order to meet our increased needs"; see RFE Research, December 29, 1972.

54. Semyonov, op. cit. The hard-currency import content of intra-bloc exports is an important bargaining point in CEMA trade (and is an issue to which practically no attention has been paid so far in the West). This is because CEMA countries find it difficult and costly to earn hard currencies, so goods that contain substantial direct or indirect inputs obtained for convertible currencies are scarce, but their relative scarcity is generally not reflected in CEMA's trading prices.

55. Hirschman, op. cit., p. 31.

56. Ibid., pp. 31-32.

57. Ibid., p. 33.

Bibliography

Ausch, Sándor. *A KGST-együttmüködés helyzete, mechanizmusa, távlatai* [CEMA Cooperation: Situation, Mechanism and Perspectives]. Budapest: Közga dasági és Jogi Könyvkiadó, 1969.

Brown, Alan A. and Paul Marer. "Foreign Trade in the East European Reforms." Working Paper No. 9. Bloomington: International Development Research Center, Indiana University, 1972.

Brown, Alan A. and Egon Neuberger. *International Trade and Central Planning.* Berkeley: University of California Press, 1968.

Brzezinski, Zbigniew K. *The Soviet Bloc: Unity and Conflict.* 2nd ed., rev. New York: Frederick A. Praeger, Inc., 1962.

Campbell, Robert W. "Some Issues in Soviet Energy Policy for the Seventies." In *Soviet Economic Perspectives for the Seventies.* Joint Economic Committee, U.S. Congress. Washington, D.C.: U.S. Government Printing Office, 1973.

Ceausescu, Nicolae. *The Romanian Communist Party–Continuer of the Romanian People's Revolutionary and Democratic Struggle, of the Traditions of the Working Class and Socialist Movement in Romania.* Bucharest: Agerpres, 1966.

Dewar, Margaret. *Soviet Trade with Eastern Europe: 1945-1949.* London: Royal Institute of International Affairs, 1951.

Freedman, Robert O. *Economic Warfare in the Communist Bloc.* New York: Praeger Publishers, Inc., 1970.

Goldman, Marshall I. *Soviet Foreign Aid.* New York: Frederick A. Praeger, Inc., 1967.

Granick, David. "The Pattern of Foreign Trade in Eastern Europe and Its Relation to Economic Development Policy," *Quarterly Journal of Economics*, Vol. XLVII, No. 3 (August 1954), pp. 377-400.

Hardt, John P. "East European Economic Development: Two Decades of Interrelationships and Interactions with the Soviet Union," *Economic Developments in Countries of Eastern Europe.* A compendium of papers submitted to the Subcommittee on Foreign Economic Policy of the Joint Economic Committee, U.S. Congress. Washington, D.C.: U.S. Government Printing Office, 1970.

Harper, Marilyn and Edwin M. Snell. "Postwar Economic Growth in East Germany: A Comparison with West Germany," *Economic Developments in Countries of Eastern Europe* (op. cit.).

Hewett, Edward A. "Foreign Trade Prices in the Council for Mutual Economic Assistance." Unpublished Ph.D. dissertation. Ann Arbor: University of Michigan, 1971.

Hirschman, Albert O. *National Power and the Structure of Foreign Trade.* Berkeley: University of California Press, 1945.

Holesovsky, Vaclav. *The Czechoslovak Economy in Transition.* Bloomington: International Development Research Center, forthcoming.

Holzman, Franklyn D. "Soviet Bloc Mutual Discrimination: Comment," *Review of Economics and Statistics*, Vol. XLI (May 1959), pp. 496-9.

_____. "Soviet Foreign Trade Pricing and the Question of Discrimination," *Review of Economics and Statistics*, Vol. XLIV (May 1962), pp. 134-47.

Horvath, Janos. "Grant Elements in Intra-Bloc Aid Programs," *ASTE Bulletin*, Vol. XIII, No. 3, Fall 1971, pp. 1-17.

Kaser, Michael. *COMECON: Integration Problems of the Planned Economies.* 2nd ed. London: Oxford University Press, 1967.

Kenwood, A.G., and A.L. Lougheed. *The Growth of the International Economy, 1820-1960.* London: George Allen & Unwin Ltd., 1971.

Köhler, Heinz. *Economic Integration in the Soviet Bloc.* New York: Frederick A. Praeger, Inc., 1965.

Loebl, Eugene. *Sentenced & Tried: The Stalinist Purges in Czechoslovakia.* London: Elek Books Limited, 1969.

Loshakov, M. "Epoch-Making Success, Good Prospects," *Foreign Trade* (Moscow), November 1971.

Marer, Paul. "Foreign Trade Prices in the Soviet Bloc: A Theoretical and Empirical Study." Unpublished Ph.D. dissertation. Philadelphia: University of Pennsylvania, 1968.

_____. *Postwar Pricing and Price Patterns in Socialist Foreign Trade.* Bloomington: International Development Research Center Report No. 1, 1972a.

_____. *Soviet and East European Foreign Trade, 1946-1969: Statistical Compendium and Guide.* Bloomington: Indiana University Press, 1972b.

Márton, Ádám. "Price Developments in Hungary's Foreign Trade: 1949-1970." Working Paper No. 10. Bloomington: International Development Research Center. Indiana University, 1972.

Mendershausen, Horst. "Terms of Trade Between the Soviet Union and Smaller Communist Countries, 1955-1957," *Review of Economics and Statistics*, Vol. XLI (May 1959), pp. 106-18.

_____. "The Terms of Soviet-Satellite Trade: A Broadened Analysis," *Review of Economics and Statistics*, Vol. XLII (May 1960), pp. 152-63.

Mieczkowski, Bogdan. "Patterns of Soviet Exploitation in Eastern Europe in the 1970s," *Federalist*, No. 1/2 (July/December 1972), pp. 1-11.

Montias, John M. *Economic Development in Communist Rumania.* Cambridge, Mass.: The M.I.T. Press, 1967.

Oslovsky, Rudolph, and Vaclav Prucha, eds. *Strucny Hospodarsky Vyvoj Ceskoslovenska Do Roku 1955.* Prague: Szvoboda, 1969.

Pryor, Frederic L. *The Communist Foreign Trade System.* Cambridge, Mass.: The M.I.T. Press, 1963.

Radio Free Europe Research. New York (Dates of reports as cited in the text).

Simai, Mihály, and Imre Vajda (eds.). *Foreign Trade in a Planned Economy.* Cambridge, England: Cambridge University Press, 1971.

Spulber, Nicolas. *The Economics of Communist Eastern Europe.* Cambridge, Mass., and New York: The Technology Press of Massachusetts Institute of Technology and John Wiley & Sons, Inc., 1957.

260

_____. "Economic Relations between the USSR and Eastern Europe." Unpublished Ph.D. dissertation. New York: New School for Social Research, 1951.

Vneshnaia torgovlia SSSR; staticheskii sbornik, 1918-1966 [Foreign Trade of the USSR, statistical volume, 1918-1966]. Moscow: Ministerstvo Vneshnei Torgovli SSSR, Planova-ekonomicheskoe upravlenie, 1967.

Whitney, Thomas P. "Russian Imperialism Today," *Economic Imperialism: A Book of Readings*, edited by Kenneth E. Boulding and Tapan Mukerjee, pp. 262-74. Ann Arbor: The University of Michigan Press, 1972.

Wiles, P.J.D. *Communist International Economics.* New York: Frederick A. Praeger, Inc., 1969.

Wszelaki, Jan. *Communist Economic Strategy: The Role of East-Central Europe.* New York: National Planning Association, 1959.

Zauberman, Alfred. *Economic Imperialism—The Lesson of Eastern Europe.* London: Ampersand, Ltd., 1955.

Zyzniewski, Stanley J. "The Soviet Economic Impact on Poland." *American Slavic and East European Review*, Vol. XVIII, No. 2, 1959, pp. 205-25.

13 Soviet Economic Penetration of China, 1945-1960: 'Imperialism' as a Level of Analysis Problem

Roy F. Grow
Brandeis University

Introduction

During the tensions preceding the outbreak of the Korean War, it became fashionable for American policy-makers to characterize the actions of the Soviet Union in China in a new and unusual light; hidden beneath the socialist facade, it seemed to many, was a form of imperialist expansion incorporating parts of Asia into an economic and military empire. Somewhat later, during the Cultural Revolution of the 1960s, many Chinese found themselves echoing the same sentiments since the activities of the Soviet leadership appeared as "imperialist and reactionary" as any on the part of the Western powers in the past.

There is certainly little doubt that the Soviet Union became involved in political and economic activities beyond its frontiers after World War II, as the course of events in East Europe, Mongolia, or the Middle East demonstrates. But is involvement evidence of a new form of economic imperialism? On this, opinion seems to differ. "The Soviet Union's economic policy toward its less powerful allies," one analyst has noted, "has been as imperialistic as anything devised by the most avaricious firms in the West toward the developing countries. By means of war reparations, joint stock companies, and discriminatory pricing, the Russians have contrived schemes that would make even such masters of intrigue as Union Minière du Haut-Katanga, United Fruit, and Standard Oil blush with shame."[1]

On the contrary, comes a disclaimer from another observer; imperialism is not a motive in Soviet foreign policy. The Soviet Union "has never sent a gunboat. Debt collection and property protection rank miles behind the questions of politics for her."[2]

Even the possibility of one socialist state acting in such a manner toward another, however, raises interesting and important questions. Was Soviet involvement in China purely a function of socialist solidarity or might there have been other motives involved such as capital extraction and the maintenance of resource flows, the enhancement of political influence, or the manipulation of a surrogate in various military activities? Any one of these, some analysts hold,

The author wishes to thank the Center for Russian and East European Studies at The University of Michigan for the use of its facilities during the preparation of this chapter.

261

would be sufficient to demonstrate an imperialist rationale for Soviet activity in China.

Our task in this chapter is therefore twofold: to demonstrate the nature of Sino-Soviet economic interaction; and then to determine the relevance of economic theories of imperialism to an understanding of this relationship. In accomplishing the first task, we will examine Sino-Soviet economic activity for the period of 1945 to 1960 and focus on capital transactions, aid, trade patterns, and commodity composition. The immediate post-World War II period is a useful place to begin a study of this sort, not only because it marks the resurgence of overt Soviet interest in North Asia after a decade of pre-emption by the Japanese but also because it was in 1945 that the provisions of the Yalta agreement were implemented in Manchuria, 1960 provides a logical stopping point as that date marks a definite "cooling off" in political relations between the two nations and, hence, a decline in economic interaction. Since 1960, the Chinese have also become noticeably more reticent in publishing complete accounts of their economic activity with the Soviet Union.

Placing this Sino-Soviet activity in the context of economic theories of imperialism is a somewhat more complex task. As we shall see, the level of analysis used in a study of this sort has an important influence on the nature of the conclusions obtained.[3] For this reason, we will attempt to conduct our analysis at two different levels: using nation-state frames of reference supported by data aggregated according to such considerations; and then on a sub-national basis, using frameworks derived from certain geographic and institutional considerations.

The divisions in this chapter reflect these concerns. The first part outlines the indicators of Soviet involvement in the Chinese economy, and assumes the relevant actors to be two nation-states. The second part looks at this data in a slightly different manner and attempts to demonstrate the impact Soviet economic involvement had on a few specific components of the Chinese polity.

Indicators of Soviet Involvement in the Chinese Economy

The basic indicators of Soviet involvement in the Chinese economy fall into two broad categories: (a) capital transfers, such as loans, grants of various types, and reparations; and (b) trade, terms, and commodity composition.

Capital Transfers

Reparations. In return for military action against the Japanese, the Yalta agreements gave the Soviet Union important rights in Manchuria: "internationalization" of Port Arthur, a naval base for the use of Soviet ships, and half interest in the Chinese Eastern Railroad. While the military activity lasted only one week, the tangible benefits were considerable as the Soviet government proceeded to unilaterally collect reparations, primarily in the form of factories and equipment, from the Japanese-held territory it occupied. One American source estimates the amount of equipment removed during this occupation at some $900 million, with replacement and repair value at about $2 billion.[4] Soviet figures, however, place the value of all machinery removed during this period at closer to $97 million.[5]

There are several difficulties in evaluating these reparations in terms of Sino-Soviet economic activity. Historically, the relationship between Manchuria and China proper has been somewhat tenuous. The traditional home of the non-Han Manchus, the area had been open to Chinese migration only since the end of the 1800s and had long been the subject of dispute between Russia, Japan, and China. During the twentieth century, a large portion of the industrial investment in the area had come from funds provided either by the Japanese government or prominent Japanese families and cartels. While profits derived from Manchurian resources were used for further investment in capital goods, there is thus some disagreement whether these assets should be attributed to the Chinese economy, as Chiang Kai-shek's Kuomintang and the People's Republic have both insisted, or regarded instead as a capital transfer between Japan and the Soviet Union.

Joint Stock Companies. Joint stock companies were not a post-World War II innovation. Dating from Witte's attempts to construct and control the sections of the Trans-Siberian Railroad that crossed Manchuria, the Czarist and Soviet bureaucracies have frequently used this device in various dealings in Asia. While the Karakhan Declaration following the 1917 revolution put the Bolshevik government on record as disavowing Czarist economic claims in non-Soviet states, this policy was soon reconsidered—that is, in 1924, Soviet interests resumed responsibility for the Chinese Eastern Railroad and controlled it until forced to sell to the Japanese in 1935.

In post-war China, this same system was resurrected for use with Chiang Kai-shek's government, particularly in Manchuria and Sinkiang. In Port Arthur, a joint commission was appointed to run the naval facility, with three of the five directors selected by the Soviet Union, while on the Chinese Eastern Railroad (later the Chinese Changchun Railroad) not only was the board of directors dominated by the Soviet Union but Russian technicians were actively engaged in running the rail lines as well. Upon the establishment of the People's Republic in 1949, these arrangements were continued, with Chinese Communists merely replacing the Nationalist members of the boards.

As a result of the negotiations concluded in Moscow by Mao Tse-tung and his delegation in the spring of 1950, several additional joint stock companies were

created; these were *Sovkitmettall*, for uranium and non-ferrous metal exploration in Sinkiang, and *Sovkitneft*, for oil-searching in the same province. In 1951,
two more companies were organized; these were *Skoga*, a civil airline with routes
between China and Mongolia, and *Sovkitsudostroi*, a shipbuilding company in
Dairen.

The exact effect of these companies on the Chinese economy is not clear, but
as one observer has noted:

... the JSC served as a bold instrument of economic penetration. By imposing
them on countries that had been friendly as well as hostile, the Russians
managed to obtain a source of steady income in the countries affected, and also
to secure priority shipment of goods to the USSR from their partially owned
companies at a time of severe international shortages.[6]

After Stalin's death, a decision was made to disband the companies in both
Asia and East Europe; in October, 1954, Khrushchev visited Peking and agreed
to turn the companies over to China the following year while also withdrawing
Soviet military forces from Port Arthur. The one provision insisted on by
Khrushchev was that China would continue to supply uranium from Sinkiang.

The Soviet Union was to be reimbursed for their share in the joint stock
companies with Chinese exports. In this regard, Dernberger estimates that the
Chinese paid $175 million for the Soviet shares in these companies.[7] In contrast
to the policy in East Europe after the Polish and Hungarian uprisings, however,
the Chinese payments were never cancelled.[8]

Aid. Soviet aid to the People's Republic took the form of either loans for the
purchase of Soviet goods or the extension of technical expertise.

In the period up to 1960, only two credit agreements were formally
publicized. The first, signed in February of 1950 during Mao's trip to Moscow,
committed the Soviet Union to deliver $300 million in goods from 1950 to 1954
at the rate of $60 million a year; repayment would be in the form of Chinese
export of certain goods to the Soviet Union over a ten-year period beginning in
1954, with a 1 percent rate of interest. The second agreement, signed in October
1954, was a supplement to the first and committed the Soviet Union to an
additional $130 million to be used and repaid in much the same manner.

These two loans would become the basis of the Soviet effort to rehabilitate
portions of China's economy devastated by the war and revolution. The bulk of
these loans were used to finance the 156 "keypoint" industrial projects
developed in China under Soviet direction. Support for these projects consisted
of either complete factories, shipped directly from the Soviet Union, or
machinery and goods for projects, developed in China with the aid of Soviet
technicians. Many of these projects would become the core of larger complexes,
such as the giant iron and steel works at Anshan in Manchuria.

Aid was extended in other ways, as well. A large number of Soviet experts and technicians were sent to China; some went to Manchuria as early as 1948. Between 1950 and 1960, about 11,000 Soviet experts worked in China.[9] Included were both *chuan-chia*, the experts in engineering and planning, and *ku-wen* who assisted the Chinese in executing the technical tasks. There were at least twenty Soviet experts in each of the 156 Soviet projects, and many more in such industries as the Changchun Railroad, which employed 1,500 Russian specialists and engineers between 1950 and 1952.[10]

In addition to the loans and technicians, by 1960 the Soviet Union had supplied China with about 10,000 sets of specifications that included 1,250 designs for capital construction projects, 4,000 blueprints for the manufacture of machines and equipment, and 4,000 sets of technical specifications.[11] A number of Chinese were also trained in the USSR, mainly in Moscow, Leningrad, Tashkent, and Baku. By 1960, some 38,000 Chinese had studied in the Soviet Union,[12] many of whom returned to work in the Soviet-sponsored industries.[13]

Soviet sources have stated frankly that all of this technical assistance was to be paid for by the Chinese, with the exception of the blueprints and specifications that were transmitted free of charge. According to statements of Japanese who returned from China, the minimum salary for these experts and specialists was no less than $6,000 a year.[14] A rough estimate of the wage value of these services, along with the cost of educating the Chinese students, would be about $100 million. It is of course difficult to estimate the benefits that accrued to the Chinese economy as a result of the technical aid; it provided that margin of expertise that is beyond calculation in absolute terms.

Additional Loans and Aid. To the best of our knowledge, the Soviet Union has not made any free grants to the People's Republic since its establishment in 1949.[15] All of the aid has been in the form of interest-deriving loans, to be repaid through Chinese exports to the Soviet Union; these repayments appear in Chinese export figures as trade deficits to the Soviet Union. According to statistics released by the Chinese Ministry of Finance, the total of the loans for the goods reflected in the trade deficits amounted to $2,250 million by 1960.[16] Although we are aware of the loans used to finance these deficits in only two cases, the 1950 agreement for $300 million and the 1954 supplement for $130 million, there were unpublicized agreements on May 15, 1953, April 7, 1956, August 8, 1958, and February 7, 1959.[17]

Military aid accounted for the major portion of the loans in this trade deficit. During the period up to 1960, this aid has been estimated at almost 60 percent of the loan total and amounts to about $1,447 million.[18] It appears that debts incurred during the Korean War were part of this amount, estimated at between $500 million[19] and $750 million.[20] These war debts were to be repaid also with Chinese exports, although at a much higher rate of interest and sooner than the ten-year period granted for other loans.[21] The bitterness engendered by these payments has frequently broken into the open, as indicated by a statement from one Chinese source:

For many years we have been paying the principle and interest of these Soviet loans, which account for a considerable amount of our yearly exports to the Soviet Union. Thus, even the war materiel supplied to China in the war to resist U.S. aggression and aid Korea has not been gratis.[22]

"This," complained General Lung Yun in 1957, "is very unfair."[23]

Trade and Commodity Composition

The repayment of the loans and aid was accomplished through trade imbalances between China and the Soviet Union. The figures for Soviet trade deliveries to China thus include not only regular forms of trade, but deliveries for military and aid programs as well. By the same token, Chinese figures for exports to the Soviet Union include regular trade deliveries, along with the delivery of goods used for payment of the principle and interest on the Soviet loans. There are therefore "unspecified" sections in the trade lists, whose exact composition can only be estimated.

As is common in the bloc, trade occurred as a result of bilateral agreements between the two governments, with lists of goods to be exchanged included in annual protocols. It is important to note that in distinction to her relations with East Europe and certain non-bloc states, China has not signed any long-term agreements with the Soviet Union.[24] Nevertheless, for the period from 1950 to 1957, constant prices and exchange rates were maintained, despite high fluctuations in the international market.[25]

While the terms of Sino-Soviet trade have been difficult to reconstruct, several analysts have concluded that in comparison with the Soviet Union's trade with West Europe, Soviet trade with China has definitely been at the disadvantage of the latter. A number of factors account for this. The Chinese have received goods of quality inferior to that of the Soviet Union's other trading partners; Soviet demand for Chinese goods has been more inelastic than Chinese demand for Soviet goods; and the transportation costs are much greater between China and the Soviet Union than between the Soviet Union and West Europe.[26]

Direction of Trade. There has been a remarkable shift in the direction of China's trade since the early 1930s. The four areas (the United States, United Kingdom, Hong Kong, and Japan) that from 1927 to 1930 accounted for 66 percent of China's foreign trade participated in 1952 to 1956 in only 9 percent. On the other hand, while accounting for only 4 percent of China's trade from 1927 to 1930, the USSR received over half of China's exports in the 1950s.[27]

Commodity Composition. Change in the direction of China's trade has coincided with changes in the commodity composition of this trade. Actually, most of this change has been in the composition of Chinese imports; if we compare

China's exports during the 1950s with figures from the 1930s, there is a remarkably stable pattern.[28]

Almost all of the important changes in the composition of trade have been in the nature of Chinese imports. Most obvious has been the declining share of consumer goods in the face of a rise in capital goods. As Soviet figures indicate, heavy industrial products such as machinery, plant installations, and oil products, have taken an increasingly large share of this trade.

Balance of Trade. As noted earlier, Soviet aid deliveries for industrial and military programs were repaid with Chinese exports in the form of raw materials and consumer goods. These aid deliveries resulted in trade surpluses in favor of the Chinese during the early 1950s.

As payment for this aid came due, the Chinese trade surpluses of the early 1950s decreased steadily and resulted in the first deficit in 1956. After 1953, the Chinese became increasingly aware of the burdens this placed on their own pattern of economic development and attempted to re-negotiate many of the trade agreements. (The first publicized attempt was apparently the negotiation directed by Li Fu-ch'un in 1953.) It is difficult to escape the implications that this trade imbalance had upon the increased tension in Sino-Soviet relations in the mid and late 1950s.

Summary

What, then, is the balance sheet? For the Chinese, the list is fairly tangible, and includes the following: (1) loans amounting to $430 million that were to be used for the purchase of Soviet machinery and factories; (2) at least $1,450 million in military aid, equipment, and support; (3) Soviet shares in the joint stock companies; and (4) Soviet experts, specialists, and technical specifications.

In return, the Soviet Union received exports to pay for the following: (1) $430 million for the factory equipment; (2) $1,450 million for military aid and equipment; (3) $175 million for the Soviet shares in the joint stock companies; (4) $100 million for the support of technicians and specialists; and (5) interest of between $50 and $100 million. In addition, there were the reparations extracted from the former Japanese territories in China, as well as several benefits not directly calculable. This list includes (1) Chinese participation in the Korean War, with aid that was repaid with interest; (2) change in the direction of Chinese trade; (3) shipment of consumer goods to the Soviet Union, during a period when such goods were extremely important for domestic political reasons; and (4) a market for certain categories of Soviet heavy industrial equipment.

In spite of these figures, however, we are struck by how little Soviet economic aid and trade there actually was in comparison to both China's needs

Table 13-1
Commodity Composition of Sino-Soviet Trade, 1950-1960: China's Exports to the Soviet Union (in per cent)

Year	Total (Millions of Dollars)	Food Products	Food	Non-ferrous Metals	Textiles, Raw	Textiles, Finished	Animal Products	Chemicals
1950	$191.3	35.6	11.5	10.7	8.9	–	5.2	0.8
1951	331.2	–	–	13.8	9.1	1.1	5.1	0.4
1952	413.8	30.2	13.8	17.7	9.4	3.5	7.6	0.5
1953	474.7	25.7	18.7	21.3	12.2	3.6	3.7	4.1
1954	578.4	–	–	18.5	9.5	6.4	4.3	3.3
1955	643.5	–	–	18.4	9.2	9.1	4.2	1.3
1956	764.2	16.6	23.8	16.4	7.7	12.3	3.4	4.1
1957	738.1	–	–	19.2	6.6	14.7	2.8	6.6
1958	881.2	–	26.1	–	4.3	–	–	–
1959	1100.3	–	19.9	–	8.3	–	–	–
1960	848.1	–	15.1	–	7.7	–	–	–

China's Imports from the Soviet Union (in per cent)

Year	Total (Millions of Dollars)	Machinery & Equipment		Ferrous Metals	Non-ferrous Metals	Oil	Chemicals
		Total	Factories Only				
1950	$388.2	10.7	0.2	5.2	0.9	2.9	–
1951	478.4	22.9	–	10.4	3.5	8.1	3.3
1952	554.2	28.2	7.3	12.0	2.8	5.8	1.8
1953	697.6	23.1	7.1	9.8	1.9	6.9	0.9
1954	756.3	26.2	12.3	11.6	2.9	5.9	1.1
1955	748.3	30.7	18.9	10.9	1.7	10.6	0.8
1956	733.0	41.6	29.6	8.5	2.4	11.7	0.7
1957	544.1	49.9	38.4	6.3	1.5	16.6	0.8
1958	634.0	50.2	26.2	9.4	2.5	14.5	0.6
1959	954.0	62.6	41.8	5.0	0.7	12.3	0.4
1960	817.0	61.7	–	7.3	1.3	13.8	1.2

Sources: Sladkovskii, M.I., *Vneshniaia Torgovlia*, v. 29, no. 10, October 1959. *Ten Years of the People's Republic of China, JPRS*, No. 2825, (June 22, 1960).

Dimensions of Soviet Economic Power (Washington, D.C.: Government Printing Office, 1962), pp. 738-9. Chu-yuan Cheng, *Economic Relations Between Peking and Moscow, 1949-1963* (New York: Praeger, 1964), pp. 58, 59, 61, 63, 65, 66. Eckstein, A., "Sino-Soviet Economic Relations: A Re-appraisal," in C.D. Cowan (ed.), *The Economic Development of China and Japan* (London: Allen and Unwin, 1964), p. 146.

Table 13-2
Value of Sino-Soviet Trade, 1949-1960

Year	China's Exports to S.U.	China's Imports, fm S.U.	Balance of Trade	Cumulative Balance
		(in millions of U.S. dollars)		
1949	117	163	−46	
1950	191	388	−197	−243
1951	331	478	−147	−390
1952	413	554	−141	−531
1953	474	697	−223	−754
1954	578	756	−178	−932
1955	643	748	−105	−1037
1956	764	733	+31	−1006
1957	738	544	+194	−812
1958	881	634	+247	−565
1959	1100	954	+146	−419
1960	848	817	+31	−388
1961	551	367	+184	−204
1962	516	233	+283	+79

Sources: Sladkovskii, M.I., *Vneshniaia Torgovlia*, v. 29, no. 10, October 1959.
Vneshniaia Torgovlia SSSR 1918-1966 (Moscow: Mezhdunarodnye Otnosheniia, 1967), pp. 66-67.

Table 13-3
Foreign Trade and National Income of China, 1953-1957

Year	Imports M	Exports E	Total Trade T	GNP Y	M/Y	E/Y	T/Y
	(in millions of yuan)				(in per cent)		
1953	2,932	2,669	5,601	82,380	3.56	3.24	6.80
1954	3,179	2,794	5,973	88,990	3.57	3.14	6.71
1955	3,221	3,283	6,504	92,100	3.50	3.56	7.06
1956	3,516	3,936	7,453	106,430	3.30	3.70	7.00
1957	3,330	3,969	7,299	114,450	2.91	3.47	6.38

Source: Derived from Alexander Eckstein, "Sino-Soviet Economic Relations: A Re-Appraisal" in C.D. Cowan, *The Economic Development of China and Japan* (London: Allen and Unwin, 1964), p. 136.

and her total economic activity. As Table 13-3 indicates, for the period from 1953 to 1957, the ratio of either total imports or exports to Chinese GNP was only about 2.9 to 3.7 percent, with the Soviet Union accounting for a little over half of this amount. If Soviet military aid is excluded, Chinese trade deficits to the Soviet Union were scheduled to amount to about $800 million for a ten-year period, certainly no great burden, even for a non-industrial nation. As Table 13-4 demonstrates, Soviet loans accounted for only about 1.5 percent of the total capital investment from 1953 through 1957. In view of all of the needs of China, concludes Feng-hua Mah, the amount of Soviet aid and loans was "surprisingly small."[29]

On the other hand, observes Walter Galenson, these economic patterns may actually had been disadvantageous to the Soviet Union since Chinese trade and aid meant a forced transfer of resources from growth to consumption. From the Russian point of view, Chinese growth was being substituted for Soviet growth.[30]

It would seem that charges of Soviet imperialism, in terms of political domination and economic extraction, are not supported by the available evidence.

Soviet Penetration of the Chinese Economy

The data presented in the first part of this chapter did not support the hypothesis that Soviet activity in China had its basis in imperialist motives. While

Table 13-4
Soviet Loans and China's Capital Investment, 1953-1957

Year	Soviet Economic Loans	Capital Investment	Soviet Economic Loans as % of Capital Invest.
	(in millions of yuan)		(in per cent)
1953	141	6,506	2.2
1954	141	7,498	1.9
1955	305	8,632	3.5
1956	117	13,986	0.8
1957	23	12,370	0.2
1953-57	727	48,777	1.5

Source: Derived from Feng-Hua Mah, "The First Five Year Plan and Its International Aspects" in C.F. Remer, *Three Essays on the International Economics of Communist China* (Ann Arbor, University of Michigan Press Monograph, 1959), p. 87.

the nature of Soviet involvement changed over time, the degree of this involvement never appeared sufficient to dominate Chinese economic or political life. Imports or exports of less than 2 percent of national income by a trading partner accounting for half of its trade certainly does not seem an impressive figure, while the loans extended to China during the 1950s were largely for payment of military goods. Although the technical help was impressive, the importance of 12,000 technicians spread over a ten-year period to a nation with a population of over 700,000,000 seems somewhat dubious.

These conclusions, however, are perhaps somewhat premature or inappropriate. Before judging these figures, let us frame the problem in a slightly different manner. If Soviet economic activity can be shown to account for only a relatively small portion of Chinese economic life in general, could it not be possible that this activity had a somewhat greater impact on specific components of the Chinese economy? And if such is indeed the case, might this then be sufficient grounds to re-evaluate the tentative conclusions reached in the Summary of the first part.

Unfortunately, pinpointing the impact of Soviet activity on specific sectors is a somewhat more difficult task than the one that confronted us in the previous section. Since the Chinese have released few figures relevant to a study of this sort, we are forced to piece together our own information. Due to the peculiarities of Chinese historical, political, and institutional development, as well as certain traditional Russian interests in Asia, it is possible to reformulate our analysis along two somewhat different dimensions: (a) the penetration of certain geographic areas; and (b) influence over specific economic sectors.

Geographic Penetration

China is a land so diverse and immense that division by geographic region has long been a political fact of life; not only have provincial boundaries existed for some time, but larger "regional" distinctions have appeared as well. These divisions continued after the establishment of the People's Republic in 1949, as China was divided into six large administrative regions each consisting of a number of contiguous provinces. (These regions were the Northeast [Manchuria], North, East, Central-South, Southwest, and Northwest Regions.) During the early years of the People's Republic, these regions had an impressive degree of autonomy in important political, economic, and military matters.

By the same token, foreign interest in China had also been somewhat regional in nature. Historically, Russian activities had centered on three areas in China—Sinkiang, Mongolia, and Manchuria. Sinkiang became tied to the Soviet Union in the 1930s, primarily as a result of the development of transportation links such as the Turkish Railway. When rebellions broke out, they were suppressed by Soviet troops, most notably in 1931 and 1937. So close was the political tutelage that Sinkiang's political strongman, General Sheng Shih-tsai, joined the CPSU in the 1930s and then granted the Soviet government significant concessions in oil, tungsten, and tin. Although General Sheng later left the party and defected to the Nationalists, Soviet pressure in this Chinese province continued after World War II.[31]

Mongolia also attracted Soviet interest. After 1917, a number of Soviet companies were established in Mongolia with the stated intention of forcing out foreign competition, especially from Chinese, British, and American firms. Joint stock companies were established to handle this task, especially for such products as wool and leather, and in state trade. These efforts were apparently quite successful, since between 1924 and 1926 the number of Chinese companies in Mongolia decreased from 470 to 270, while English and American companies decreased from twelve to nine.[32] "Prior to World War II," one observer has stated, "the Russians had penetrated into virtually every sector of the Mongolian economy."[33]

Manchuria (the Northeast), however, was by far the most interesting and important case. An object of Russian interest since before the Treaty of Nirchinsk in the seventeenth century, the area had become important to Witte and the Czarist military as a route to Vladivostok for the Trans-Siberian Railroad. The completion of this railroad, along with the economic and military advantages it implied, would become a major factor in the Russo-Japanese War of 1905. Although the Japanese would dominate the competition in this area during the 1930s and 1940s, after World War II the joint stock company arrangement with the Kuomintang would place the Soviet Union in control of virtually the same rail system envisioned by Witte at the end of the nineteenth century.

After the establishment of the People's Republic in 1949, Manchuria would continue to play an important role in the Soviet Union's Far Eastern calculations. Due to its strategic location at a juncture between China, the Soviet Union, and Korea, the military hostilities of the early 1950s would reinforce its significance in the minds of Soviet decision-makers.

There was another factor that made Manchuria important in the early 1950s. Due to its history of Japanese economic development, it was a natural site for future industrial growth. Even after the disastrous reparations policy of 1945-46, the basis of industrial activity remained—developed centers of resource exploitation; complex transportation systems; and an urbanized, technically sophisticated population. Manchuria was an obvious location for the economic rehabilitation needed for China's efforts in the Korean conflict.

From a geographic standpoint, therefore, a clear pattern emerges in the early Sino-Soviet economic relationship. Of the Soviet advisors we have been able to identify in China, over 60 percent were located in the Northeast (Manchuria);[34] of the 156 projects being developed with Soviet aid, most were in the Northeast;[35] of the joint stock companies, the most important were in the

Northeast; and Port Arthur was the sole military base in China occupied and managed by Soviet troops.

Manchuria's economic rehabilitation was also occurring at a much faster rate than in the rest of China. In the early 1950s, the Northeast was the only region held up as a "vanguard" model for the rest of the nation; in concrete terms, the Northeast had developed so rapidly that in 1952 it accounted for 52 percent of China's gross industrial product.[36]

Not surprisingly, this pattern of regional economic development had implications for China's internal political processes. Due to the economic successes of the Northeast, the man who headed the Northeastern regional bureaucracy, Kao Kang, climbed to a position of prominence just behind Mao Tse-tung, Chou En-lai, and Liu Shao-ch'i. So impressive were Kao's successes in Manchuria, in fact, that in 1952 he "moved to the center" and left the Northeast for Peking. There he directed the new and important State Planning Committee, one of the major agencies responsible for the planning and implementation of China's First Five-Year Plan, (1953-1957).

Soviet Penetration by Economic Sector

Due to its geographic location, previous economic history, and concentration of Soviet aid, the Northeast developed in a somewhat different manner than the other regions after 1949. Manchurian industry, for example, was not only rehabilitated more rapidly, it was also re-organized along Soviet lines to a greater degree than in the rest of China, especially in such industries as steel and iron, coal, and the various railroads. Significantly, it was not until Kao moved to the State Planning Committee in late 1952 that these industries in other areas of China began to implement the same Soviet strategies.[37]

If the State Planning Committee was a mechanism through which the Chinese industrial system reorganized itself along Soviet lines, the First Five-Year Plan (FFYP) beginning in 1953 would give coherence and guidance to this effort. The plan itself was both remarkable and ambitious and marked China's first attempt at central direction of the increasingly dominant socialist sector while emphasizing an increase in industrial capacity, especially in such areas as machine building, iron, steel, coal, and rail transportation. Organizationally, a number of new ministries were formed to aid in the implementation of the plan, with the State Planning Committee under Kao Kang (and responsible directly to the Central People's Government) in charge of the planning, coordination, and execution of its major sections.

For the purposes of this chapter, we are interested in two aspects of the FFYP: its relevance to specific sectors of the economy, and the importance of Soviet aid and loans in its execution. In gross terms, as we have seen, Soviet aid and trade was not of overwhelming significance; as indicated earlier, trade from all partners amounted to something under 7 percent of China's national income. Moreover, if we look at Soviet loans to China during the FFYP as a percentage of total investment, we see that they accounted for only 11.2 percent of the total machinery and equipment to be imported by the Chinese during this period.[38]

These figures, however, present a somewhat distorted picture. As the Chinese emphasized over and over, the key to their plans for economic development were 694 "above norm" projects, of which the 156 Soviet industrial projects would be the core. So important were the Soviet projects, in fact, that during the first year of the plan (1953), the plan itself consisted of nothing more than the estimated capacities of the Soviet projects.[39] As Table 13-5 indicates, these projects were concentrated mainly in the metal, power, chemical, and coal industries, and were responsible for most of the increase in productivity in these industries.

The Chinese had planned to invest 11,000 million yuan in these projects, or 44.3 percent of the planned industrial investment during the five-year period. In addition, 1,800 million yuan, or 7.2 percent of the total industrial development would be spent on 143 "above norm" projects that supplemented the primary Soviet-aided ones.[40] Together, investment in these two groups was scheduled to take 55.5 percent of the five-year total, which indicates the importance of the Soviet designed projects to the FFYP. In these projects, the Russians were to provide some 60 percent of the machinery and equipment used.[41]

As in the case of regional economic growth, the Soviet influence in the FFYP would also have important political consequences. At the beginning of the plan, Kao Kang would be among the most prominent and rapidly rising politicians in China. As a result of the tensions accompanying the implementation of the new industrial strategies, however, Kao became involved in a serious political controversy and lost his life in the purge that culminated in 1955. Significantly, although the plan itself was announced in 1952, details were not released until much later; in fact, they were announced on the same day as the announcement of Kao's purge and death in 1955, an indication of the relationship between the two events.

The plan was thus apparently having a leverage effect in both Chinese economic and political life. In industry, the Soviet projects were being used as the basis of a scheme to convert most of Chinese heavy industry from the rather diverse and eclectic styles inherited from previous periods into an integrated system patterned after Soviet organizational models.[42] In early 1953, the Soviet organizational strategy was becoming an increasingly dominant paradigm in Chinese heavy industry, while many of the strategies associated with certain aspects of the Chinese revolutionary heritage were being placed on the defensive.[43]

It seems possible to say, therefore, that Soviet aid and loans were not only aiding the development of heavy industry in China, it was dominating this

Table 13-5
Soviet Aid and Chinese Industry

(A) Soviet Aid Projects: Distribution by Sector

	"Above-Norm" Enterprises	Soviet Projects
Heavy Industry		
Iron and Steel	15	7
Non-ferrous Metals	18	14
Power Stations	107	24
Machine Building	63	63
Coal	194	27
Oil	13	2
Chemicals	15	5
Building Materials, Lumber	27	0
Light Industry		
Pharmeceuticals	4	2
Paper	10	1
Textiles	53	1
Water Conservation	1	1
State Farms	1	1
Transportation	1	5
Food	34	0
Other	138	3
	694	156

(B) Role of Soviet Projects in Productivity Increase in Chinese Industry, 1953-1957

	Productivity Increase During FFYP (1952 = 100)	Percentage of this Increase Derived from the 156 Soviet Projects
Iron	246	92.1
Steel	306	82.8
Steel Products		90.4
Coal	178	22.7
Trucks		100.0
Power Equipment		45.0
Fertilizer		28.5
Crude Oil	462	51.4
Metallurgical Equip.	180	50.3

Sources: *First Five-Year Plan for the Development of the National Economy of the People's Republic of China* (Peking: Foreign Language Press, 1956), pp. 48-94, 115.

Huang Ch'en-ming and Huang Yung-ting, *Ts'ung Chung-su Ching-chi Ho-tso Kan Chung-su Jen-min wei-ta yu-i* (Peking: Ts'ai-cheng Ching-chi Chu-pan-she, 1956), p. 9.

industry to the degree that it was being reshaped in a Soviet image. The Chinese industrial sector, it appeared in the early 1950s, was definitely embarking on a developmental path influenced by the Soviet experience.

Even with Soviet aid, however, heavy industry in China could not develop in a vacuum, unconnected with other sectors; rather, it continued to stand in symbiotic relationship to agriculture. While heavy industry might increasingly have been following the Soviet model, several analyses have shown that Chinese agriculture was proceeding on a distinctly separate course. The procurement of grain by the state (the rate of taxation) during the 1950s at no time approached the levels obtained in the Soviet Union during the collectivization of the 1930s, a level which the Soviet industrial model in China would most likely require for its continued development.[44]

These antinomic patterns forecast a period of intense debate and political controversy, as the new Soviet industrial demands ran headlong into the more dynamic and visceral concerns of the Chinese revolutionary experience in the agricultural sector. It borders on the obvious to point out that a revolutionary tradition with such strong roots in this rural heritage would be somewhat loathe to apply the same rates of taxation and coercion that had characterized the Soviet drive to industrialize under Stalin. Thus, as Soviet patterns in industry became more pronounced in China, it appears that somewhat contrary, non-Soviet trends were also increasingly emphasized in agriculture.[45]

Soviet economic activity in China during the early 1950s, therefore, was tied to support of a Soviet-style industrial base whose increased growth and influence threatened agricultural priorities and strategies that had evolved out of the agricultural heritage. Soviet involvement increased the tension between these sectors, with the aid representing possibly a crucial margin for the industrial interests.

The basis of this heavy industrial development, however, was the Soviet political system, with Stalin at its center. With his death in March 1953, the linchpin that had held all of the diverse elements of the Soviet polity together for so long was removed, which disrupted working political arrangements not only within the Soviet Union but in the larger bloc as well. As we now know, during the inter-regnum that followed, there was a period of intense negotiation between various Soviet and bloc factions in 1953 and 1954 that was followed by the rise of new political coalitions in both China and the Soviet Union the next year.[46] The level at which this cross-national bargaining occurred is indicated in the agreements that came out of Khrushchev's 1954 trip to Peking. These agreements covered such topics as aid and repayment, return of the joint stock companies and Port Arthur, and an implicit Soviet agreement to drop support of such anti-Maoist politicians as Kao Kang.

The question of Soviet economic and organizational penetration, however, remains one of China's most difficult problems, largely unresolved even after the 1954 agreements. The question of loan repayment and the problem of deciding what sort of exports could be used for this repayment were only surface indications of this fundamental cleavage. The tension between the groups associated with these different strategies has periodically flared into the open, as during the experiments associated with the Great Leap Forward, the purge of General P'eng Teh-huai for his Soviet leanings, and the controversies associated with the Cultural Revolution.

Summary

On the basis of the data presented in this chapter, a number of conclusions may seem warranted. As a result of the analysis presented in the first part, Soviet policies in China might well have been viewed in terms of an effort to create a degree of coherence and rationality in the Chinese economic system, coupled with a desire to integrate China into the larger bloc system. In terms of an effort to create patterns of economic dependence or political domination, however, Soviet efforts seemed negligible. In fact, when seen in the context of costs to Soviet economic development, some analysts have indicated that the efforts may even have been dysfunctional.

A re-analysis of this same data, however, in terms of its importance to specific economic sectors, demonstrated the impact that this relationship had on certain components of the Chinese polity. Soviet economic policies, especially before the death of Stalin, seemed concerned equally with problems of political influence and manipulation, not to mention the possibility of economic domination and extraction. By the same token, a chief concern in Chinese politics throughout the 1950s was the relative importance of this "Soviet sector" to the entire Chinese economy.

The level of analysis one brings to a study of imperialism is thus as important as the general theory itself. As we have seen, to judge a trans-national economic relationship solely in terms of data aggregated in terms of nation-state frames of reference is to posit relationships that are at best superficial and are often quite misleading. As even this cursory examination has shown, quite different results and conclusions can be obtained by disaggregating the data, demonstrating the impact that economic activity has on specific sectors, and then relating these sectors back to the larger political and economic system.

Using what might be termed a sub-national level of analysis, therefore, it is possible to outline a number of quite distinct and separate periods of Sino-Soviet economic interaction:

1. 1945-1949. This period was characterized by dual priorities in Soviet policy—that is, extraction of reparations from the so-called Japanese areas of China, while supporting the Kuomintang government as the best means of protecting general Soviet interests in East Asia.
2. 1950-1953. This period was dominated by the efforts to remake portions of

the Chinese economy in the Soviet image, while maintaining China as a viable military force in the Korean conflict.

3. 1953-1955. This period was dominated by Soviet factional struggles in the inter-regnum following Stalin's death and an intense debate over economic priorities in China. The period ended with the rise of Khrushchev in the Soviet Union and the fall of Kao Kang in China.

4. 1955-1959. This is the period during which the Chinese faced up to the implications of the Soviet economic relationship and during which—to Khrushchev's chagrin—China began to experiment with somewhat unique non-Soviet economic forms.

In summary, it appears that the charges of imperialism leveled at the Soviet Union might have some factual basis, depending, of course, on the level of analysis used in ordering the data. But as many studies have shown, while economic considerations may have provided one of the motives for Soviet activity during certain brief periods, additional factors must also be taken into account. These include the attempt to use economic relationships as a means of political domination and the utilization of this domination to insure China's continued role as a military surrogate in Asia.

Notes

1. Marshall Goldman, *Soviet Foreign Aid* (New York: Praeger, 1967), p. 3.

2. P.J.D. Wiles, *Communist International Economics* (New York: Praeger, 1969), p. 2.

3. See, for example, J. David Singer, "The Global System and Its Subsystems: A Developmental View" in *Linkage Politics*, ed. by James Rosenau (New York: Free Press, 1969), pp. 13-14.

4. Edwin Pauley, "Report on Japanese Assets in Manchuria to the President of the United States," United States Department of State, July, 1946.

5. Goldman, op. cit., p. 5.

6. Ibid., p. 21.

7. Robert Dernberger, "The International Trade of Communist China" in *Three Essays on the International Economics of Communist China*, ed. by C.F. Remer (Ann Arbor: University of Michigan Press Monograph, 1959), pp. 151-2.

8. Goldman, op. cit., p. 20.

9. *Pravda*, September 30, 1960; and Chou En-lai, *Ten Great Years* (Peking: Foreign Language Press, 1959), p. 65.

10. Chu-yuan Cheng, *Economic Relations Between Peking and Moscow* (New York: Praeger, 1964), pp. 36-37.

11. Ibid., p. 38.

12. *Sinkiang Jih Pao*, February 14, 1960.

13. Cheng, op. cit., p. 39.

14. Dernberger, op. cit., p. 152.

15. Alexander Eckstein, "Sino-Soviet Economic Relations," in *The Economic Development of China and Japan*, ed. by C.D. Cowan (London: George Allen and Unwin, Ltd., 1964), p. 149.

16. Cheng, op. cit., pp. 28-29; Eckstein, op. cit., p. 150.

17. Goldman, op. cit., p. 41.

18. Cheng, op. cit., p. 81.

19. Goldman, op. cit., p. 43.

20. Dernberger, op. cit., p. 151.

21. Cheng, op. cit., p. 83.

22. *Peking Review*, May 8, 1964, p. 14.

23. *Kuang Ming Jih Pao*, June 19, 1957.

24. Cheng, op. cit., pp. 52-53.

25. Ibid., p. 51.

26. Alexander Eckstein, "Moscow-Peking Axis: The Economic Pattern," in *Moscow-Peking Axis: Strengths and Strains*, ed. by H. Boorman (New York, 1957), p. 84.

27. Alexander Eckstein, *Communist China's Economic Growth and Foreign Trade* (New York: McGraw-Hill, 1966), p. 27.

28. Dernberger, op. cit., pp. 138-142.

29. Feng-hua Mah, "The First Five Year Plan and Its International Aspects," in *Three Essays on the International Economics of Communist China* (Ann Arbor: University of Michigan Press Monograph, 1959), p. 87.

30. Walter Galenson, "Economic Relations Between the Soviet Union and Communist China," in *Study of the Soviet Economy*, ed. by Nicholas Spulber (Bloomington: University of Indiana Press, 1961), p. 136.

31. Allen S. Whiting and Sheng Shih-tsai, *Sinkiang: Pawn or Pivot?* (East Lansing: Michigan State University, 1959).

32. Goldman, op. cit., p. 32.

33. Ibid., p. 12.

34. Derived from a listing by Cheng, op. cit., pp. 36-37.

35. One source places 89 of 141 projects in the Northeast. See Yuan-li Wu, *An Economic Survey of Communist China* (New York: Bookman, 1956), pp. 265-269; and Ronald Hsia, "Changes in the Location of China's Steel Industry," in *Industrial Development in Communist China*, ed. by Choh-ming Li (New York: Praeger, 1964), pp. 125-33.

36. *Jen-Min Jih Pao*, May 15, 1952.

37. Roy F. Grow, "The Politics of Industrial Development in China and the Soviet Union." Unpublished Ph.D. Dissertation. Ann Arbor: The University of Michigan, Department of Political Science, 1973. As this study has shown, there are important differences between Soviet organizational strategies and the industrial technologies of Western Europe and North America. These differences

are especially evident in heavy industrial sectors such as coal, steel, and rail transportation.

38. Dernberger, op. cit., p. 87.

39. Ibid., p. 43.

40. Ibid., p. 87.

41. Ibid., p. 88.

42. Grow, op.cit.

43. Ibid.

44. David Denny, "Rural Policies and the Distribution of Agricultural Products in China: 1950-1959." Unpublished Ph.D. Dissertation. Ann Arbor: The University of Michigan, 1971, and Thomas P. Bernstein, "Leadership and Collectivization of Agriculture in China and Russia: A Comparison." Unpublished Ph.D. Dissertation. New York: Columbia University, 1970.

45. Grow, op. cit.

46. Ibid.

About the Contributors

James Caporaso is Associate Professor of Political Science at Northwestern University. He is coeditor of *Quasi-Experimental Approaches: Testing Theory and Evaluating Policy* (Northwestern University Press, 1973) and author of *The Structure and Function of European Integration* (Goodyear, 1974), among other publications.

Karl W. Deutsch is Professor of Government at Harvard University. He is the author of *The Analysis of International Relations* (Prentice-Hall, 1968), and of many other books on international politics and comparative politics.

Walter Goldstein is Professor of Political Science at the Graduate School of Public Affairs, State University of New York at Albany. He has written extensively on the multinational corporation and on problems of arms control and military strategy.

Roy F. Grow is Assistant Professor of Politics at Brandeis University; he specializes in the politics of China and the USSR. Among his other work is his 1973 Ph.D. dissertation at the University of Michigan, "The Politics of Industrial Development in China and the Soviet Union."

Stephen D. Krasner is Assistant Professor of Government at Harvard University; he specializes in international politics and international economics. His publications include "Are Bureaucracies Important?" in *Foreign Policy* (Summer 1972); "Business-Government Relations: The Case of the International Coffee Agreement," in *International Organization* (Autumn 1973); and "The Great Oil Sheikdown," in *Foreign Policy* (Winter 1973-74). Professor Krasner is also writing a book concerning international commodity trade.

James R. Kurth is Associate Professor of Political Science at Swarthmore College. His publications include "Why We Buy the Weapons We Do," in *Foreign Policy* (Summer 1973); and "United States Foreign Policy and Latin American Military Rule," in Philippe C. Schmitter, ed., *Military Rule in Latin America* (Sage, 1973). Professor Kurth is writing a book about competing theories of American foreign policy.

Andrew Mack is Research Administrator at the Richardson Institute for Conflict and Peace Research in London; his professional interest is political sociology. Among his publications is *War Without Weapons: Nonviolence in National Defence* (London: Frances Pinter, 1974).

Harry Magdoff is coeditor of the *Monthly Review*. He is the author of *The Age of Imperialism* (Monthly Review Press, 1969) and many articles on economic analysis of U.S. foreign policy.

Paul Marer is Director of the East Europe Program at the International Development Research Center and a visiting associate professor in the department of economics at Indiana University. He is the author of *Soviet and East European Foreign Trade* (Indiana University Press, 1972); *Postwar Pricing and Price Patterns in Socialist Foreign Trade* (IDRC, 1972); and numerous articles and studies on socialist economies and trade.

Donald E. Milsten is Assistant Professor of Political Science at the University of Maryland Baltimore County, specializing in international politics. He is the author of several articles on the politics of the oceans.

Theodore H. Moran is a research associate for the Project on Multinational Corporations and U.S. Foreign Policy at the Brookings Institution. His publications include "Foreign Expansion as an 'Institutional Necessity' for U.S. Corporate Capitalism: The Search for a Radical Model," in *World Politics* (April 1973); and *Economic Nationalism and the Politics of International Dependence: The Case of Copper in Chile, 1945-1973* (Princeton University Press, 1974).

John S. Odell is a graduate student in political science at the University of Wisconsin, specializing in American foreign policy.

Steven J. Rosen is Assistant Professor of Politics at Brandeis University, specializing in the theory of international conflict. He is the editor of *Testing the Theory of the Military-Industrial Complex* (Lexington Books, D.C. Heath and Company, 1973), coauthor of *The Logic of International Relations* (Winthrop, 1974), and author of numerous other studies on international political economy and conflict.

Thomas E. Weisskopf is Professor of Economics at the Center for Research on Economic Development, University of Michigan. He is coeditor of *The Capitalist System* (Prentice-Hall, 1972), and author of, among other studies, "Capitalism, Underdevelopment, and the Future of the Poor Countries," in Jagdish N. Bhagwati, ed., *Economics and World Order* (Macmillan, 1972).